CALIFORNIA EDITION

HOUGHTON MIFFLIN

Math Steps

HOUGHTON MIFFLIN

Boston • Atlanta • Dallas • Denver • Geneva, Illinois • Palo Alto • Princeton

Grateful acknowledgment is given for the contributions of

Student Book

Rosemary Theresa Barry
Karen R. Boyle
Barbara Brozman
Gary S. Bush
John E. Cassidy
Dorothy Kirk
Sharon Ann Kovalcik
Bernice Kubek
Donna Marie Kvasnok
Ann Cherney Markunas
Joanne Marie Mascha
Kathleen Mary Ogrin
Judith Ostrowski
Jeanette Mishic Polomsky
Patricia Stenger
Annabelle L. Higgins Svete

Teacher Book
Contributing Writers

Dr. Judy Curran Buck
Assistant Professor of Mathematics
Plymouth State College
Plymouth, New Hampshire

Dr. Richard Evans
Professor of Mathematics
Plymouth State College
Plymouth, New Hampshire

Dr. Mary K. Porter
Professor of Mathematics
St. Mary's College
Notre Dame, Indiana

Dr. Anne M. Raymond
Assistant Professor of Mathematics
Keene State College
Keene, New Hampshire

Stuart P. Robertson, Jr.
Education Consultant
Pelham, New Hampshire

Dr. David Rock
Associate Professor,
Mathematics Education
University of Mississippi
Oxford, Mississippi

Michelle Lynn Rock
Elementary Teacher
Oxford School District
Oxford, Mississippi

Dr. Jean M. Shaw
Professor of Elementary Education
University of Mississippi
Oxford, Mississippi

Printed in the U.S.A.

ISBN-13: 978-0-395-98012-5 ISBN-10: 0-395-98012-7

18 19 20 21 22 -POO- 10 09 08 07 06

Contents

UNIT 1 • TABLE OF CONTENTS

Place Value and Addition and Subtraction of Whole Numbers

UNIT 1 • TABLE OF CONTENTS

We will be using this vocabulary:

place value the value given to the place, or position, of a digit in a number

round to replace an exact number with another number that is easier to use

addend a number used in an addition problem

sum the answer to an addition problem

variable a letter that is used to represent one or more numbers

exponent a number that tells how many times a base is to be used as a factor

Dear Family,

During the next few weeks, our math class will be learning about comparing, ordering, adding, and subtracting whole numbers.

You can expect to see homework that provides practice with comparing whole numbers. Here is a sample you may want to keep handy to give help if needed.

Comparing Whole Numbers

To compare whole numbers such as **607,760** and **608,706**, first align the numbers.

607,760

608,706

Then, beginning at the left or at the greatest place value of each number, compare the digits until you find two digits that are different.

↓

607,760

608,706

Since **7** is less than **8, 607,760** is less than **608,706**. Because the symbol < represents "is less than," we can write **607,760 < 608,706**.

During this unit students will need to continue to practice comparing whole numbers.

Sincerely,

Name ______________________________

Place Value Through Billions

STANDARD

There are many ways to express a number such as **4,367.**

Standard Form: 4,367

Expanded Form: 4,000 + 300 + 60 + 7

Word Form: four thousand, three hundred sixty-seven

Place-value Chart			
Th	H	T	Ones
4	**3**	**6**	**7**

The place-value table below shows **398,412,567,103.**

Billions			Millions			Thousands			Ones			
Hundred Billions	Ten Billions	Billions	Hundred Millions	Ten Millions	Millions	Hundred Thousands	Ten Thousands	Thousands	Hundreds	Tens	Ones	← Place Values
3	**9**	**8**	**4**	**1**	**2**	**5**	**6**	**7**	**1**	**0**	**3**	← Digits

← Periods

398 billion, **412** million, **567** thousand, **103** ← Short Word Form

Read: Three hundred ninety-eight *billion*, four hundred twelve *million*, five hundred sixty-seven *thousand*, one hundred three. ← Word Form

The number has been separated into **4** groups of **3** digits each, called **periods.** When you write a number in standard form, separate the periods with commas.

Separate each number into periods with commas. Then read each number.

1.	45061	2830375	7829
2.	10000000	600000000	300000
3.	200000000000	8000000000	4639521
4.	269450616	600000000	1000000001
5.	146272915412	68390030050	200002
6.	627291542	7893896850 0	1500004
7.	7691004	100000000000	98000123

STANDARD

Complete.

8. In the number **916,853,274**

the ___ shows the number of hundred thousands
the ___ shows the number of millions
the ___ shows the number of tens
the ___ shows the number of ten millions
the ___ shows the number of hundred millions

Write in standard form.

9. Ninety thousand, four hundred eight ________

10. Nine hundred thousand, five hundred five ________

11. Seven million, twenty-two thousand, two hundred ________

Write in words. Use commas and hyphens.

12. 38,492 ________________________

13. 276,023 ________________________

14. 28,005,010,035 ________________________

Write in expanded form.

15. 45 = ____________ 333 = ____________ 527 = ____________

16. 7,891 = ____________ 67,807 = ____________

Problem Solving Reasoning Solve.

17. What number in standard form represents one thousand millions?

____

18. What number in standard form represents one million thousands?

____

Test Prep ★ Mixed Review

19 What number sentence is in the same family of facts as 8 + 4 = □?

A 8 × 4 = □

B 8 − 4 = □

C □ ÷ 4 = 8

D □ − 4 = 8

20 What number comes next in this pattern?
40, 38, 36, 34, ______

F 33 H 31

G 32 J 30

Name ____________________

Rounding Whole Numbers

STANDARD

Round **32** to the nearest ten.

The number line shows that **32** is between **30** and **40**.
It is nearer to **30** than to **40.** Round **32** *down* to **30.**

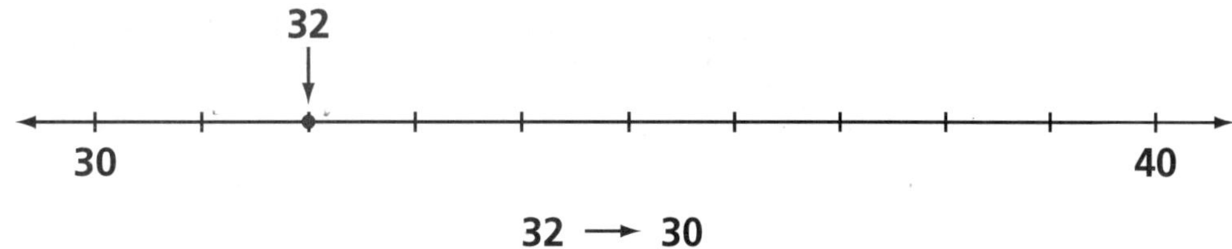

32 → 30

Round **250** to the nearest hundred.

The number line shows that **250** is halfway between **200** and **300.**
A number halfway is rounded up. Round **250** *up* to **300.**

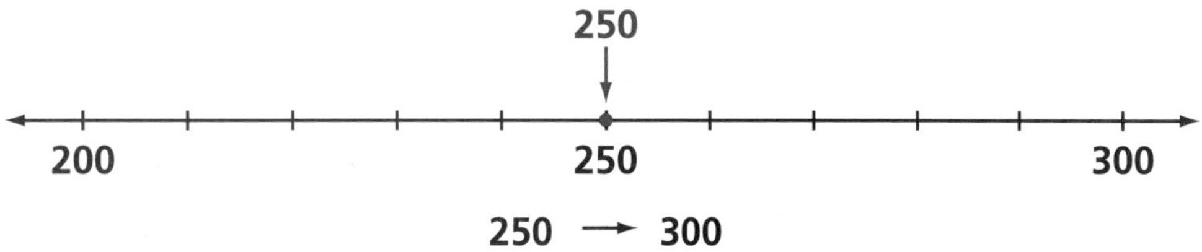

250 → 300

Round **2,843** to the nearest thousand.

The number line shows that **2,843** is between **2,000** and **3,000.**
It is nearer to **3,000** than to **2,000.** Round **2,843** *up* to **3,000.**

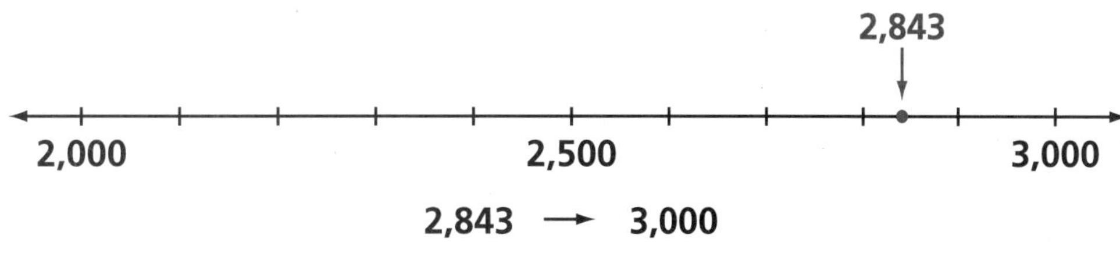

2,843 → 3,000

Round each number to the nearest ten.

1. 13 ______ 23 ______ 55 ______ 49 ______ 77 ______

Round each number to the nearest hundred.

2. 267 ______ 850 ______ 640 ______ 99 ______ 734 ______

Round each number to the nearest thousand.

3. 967 ______ 8,500 ______ 3,499 ______ 1,300 ______

4. 3,290 ______ 2,821 ______ 3,500 ______ 3,700 ______

STANDARD

You can round numbers without using a number line.

Round **1,238** to the nearest hundred.

Round to this place.

1 2 3 8 → 1,200

less than 5, round *down*

Round **1,278** to the nearest hundred.

Round to this place.

1 2 7 8 → 1,300

greater than 5, round *up*

A rounded number is not exact – it is an **estimate.** Use estimates when:

- an estimate is just as valuable as an exact answer. For example:

  About how many people live in a city?

- an exact answer is not possible. For example:

  How many stars are in the sky?

- an exact answer is possible, but it may be difficult to obtain. For example:

  How many students were absent last year?

Round to the

	nearest ten thousand	**nearest hundred thousand**	**nearest million**
5.	**4,761,742** _______	**4,761,742** _______	**4,761,742** _______
6.	**6,757,963** _______	**6,757,963** _______	**6,757,963** _______
7.	**1,080,555** _______	**1,080,555** _______	**1,080,555** _______
8.	**5,555,555** _______	**5,555,555** _______	**5,555,555** _______

Problem Solving Reasoning

Which of the following represent an exact number? Which represent an estimate? Explain your reasoning.

9. The circumference of the earth at its equator is **24,910** miles.

____

10. I am almost **12** years old.

____

11. The speed limit on some highways is **65** miles per hour.

____

12. My telephone number is **555–1094.**

____

Test Prep ★ Mixed Review

13 **What is the value of the 9 in 1,395,273?**

A 9 millions

B 9 hundred thousands

C 9 ten thousands

D 9 thousands

14 **$4000.00 + $300.00 + $0.80 + $0.09 =**

F $4,389.00

G $4,380.09

H $4,308.09

J $4,300.89

Name ______________________

Comparing and Ordering Whole Numbers

STANDARD

Compare. Tell which is greater. **3,749** ◯ **3,758.**

1. Line up the digits.
2. Compare digits in each place until they are different.

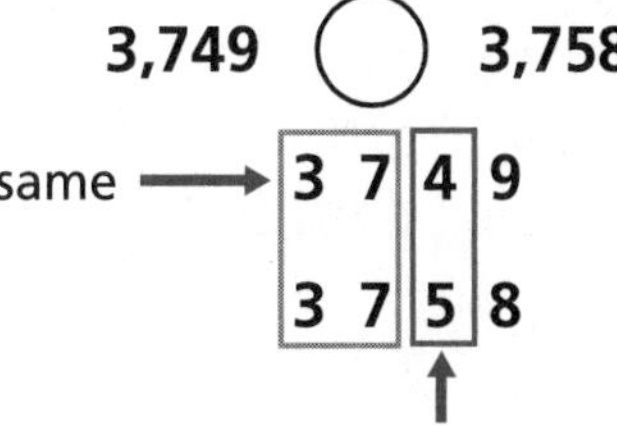

The digits are different: 4 is less than 5

So, 3,749 is less than 3,758. **3,749 < 3,758**

< is less than
> is greater than
= is equal to

Complete. Write <, >, or =.

1. **63** ◯ **65**   **78** ◯ **87**   **200** ◯ **212**

2. **437** ◯ **428**   **919** ◯ **922**   **1,014** ◯ **1,041**

3. **5,021** ◯ **5,021**   **10,155** ◯ **10,135**   **212,697** ◯ **212,687**

Write the numbers in order from least to greatest.

4. **150; 138; 156; 131; 146; 135** ______________________

5. **6,017; 6,907; 6,871; 6,107; 6,697; 6,077** ______________________

6. **5,683; 5,428; 8,548; 5,863; 8,508; 8,458** ______________________

Complete.

College Football Stadium	Seating Capacity
Ohio State	89,841
Michigan	102,501
Oklahoma State	50,614
Penn State	93,967
Auburn	85,214

7. Arrange the seating capacities in order from least to greatest.

____

8. Which stadium has a seating capacity closest to **90,000?**

____

9. Which stadium holds **10,000** fewer fans than **95,214?**

____

10. Suppose a game was played last Saturday and **97,541** spectators attended. In which stadium was the game played? Explain.

____

STANDARD

Problem Solving Reasoning **Use this table to solve each problem below.**

Population of Six Continents	
Africa	731,500,000
Asia	3,428,300,000
Australia	28,900,000
Europe	799,600,000
North America	295,400,000
South America	488,600,000

11. Arrange the six continents in order according to population. Begin with the continent that has the greatest population.

____

____

12. Do you think the population data are exact or estimated? Explain.

____

13. Which continent now has a population nearest a half billion people? Explain.

____

14. For every person who lives in Australia, about how many people live in North America?

____

Quick Check

15. Write **6** billion **472** million in standard form.

____

16. What is the value of the **6** in the number **2,869,472,508**?

____

17. Write the number **4,520,000,017** in short word form.

____

Round each number to the nearest thousand, then to the nearest million.

18. 5,294,376 ____________ ____________

19. 23,459,622 ____________ ____________

Complete. Write <, >, or =.

20. 387 ◯ 372 **21.** 7,437 ◯ 8,200 **22.** 14,462 ◯ 14,398

Work Space

Name ______________________

Problem Solving Application: Use a Graph

STANDARD

This bar graph shows the results of a survey of the number of each type of pet some people have.

In this lesson, you will need to use the graph to draw conclusions about the data.

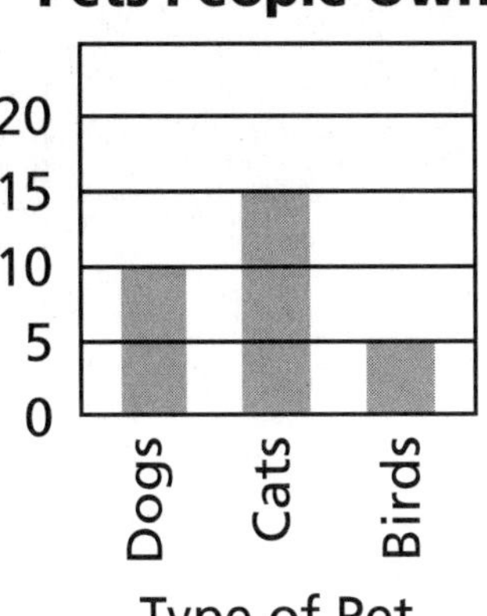

Tips to Remember

1. Understand 2. Decide 3. Solve 4. Look back

- Ask yourself: Have I solved a problem like this before? If so, how did I solve it?
- Compare the labels on the graph with the words and numbers in the problem. Find the facts you need from the graph.
- When you can, make a prediction about the answer. Then compare your answer with your prediction.

Solve. Use the bar graph above.

1. What is the total number of pets that the people who were surveyed own?

Think: How can the bars in the graph help you find the number?

____

____

Answer ______________________

2. The number of people surveyed was 15. Is it true that each person surveyed has 2 pets? Explain.

Think: Does each person surveyed own a pet?

____

Answer ______________________

____

____

3. The people surveyed own the least number of which pet?

____

____

4. The number of cats people own is double the number of birds. Is this statement true or false? Explain.

____

____

STANDARD

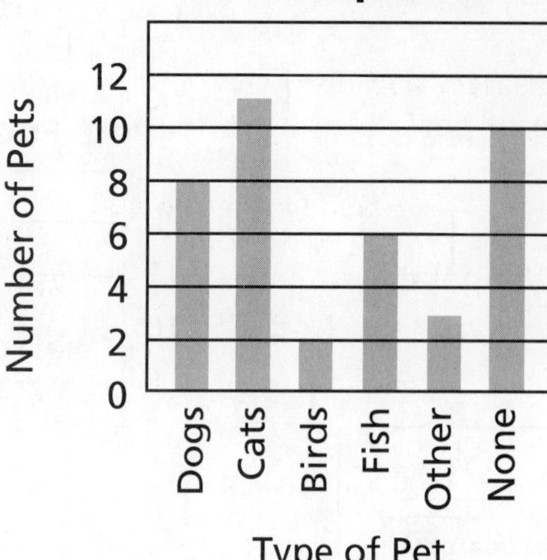

Solve. Use the bar graph above.

5. The bar graph shows the results of a survey in which people were asked what pets they own and how many. Do people own more dogs than fish? Explain your answer.

6. The people surveyed own the greatest number of which pet? Explain.

7. The number of fish the people own is three times the number of birds. Is this statement true or false? Explain.

8. Of the people surveyed, one person owned 3 pets: a goat, a sheep, and a horse. Which bar above shows the pets that this person owned? Explain.

Extend Your Thinking

9. Suppose one person in the survey bought 4 more dogs. How would this change the data? How would you change the graph to reflect this data? Explain.

Name ___________________________

Adding and Subtracting Whole Numbers

STANDARD

Use what you learned last year to review addition.
Find **437 + 186.**

Estimate first: **437** rounds to **400** **186** rounds to **200** **400 + 200 = 600**

1. Add the ones and regroup **10** ones as **1** ten.

$$\begin{array}{r} {}^{1}\\ 437 \\ +\,186 \\ \hline 3 \end{array}$$

2. Add the tens and regroup **10** tens as **1** hundred.

$$\begin{array}{r} {}^{1\,1}\\ 437 \\ +\,186 \\ \hline 23 \end{array}$$

3. Add the hundreds.

$$\begin{array}{r} {}^{1}\\ 437 \\ +186 \\ \hline 623 \end{array}$$

The sum, **623**, is close to the estimate, **600**. The answer is reasonable.

Add. Estimate first. Then use your estimate to check whether your answer is reasonable.

1. 783 + 149 ; 585 + 258 ; 148 + 664 ; 736 + 177 ; 959 + 172

	a	b	c	d	e
1.	783 + 149	585 + 258	148 + 664	736 + 177	959 + 172
2.	5,728 + 3,307	3,914 + 2,843	6,051 + 3,572	3,798 + 2,473	7,140 + 3,695
3.	29,132 + 30,567	75,213 + 75,213	59,604 + 31,572	72,092 + 45,358	60,380 + 27,294
4.	63 42 78 + 91	45 45 45 + 45	258 346 91 + 759	7,425 6,813 4,259 + 647	24,752 76,874 80,257 + 323
5.	51 38 29 74 + 51	59 61 58 62 + 60	272 353 438 686 + 147	3,456 2,851 1,234 659 + 154	76,325 81,804 97,325 936 + 5,563

STANDARD

Now review subtraction: find **703 – 329**.
Estimate first: **700 – 300 = 400.**

1. Regroup **1** hundred for **10** tens.

```
 6 10
 7 0 3
-3 2 9
```

2. Regroup **1** ten for **10** ones.

```
     9
 6 10 13
 7 0 3
-3 2 9
```

3. Subtract.

```
     9
 6 10 13
 7 0 3
-3 2 9
 3 7 4
```

The difference, **374,** is close to **400**. The answer is reasonable.

Subtract. Estimate first. Then use your estimate to check if your answer is reasonable.

6.	407 − 348	500 − 329	592 − 327	904 − 457	300 − 258
7.	6,000 − 5,532	4,780 − 2,219	6,051 − 1,883	5,210 − 3,782	6,400 − 2,588
8.	9,717 − 7,138	9,512 − 2,638	7,115 − 2,968	8,433 − 5,851	9,246 − 1,056

Quick Check

Write the standard numeral.

9. 2^3 ________ **10.** 6×10^5 ________

11. $(9 \times 10^6) + (5 \times 10^0)$ ________

Find the sum.

12. 46,802 + 51,732

13. 50,709 + 64,757

14. 94,466 + 18,833 + 2,346 + 35,276

Find the difference.

15. 14,080 − 13,783

16. 6,090 − 2,987

17. 498,541 − 372,639

Work Space

Name ___________________________

Addition and Subtraction Expressions

STANDARD

A **variable** is a letter or a symbol that is used to represent an unknown quantity.

Although the letters x and n are often used as variables, you can use any letter of the alphabet.

When you write an **algebraic expression** for a word phrase, you use numbers, operation signs, and variables.

word phrase	algebraic expression
the sum of a number and **4**	$n + 4$
a number decreased by **10**	$x - 10$
8 more than a number	$h + 8$
25 less than a number	$w - 25$

Write an algebraic expression for the word phrase. Use n to represent a variable.

1. twelve more than a number ____________

2. a number decreased by **100** ____________

3. thirty-four less than a number ____________

4. a number increased by **75** ____________

Write an algebraic expression for the word phrase.

5. forty decreased by a number x ____________

6. the sum of a number b and **1** ____________

7. a number z decreased by itself ____________

8. a number p plus $\frac{1}{2}$ ____________

9. a number r less **1** ____________

10. fourteen increased by a number q ____________

11. a number g increased by itself ____________

12. a number m decreased by **2** ____________

13. three more than a number y ____________

14. sixty decreased by a number u ____________

STANDARD

It is possible to evaluate an algebraic expression if the value of a variable is known. To **evaluate** an expression you substitute numbers for variables.

Example: Evaluate the algebraic expression $n - 11$ for $n = 30$.

1. Write the expression. $n - 11$
2. Substitute **30** for n. $30 - 11$
3. Simplify. **19**

Evaluate each algebraic expression for $x = 25$.

15. $x + 9$ ______ $x - 13$ ______ $250 + x$ ______

16. $x + 29$ ______ $x + x$ ______ $x - x$ ______

Complete each table.

17.

n	$n - 1$
20	
15	
10	
5	

18.

k	$k + 17$
0	
1	
2	
3	

19.

x	$x - 6$
12	
11	
10	
9	

Problem Solving Reasoning

Write an algebraic expression to represent each situation. For each expression you write, explain what the variable you chose represents.

20. Jamie's brother is two years younger than Jamie.

What is her brother's age? ______

21. The sum of two different numbers is **14**.

______

22. The difference between two different numbers is **1**.

______

Test Prep ★ Mixed Review

23 **Mr. Gomez read 128 pages in his book on Friday and 273 pages on Saturday. About how many more pages did he read on Saturday?**

A 50 **C** 250

B 150 **D** 350

24 **What is this number in standard form? 7×10^5**

F 7,000

G 70,000

H 700,000

J 7,000,000

Name ________________________________

Equations

STANDARD

A mathematical sentence with an equals sign (=) is an **equation**. There are three kinds of equations: true, false, and open.

True equation	False Equation	Open equation
$15 - 15 = 0$	**$1 + 1 = 9$**	**$n - 2 = 6$**

When you find a number for ***n*** that makes an open equation true, you **solve** the equation.

To solve an addition equation, think of a related subtraction equation.

$n + 1 = 4$
Think: $n = 4 - 1$
$n = 3$

Subtraction is the opposite of addition.
Think: **4** minus **1** is what number?

To solve a subtraction equation, think of a related addition equation.

$n - 5 = 2$
Think: $n = 2 + 5$
$n = 7$

Addition is the opposite of subtraction.
Think: **2** plus **5** is what number?

Identify each equation. Write *True*, *False*, or *Open*.

1. $10 - 2 = 4$ ________ $n + 3 = 5$ ________

2. $12 - 3 = 9$ ________ $7 + 6 = 13$ ________

3. $5 + a = 20$ ________ $8 - 4 = 1$ ________

Complete.

4. $n + 2 = 6$
Think: $n = 6 -$ ______
$n = 4$

$n - 4 = 5$
Think: $n = 5 + 4$
$n =$ ______

$n - 3 = 3$
Think: $n = 3 +$ ______
$n = 6$

5. $n - 2 = 7$
Think: $n = 7 + 2$
$n =$ ______

$7 + n = 15$
Think: $n = 15 -$ ______
$n = 8$

$n + 8 = 13$
Think: $n = 13 - 8$
$n =$ ______

6. $n - 6 = 2$
Think: $n = 2 +$ ______
$n = 8$

$n - 15 = 21$
Think: $n = 21 + 15$
$n =$ ______

$10 + n = 20$
Think: $n = 20 -$ ______
$n = 10$

STANDARD

Sometimes the properties of addition can help you solve equations.

Commutative Property of Addition		Identity Property of Addition	
Arithmetic	Algebra	Arithmetic	Algebra
$3 + 2 = 2 + 3$	$a + b = b + a$	$7 + 0 = 7$	$n + 0 = n$

The rules for subtraction can help, too.

Rules for Subtraction	
Arithmetic	Algebra
$8 - 8 = 0$	$n - n = 0$
$6 - 0 = 6$	$n - 0 = n$

Find the value of *n*.

7. $n + 7 = 7 + 3$ ________ $19 + n = 54$ ________ $n - 18 = 40$ ________

8. $n - 9 = 0$ ________ $5 + n = 25$ ________ $100 + n = 500$ ________

9. $n - 0 = 8$ ________ $n - 7 = 11$ ________ $n - 15 = 135$ ________

10. $21 + n = 31$ ________ $n + 12 = 39$ ________ $n + 14 = 33$ ________

Problem Solving Reasoning **Solve.**

11. At rest, Mark's heart beats **72** times per minute. When he jogs, his heartbeat increases to **95** beats per minute. How can you show this using a variable?

____

12. Write a problem involving addition or subtraction. Then write an equation to represent the problem.

____

Test Prep ★ Mixed Review

13 A large cement block weighed 1,548 pounds. What is that number rounded to the nearest thousand pounds?

A 2,000

B 1,150

C 1,140

D 1,000

14 Sarita bought a sandwich for $4.95, a drink for $.75, and an apple for $.35. She gave the clerk a $10 bill. What was her change?

F $3.95

G $4.05

H $4.95

J $6.05

Name ______________________

Problem Solving Strategy: Write an Equation

STANDARD

Sometimes it is helpful to write an equation to solve a problem.

Problem

Matt had 12 marbles. Mindy gave him some of her marbles. Now he has 20 marbles. How many marbles did Mindy give him?

---

1 Understand As you reread, ask yourself questions.

- What do you know about the number of marbles?

  Matt had 12 marbles.
  Now he has 20 marbles.

  What do you need to find?

  ____

---

2 Decide Choose a method for solving.

- Try the strategy Write an Equation.

  Pick a variable to represent what you need to find.

  What variable did you select?

  ____

---

3 Solve Try to write a word equation first.

- What equation can you use to help you solve the problem?

  ____

  What is the solution to the equation?

  ____

---

4 Look back Check your answer. Replace the variable with its value.

  Write your answer below.

  Answer: ______________________

  Does your answer make sense? Explain.

  ____

STANDARD

Use the Write an Equation strategy or any other strategy you have learned.

1. Lorna had **$58.73** in her savings account. She made a deposit. Her new balance was **$92.09**. How much was the deposit?

Think: What does it mean to make a deposit?

____

Answer: ______________________

2. Jamel collects baseball cards. He sold **17** to his friend Mia. Now he has **83** cards left. How many cards did Jamel start with?

Think: Did Jamel start with more cards or fewer cards?

____

Answer: ______________________

3. Together Timothy and Lili have **$117**. If Timothy has **$59**, how much does Lili have?

____

4. Miguel has three times as many CDs as Chen. If Chen has **19** CDs, how many CDs does Miguel have?

____

5. Gloria has half as many seashells as George. If George has **54** shells, how many shells does Gloria have?

____

6. A square has a perimeter of **24** inches. What is the length of each side of the square?

____

7. Taniqua baked **76** cookies. If there were **19** cookies in each batch, how many batches did she bake?

____

8. One year a fire department responded to fires on **289** days. On how many days were there no fires to put out?

____

9. I'm thinking of a number. If I subtract **65** from it, the result is **56**. What number am I thinking of?

____

10. I'm thinking of a number. If I multiply it by **13**, the result is **117**. What number am I thinking of?

____

Name ______________________________

Using Grouping Symbols

STANDARD

You can use parentheses to group numbers. In addition, the way you group the numbers does not change the sum. This is called the **associative property of addition**.

$$2 + (3 + 4) = (2 + 3) + 4$$

$$2 + 7 = 5 + 4$$

$$9 = 9$$

In mathematics, parentheses are **grouping symbols**. When parentheses are used in an expression or an equation, you must do the operations inside parentheses first.

grouping symbols

$(9 - 4) + 3 = ?$

$5 \quad + 3 = 8$

grouping symbols

$9 - (4 + 3) = ?$

$9 - \quad 7 \quad = 2$

Solve. Remember to work inside the parentheses ( ) first.

1. $(95 - 23) + 47 =$ ______ $95 - (23 + 47) =$ ______

2. $90 - (56 - 29) =$ ______ $(90 - 56) - 29 =$ ______

3. $(349 + 526) - 235 =$ ______ $349 + (526 - 235) =$ ______

4. $290 + (63 + 159) =$ ______ $(290 + 63) + 159 =$ ______

Solve. Let $n = 8$.

5. $n - (4 + 1) =$ ______ $(n + 12) - 3 =$ ______

6. $(16 - n) + 3 =$ ______ $25 - (n + 2) =$ ______

7. $(n + 1) - 5 =$ ______ $(n - 7) - 1 =$ ______

8. $(n + n) - 10 =$ ______ $n + (n - n) =$ ______

9. $(n + 7) - n =$ ______ $(n - 1) + 9 =$ ______

10. $(3 + n) + (10 - n) =$ ______ $(n + 5) - (n - n) =$ ______

STANDARD

Solve. Let $x = 2$.

11. $x - (0 + 1) =$ ______ $(9 - x) - 5 =$ ______

12. $(x + x) - 3 =$ ______ $14 - (x + 7) =$ ______

13. $17 - (8 + x) =$ ______ $(x + 3) - x =$ ______

14. $(x + 5) - (x + 3) =$ ______ $10 - (x - x) - 10 =$ ______

Problem Solving Reasoning Insert parentheses ( ) to make each equation true.

15. 10 − 4 + 1 = 7 8 − 5 + 2 = 1

16. 2 + 9 − 3 + 4 = 4 14 − 6 + 1 − 5 = 2

17. Explain why these expressions have different values.

5 + (3 − 2) + 1 and 5 + 3 − (2 + 1)

____

____

18. Is this a true equation? Explain.

6 − 4 + 9 = 15 − 9 + (3 + 2)

____

____

Quick Check

Evaluate for $r = 5$.

19. $r + 3$ ______ **20.** $16 - r$ ______

21. $r + r$ ______

Find the value of the variable.

22. $77 - v = 0$ ______ **23.** $29 + h = 40$ ______

24. $49 + 27 = c + 49$ ______

Evaluate.

25. 509 + (127 − 23) ______ **26.** (250 + 988) + 750 ______

27. 500 − (819 − 342) ______

Work Space

Name ____________________

Unit 1 Review

Write each number in standard form.

1. 3^3 ______ **2.** two million, sixteen thousand, five ______

3. Write **6,450** in word form. ______

Compare. Write <, >, or =.

4. 4,000 ◯ 4,100

5. 1,745 ◯ 1,745

6. 798,555 ◯ 789,555

Round to the nearest million.

7. 2,354,768 ______

8. 5,664,890,722 ______

Add or subtract.

9. $467 + 398$

10. $709 - 271$

11. $6{,}020 - 2{,}354$

12. $5{,}001 - 687$

13. $65{,}000 + 32{,}000 + 6{,}451$

Evaluate each expression for $x = 15$.

14. $x + 30$ ______

15. $x - 12$ ______

16. $75 + x$ ______

17. $x - x$ ______

Solve each equation for n.

18. $20 - n = 14$ ______

19. $n - 6 = 0$ ______

20. $8 + n = 4 + 8$ ______

21. $12 - n = 12$ ______

Use the graph to solve each problem.

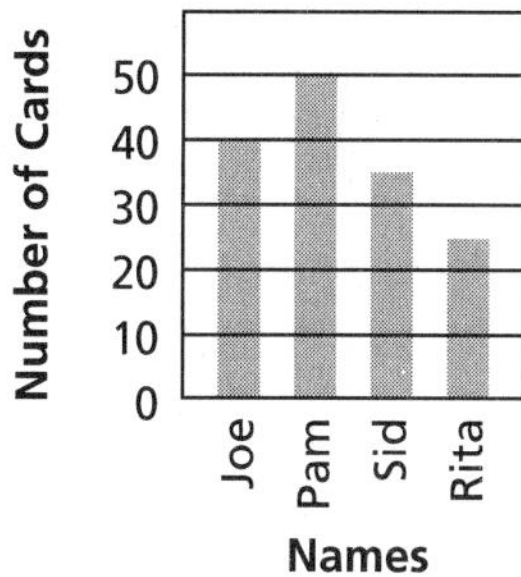

22. How many more baseball cards does Joe have than Rita? ______

23. How many baseball cards do Joe and his friends have in all? ______

Write an equation to solve the problem. Then solve the equation.

24. Melissa had **9** stamps after she sold **4** stamps at the stamp show. How many stamps did she have before the show? ______

Name ______________________________

Total Acreage in California

Year	Grapes	Almonds
1996	744,786	466,777
1997	772,973	472,053

1 **Which is the almond acreage for 1997 rounded to the nearest ten thousand?**

A 770,000 **C** 472,000

B 700,000 **D** 470,000

2 **What is the difference in total grape acreage between 1996 and 1997?**

F 5,276 acres

G 28,187 acres

H 30,000 acres

J 744,786 acres

K 772,973 acres

3 **Which value for x makes this equation true? $15{,}692 - x = 4{,}000 + 10{,}692$**

A 11,000 **C** 1,000

B 10,000 **D** 100

4 **What is the value of the 4 in 246,791,539?**

A 4×10^6

B 4×10^7

C 4×10^8

D 4×10^9

5 **This graph shows the number of miles Anne rode her bike each day for four days.**

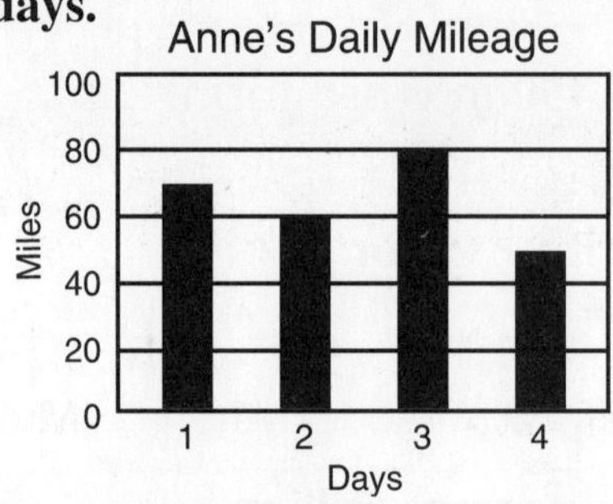

On which day did Anne ride the greatest number of miles?

F Day 1

G Day 2

H Day 3

J Day 4

6 **Dylan lost one piece of his design. Which piece could be used to complete the pattern?**

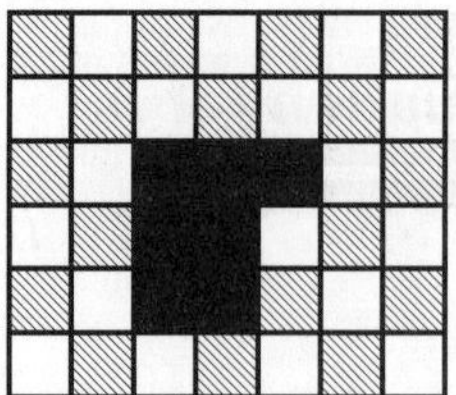

F

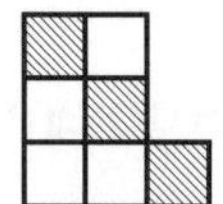

H

G

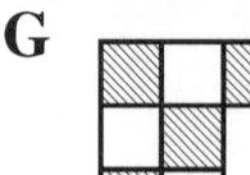

J

UNIT 2 • TABLE OF CONTENTS

Multiplication of Whole Numbers

We will be using this vocabulary:

factors numbers that are multiplied
product the answer in a multiplication problem
equation a number sentence with an equals (=) sign
multiple a number that is a product of itself and a counting number
distributive property the answer will be the same whether you add first and then multiply or multiply first and then add

Dear Family,

During the next few weeks, our math class will be learning and practicing multiplication of whole numbers.

You can expect to see homework that provides practice with multiplying whole numbers. Here is a sample you may want to keep handy to give help if needed.

Multiplying By Tens and Hundreds

These patterns can help a student understand how to multiply by tens and hundreds.

$$\begin{array}{r} 48 \\ \times\ 1 \\ \hline 48 \end{array} \qquad \begin{array}{r} 48 \\ \times\ 10 \\ \hline 480 \end{array} \begin{array}{l} \\ \text{"one zero"} \\ \text{"one zero"} \end{array} \qquad \begin{array}{r} 48 \\ \times\ 100 \\ \hline 4{,}800 \end{array} \begin{array}{l} \\ \text{"two zeros"} \\ \text{"two zeros"} \end{array}$$

The number of zeros in the factors is equal to the number of zeros in the answer, or product.

So, to multiply **800 × 200**, first think **8 × 2 = 16**, then add **4** zeros to the product because the factors **800 × 200** contain **4** zeros.

$$\begin{array}{r} 800 \\ \times\ 200 \\ \hline 16 \end{array} \qquad \begin{array}{r} 800 \\ \times\ 200 \\ \hline 160{,}000 \end{array}$$

During this unit, students will need to continue practicing multiplying by tens and hundreds.

Sincerely,

Name ______________________________

Multiplication Expressions

STANDARD

Some word phrases involve multiplication. These word phrases can be written as algebraic expressions.

Word Phrase	Algebraic Expression
the product of **4** and a number *b*	$4 \times b$
seven times a number *r*	$7 \times r$
10 multiplied by a number *c*	$c \times 10$

There are different ways to simplify an algebraic expression that contains multiplication.

Algebraic Expression		Rewritten Algebraic Expression
$4 \times b$	Eliminate the multiplication sign.	$4b$
$7 \times r$	Use parentheses.	$7(r)$ or $(7)r$ or $(7r)$
$c \times 10$	Multiplication is commutative, so write the variable after the numeral.	$10c$

Write another algebraic expression for the word expression. Let *n* represent the number.

1. **25** multiplied by a number ______

2. a number multiplied by **2** ______

3. the product of **100** and a number ______

4. **12,400** times a number ______

5. the product of a number and **19** ______

6. Multiply the value of ***n*** by **9** ______

Write a word phrase for each algebraic expression.

7. $34 \times h$ ______________________________

8. $480u$ ______________________________

9. $16x$ ______________________________

STANDARD

Look at the table. Decide what is done to *x* each time to find *y*. Write a rule. Then write your rule as an algebraic expression.

10.

x	*y*
2	10
6	30
4	20
5	25

What's my rule?

______

______

______

Expression:

______

11.

x	*y*
0	3
1	4
2	5
3	6

What's my rule?

______

______

______

Expression:

______

12.

x	*y*
15	30
25	50
35	70
45	90

What's my rule?

______

______

______

Expression:

______

Problem Solving Reasoning **Write an algebraic expression for the situation.**

13. Let ***n*** represent the average number of hours you study each day. How many hours do you spend studying in **5** days? ______

14. Let ***b*** represent the average number of times you blink your eyes each hour. How many times do you blink your eyes in **8** hours? ______

Test Prep ★ Mixed Review

15 **Which expression is equivalent to $(n + 3) + 8$?**

A $n + 3 + 8$

B $11n$

C $3n + 8$

D $24 \times n$

16 **What value for n makes the equation true? $n + 56 = 83$**

F 149

G 139

H 33

J 27

Name ______________________

Multiplication Equations

STANDARD

The properties of multiplication can help you solve equations.

Commutative Property of Multiplication	
Arithmetic	**Algebra**
$3 \times 2 = 2 \times 3$	$ab = ba$

The order of the factors does not change the product.

Associative Property of Multiplication	
Arithmetic	**Algebra**
$3(2 \times 5) = (3 \times 2) \times 5$	$a \cdot (bc) = (ab) \cdot c$

The grouping of the factors does not change the product.

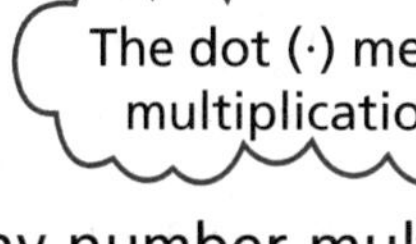

Property of One for Multiplication	
Arithmetic	**Algebra**
$1 \times 7 = 7$	$1 \times n = n$

Any number multiplied by one equals that number.

Zero Property of Multiplication	
Arithmetic	**Algebra**
$0 \times 5 = 0$	$0 \times n = 0$

Any number multiplied by zero equals zero.

Complete.

1. $7 \times 28 =$ ______ $\times 7$ $\quad$ $(ab) \cdot c =$ ______ (bc)

2. $5 \times 1 =$ ______ $\quad$ $d \cdot 1 =$ ______

3. $4 \times$ ______ $= 5 \times 4$ $\quad$ $(5a) \times$ ______ $= 1 \times 5a$

4. $9 \times 0 =$ ______ $\quad$ $ab \cdot 0 = 0 \cdot$ ______

5. $3(4 \times 5) = (3 \times$ ______$) \times 5$ $\quad$ $bdn = n$ ______ b

Complete. Let $n = 6$.

6. $6n =$ ______ $\quad$ $19 + n =$ ______ $\quad$ $n - 2 =$ ______ $\quad$ $5n =$ ______

7. $n \times 0 =$ ______ $\quad$ $52 - n =$ ______ $\quad$ $21n =$ ______ $\quad$ $n(10n) =$ ______

STANDARD

Complete. Let $x = 5$.

8. $x^2 =$ ______ $10 \cdot x =$ ______

9. $x - (1 - 0) =$ ______ $(9x) - 5 =$ ______

10. $(x^2) - 5 =$ ______ $36 - (x + 7) =$ ______

11. $(15 + x) + 20 =$ ______ $(x + 3) - x =$ ______

12. $(2x) - (x + 3) =$ ______ $100 - (x^2) - 10 =$ ______

Problem Solving
Reasoning

Write an equation.

13. The Moreles family plans to mail order a scanner for their computer. It costs **\$250.** The tax will be **\$12.50.** They don't know what the shipping and handling will cost. Write an equation to show the total cost. ______

14. Jamal wants to buy **\$70**-speakers for his computer. He plans to save **\$5** a week for **10** weeks. His father said he would give Jamal **\$25.** Write an equation to show how much Jamal will have after **10** weeks. ______

15. Marcia is saving money to buy a computer. She has saved **\$120** each month for **10** months. Write an equation to show how much more she needs to buy a **\$2,400** computer. ______

16. Jan ran **6** miles each day, Monday through Friday. Write an equation to show how many miles she ran this week. ______

Test Prep ★ Mixed Review

17 In air miles, Los Angeles is 6,296 miles from Rio de Janeiro. What is that number rounded to the nearest 100 miles?

A 7,000 mi

B 6,400 mi

C 6,300 mi

D 6,000 mi

18 Which symbol makes the statement true?
2,600,000 ? 2 million, 6 hundred thousand

F +

G =

H <

J >

Name ______________________________

The Distributive Property

STANDARD

You can use the **Distributive Property** to "break apart" multiplication expressions. Here are two ways to write **2 × 9**.

Multiply. Then add.

$2 \times 4 \quad + \quad 2 \times 5$

$(2 \times 4) + (2 \times 5)$

$8 + 10$

18

There are **18** stars in all.

Add. Then multiply.

$2 \times (4 + 5)$

$2 \times (4 + 5)$

2×9

18

Distributive Property	
Arithmetic	**Algebra**
$6 \times (5 + 4) = (6 \times 5) + (6 \times 4)$	$a \times (b + c) = (a \times b) + (a \times c)$
$6 \cdot (5 + 4) = (6 \cdot 5) + (6 \cdot 4)$	$a \cdot (b + c) = a \cdot b + a \cdot c$
$6(5 + 4) = (6)(5) + (6)(4)$	$a(b + c) = (ab) + (ac)$

Use the distributive property to "break apart" the multiplication expression.

1. $7 \times 9 = 7 \times (3 + 6)$ and $(7 \times 3) + (7 \times$ ______$)$

2. $8 \times 13 =$ ______ $\times (10 + 3)$ and $(8 \times 10) + (8 \times 3)$

3. $5 \times 14 = 5 \times (10 + 4)$ and $(5 \times$ ______$) + (5 \times 4)$

4. $x \cdot 16 = x \cdot (10 +$ ______$)$ and $(x \cdot 10) + (x \cdot$ ______$)$

5. $2 \times 42 =$ ______ $\times (40 + 2)$ and $($______ $\times 40) + ($______ $\times 2)$

6. $n \cdot 34 = n \cdot ($______ $+ 4)$ and $(n \cdot$ ______$) + ($______ $\cdot 4)$

7. $3 \times 21 = 3 \times (20 + 1)$ and $(3 \times$ ______$) + (3 \times 1)$

8. $18 \times 2 = 2 \times ($______ $+ 8)$ and $(2 \times 10) + (2 \times$ ______$)$

9. $51 \cdot p = p(50 + 1)$ and $($______ $\cdot 50) + (p \cdot$ ______$)$

STANDARD

When you multiply using the short form, you are also using the distributive property.

Expanded form	Short form
$\begin{array}{r} 10 + 5 \\ \times \quad 6 \\ \hline 60 + 30 = 90 \end{array}$	$\begin{array}{r} \overset{3}{1}5 \\ \times\ 6 \\ \hline 90 \end{array}$

Multiply.

10. $\begin{array}{r} 29 \\ \times\ 9 \\ \hline \end{array}$ $\begin{array}{r} 83 \\ \times\ 4 \\ \hline \end{array}$ $\begin{array}{r} 65 \\ \times\ 5 \\ \hline \end{array}$ $\begin{array}{r} 664 \\ \times\ 7 \\ \hline \end{array}$ $\begin{array}{r} 559 \\ \times\ 3 \\ \hline \end{array}$ $\begin{array}{r} 859 \\ \times\ 4 \\ \hline \end{array}$

11. $\begin{array}{r} 4{,}126 \\ \times\ 6 \\ \hline \end{array}$ $\begin{array}{r} 4{,}562 \\ \times\ 7 \\ \hline \end{array}$ $\begin{array}{r} 8{,}395 \\ \times\ 2 \\ \hline \end{array}$ $\begin{array}{r} 9{,}517 \\ \times\ 8 \\ \hline \end{array}$ $\begin{array}{r} 3{,}084 \\ \times\ 3 \\ \hline \end{array}$ $\begin{array}{r} 7{,}652 \\ \times\ 5 \\ \hline \end{array}$

Problem Solving
Reasoning

Use the distributive property and mental math to solve.

12. Each car of a train holds **158** people. About how many people can ride on a **6**-car train?

______

13. A group of ***n*** people paid ***n*** × **$5** for a boat ride and ***n*** × **$7** for lunch. Write an expression for the total expense.

______

Quick Check

Find the value of the expression when $n = 5$.

14. $n \times 3$ ______ **15.** $n + n$ ______ **16.** $n \times n$ ______

Solve.

17. $3n = 24$ **18.** $15 = 3 \cdot p$ **19.** $8 \cdot y = 4 \cdot 8$

______ ______ ______

Multiply. Use the distributive property.

20. 602×3 ______ **21.** $\begin{array}{r} 527 \\ \times\ 8 \\ \hline \end{array}$ **22.** $\begin{array}{r} 432 \\ \times\ 6 \\ \hline \end{array}$

Work Space

Name ___________________________

Multiples of 10, 100, and 1,000

STANDARD

These examples show how to multiply by **10, 100,** or **1,000.**

28 × 10 = 280 ← 1 zero	28 × 100 = 2,800 ← 2 zeros	28 × 1,000 = 28,000 ← 3 zeros
Multiplying **28 × 10** is the same as multiplying **28 × 1** and writing one **0** in the product.	Multiplying **28 × 100** is the same as multiplying **28 × 1** and writing two **0**s in the product.	Multiplying **28 × 1,000** is the same as multiplying **28 × 1** and writing three **0**s in the product.

To multiply a number by **10, 100,** or **1,000**, write as many zeros in the product as there are in **10, 100,** or **1,000.**

Multiply.

1. 45 × 10   45 × 100   45 × 1,000   77 × 10   77 × 100   77 × 1,000

2. 823 × 10   823 × 100   823 × 1,000   961 × 10   961 × 100   961 × 1,000

3. 4 × 1,000   7 × 10   2 × 100   64 × 10   275 × 1,000   3193 × 100

Circle the greater product.

4. 36 × 10 or 4 × 100
73 × 10 or 6 × 100
372 × 10 or 41 × 100

5. 804 × 10 or 79 × 100
57 × 100 or 6 × 1,000
26 × 100 or 2 × 1,000

6. 60 × 10 or 5 × 100
800 × 10 or 90 × 100
70 × 100 or 6 × 1,000

7. 47 × 10 or 5 × 100
62 × 100 or 605 × 10
99 × 10 or 10 × 100

8. 702 × 10 or 70 × 100
17 × 1,000 or 105 × 100
76 × 100 or 709 × 10

9. 10 × 1,000 or 100 × 90
906 × 10 or 9 × 1,000
43 × 1,000 or 50 × 100

STANDARD

This pattern shows how to multiply by multiples of 10 and 100.

$\begin{array}{r} {}^{1\,2} \\ 258 \\ \times\ 3 \\ \hline 774 \end{array}$ Remember to regroup.	$\begin{array}{r} 258 \\ \times\ 30 \\ \hline 7{,}740 \end{array}$ There is one **0** in the ones place.	$\begin{array}{r} 258 \\ \times\ 300 \\ \hline 77{,}400 \end{array}$ There are two **0**s.

Multiply.

10. $\begin{array}{r} 372 \\ \times\ 4 \\ \hline \end{array}$ $\begin{array}{r} 372 \\ \times\ 40 \\ \hline \end{array}$ $\begin{array}{r} 703 \\ \times\ 6 \\ \hline \end{array}$ $\begin{array}{r} 703 \\ \times\ 60 \\ \hline \end{array}$ $\begin{array}{r} 393 \\ \times\ 7 \\ \hline \end{array}$ $\begin{array}{r} 393 \\ \times\ 70 \\ \hline \end{array}$

11. $\begin{array}{r} 352 \\ \times\ 50 \\ \hline \end{array}$ $\begin{array}{r} 352 \\ \times\ 500 \\ \hline \end{array}$ $\begin{array}{r} 720 \\ \times\ 60 \\ \hline \end{array}$ $\begin{array}{r} 720 \\ \times\ 600 \\ \hline \end{array}$ $\begin{array}{r} 892 \\ \times\ 90 \\ \hline \end{array}$ $\begin{array}{r} 892 \\ \times\ 900 \\ \hline \end{array}$

12. $\begin{array}{r} 409 \\ \times\ 70 \\ \hline \end{array}$ $\begin{array}{r} 409 \\ \times\ 700 \\ \hline \end{array}$ $\begin{array}{r} 390 \\ \times\ 40 \\ \hline \end{array}$ $\begin{array}{r} 390 \\ \times\ 400 \\ \hline \end{array}$ $\begin{array}{r} 503 \\ \times\ 30 \\ \hline \end{array}$ $\begin{array}{r} 503 \\ \times\ 300 \\ \hline \end{array}$

Multiply.

13. 50 × 30 = ________

80 × 700 = ________

800 × 600 = ________

14. 60 × 70 = ________

90 × 400 = ________

700 × 300 = ________

15. 80 × 50 = ________

40 × 500 = ________

500 × 600 = ________

Test Prep ★ Mixed Review

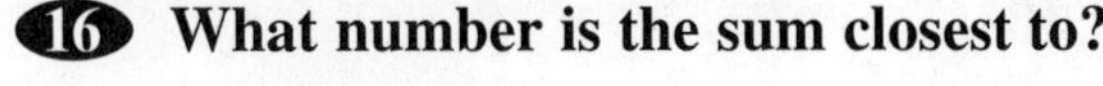

16 **What number is the sum closest to?**

$\begin{array}{r} 234{,}629 \\ +\ 492{,}616 \\ \hline \end{array}$

A 7,000,000

B 700,000

C 70,000

D 7,000

17 **Your total is $3.62. You give the clerk 3 $1 bills and 3 quarters. What is your change?**

F 3 dimes, 1 nickel, 3 pennies

G 4 nickels

H 1 dime and 3 pennies

J 3 pennies

Name ______________________________

Multiplying by Two-Digit Numbers

STANDARD

This example shows how to multiply **643** by **35.**

1. Multiply by the ones digit.

```
 2 1
 643
× 35
3215  ← 5 × 643
```

Remember to regroup.

2. Multiply by the tens digit.

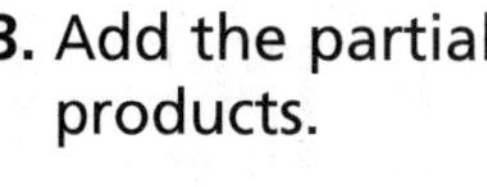

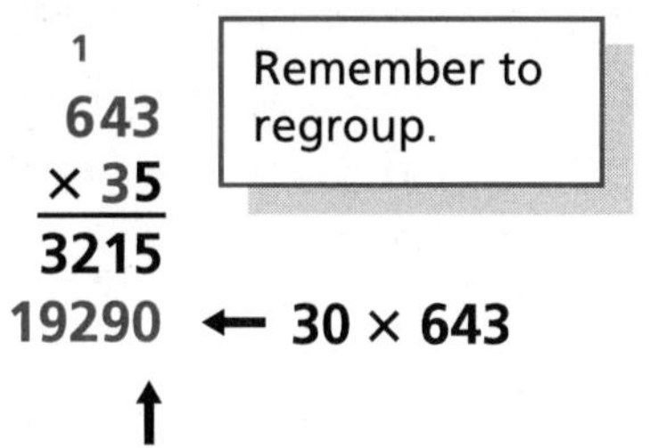

```
    1
  643
 × 35
 3215
19290  ← 30 × 643
```

Remember to regroup.

You do not have to write the zero. Start the answer in the tens place.

3. Add the partial products.

```
   643
  × 35
  3215
+ 1929
22,505
```

Multiply.

1.	404 × 83	567 × 42	390 × 56	770 × 35	371 × 50
2.	408 × 62	573 × 44	608 × 55	725 × 68	937 × 46
3.	685 × 24	393 × 37	408 × 67	380 × 54	609 × 58

4.	75 × 84	29 × 36	47 × 18	630 × 49	504 × 35	480 × 17
5.	158 × 31	296 × 45	342 × 62	506 × 51	821 × 78	142 × 46

STANDARD

Round each factor to the place indicated. Multiply the rounded numbers to find the estimated product.

Factors	Rounded factors	Estimated product
56; 23		
31; 32		
24; 11		
42; 22		
47; 803		

Problem Solving
Reasoning

Decide whether you need an exact answer or an estimated answer. Then solve.

6. An egg carton contains **12** eggs. A shipment of eggs contains **310** cartons. How many eggs are in the shipment?

____

7. A museum is open for **14** hours each day. If an average of **135** people visit the museum per hour, how many people visit the museum each day?

____

8. A mail carrier estimates she drives **750** miles each month. At that rate, how many miles does she drive in **1** year?

____

9. Each week, a courier works Monday through Saturday and estimates he drives **225** miles each day. At that rate, how many miles does he drive in **4** weeks?

____

Quick Check

Use mental math to multiply.

10. 100×97

11. 80×30

12. 200×90

Find the products.

13. 48×57

14. 362×24

15. 89×63

Work Space

Name ______________________

Problem Solving Strategy: Find a Pattern

STANDARD

Sometimes it is helpful to make a table to help you find a pattern.

When you make a table, look for the rule that describes the relationship between the numbers in the pattern.

Problem

Miss Kelly played a game with her class. She asked four students to name a number and then Miss Kelly named another number. When Eva said 2, Miss Kelly said 6. When Joe said 5, Miss Kelly said 15. When Lou said 7, Miss Kelly said 21. When Ryan said 10, what did Miss Kelly say?

1 Understand

As you reread, ask yourself questions.

- Are Miss Kelly's numbers greater than or less than the students' numbers?

____

2 Decide

Choose a method for solving.

- Try the strategy Find a Pattern.

Students	2	5	7	10
Miss Kelly	6	15	21	

3 Solve

Analyze the numbers in the table.

- Does the pattern appear to be an addition pattern or a multiplication pattern? How can you tell?

____

- What did Miss Kelly multiply each student's number by?

______

- What will Miss Kelly's answer be for 10? ______

4 Look back

Check your answer. Write your answer below.

Answer: ______________________

STANDARD

Use the Find a Pattern strategy or any other strategy you have learned.

1. If Robert saves **$1** on Sunday, **$2** on Monday, and **$4** on Tuesday, and if the pattern continues, how much will he save on Saturday?

2. Mary bought **2** muffins for **$3**, Jenna bought **4** muffins for **$6**, and Maurice bought **6** muffins for **$9**. How much does a dozen muffins cost?

3. Ray played a number-guessing game with Jay. When Jay said **9**, Ray said **18**. When Jay said **3**, Ray said **12**. When Jay said **1**, Ray said **10**. What was Ray's rule?

4. To make **6** servings of rice, you use **2** cups of water. For **12** servings, you use **4** cups of water. How many cups of water would you need for **24** servings?

5. Emily is **11** years old and her brother is **22**. How old will Emily be when her brother is **44**?

6. A grandfather clock chimes on the hour and then every **15** minutes. How many times does the clock chime in **24** hours?

7. There are **5** children in a family. The oldest gets an allowance of **$20** per week. Each younger child gets **$3** less than the next older brother or sister. How much allowance does the youngest child get?

8. Bath towels are on sale at **2** for **$15**, hand towels are **2** for **$9**, and wash cloths are **2** for **$5**. What is the total cost if you buy **6** of each type of towel?

9. Write a rule for a number pattern. Then fill in the table showing how your pattern works.

Rule ______________________

First Number						
Second Number						

Name ______________________________

Multiplying by Three-Digit Numbers

STANDARD

This example shows how to find **187 × 298.**

Estimate first. **200 × 300 = 60,000**

1. Multiply by the ones digit.

```
  298
× 187
 2086
```

2. Multiply by the tens digit.

```
  298
× 187
 2086
2384
```

3. Multiply by the hundreds digit.

```
   298
 × 187
  2086
 2384
298
```

4. Add the partial products.

```
   298
 × 187
  2086
 2384
+298
55,726
```

Remember to regroup!

Multiply.

1. 643×176 142×723 698×293 594×685 328×286

2. 754×215 976×234 188×368 576×265 739×426

3. 283×276 543×911 638×419 527×372 293×872

4. 527×468 831×662 391×125 615×281 302×469

STANDARD

Multiply.

5. $\begin{array}{r} 318 \\ \times\ 244 \\ \hline \end{array}$ $\begin{array}{r} 651 \\ \times\ 298 \\ \hline \end{array}$ $\begin{array}{r} 342 \\ \times\ 723 \\ \hline \end{array}$ $\begin{array}{r} 819 \\ \times\ 126 \\ \hline \end{array}$ $\begin{array}{r} 489 \\ \times\ 321 \\ \hline \end{array}$

6. $\begin{array}{r} 629 \\ \times\ 138 \\ \hline \end{array}$ $\begin{array}{r} 721 \\ \times\ 385 \\ \hline \end{array}$ $\begin{array}{r} 915 \\ \times\ 211 \\ \hline \end{array}$ $\begin{array}{r} 853 \\ \times\ 491 \\ \hline \end{array}$ $\begin{array}{r} 276 \\ \times\ 186 \\ \hline \end{array}$

7. $\begin{array}{r} 836 \\ \times\ 358 \\ \hline \end{array}$ $\begin{array}{r} 125 \\ \times\ 581 \\ \hline \end{array}$ $\begin{array}{r} 439 \\ \times\ 682 \\ \hline \end{array}$ $\begin{array}{r} 385 \\ \times\ 224 \\ \hline \end{array}$ $\begin{array}{r} 721 \\ \times\ 216 \\ \hline \end{array}$

Problem Solving
Reasoning

Solve.

8. A supermarket is open every day of the year. An average of **420** people shops in the supermarket per day. In one year, how many shoppers can the supermarket expect to serve? (Hint: **1** year = **365** days)

____

9. A non-leap year is **365** days long. A leap year is **366** days long. In a leap year, how many shoppers can the supermarket in exercise 8 expect to serve?

____

Test Prep ★ Mixed Review

10 **Which value of *n* makes the equation true? 75 × 77 = 75 × (*n* + 7)**

A 77

B 75

C 70

D 7

11 **Seventy-seven students paid 75¢ for a ticket to a school play. About how much money did they pay for tickets?**

F More than $77

G Between $70 and $77

H Between $60 and $70

J Between $50 and $60

Name ______________________

Multiplying with Zeros

STANDARD

Sometimes factors contain one or more zeros.

```
    643      Write zero in the
  × 201      partial product to
    643      show 0 tens. Then
  12860  ←   multiply by hundreds.
129,243
```

```
    376      Write zero in the
  × 240  ←   partial product to
  15040  ←   show 0 ones. Then
  + 752      multiply by tens.
 90,240
```

Multiply.

1.	729 × 603	694 × 630	428 × 702	376 × 240	865 × 409
2.	421 × 402	615 × 109	726 × 305	843 × 206	908 × 406
3.	662 × 470	753 × 360	835 × 290	444 × 130	633 × 520
4.	842 × 460	953 × 320	657 × 590	570 × 260	398 × 180
5.	3,007 × 717	5,600 × 906	9,080 × 652	4,770 × 530	1,919 × 381

STANDARD

Multiply.

6. 385 × 728 | 430 × 637 | 842 × 160 | 609 × 850 | 826 × 529

7. 703 × 806 | 381 × 316 | 834 × 503 | 809 × 845 | 394 × 671

Problem Solving Reasoning

Solve.

8. A book is **320** pages long and has an average of **483** words per page. At that rate, how many words would you expect the book to have?

______

9. An outdoor theater has **160** rows of seats. Each row has **130** seats. If a person is sitting in each seat, how many people are seated in the theater?

______

Quick Check

Multiply.

10. 615 × 114

11. \$3.82 × 264

12. \$3.99 × 125

Find the product.

13. 516 × 901

14. 308 × 604

15. 860 × 904

Work Space

Name ______________________

Problem Solving Application: Is the Answer Reasonable?

STANDARD

After you solve a problem, check whether the answer makes sense. Is the answer too great? Is the answer too small? Or is it just about right?

In this lesson, use estimation when you can to check whether your answer is reasonable.

Tips to Remember

1. Understand 2. Decide 3. Solve 4. Look back

- Ask yourself questions about the numbers in each statement. Should the answer be an exact answer or an estimate?
- Think about strategies you have learned and use them to help you solve the problem.
- Think about the answer. Is it reasonable?

Solve. Check that your answer is reasonable.

1. A school cafeteria has **15** tables. Each table can seat **12** students. How many students can eat in the cafeteria at one time?

Think: Should you add or multiply? How can you use rounding to estimate?

____

____

Answer ______________________

____

2. The school is having a book fair. The first book you buy costs **$6** and each additional book is half of this price. What is the cost of **3** books?

Think: How much does each additional book cost?

____

Answer ______________________

STANDARD

Solve. Check that your answer is reasonable.

3. There are **375** seats in the school's auditorium. The school play was sold out for each of the **3** performances. How many people saw the play?

____

4. The students rehearsed **2** hours after school every day for **3** weeks. What was the total number of hours the students rehearsed?

____

5. The **9** students in the play bought flowers for the play's director. If each student's share was **$4.50**, was the cost of the flowers closer to **$36** or **$40**?

____

6. The proceeds from a cake and cookie sale at the play were **$33**. Nine cakes sold for **$3** each and cookies sold for **$.50** each. Were there **6** cookies or **12** cookies sold?

____

7. Tickets for the school play cost **$8** each for adults and **$3** each for students. What was the cost of **2** adult tickets and **1** student ticket?

____

8. For one performance, **212** adult tickets and **163** student tickets were sold. Was the total amount of money taken in that night closer to **$2,000** or **$3,000**?

____

Extend Your Thinking

9. There were **225** adult tickets sold for the play one night. What was the total amount of money taken in from ticket sales that night? (Use the information in problem **7** to solve.)

____

10. Explain your method for solving problem 6. Did you use more than one operation?

____

____

____

Name ______________________

Unit 2 Review

Write an algebraic expression for each word expression. Let n represent each variable.

1. 12 multiplied by a number ______

2. the product of a number and 35 ______

Complete each equation.

3. $4 \times 9 =$ ______ $\times 4$

4. $0 \cdot x =$ ______

5. $2\,(6 \times 3) = 2 \times ($______$)$

6. $1d =$ ______

7. $r(st) = (rs)$ ______

8. $abc = c$ ______

Solve each equation for $n = 3$.

9. $n^3 =$ ______

10. $6n =$ ______

11. $(8n) - 4 =$ ______

Use the distributive property to break apart each multiplication.

12. $5 \times 13 = 5 \times (6 +$ ______$) = (5 \times$ ______$) + ($______ $\times 7)$

13. $24 \times 3 =$ ______ $\times (20 + 4) = (3 \times$ ______$) + ($______ $\times 4)$

Multiply.

14. 34×4

15. 807×5

16. $1{,}044 \times 3$

17. 525×100

18. 78×10

19. 372×40

20. 782×45

21. 470×944

22. $2{,}066 \times 649$

23. $1{,}000 \times 360$

Solve.

24. Before multiplying **1,999** × **19,** Jim estimated the product to be **400,000**. Is **400,000** a reasonable estimate? Explain.

____

25. What amount comes next in this pattern? ______

$.50 $1.05 $2.15 $4.35 $8.75 ______

Name ______________________________

Cumulative Review
★ Test Prep

1 **What is another way to express 10^9?**

A 1 followed by 6 zeros

B 10 followed by 6 zeros

C 100 followed by 6 zeros

D 1,000 followed by 6 zeros

2 **Which number is the product for $n \cdot 57 = (n \cdot 50) + (3 \cdot 7)$?**

F 570 **H** 150

G 171 **J** 21

3 **The product p of each of these three equations will be the same if the places of two circled numbers are switched.**

(12) × (2) = p
(18) × (3) = p
(4) × (9) = p

The places of which two numbers should be switched?

A 18 and 4 **C** 3 and 2

B 9 and 12 **D** 4 and 12

4 **Which value for x makes this equation true? $x + 2{,}453 = 3{,}542$**

F 5,995 **H** 1,089

G 1,111 **J** 144

5 **Shaina wants to buy a hat that costs $7.59. If she buys a hat for herself and one hat for each of her two sisters, how much money will she spend?**

A $7.59 **C** $27.59 **E** Not here

B $22.77 **D** $30.36

6 **This table shows the prices of a 19-inch color television in three different years.**

Television Prices

1964	$179.95
1972	$220.00
1987	$209.99

How much more did a 19-inch color television cost in 1972 than in 1987?

F $70.95 **H** $29.00 **K** Not here

G $29.05 **J** $21.00

7 **Which number sentence shows the cost of two televisions in 1987?**

A 2 × $179.95 = $359.90

B 2 × $209.99 = $419.98

C $440.00 + 2 = $442.00

D $359.90 − 2 = $357.90

8 **Which number shows how many pencils are in 100 boxes?**

F 14,400,000 **H** 144,000 **K** 1,440

G 1,440,000 **J** 14,400

9 **Louis walks three miles each day. How many miles does he walk in one year (365 days)?**

A 3,650 miles **C** 90 miles **E** 21 miles

B 1,095 miles **D** 30 miles

UNIT 3 • TABLE OF CONTENTS

Division of Whole Numbers

We will be using this vocabulary:

divisor the number by which a number is divided

dividend the number that is divided

quotient the number of groups or the number in each group

remainder the number left over after you find the quotient

Dear Family,

During the next few weeks, our math class will be learning and practicing the division of whole numbers.

You can expect to see homework that provides practice with dividing and checking whole numbers. Here is a sample you may want to keep handy to give help if needed.

Checking Division

To divide **407** by **23**, first think about how many digits will be in the quotient.

$23\overline{)407}$

Think about hundreds.
23 > 4
The quotient will not have hundreds.

There will be two digits in the quotient. The first digit will be in the tens.

$$\begin{array}{r} 17 \text{ R16} \\ 23\overline{)407} \\ -23 \\ \hline 177 \\ -161 \\ \hline 16 \end{array}$$

To check if the answer is correct, multiply the divisor **(23)** by the quotient **(17)**. Then add the remainder **(16)**. The result should be the same as the dividend **(407)**.

$$\begin{array}{r} 17 \\ \times 23 \\ \hline 51 \\ 340 \\ \hline 391 \\ +\ 16 \\ \hline 407 \end{array}$$

During this unit, students will need to continue practicing addition, subtraction, multiplication, and division facts.

Sincerely,

Name ______________________________

Multiplication and Division Equations

STANDARD

You know that you can use opposite or **inverse** operations to solve an equation.

To solve a division equation, use multiplication.

$n \div 4 = 8$

Think: $n = 8 \times 4$

$n = 32$

Multiplication is the inverse of division.
Think: 8 times **4** is what number?

To solve a multiplication equation, use division.

$y \times 3 = 15$

Think: $y = 15 \div 3$

$y = 5$

Division is the inverse of multiplication.
Think: 15 divided by **3** is what number?

Complete.

1. $n \div 5 = 9$
Think: $n = 9 \times$ ______
$n = 45$

$y \div 6 = 7$
Think: $y =$ ______ $\times 6$
$y = 42$

$a \div 5 = 6$
Think: $a = 6 \times 5$
$a =$ ______

2. $b \times 4 = 12$
Think: $b = 12 \div 4$
$b =$ ______

$7 \times n = 21$
Think: $n = 21 \div$ ______
$n = 3$

$9 \times y = 27$
Think: $y = 27$ ______ 9
$y = 3$

3. $n \div 9 = 7$
Think: $n = 7 \times$ ______
$n =$ ______

$8 \times a = 40$
Think: $a = 40 \div$ ______
$a =$ ______

$h \times 4 = 28$
Think: $h =$ ______ $\div 4$
$h =$ ______

4. $a \div 5 = 7$
Think: $a = 7$ ______ 5
$a =$ ______

$n \times 4 = 24$
Think: $n = 24$ ______ 4
$n =$ ______

$y \div 8 = 2$
Think: $y =$ ______ $\times$ ______
$y =$ ______

Find the value of *y*.

5. $y \div 6 = 2$ $\quad$ $y \times 4 = 20$ $\quad$ $y \div 8 = 7$ $\quad$ $4 \times y = 36$

6. $y \times 4 = 16$ $\quad$ $y \div 9 = 2$ $\quad$ $3 \times y = 18$ $\quad$ $y \div 6 = 9$

STANDARD

Find the value of h.

7. $h \times 4 = 40$ $h \div 7 = 2$ $5 \times h = 25$ $h \div 7 = 7$

8. $h \div 9 = 9$ $h \times 5 = 10$ $h \div 8 = 10$ $3 \times h = 9$

9. $h \times 4 = 8$ $h \div 3 = 9$ $h \div 9 = 10$ $3 \times h = 6$

Problem Solving Reasoning

Circle the equation that represents the problem. Then find the value of t.

10. Members of a hiking club hiked **54** miles in **6** days. They hiked the same number of miles each day. How many miles did they hike each day?

$t \div 6 = 54$

$t \times 6 = 54$

$t =$ ______

11. Three hikers sleep in each of **6** tents. How many hikers are there?

$h \div 3 = 6$

$h \times 3 = 6$

$h =$ ______

Write a problem that could be represented by the equation $n \div 7 = 3$. Then find the value of n.

12. ____

____

____

Test Prep ★ Mixed Review

13 What number sentence is in the same family of facts as $6 \times 4 = \square$?

A $6 + 4 = \square$

B $\square \times 4 = 6$

C $\square = 6 \div 4$

D $\square \div 4 = 6$

14 A pad and pencil costs $7.83. You give the clerk a $10 bill and 3 pennies. What change do you get?

F 3 $1 bills

G 2 dimes, 2 $1 bills

H 2 pennies, 1 nickel, 1 dime, 2 $1 bills

J 2 pennies, 2 dimes, 2 $1 bills

Name ______________________________

Order of Operations

STANDARD

To evaluate an expression that has more than one operation, follow the rules for the order of operations.

Evaluate $72 \div x^2 + (4 - 2)$ for $x = 3$.

1. Perform all operations inside parentheses first.
2. Evaluate exponents.
3. Multiply and divide from left to right.
4. Add and subtract from left to right.

$72 \div x^2 + (4 - 2)$
↓
$72 \div x^2 + 2$
↓
$72 \div 9 + 2$
↓
$8 + 2$
↓
10

> **Remember:** When you **evaluate an expression,** you substitute the value of the variable in the expression.

Write the operation you would perform first to evaluate each expression for $n = 3$.

1. $3 + 9 \times n$ ________ $18 - n^2 \div 3$ ________ $8 \times (9 - n)$ ________

2. $n - 2 \div 2$ ________ $36 \div (n + 1)$ ________ $8 - n \times 2^2$ ________

Complete to evaluate each expression for $a = 2$.

3. $10 - 4 \div a$ → $10 -$ ______ → ______

$6 + 4 \times a$ → $6 +$ ______ → ______

$13 - 6 + a$ → ______ $+ a$ → ______

4. $6 \times (10 - a) \div 8$ → $6 \times$ ______ $\div 8$ → ______ $\div 8$ → ______

$a + 3^2 - 7$ → $a +$ ______ $- 7$ → ______ $- 7$ → ______

$a^3 + (7 - 1) \div a$ → ______ $+$ ______ $\div a$ → ______ $+$ ______ → ______

STANDARD

You can use the division rules for **0** and **1** when you evaluate expressions.

- When you divide a number by **1**, $9 \div 1 = 9$ the quotient is that number.
- When you divide any number except **0** by itself, $12 \div 12 = 1$ the quotient is **1**.
- When you divide **0** by any number except **0**, $0 \div 4 = 0$ the quotient is **0**.

  But remember, you cannot divide a number by **0**.

Evaluate each expression. Replace the variable with the given value.

5. $3^2 \div (3 + a)$ for $a = 6$ ______ $(s - 3^2) \div 6$ for $s = 9$ ______

6. $15 \div s + 2$ for $s = 3$ ______ $x - (3 \times 3)$ for $x = 18$ ______

7. $4 - 2 \times 6 \div s$ for $s = 3$ ______ $a \times (3 + 2)^2$ for $a = 1$ ______

8. $5 \times 2 - (2 + x)$ for $x = 3$ ______ $(n \div 2)^2 - 7$ for $n = 8$ ______

9. $n \div 4 + 9 \times 2$ for $n = 0$ ______ $(2 + s - 1) \times 2 \div 8$ for $s = 3$ ______

10. $11 \div (9 - y)$ for $y = 8$ ______ $0 \div y^2$ for $y = 5$ ______

Problem Solving Reasoning

Write an expression that represents the problem. Use *x* for the variable. Evaluate the expression for *x* = $25.

11. Jamie donated her award money to her 5 favorite charities. She gave the same amount to each charity. How much did she give to each charity?

____

12. Sean put $10 of his award money in a savings account. He gave the rest to 3 charities. He gave the same amount to each charity. How much money did he give to each charity?

____

Test Prep ★ Mixed Review

13 **Which numbers complete the pattern?**

Pattern: 20, 19, 17, 14, ___, ___

A 18, 23

B 113, 12

C 10, 5

D 10, 1

14 **It is 154 miles to the beach and 196 miles to the mountains. What is the best estimate of how much farther it is to travel to the mountains?**

F 50 miles

G 100 miles

H 300 miles

J 350 miles

Name ______________________

Dividing by One-Digit Numbers

STANDARD

Follow these steps to divide by a one-digit number.

1. Look at the dividend and the divisor. Decide if you can divide.

$$6\overline{)85} \quad \text{quotient: } 1$$

Think: **6)8**
Try **1** in the quotient.

2. Multiply. Then compare the product to the dividend number.

$$\begin{array}{r} 1 \\ 6\overline{)85} \\ -6 \end{array}$$

1 × 6 = 6
6 < 8 If the product is greater than the dividend digit, try a lesser digit in the quotient.

3. Subtract. Then compare the difference to the divisor.

$$\begin{array}{r} 1 \\ 6\overline{)85} \\ -6 \\ \hline 2 \end{array}$$

Since **2 < 6** you cannot divide until you bring down another digit.

4. Bring down the next digit in the dividend. Subtract. Repeat these steps until there are no numbers left to bring down.

$$\begin{array}{r} 14\ \text{R1} \\ 6\overline{)85} \\ -6 \\ \hline 25 \\ -24 \\ \hline 1 \end{array}$$

quotient: 14; remainder: R1; divisor: 6; dividend: 85; remainder: 1

- To check the answer:
- Multiply the quotient by the divisor. Then add the remainder.
- The result should be the same as the dividend.

$$\begin{array}{r} 14 \\ \times\ 6 \\ \hline 84 \\ +\ 1 \\ \hline 85 \end{array}$$

14 ←**quotient**
× 6 ←**divisor**
+ 1 ←**remainder**
85 The dividend is **85**.
So the answer is correct.

Divide.

1. 6)59 3)98 4)85 8)70 6)87

2. 5)93 7)43 6)75 3)45 2)51

STANDARD

Divide. Use multiplication to check.

3. $3\overline{)126}$ $6\overline{)504}$ $5\overline{)408}$ $5\overline{)762}$

4. $6\overline{)416}$ $3\overline{)498}$ $7\overline{)628}$ $6\overline{)958}$

Problem Solving Reasoning

Solve. If there is a remainder, explain how you got your answer.

5. One hundred seventy people are going on a bus tour. They will fill **5** buses. How many people will be on each bus?

____

____

____

6. To reach the mountain top, sightseers can ride in cable cars. Each cable car seats **8** people. One hundred people want to reach the mountain top. How many cable cars will they need?

____

____

Quick Check

Find the value of the variable in the equation.

7. $5 = s \div 5$ ______ **8.** $x \div 3 = 9$ ______ **9.** $t \times 6 = 54$ ______

Use the order of operations to find the value of the expression.

10. $(7 + 7^2) \div 7$ ______

11. $2 + 11 - (13 - 4)$ ______

12. $5^2 - 7 \times 3$ ______

Divide.

13. $9\overline{)369}$ **14.** $6\overline{)381}$ **15.** $7\overline{)203}$

Work Space

Name ____________________

Dividing Money

STANDARD

Here are some examples of dividing money. Remember to place the cent sign, dollar sign, and decimal point in the quotient as necessary.

$$\begin{array}{r} 43¢ \\ 2\overline{)86¢} \\ -8 \\ \hline 6 \\ -6 \\ \hline 0 \end{array}$$

Divide as you would with whole numbers.

$$\begin{array}{r} \$25 \\ 5\overline{)\$125} \\ -10 \\ \hline 25 \\ -25 \\ \hline 0 \end{array}$$

$$\begin{array}{r} \$.14 \\ 7\overline{)\$.98} \\ -7 \\ \hline 28 \\ -28 \\ \hline 0 \end{array}$$

Write the decimal point in the quotient above the decimal point in the dividend.

$$\begin{array}{r} \$2.45 \\ 3\overline{)\$7.35} \\ -6 \\ \hline 13 \\ -12 \\ \hline 15 \\ -15 \\ \hline 0 \end{array}$$

Divide.

1. $8\overline{)96¢}$ $4\overline{)\$60}$ $3\overline{)72¢}$ $4\overline{)\$88}$

2. $4\overline{)\$.96}$ $2\overline{)\$58}$ $2\overline{)\$.76}$ $3\overline{)\$75}$

3. $4\overline{)\$5.64}$ $3\overline{)\$8.10}$ $4\overline{)\$5.00}$ $2\overline{)\$7.06}$

4. $6\overline{)\$4.74}$ $7\overline{)\$5.53}$ $5\overline{)\$2.90}$ $8\overline{)\$7.76}$

STANDARD

Divide.

5. $4\overline{)\$7.64}$ $8\overline{)\$496}$ $3\overline{)\$813}$ $9\overline{)\$6.66}$

6. $9\overline{)\$8.64}$ $7\overline{)\$595}$ $2\overline{)\$918}$ $4\overline{)\$9.00}$

7. $4\overline{)76¢}$ $6\overline{)\$9.96}$ $2\overline{)\$.74}$ $5\overline{)\$110}$

Problem Solving
Reasoning

Solve. Explain your answer.

8. A basket of chicken wings costs **$9.99.** If **4** people share **1** basket, what is the cost per person?

____

____

____

9. An order of vegetables costs **$8.50**. If six people share the order, what is the cost per person?

____

____

____

Test Prep ★ Mixed Review

10 **Which pair of numbers when rounded will give a sum of about 100 and a product of about 2,100?**

A 45 and 42

B 56 and 41

C 65 and 32

D 75 and 29

11 **There are 48 cartons on a shelf. Each carton contains 64 books. What is a good estimate of how many books there are?**

F 10

G 100

H 2,400

J 3,000

Name ______________________________

Zero in the Quotient

STANDARD

Sometimes when you divide, you must write a zero in the quotient.

Divide **2,013** by **4**.

1. Divide hundreds. **2.** Divide tens. **3.** Bring down the next digit. Divide ones. **4.** Multiply to check.

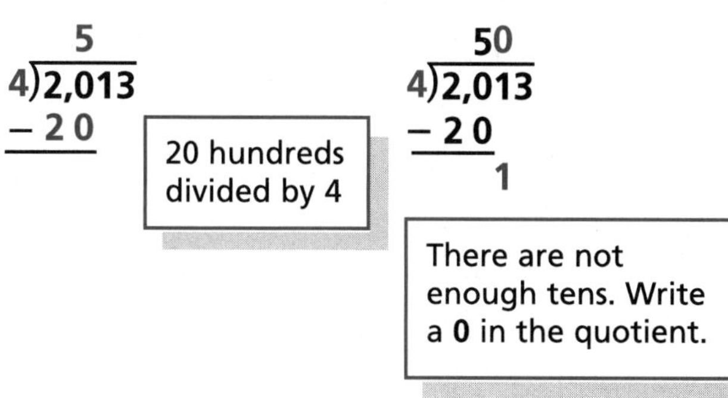

503 ← quotient
× 4
2,012
+ 1 ← remainder
2,013 ← dividend

It checks. The answer, **503 R1,** is correct.

Divide. Use multiplication to check.

1. 4)836	5)$5.20	3)962
2. 2)$6.10	7)743	8)645
3. 6)542	4)428	8)$8.72
4. 5)1,520	6)1,255	8)4,856

STANDARD

Divide. Use multiplication to check.

5. $3\overline{)1,521}$ $4\overline{)1,234}$ $2\overline{)\$14.18}$

6. $6\overline{)2,448}$ $9\overline{)\$27.54}$ $7\overline{)3,539}$

Problem Solving Reasoning Solve.

7. There are **3,654** people seated in **6** sections of a stadium. An equal number is in each section. How many people are in each section?

____

8. Three season passes to football games cost **$306.** How much does **1** season pass cost?

____

9. Each team van can seat **6** people. How many vans are needed for **125** people? Explain what you did with the remainder.

____

____

Test Prep ★ Mixed Review

10 What is the value of the expression $4 \times (15 - 2) \div 13$?

A 30

B 26

C 17

D 4

11 A Thanksgiving turkey weighs 18 pounds. If 1 pound = 16 ounces, what is the weight of the turkey in ounces?

F 288

G 34

H 22

J 2

Name ______________________

Averages

STANDARD

This **line plot** shows the number of pennies **8** students have in their pockets. What is the average number of pennies the students have?

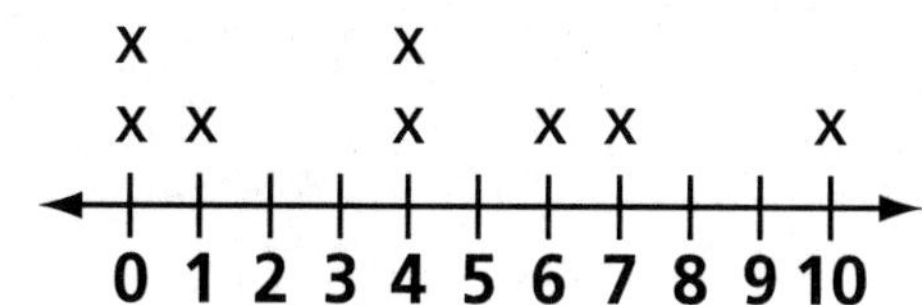

To find the **average** or **mean** of a set of numbers:

1. Add the numbers.

0 + 0 + 1 + 4 + 4 + 6 + 7 + 10 = 32

8 addends — sum

2. Divide the sum by the number of addends.

32 ÷ 8 = 4

The average number of pennies is **4.**

Find the average of each group of numbers.

1. 3, 6, 9 ______ 0, 2, 4 ______ 1, 5, 9 ______

2. 7, 11, 30 ______ $11, $13 ______ 100, 200 ______

3. 42, 76, 83 ______ 1, 2, 3, 4, 5 ______ 5, 12, 15, 8 ______

4. 6, 8, 19, 15 ______ 59¢, 42¢, 58¢ ______ 19, 42, 31, 8 ______

5. 183, 157, 170 ______ 562, 571, 538, 573 ______

6. 110, 108, 98, 60, 139 ______ 80, 59, 43, 46 ______

7. 79, 95, 80, 66, 77, 77 ______ 72, 65, 36, 57, 87, 97, 57, 65 ______

8. 86, 95, 59, 74, 58, 83, 70 ______ 125, 240, 360, 255, 190 ______

9. 65, 37, 45, 18, 21, 44 ______ 100, 112, 114, 118, 106 ______

STANDARD

Problem Solving
Reasoning

Solve.

10. Susan's test scores in mathematics for the past eight weeks are: **80, 85, 90, 75, 75, 100, 85,** and **90.**

What is Susan's average test score? ______

11. During the four periods of a basketball game, the Jets scored **24, 17, 29,** and **26** points. What is the average number of points the Jets scored in a period?

____

12. Ben's bowling scores for the past seven weeks are: **150, 124, 115, 160, 130, 140, 140.** What is Ben's average bowling score?

____

13. The average temperature during one week in January was **17°F**. Write **7** different temperatures that could have an average of **17°F.**

____

Quick Check

Divide.

Work Space

14. 2)$4.70 **15.** 7)$1.40 **16.** 3)$0.18

17. 5)815 **18.** 6)6,581 **19.** 7)915

Find the average.

20. 26, 35, 60, 31, 26, 50 ______

21. $8, $0, $6, $14, $7, $10, $4 ______

22. 236, 473, 286, 505 ______

Name ______________________

Problem Solving Application: Too Much or Not Enough Information

STANDARD

Sometimes a problem may give you more facts than you need. You have to decide which facts you need to answer the question.

Other times you may not have enough facts.

In this lesson you will identify the extra information or name the fact or facts that you need to solve a problem.

Tips to Remember

1. Understand 2. Decide 3. Solve 4. Look back

- Write down the facts in the problem. Decide if there are extra facts. Is any information missing?
- Read each problem more than once. Circle the important words and numbers. Cross out the words and numbers that you don't need.
- Think about each fact in the problem. Ask yourself: Is this an extra fact? Or do I need it to find a solution?

Cross out the extra information. Then solve the problem. If information is missing, name the fact or facts needed on the answer lines.

1. The fifth grade at the Lakewood School is taking a field trip to the zoo. If there are **135** people going on the trip, how many buses are needed?

Think: What two pieces of information do you need to answer the question?

____

____

Answer

____

____

2. Judy's father bought a living room rug. How much did the rug cost if he paid **$31.50** a month for **24** months?

Think: What two pieces of information do you need to find the total cost of the rug?

____

____

Answer

____

STANDARD

Cross out the extra information. Then solve the problem.
If information is missing, name the fact or facts that you need.

3. There are **28** seats in each row of a section of a baseball stadium. There are **336** seats in a section. How many seats are there in the stadium?

4. Carla earns **$84** each day that she works. Last week she worked on Monday, Tuesday, and Friday for **4** hours each day. How much did she earn last week?

5. Mr. Howard cut **15** pieces of silk from a large roll of **1,000** yards. How much was left?

6. Last week, Tom, David, and Jackie earned **$316.98, $271.02**, and **$183.45** respectively. How much did Tom and David earn together?

7. Mrs. Balch's class had **1** package of red paper and **2** packages of green paper. How many sheets of red paper were used if there were **45** sheets left in a pack of **500** sheets?

8. The Wallaces bought **3** sandwiches, a salad, and **3** drinks to take to the beach. Each sandwich cost **$2.95** and each drink was **$.85**. How much did they spend on food for the beach?

Extend Your Thinking

9. How can you find the number of square yards in the area of the rug in problem **2**? Find the area of the rug

10. Look back at problem **8**. Explain the method you used to solve the problem.

Name ______________________________

Divisibility

STANDARD

A number is **divisible** by another number when the quotient is a whole number and the remainder is zero.

Here are ways to test if a number is divisible by another number.

If a number is divisible by **2**, it is even. If it is not divisible by **2**, the number is odd.

564
4 is divisible by **2,** so
564 is divisible by **2.**

465
5 is not divisible by **2,** so
465 is not divisible by **2.**

A number is divisible by **3** if the sum of the digits is divisible by **3**.

243
2 + **4** + **3** = **9**
9 is divisible by **3,** so
243 is divisible by **3.**

A number is divisible by **9** if the sum of the digits is divisible by **9**.

891
8 + **9** + **1** = **18**
18 is divisible by **9,** so
891 is divisible by **9.**

A number is divisible by **4** if the last two digits are divisible by **4**.

132
32 is divisible by **4,** so
132 is divisible by **4.**

218
18 is not divisible by **4,** so
218 is not divisible by **4.**

Place a ✔ by each number that is divisible by 2.

1. 23 54 90 233 127 1,124

2. 12 97 45 234 721 4,112

Put a ✔ in the box to show that the number is divisible by 2, 4, 3, or 9.

		2	4	3	9
3.	164				
4.	45				
5.	503				

		2	4	3	9
6.	71				
7.	252				
8.	116				

STANDARD

A number is divisible by **5** if the digit in the ones' place is **0** or **5**.

365 is divisible by **5.**
563 is not divisible by **5.**

A number is divisible by **10** if the digit in the ones' place is **0.**

470 is divisible by **10.**
407 is not divisible by **10.**

Place a ✔ in the box to show that the number is divisible by 2, 3, 4, 5, 9, or 10.

		2	3	4	5	9	10
9.	108						
10.	130						
11.	246						
12.	333						
13.	782						
14.	880						

Problem Solving Reasoning **Solve.**

15. One hundred thirty students will attend a school party. Can they all be seated at tables of **5**? Can they all be seated at tables of **10**? Explain your answers.

____

____

16. Can **130** students all be seated at tables of **6**? Explain your answer.

____

____

Test Prep ★ Mixed Review

17 In which number does the 6 have the greatest value?

A 99,246,072

B 840,506

C 640,508

D 57,600

18 Maria is 3 years older than her sister. If her sister is s years old, then which expression tells how old Maria is?

F $s + 3$

G $s - 3$

H $s \times 3$

J $s \div 3$

Name ______________________________

Prime and Composite Numbers

STANDARD

Every counting number **(1, 2, 3, . . .)** has at least one pair of **factors.** A factor of a number is also a **divisor** of that number.

24 = 3 × 8   24 = 8 × 3

3 and **8** are *factors* of **24.**

3 and **8** are *divisors* of **24.**

Write each number as a product of a pair or pairs of factors.

1.

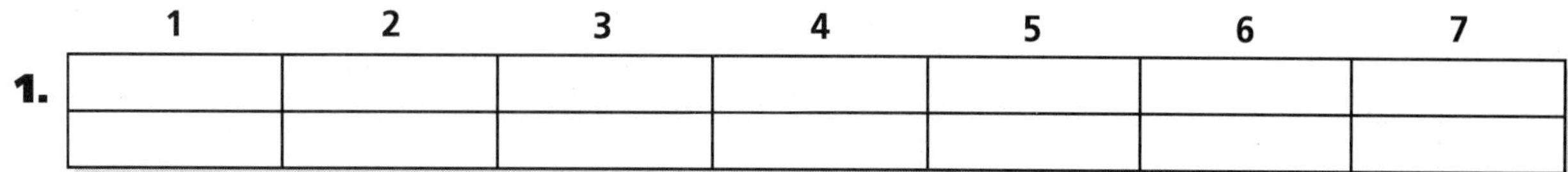

1	2	3	4	5	6	7

2.

8	9	10	11	12	13	14

3.

15	16	17	18	19	20	21

Notice that some of the numbers above have only **2** factors.

- If a counting number has only two factors (itself and **1**), then it is called a **prime number**.
- The numbers above that are prime numbers are: **2, 3, 5, 7, 11, 13, 17,** and **19.**
- The number **1** has only one factor. It is therefore neither prime nor composite.

Notice that the other numbers above have more than **2** factors.

- If a counting number has more than two factors, then it is called a **composite number**.
- The numbers above that are composite numbers are: **4, 6, 8, 9, 10, 12, 14, 15, 16, 18, 20,** and **21.**

Complete by writing the products with as many different pairs of factors as you can. Circle the prime numbers.

4.

23	25	27	29	31	33	35

STANDARD

Write *P* for prime or *C* for composite. If the number is composite, then write it as a product of a pair of factors other than itself and 1.

5. 32 ______ 17 ______

6. 31 ______ 57 ______

7. 97 ______ 42 ______

8. 99 ______ 29 ______

9. 63 ______ 51 ______

Write *E* for even numbers, *O* for odd numbers. Then write *P* for prime or *C* for composite.

10. 14 ___ ___ 15 ___ ___ 16 ___ ___

11. 18 ___ ___ 20 ___ ___ 21 ___ ___

12. 22 ___ ___ 23 ___ ___ 34 ___ ___

13. 40 ___ ___ 42 ___ ___ 45 ___ ___

14. 1 ___ ___ 57 ___ ___ 62 ___ ___

15. 64 ___ ___ 72 ___ ___ 75 ___ ___

Problem Solving
Reasoning

Write *True* or *False*. Then explain your answer.

16. All prime numbers are odd. ______

17. All composite numbers are even. ______

Solve.

18. Predict which of the numbers to the right will have the *greatest* number of pairs of factors. Which will have the *least*? Then test your prediction by finding the pairs of factors for each number.

32 33 34

35 36 37

______

Test Prep ★ Mixed Review

19. A can of cat food costs 33¢ + 1¢ tax. Which expression shows how much 16 cans will cost?

A 16 × 33¢ + 1¢

B \$16 × 33 + \$1

C \$16 × 33 + \$16 × 1

D 16 × (33¢ + 1¢)

20. Edda is 3 times older than her nephew. If Edda is d years old, then which expression tells how old her nephew is?

F $d \div 3$

G $d - 3$

H $d \times 3$

J $d + 3$

Name ____________________

Prime Factorization

STANDARD

When you write a composite number as the product of prime factors, it is called **prime factorization.**

You can make a **factor tree** to find the prime factorization of a composite number.

Follow these steps to make a factor tree for **36**.

1. Write a pair of factors for **36.**

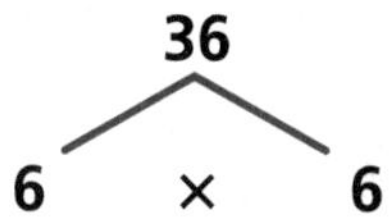

2. Write each factor as a pair of factors until all the factors are prime numbers.

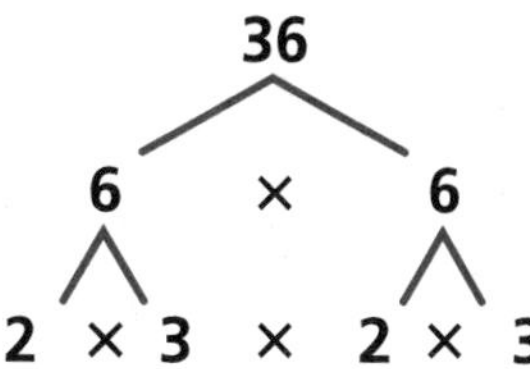

3. Use exponents, when you can, to write the prime factorization.

$36 = 2 \times 2 \times 3 \times 3$

$36 = 2^2 \times 3^2$

Write the factors in order, from least to greatest.

Complete the factor trees for each number. Notice that the prime factors are the same. Then use exponents to write the prime factorization.

1. 70: 7 × 10; _ × _ × _

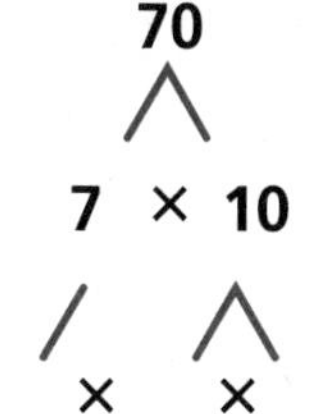

70: 5 × 14; _ × _ × _

70 = ____________________

2. 45: 5 × 9; _ × _ × _

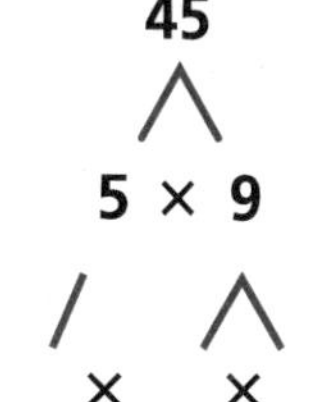

45: 3 × 15; _ × _ × _

45 = ____________________

3. 48: 4 × ___

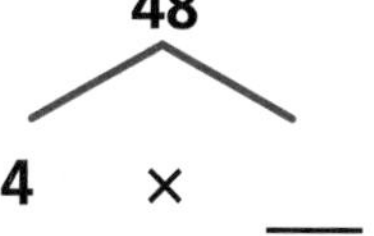

48: 6 × ___

48 = ____________________

4. 84: 2 × ___

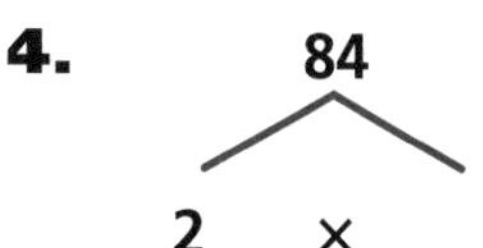

84: ___ × ___

84 = ____________________

STANDARD

Write each prime factorization. Use exponents when you can.

5. 12 = ________ 15 = ________ 16 = ________

6. 18 = ________ 20 = ________ 21 = ________

7. 22 = ________ 24 = ________ 25 = ________

8. 26 = ________ 27 = ________ 28 = ________

Problem Solving **Reasoning** Write *True* or *False.* Explain your answer.

9. The prime factorization of any composite number includes prime and composite numbers.

____

____

10. The prime factorization of any composite number includes three or more prime numbers.

____

____

Quick Check

Put a ✔ in the box to show that the number is divisible by 2, 3, 4, 5, or 10.

		2	3	4	5	10
11.	450					
12.	184					
13.	90					

Write prime or composite. If the number is composite, then write it as a product of factors other than itself and 1.

14. 36 **15.** 57 **16.** 43

________ ________ ________

Use factor trees to write the prime factorization in exponent form.

17. 72 **18.** 60 **19.** 48

________ ________ ________

Work Space

Name ______________________

Common Factors

STANDARD

When two or more numbers have some factors that are the same, then those factors are called **common factors**. To find the common factors of two numbers:

1. List all the factors of each number.
2. Identify the factors that are in **both** lists.

Factors of **14**: **1, 2, 7, 14**

Factors of **35**: **1, 5, 7, 35**

Common factors of **14** and **35**: **1, 7**

Factors of **27**: **1, 3, 9, 27**

Factors of **45**: **1, 3, 5, 9, 15, 45**

Common factors of **27** and **45**: **1, 3, 9**

Write all the factors of each number. Then write the common factors of the numbers.

1. Factors of **12**: ______
Factors of **20**: ______
Common factors: ______

Factors of **10**: ______
Factors of **12**: ______
Common factors: ______

2. Factors of **14**: ______
Factors of **56**: ______
Common factors: ______

Factors of **15**: ______
Factors of **16**: ______
Common factors: ______

3. Factors of **7**: ______
Factors of **32**: ______
Common factors: ______

Factors of **21**: ______
Factors of **28**: ______
Common factors: ______

4. Factors of **9**: ______
Factors of **45**: ______
Common factors: ______

Factors of **13**: ______
Factors of **53**: ______
Common factors: ______

5. Factors of **25**: ______
Factors of **40**: ______
Common factors: ______

Factors of **14**: ______
Factors of **18**: ______
Common factors: ______

STANDARD

The **greatest common factor**, or **GCF**, of two numbers is the greatest number in the lists of common factors.

Factors of **12**: **1, 2, 3, 4, 6, 12**	Factors of **9**: **1, 3, 9**
Factors of **20**: **1, 2, 4, 5, 10, 20**	Factors of **16**: **1, 2, 4, 8, 16**
Common factors: **1, 2, 4**	Common factors: **1**
The **GCF** of **12** and **20** is **4.**	The **GCF** of **9** and **16** is **1.**

Find the GCF of each pair of numbers.

6. 10, 12 ______ 25, 9 ______ 15, 25 ______

7. 20, 38 ______ 26, 34 ______ 15, 18 ______

8. 32, 48 ______ 30, 45 ______ 18, 24 ______

9. 14, 21 ______ 24, 15 ______ 40, 25 ______

10. 21, 51 ______ 13, 17 ______ 26, 34 ______

Problem Solving Reasoning **Solve.**

11. Ellen is making corsages of red and white roses. She has **24** red roses and **16** white roses. She wants to put the same number of red roses and the same number of white roses in each corsage. What is the greatest number of corsages she can make and not have any roses left over?

____

12. Mark is making balloon bouquets for a birthday party. He **20** yellow balloons and **10** green balloons. He wants to put the same number of yellow balloons and the same number of green balloons in each bouquet. What is the greatest number of bouquets he can make and not have any balloons left over?

____

Test Prep ★ Mixed Review

13 **A year has 365 days. A leap year has 366 days. How many days are there in 4 years, that is, 3 years and 1 leap year?**

A 2,921 **C** 1,463

B 1,826 **D** 1,461

14 **What is the value of the expression $6 + 4^3 \div 8 - 6$?**

F 500

G 119

H 8

J 6

Name ___________________________

Dividing by Two-Digit Numbers

STANDARD

Before you divide, think about how many digits will be in the quotient. For example, think about finding 659 ÷ 21.

1. Start with hundreds.

21)659

Think: **21 > 6**
The quotient will not have hundreds.

Then look at tens.

□□
21)659

Think: **21 < 65**
The first digit will be in the tens' place.

2. Estimate. Then multiply.

```
    3
21)659
   63
```

3 × 21 = 63

Think: **65 ÷ 21**
↓ ↓
70 ÷ 20 is about **3**.

3. Subtract.

```
    3
21)659
  − 63
     2
```

4. Bring down the next digit in the dividend. Repeat the steps until there are no digits left to bring down.

```
    31 R8
21)659
  − 63↓
     29
   − 21
      8 ← remainder
```

Check the answer.
- **Multiply** the quotient by the divisor. Then **add** the remainder.

659 is the dividend.
So the answer is correct.

```
   31 ← quotient
 × 21 ← divisor
   31
 + 62
  651
  + 8 ← remainder
  659
```

Divide. Use multiplication to check.

1. 13)39   24)49   44)50

2. 32)99   19)76   23)95

STANDARD

Divide. Use multiplication to check.

3. $10\overline{)114}$ $20\overline{)346}$ $45\overline{)738}$

4. $44\overline{)469}$ $32\overline{)352}$ $19\overline{)564}$

5. $65\overline{)567}$ $59\overline{)531}$ $74\overline{)917}$

Problem Solving
Reasoning

Solve. Check to make sure your answer is reasonable.

6. A theater has **418** seats arranged in rows of **19** seats each. How many rows are in the theater?

____

7. Tickets for a play cost **$12** each. If the box office received **$648** for ticket sales, how many tickets were sold?

____

8. Mr. Jackson paid **$960** for **15** CD players to sell in his store. How much did each CD player cost?

____

9. Mr. Jackson has **20** boxes ready to be unpacked. There are **18** radios in each box. How many radios are there altogether?

____

Test Prep ★ Mixed Review

10 **What is $2^3 \times 3^2$ equivalent to?**

A 734

B 216

C 144

D 72

11 **$8 \times n = 6{,}400$**
What is the missing number *n*?

F 10

G 80

H 800

J 1000

Name ______________________

Quotients Too Large or Too Small

STANDARD

Sometimes when you divide, your first estimate is too large.

Find **24)829**.

1. The first digit in the quotient will be in the tens' place. Try **4**.

```
     4
24)829
 - 96
```

Think: **96** > **82**, so **4** is too large.

2. Try **3** in the quotient. Multiply.

```
     3
24)829
 - 72
```

Think: **72** < **82**, so **3** is correct.

3. Subtract. Bring down the next digit. Try **5**.

```
    35
24)829
 - 72
   109
 - 120
```

Think: **120** > **109**, so **5** is too large.

4. Try **4** in the quotient.

```
    34 R13
24)829
 - 72
   109
 - 96
    13
```

Think: **96** < **109**, so **4** is correct. Remember to check the answer.

Is the quotient too large? Write *Yes* or *No.*

1. 9)56 with quotient 7 ______   31)91 with quotient 3 ______   14)70 with quotient 5 ______   18)67 with quotient 3 ______

2. 27)379 with quotient 15 ______   61)782 with quotient 12 ______   45)742 with quotient 17 ______   28)745 with quotient 28 ______

Divide.

3. 35)140   13)117   19)144   79)478   51)275

4. 71)891   14)439   32)767   59)828   32)581

STANDARD

Sometimes when you divide, your first estimate is too small. When you subtract, the result must always be less than the divisor.

1. The first digit in the quotient will be in the tens' place. Try **3**.

```
    3
17)821
  - 51
    31
```

Think: **31** > **17**, so **3** is too small.

2. Try **4**. Multiply and subtract.

```
    4
17)821
  - 68
    14
```

Think: **14** < **17**, so **4** is correct.

3. Bring down the next digit. Try **7**.

```
     47
17)821
  - 68
    141
  - 119
     22
```

Think: **22** > **17**, so **7** is too small.

4. Try **8** in the quotient.

```
     48 R5
17)821
  - 68
    141
  - 136
remainder → 5
```

Think: **5** < **17**, so **8** is correct. Remember to check the answer.

Divide.

5. 45)289   73)611   89)827   91)737

6. 12)568   24)955   22)747   19)496

Quick Check

Find the greatest common factor of the numbers.

7. 20, 45 ______

8. 14, 28, 63 ______

9. 16, 56, 64 ______

Divide.

10. 33)860

11. 64)390

12. 43)165

13. 26)1,456

14. 57)3,898

15. 38)2,940

Work Space

Name ______________________________

Dividing Greater Numbers

STANDARD

Follow the same steps to divide greater numbers as you have with 2- and 3-digit numbers. For example, find 19,859 ÷ 32.

1. The first digit in the quotient will be in the ones' place.

$$32\overline{)19{,}859}\quad 6$$

Think **200** ÷ **30** is about **6**.

2. Multiply.

Think: **6** × **32** = **192**

$$\begin{array}{r} 6 \\ 32\overline{)19{,}859} \\ -19\,2 \end{array}$$

Think: **192** < **198**.

3. Subtract. Then compare the difference to the divisor.

$$\begin{array}{r} 6 \\ 32\overline{)19{,}859} \\ -19\,2 \\ \hline 6 \end{array}$$

Think: **6** < **32**.

4. Bring down the next digit in the dividend. Repeat these steps until there are no digits left to bring down.

$$\begin{array}{r} 620 \text{ R19} \\ 32\overline{)19{,}859} \\ -19\,2 \\ \hline 65 \\ -64 \\ \hline 19 \\ -0 \\ \hline 19 \end{array}$$

Remember to check the answer.

Divide.

1. $48\overline{)2{,}496}$ $38\overline{)5{,}375}$ $42\overline{)5{,}420}$ $36\overline{)8{,}319}$

2. $32\overline{)1{,}664}$ $43\overline{)1{,}078}$ $64\overline{)2{,}176}$ $23\overline{)1{,}104}$

STANDARD

Divide.

3. $17\overline{)6,021}$ $53\overline{)5,726}$ $31\overline{)8,063}$ $26\overline{)4,655}$

4. $19\overline{)81,035}$ $41\overline{)64,087}$ $33\overline{)48,679}$ $23\overline{)87,264}$

5. $43\overline{)31,965}$ $25\overline{)10,600}$ $53\overline{)14,628}$ $89\overline{)72,561}$

Problem Solving Reasoning Solve.

6. Reggie delivers **1,495** newspapers in **65** days. He delivers the same number of newspapers each day. How many newspapers does he deliver each day?

____

7. The Bradleys pay a subscription price of **$39.00** for **52** newspapers. What is the cost of each newspaper?

____

Test Prep ★ Mixed Review

8 **Which expression is equivalent to $3 \times (80 + x)$?**

A $3 \times 80 + x$

B $3 \times 80 + 3 \times x$

C $(3 \times 80) + x$

D $(3 + x) \times 80$

9 **Sal is going on vacation for 19 days. Which equation shows how many weeks this is?**

F $19 + 7 = w$

G $19 - 7 = w$

H $19 \times 7 = w$

J $19 \div 7 = w$

Name ______________________

Estimating Quotients

STANDARD

You can use **compatible numbers** to estimate quotients.

Compatible numbers are numbers that are easy to divide mentally.

You should choose compatible numbers that are close to the actual numbers.

$7\overline{)418}$ →	$\begin{array}{r}60\\7\overline{)420}\end{array}$	$78\overline{)317}$ →	$\begin{array}{r}4\\80\overline{)320}\end{array}$	$62\overline{)1,860}$ →	$\begin{array}{r}30\\60\overline{)1,800}\end{array}$

Rewrite each exercise using compatible numbers that are close to the actual numbers. Then estimate each quotient.

1. $6\overline{)38}$ $7\overline{)50}$ $8\overline{)74}$

2. $3\overline{)272}$ $5\overline{)241}$ $2\overline{)170}$

3. $4\overline{)3,434}$ $8\overline{)6,188}$ $2\overline{)1,196}$

4. $32\overline{)684}$ $21\overline{)181}$ $42\overline{)761}$

5. $35\overline{)2,850}$ $57\overline{)5,623}$ $74\overline{)6,243}$

6. $72\overline{)20,967}$ $48\overline{)19,901}$ $56\overline{)42,332}$

STANDARD

Estimate each quotient.

7. 2)98 | 4)39 | 5)433 | 8)705

8. 6)238 | 4)3,503 | 9)5,281 | 8)2,290

9. 62)545 | 41)3,774 | 59)3,742 | 63)5,991

10. 57)42,305 | 71)47,101 | 82)41,163 | 45)11,782

Problem Solving
Reasoning

Solve.

11. A garden supply company ships flower bulbs in boxes of **46** bulbs. About how many boxes will they need to fill an order for **490** bulbs?

____

12. Roger is planting **5,701** seeds in **81** pots. He wants to plant about the same number of seeds in each pot. About how many seeds will he plant in each pot?

____

Quick Check

Divide.

13. 24)7,006 **14.** 15)11,405 **15.** 49)9,803

Estimate. Then divide.

16. 35)54,780 **17.** 81)64,344 **18.** 74)72,529

Work Space

Name ______________________

Problem Solving Strategy: Make a Table

STANDARD

Sometimes it is helpful to make a table in order to solve a problem.

Problem

Mrs. Red, Mrs. Black, and Mrs. White each is wearing a different color dress. One dress is red, one is black, and one is white. Use the clues to match each woman with the color of her dress.
Clues:
No woman's dress is the same color as her last name.
Mrs. White does not own a red dress.

1 Understand As you reread, ask yourself questions.

- What do you know about the given clues?

No woman's dress is the same color as her last name.
Mrs. White does not own a red dress.

- What do you need to do?

____

2 Decide Choose a method for solving. Try the strategy Make a Table.

	Mrs.Red	Mrs.Black	Mrs.White
Red			
Black			
White			

3 Solve Use the clues to put X's in the table.

- From the clues, we can write the following X's.

	Mrs.Red	Mrs.Black	Mrs.White
Red	X		X
Black		X	
White			X

4 Look back Check your answer. Write the answer below.

____

STANDARD

Use the Make a Table strategy or any other strategy you have learned.

1. Find **2** numbers less than **50** that are divisible by both **2** and **9**.
Think: How do you know a number is divisible by **9**?

____

Answer ______________________

____

2. Find a composite number between **40** and **50** that is divisible by **2, 3,** and **4.**

Think: Which prime numbers can you immediately eliminate?

____

Answer ______________________

3. Paul, Arthur, and Jim are each the captain of a team. One is the soccer captain, one is the baseball captain, and one is the basketball captain. Use the clues to match the boys with their sports.

Clues:
Arthur and the baseball captain both like to swim.
The baseball captain and the basketball captain are brothers.
Jim is an only child.

____

____

____

4. Betty, Nina, Carol, and Dot each live in one of these cities: Boston, New York, Chicago, and Denver. Use the clues to match the girls with the cities.
Clues:
No girl lives in a city that begins with the same letter as her first name.
Nina and Carol have never been to Boston.
Betty has never been to New York or Chicago.

____

____

____

____

5. A school bus can hold **45** children. How many school buses will be needed to take **354** children to school?

____

6. How much change would you get from a **$20** bill if you bought some ground beef for **$3.75** and a package of buns for **$1.69?**

____

7. Find all the numbers less than **60** that are prime and have a remainder of **3** when they are divided by **7**.

____

8. Jeremy read **43** library books. Jill read **29** more books than Jeremy. How many books did they read altogether?

____

Name ______________________

Unit 3 Review

Complete.

1. $4 \times n = 36$

$n =$ ___ $\div$ ___

$n =$ ___

2. $a \div 4 = 8$

$a =$ ___ $\times$ ___

$a =$ ___

Evaluate using the order of operations.

3. $42 + n \div 4$ for $n = 8$ ______

4. $a - 3 \times 2 + 1$ for $a = 10$ ______

Divide.

5. $7\overline{)459}$

6. $5\overline{)5{,}216}$

7. $68\overline{)479}$

8. $35\overline{)7{,}084}$

Find the average of each group of numbers.

9. 18, 56, 34 ______

10. 465, 89, 123, 557, 77, 117 ______

Write all the factors of each number. Then write the common factors of each pair of numbers.

11. Factors of **32**: ______________

Factors of **40**: ______________

Common factors: ______________

12. Factors of **25**: ______________

Factors of **35**: ______________

Common factors: ______________

Use exponents to write each prime factorization.

13. 63 = ______

14. 40 = ______

Solve. If information is missing, name the fact or facts needed.

15. Juanita has **$70** to buy certificates for the contestants in the math contest. How much will each certificate cost? ______________

16. Suppose each certificate for participants in the Science Fair costs **$1.50**. On another sheet of paper, make a table that shows the different numbers of certificates you could buy if you spent **$10.00** or less.

____

Name ______________________________

Cumulative Review ★ Test Prep

1 **If $1 \times (10 - a) = 8$, then what does a equal?**

A 0   C 2   E 10

B 1   D 8

2 **What is the average, or mean, of these data?**

2, 3, 3, 4, 4, 4, 4, 4, 5, 5
5, 5, 6, 6, 6, 6, 6, 6, 8, 8

F between 2 and 3   H exactly 5

G exactly 3   J more than 5

3 **A number machine used a rule to change an input number into an output number.**

Input number	1	2	3	5	6
Output number	3	5	7	11	?

What would the number machine change 6 into?

A 13   C 15

B 14   D 20

4 **Jordan bought a cheese sandwich for $2.49 and a fruit drink for $0.75. What information do you need to know in order to find out how much change he got?**

F The price of a tuna sandwich

G The price of fruit

H The amount of money Jordan has in his wallet

J The amount of money Jordan gave to the clerk

5 **A trail is 1,344 meters long. If you walked an average of 16 meters a minute, how long would it take you to walk the entire trail?**

A 94 minutes

B 94 meters

C 1,328 minutes

D 1,328 meters

E Not here

6 **In 1980, the state of California had a population of 23,668,562. What is that number rounded to the nearest million?**

F 24,000,000

G 23,000,000

H 23,700,000

J 23,670,000

K 23,660,000

7 **There are 24 classes in the school. Ten of the classes have an average of 25 students in each class. The rest have an average of 22 students. How many students are enrolled in the school?**

A 71   C 558

B 81   D 1,340   E Not here

8 **A student spent $2.75 and bought 3 pads of paper and 2 erasers. The pads of paper are 75¢ each. How much does each eraser cost?**

F $2.25   H 55¢

G $2.00   J 50¢   K 25¢

UNIT 4 • TABLE OF CONTENTS

Addition and Subtraction of Fractions and Mixed Numbers

We will be using this vocabulary:

numerator the top number in a fraction; names the number of parts being considered

denominator the bottom number in a fraction; names the number of equal parts in the whole

simplest form a fraction in which the only common factor of the numerator and denominator is 1 and the numerator is less than the denominator

equivalent fractions sometimes called *equal fractions*: two or more fractions that name the same number

Dear Family,

During the next few weeks, our math class will be learning and practicing the addition and subtraction of fractions and mixed numbers.

You can expect to see homework that provides practice with writing fractions in simplest form. Here is a sample you may want to keep handy to give help if needed.

Simplest Form

Example Write $\frac{2}{8}$ in simplest form.

To write *some* fractions in simplest form, divide the numerator (top number) and the denominator (bottom number) by the numerator.

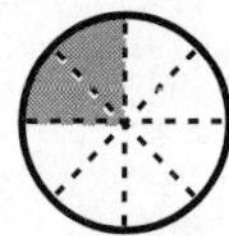

$$\frac{2}{8} = \frac{2 \div 2}{8 \div 2} \rightarrow \frac{1}{4}$$

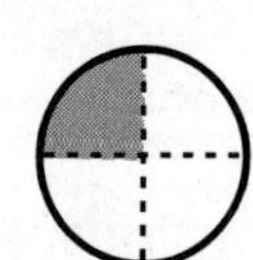

For other fractions, dividing by the numerator is not possible. For these fractions, choose a number that is a common factor of the numerator and the denominator and divide the numerator and denominator by that number.

Example Write $\frac{6}{9}$ in simplest form.

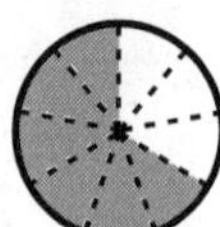

$$\frac{6}{9} = \frac{6 \div 3}{9 \div 3} \rightarrow \frac{2}{3}$$

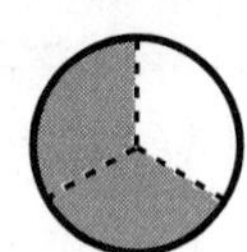

A fraction is in simplest form when the only number that divides the numerator and the denominator is **1**.

During this unit, students will need to continue practicing division, addition, and subtraction facts.

Sincerely,

Name ________________________________

Finding Equivalent Fractions

STANDARD

Operations with fractions often involve finding **equivalent fractions** first. Fractions that are equivalent name the same number. You can use *fraction models* to find equivalent fractions.

Example Write three fractions that are equivalent to $\frac{1}{2}$.

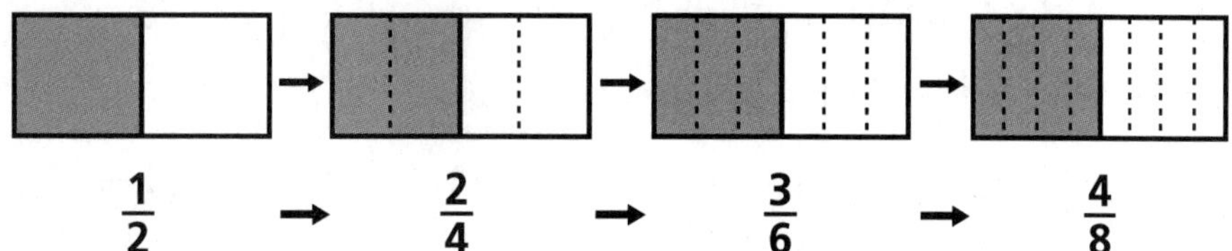

$\frac{1}{2} \rightarrow \frac{2}{4} \rightarrow \frac{3}{6} \rightarrow \frac{4}{8}$

The fractions $\frac{1}{2}$, $\frac{2}{4}$, $\frac{3}{6}$, and $\frac{4}{8}$ are equivalent fractions.

You can also use *multiplication* to find equivalent fractions. To use multiplication, choose a number and multiply the numerator and the denominator by that number.

Example Write three fractions that are equivalent to $\frac{2}{5}$.

$\frac{2 \times 2}{5 \times 2} = \frac{4}{10}$ $\frac{2 \times 3}{5 \times 3} = \frac{6}{15}$ $\frac{2 \times 10}{5 \times 10} = \frac{20}{50}$

The fractions $\frac{4}{10}$, $\frac{6}{15}$, and $\frac{20}{50}$ are all equivalent to $\frac{2}{5}$.

What equivalent fractions are shown by these models?

1. 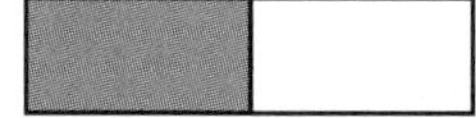

____

2. 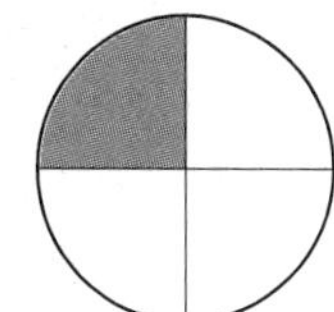 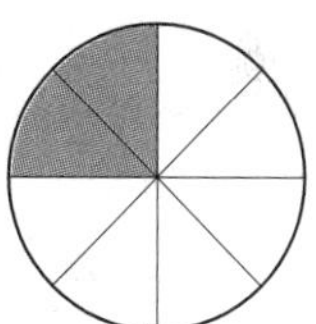

____

Complete.

3. $\frac{1 \times 3}{2 \times 3} = \frac{3}{\_\_}$ $\frac{3 \times 5}{4 \times 5} = \frac{15}{\_\_}$ $\frac{5 \times 4}{8 \times 4} = \frac{\_\_}{32}$ $\frac{1 \times 6}{4 \times 6} = \frac{6}{\_\_}$

Write five equivalent fractions.

4. $\frac{1}{3}$ ______ ______ ______ ______ ______ $\frac{3}{5}$ ______ ______ ______ ______ ______

5. $\frac{1}{8}$ ______ ______ ______ ______ ______ $\frac{1}{10}$ ______ ______ ______ ______ ______

STANDARD

You can also use *division* to find one or more equivalent fractions.

To write three fractions that are equivalent to $\frac{12}{18}$, choose a number that is a **common factor** of the numerator and denominator, and divide the numerator and the denominator by that number.

Remember: A common factor of two numbers divides each number without having a remainder.

Choose 2: $\frac{12 \div 2}{18 \div 2} = \frac{6}{9}$ Choose 3: $\frac{12 \div 3}{18 \div 3} = \frac{4}{6}$ Choose 6: $\frac{12 \div 6}{18 \div 6} = \frac{2}{3}$

The fractions $\frac{6}{9}$, $\frac{4}{6}$, and $\frac{2}{3}$ are equivalent to $\frac{12}{18}$.

Use division to write three equivalent fractions.

6. $\frac{24}{30}$ ____ ____ ____ $\frac{20}{40}$ ____ ____ ____

7. $\frac{36}{48}$ ____ ____ ____ $\frac{60}{100}$ ____ ____ ____

8. $\frac{50}{80}$ ____ ____ ____ $\frac{64}{96}$ ____ ____ ____

Problem Solving Reasoning

Complete the table. Describe the rule.

9.

Input	$\frac{1}{6}$	$\frac{2}{6}$	$\frac{3}{6}$	$\frac{4}{6}$	$\frac{5}{6}$
Output	$\frac{3}{18}$	$\frac{6}{18}$			

Rule: ________

10.

Input	$\frac{1}{8}$	$\frac{2}{4}$			
Output	$\frac{2}{16}$	$\frac{4}{8}$	$\frac{6}{12}$		

Rule: ________

Test Prep ★ Mixed Review

11 Lincoln school has 256 students. On Monday, 78 students were absent. Which equation can be used to find the number of students who were present on Monday?

A $m - 78 = 256$
B $256 + m = 78$
C $256 = m - 78$
D $256 = m + 78$

12 What is the value of the expression $20 \times a$ when $a = 14$?

F 28
G 34
H 280
J 300

Name ______________________________

Fractions and Mixed Numbers

STANDARD

Some fractions name whole numbers.

This number line shows that $\frac{3}{3} = 1$, $\frac{6}{3} = 2$, and $\frac{9}{3} = 3$.

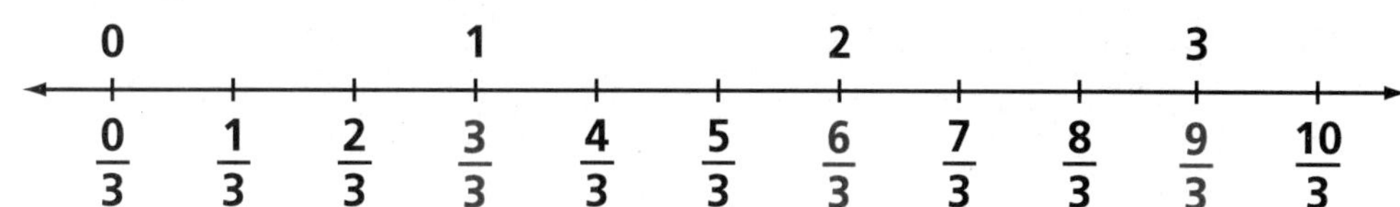

On the number line, the fractions $\frac{0}{3}$, $\frac{1}{3}$, and $\frac{2}{3}$ *are less than* **1.**

All of the other fractions on the number line *are equal to or greater than* **1.**

You can use division to rewrite a fraction as a whole number.

Example: $\frac{12}{4} = 12 \div 4 \rightarrow 3$

Read $\frac{12}{4}$ as "twelve divided by four" or "twelve fourths."

Example: $\frac{35}{7} = 35 \div 7 \rightarrow 5$

Read $\frac{35}{7}$ as "thirty-five divided by seven" or "thirty-five sevenths."

Write each missing fraction for the whole numbers.

1.

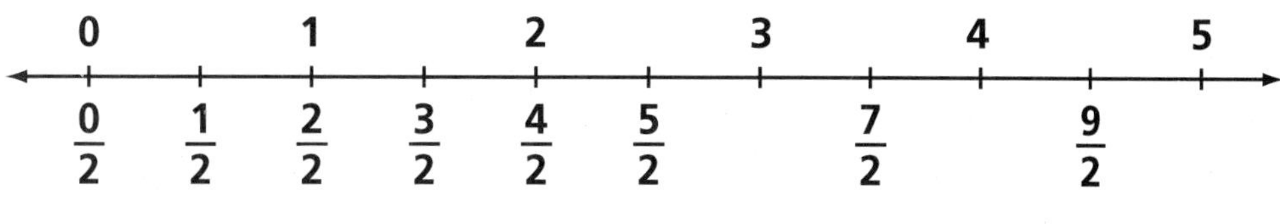

______ ______ ______

Write each whole number.

2.

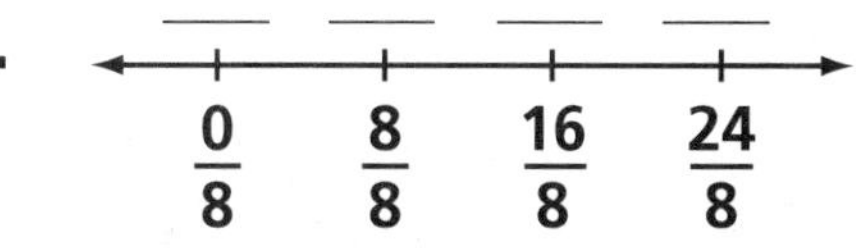

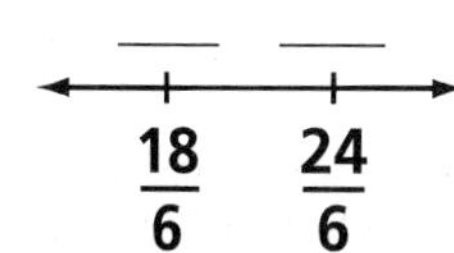

$\frac{18}{6}$ $\frac{24}{6}$

Write each missing numerator.

3. $1 = \frac{\quad}{2}$ $2 = \frac{\quad}{2}$ $3 = \frac{\quad}{2}$ $1 = \frac{\quad}{3}$ $2 = \frac{\quad}{3}$

4. $5 = \frac{\quad}{3}$ $4 = \frac{\quad}{4}$ $6 = \frac{\quad}{2}$ $8 = \frac{\quad}{3}$ $8 = \frac{\quad}{4}$

STANDARD

A **mixed number** is made up of a whole number and a fraction. $1\frac{3}{4}$

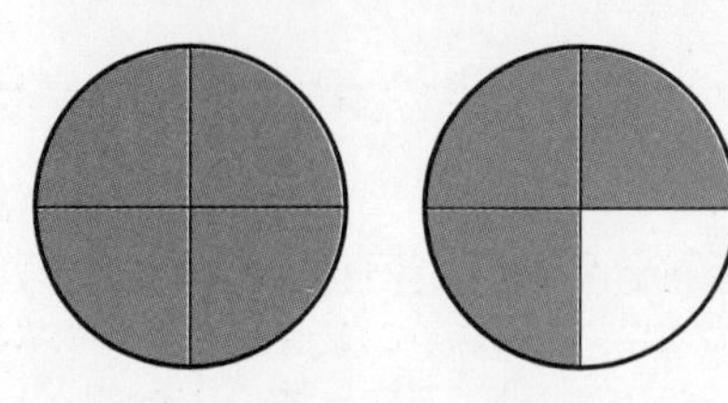

To write a mixed number as a fraction, follow these steps.

Write $4\frac{1}{2}$ as a fraction.

1. Multiply the whole number by the denominator. 2×4
2. Add the numerator to the product. $8 + 1$
3. Write the sum over the denominator. $\frac{9}{2}$ So, $4\frac{1}{2} = \frac{9}{2}$.

To write a fraction as a mixed number, divide. Write the remainder over the denominator.

Write $\frac{14}{5}$ as a mixed number

$14 \div 5 = 2\frac{4}{5}$

Write each mixed number as a fraction and write each fraction as a mixed number.

5. $2\frac{1}{4}$ ______ $\frac{7}{2}$ ______ $1\frac{3}{8}$ ______ $\frac{10}{3}$ ______

6. $\frac{12}{5}$ ______ $3\frac{1}{16}$ ______ $\frac{17}{9}$ ______ $4\frac{9}{10}$ ______

Problem Solving
Reasoning

Solve.

7. After every $\frac{1}{3}$ mile of a nature trail, there is a place to rest. How many places to rest are there on a trail that is $1\frac{2}{3}$ mile long?

____

____

Test Prep ★ Mixed Review

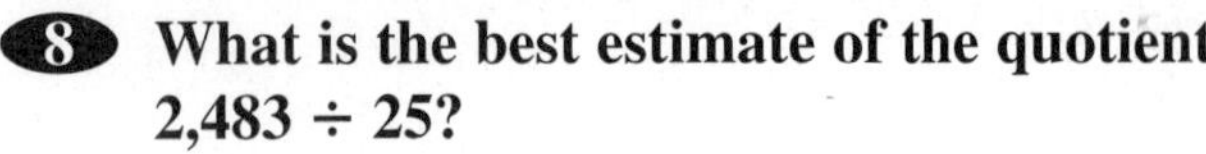

8 What is the best estimate of the quotient 2,483 ÷ 25?

A 1

B 10

C 100

D 1,000

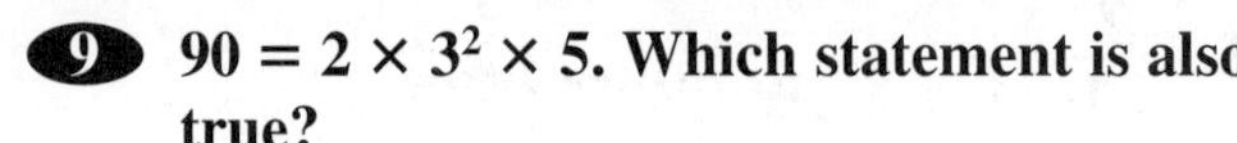

9 $90 = 2 \times 3^2 \times 5$. Which statement is also true?

F 90 is a multiple of 20

G 90 is divisible by 12

H 10 is a factor of 90

J 4×10 is a factor of 90

Name ______________________________

Simplest Form

STANDARD

When the only common factor of the numerator and the denominator of a fraction is 1, the fraction is in **simplest form.**

If a fraction such as $\frac{12}{18}$ is not in simplest form, divide the numerator and the denominator by the **greatest common factor** (GCF) to simplify it.

> Remember: To find an equivalent fraction, you can divide the numerator and denominator by a common factor.
>
> $\frac{10}{12} \rightarrow \frac{10 \div 2}{12 \div 2} = \frac{5}{6}$

1. Find the factors of **12** and **18.**

   Factors of **12**: **1, 2, 3, 4, (6), 12**

   Factors of **18**: **1, 2, 3, (6), 18**

   The **GCF** of **12** and **18** is **6.**

> Circle the greatest factor that is in both lists.

2. Divide **12** and **18** by **6**, the **GCF.**

   $\frac{12 \div 6}{18 \div 6} = \frac{2}{3}$ In simplest form, $\frac{12}{18}$ is $\frac{2}{3}$.

You can write a fraction such as $\frac{14}{10}$ in simplest form by following these steps.

1. Write $\frac{14}{10}$ as a mixed number. $\frac{14}{10} = 1\frac{4}{10}$

2. Simplify $1\frac{4}{10}$. $= 1\frac{4}{10} \rightarrow 1\frac{4 \div 2}{10 \div 2} \rightarrow 1\frac{2}{5}$

Write the fraction in simplest form.

1.	$\frac{6}{18}$ = ______	$\frac{9}{21}$ = ______	$\frac{6}{9}$ = ______	$\frac{12}{16}$ = ______
2.	$\frac{4}{6}$ = ______	$\frac{2}{4}$ = ______	$\frac{8}{14}$ = ______	$\frac{2}{6}$ = ______
3.	$\frac{6}{12}$ = ______	$\frac{8}{12}$ = ______	$\frac{10}{15}$ = ______	$\frac{7}{28}$ = ______
4.	$\frac{2}{8}$ = ______	$\frac{3}{6}$ = ______	$\frac{6}{8}$ = ______	$\frac{10}{16}$ = ______
5.	$\frac{7}{21}$ = ______	$\frac{8}{10}$ = ______	$\frac{3}{12}$ = ______	$\frac{15}{20}$ = ______
6.	$\frac{9}{12}$ = ______	$\frac{12}{20}$ = ______	$\frac{10}{18}$ = ______	$\frac{6}{10}$ = ______
7.	$\frac{8}{16}$ = ______	$\frac{10}{25}$ = ______	$\frac{15}{24}$ = ______	$\frac{16}{48}$ = ______

STANDARD

You can write a mixed number such as $2\frac{9}{15}$ in simplest form.

1. Divide **9** and **15** by **3**, the **GCF**. $\frac{9 \div 3}{15 \div 3} = \frac{3}{5}$
2. Write the mixed number in simplest form. $2\frac{9}{15} = 2\frac{3}{5}$

Write the mixed number in simplest form.

8. $1\frac{4}{12}$ ______ $3\frac{6}{8}$ ______ $4\frac{6}{16}$ ______ $7\frac{2}{4}$ ______

9. $2\frac{12}{18}$ ______ $5\frac{5}{20}$ ______ $1\frac{8}{10}$ ______ $2\frac{10}{12}$ ______

Problem Solving Reasoning **Solve.**

10. A paper clip is $\frac{12}{16}$ inch long. If you measured it with a ruler marked in $\frac{1}{4}$ inches, what would the measurement be? Is your answer in simplest form?

Explain. ______________________

____

11. A pencil eraser is $\frac{16}{32}$ inch long. If you measured it with a ruler marked in $\frac{1}{8}$ inches, what would the measurement be? Is your answer in simplest form?

Explain. ______________________

____

Quick Check

Find the missing numerator or denominator.

12. $\frac{?}{4} = \frac{4}{16}$ ______ **13.** $\frac{2}{?} = \frac{8}{12}$ ______ **14.** $\frac{?}{5} = \frac{12}{30}$ ______

Rename the fraction as a whole number or mixed number.

15. $\frac{28}{7}$ ______ **16.** $\frac{14}{3}$ ______ **17.** $\frac{39}{5}$ ______

Write the fraction in simplest form.

18. $\frac{18}{36}$ ______ **19.** $\frac{8}{6}$ ______ **20.** $\frac{18}{9}$ ______

Work Space

Name ______________________________

Adding with Like Denominators

STANDARD

The region is divided into **9** equal parts.

Each part is $\frac{1}{9}$ of the whole.

How much of the whole region is shaded?

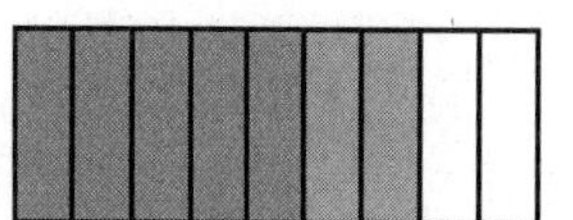

$\frac{5}{9}$ shaded red $\frac{2}{9}$ shaded gray

To solve this problem, you can add fractions that have **like denominators**:

1. Add the numerators.

2. Write the sum over the denominator.

$\frac{5}{9} + \frac{2}{9} = \frac{7}{9}$

$\frac{7}{9}$ of the whole is shaded.

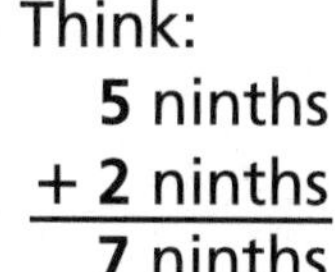

Think:
5 ninths
+ 2 ninths
7 ninths

Add. Use the shaded region. Simplify your answers if possible.

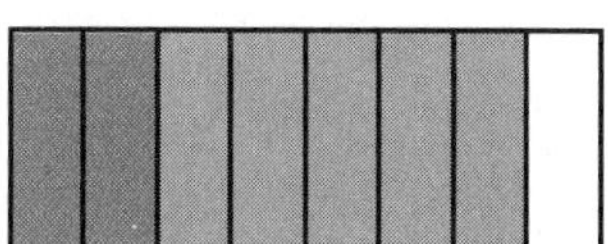

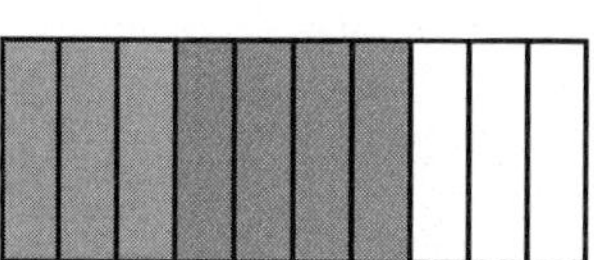

1. $\frac{1}{4} + \frac{2}{4} =$ ______ $\frac{2}{8} + \frac{5}{8} =$ ______ $\frac{3}{10} + \frac{4}{10} =$ ______

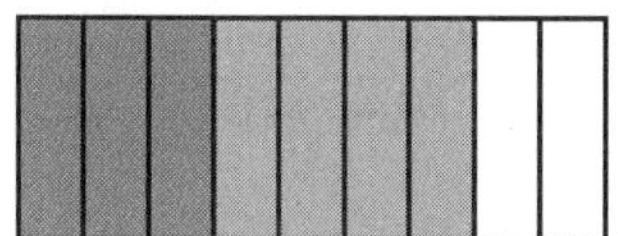

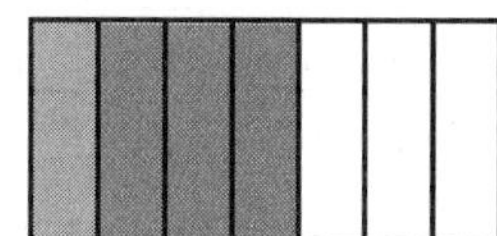

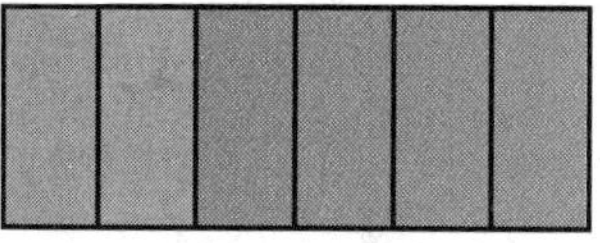

2. $\frac{3}{9} + \frac{4}{9} =$ ______ $\frac{1}{7} + \frac{3}{7} =$ ______ $\frac{2}{6} + \frac{4}{6} =$ ______

Add. Simplify your answers if possible.

3. $\frac{1}{3} + \frac{1}{3} = \frac{2}{3}$ $\frac{4}{6} + \frac{1}{6} = \frac{5}{6}$ $\frac{2}{5} + \frac{2}{5} = \frac{4}{5}$ $\frac{3}{8} + \frac{4}{8} = \frac{7}{8}$

4. $\frac{4}{9} + \frac{1}{9} = \frac{5}{9}$ $\frac{3}{10} + \frac{6}{10} = \frac{9}{10}$ $\frac{3}{7} + \frac{2}{7} = \frac{5}{7}$ $\frac{1}{10} + \frac{3}{10} = \frac{4}{10}$

5. $\frac{5}{12} + \frac{3}{12} = \frac{8}{12}$ $\frac{2}{7} + \frac{1}{7} = \frac{3}{7}$ $\frac{1}{5} + \frac{1}{5} = \frac{2}{5}$ $\frac{7}{8} + \frac{1}{8} = \frac{8}{8} = 1$ $\frac{1}{2} + \frac{1}{2} = \frac{2}{2} = 1$

STANDARD

To add two mixed numbers, follow these steps: $3\frac{5}{8} + 4\frac{1}{8}$

Add the fractions.	Add the whole numbers.	Simplify if possible.
$\begin{array}{r} 3\frac{5}{8} \\ +\,4\frac{1}{8} \\ \hline \frac{6}{8} \end{array}$	$\begin{array}{r} 3\frac{5}{8} \\ +\,4\frac{1}{8} \\ \hline 7\frac{6}{8} \end{array}$	$\begin{array}{r} 3\frac{5}{8} \\ +\,4\frac{1}{8} \\ \hline 7\frac{6}{8} = 7\frac{3}{4} \end{array}$ ← simplest form

Add. Write the sum in simplest form.

6. $\begin{array}{r} 5\frac{4}{9} \\ +\,1\frac{1}{9} \\ \hline \end{array}$ $\begin{array}{r} 1\frac{3}{8} \\ +\,4\frac{1}{8} \\ \hline \end{array}$ $\begin{array}{r} 5\frac{1}{7} \\ +\,\frac{3}{7} \\ \hline \end{array}$ $\begin{array}{r} 4\frac{1}{3} \\ +\,1\frac{1}{3} \\ \hline \end{array}$ $\begin{array}{r} 3\frac{1}{4} \\ +\,\frac{2}{4} \\ \hline \end{array}$ $\begin{array}{r} 1\frac{7}{8} \\ +\,3 \\ \hline \end{array}$

7. $\begin{array}{r} 7\frac{1}{5} \\ +\,\frac{3}{5} \\ \hline \end{array}$ $\begin{array}{r} 6\frac{1}{9} \\ +\,1\frac{2}{9} \\ \hline \end{array}$ $\begin{array}{r} 3\frac{1}{7} \\ +\,1\frac{1}{7} \\ \hline \end{array}$ $\begin{array}{r} \frac{5}{8} \\ +\,\frac{2}{8} \\ \hline \end{array}$ $\begin{array}{r} 3\frac{1}{3} \\ +\,\frac{1}{3} \\ \hline \end{array}$ $\begin{array}{r} 2\frac{3}{5} \\ +\,4\frac{0}{5} \\ \hline \end{array}$

Problem Solving Reasoning **Solve.**

8. Bike Trail A is $4\frac{9}{10}$ miles long, Trail B is $3\frac{3}{4}$ miles long, and Trail C is $5\frac{5}{8}$ miles long. Which two trails should Derrick ride if he wants to ride between **9** and **10** miles?

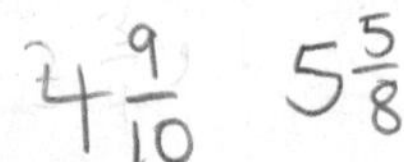

Test Prep ★ Mixed Review

9 **Which fractions are in order from least to greatest?**

A $\frac{2}{3}, \frac{9}{12}, \frac{1}{2}, \frac{5}{6}$

B $\frac{1}{2}, \frac{2}{3}, \frac{9}{12}, \frac{5}{6}$

C $\frac{1}{2}, \frac{9}{12}, \frac{2}{3}, \frac{5}{6}$

D $\frac{9}{12}, \frac{2}{3}, \frac{1}{2}, \frac{5}{6}$

10 **12 is the GCF of which numbers?**

F 24 and 36

G 12 and 30

H 24 and 48

J 30 and 48

Name ______________________

Subtracting with Like Denominators

STANDARD

You can see that $\frac{7}{9}$ of the whole is shaded. What part of the whole is shaded red?

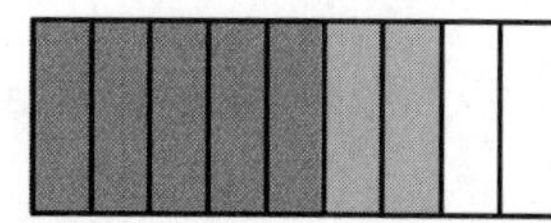

$\frac{7}{9}$ shaded $\frac{2}{9}$ shaded gray

Think:
7 ninths
− 2 ninths
5 ninths

To solve this problem, you can subtract fractions with **like denominators:**

1. Subtract the numerators. $\frac{7}{9} - \frac{2}{9} = \frac{5}{9}$

2. Write the difference over the denominator. $\frac{5}{9}$ are shaded red.

Subtract. Use the shaded regions.

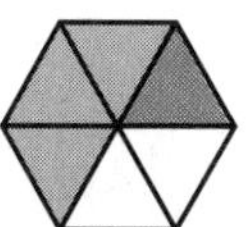

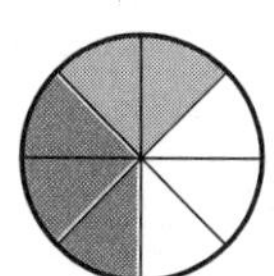

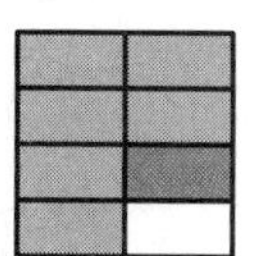

1. $\frac{4}{6} - \frac{3}{6} =$ ______ $\frac{5}{8} - \frac{2}{8} =$ ______ $\frac{7}{8} - \frac{6}{8} =$ ______

Subtract. Simplify your answer if possible.

2. $\frac{5}{6} - \frac{4}{6} =$ ______ $\frac{3}{5} - \frac{2}{5} =$ ______ $\frac{4}{8} - \frac{1}{8} =$ ______ $\frac{5}{9} - \frac{4}{9} =$ ______

3. $\frac{3}{8} - \frac{1}{8} =$ ______ $\frac{3}{4} - \frac{1}{4} =$ ______ $\frac{5}{8} - \frac{3}{8} =$ ______ $\frac{11}{16} - \frac{7}{16} =$ ______

4. $\frac{6}{7} - \frac{1}{7} =$ ______ $\frac{2}{3} - \frac{1}{3} =$ ______ $\frac{9}{10} - \frac{6}{10} =$ ______ $\frac{1}{4} - \frac{1}{4} =$ ______

5. $\frac{5}{6} - \frac{4}{6}$ $\frac{11}{12} - \frac{1}{12}$ $\frac{3}{5} - \frac{1}{5}$ $\frac{4}{4} - \frac{1}{4}$ $\frac{7}{8} - \frac{4}{8}$ $\frac{6}{9} - \frac{2}{9}$

6. $\frac{7}{8} - \frac{1}{8}$ $\frac{9}{10} - \frac{1}{10}$ $\frac{2}{3} - \frac{2}{3}$ $\frac{5}{7} - \frac{2}{7}$ $\frac{8}{9} - \frac{4}{9}$ $\frac{7}{12} - \frac{1}{12}$

STANDARD

To find the difference between two mixed numbers, such as $8\frac{5}{6} - 7\frac{1}{6}$, follow these steps:

Subtract the fractions.

$$\begin{array}{r} 8\frac{5}{6} \\ -\,7\frac{1}{6} \\ \hline \frac{4}{6} \end{array}$$

Subtract the whole numbers.

$$\begin{array}{r} 8\frac{5}{6} \\ -\,7\frac{1}{6} \\ \hline 1\frac{4}{6} \end{array}$$

Write the difference in simplest form.

$$\begin{array}{r} 8\frac{5}{6} \\ -\,7\frac{1}{6} \\ \hline 1\frac{4}{6} = 1\frac{2}{3} \end{array} \leftarrow \text{simplest form}$$

Subtract. Write the difference in simplest form.

7. $\begin{array}{r} 3\frac{7}{8} \\ -\,2\frac{1}{8} \\ \hline \end{array}$ $\begin{array}{r} 9\frac{7}{10} \\ -\,6\frac{3}{10} \\ \hline \end{array}$ $\begin{array}{r} 8\frac{4}{5} \\ -\,7\frac{2}{5} \\ \hline \end{array}$ $\begin{array}{r} 7\frac{11}{12} \\ -\,4\frac{5}{12} \\ \hline \end{array}$ $\begin{array}{r} 5\frac{6}{7} \\ -\,3\frac{1}{7} \\ \hline \end{array}$ $\begin{array}{r} 6\frac{1}{2} \\ -\,2\frac{1}{2} \\ \hline \end{array}$

8. $7\frac{9}{10} - 2\frac{7}{10} =$ ______ $8\frac{4}{5} - 6\frac{4}{5} =$ ______ $2\frac{13}{16} - 1\frac{7}{16} =$ ______

Problem Solving Reasoning Solve.

9. Sam has a board $4\frac{3}{4}$ feet long. He cuts $2\frac{1}{4}$ feet from the board to make a shelf. Will he have enough wood left to make another shelf the same length? Explain. ______________________________

____

Test Prep ★ Mixed Review

10 Which number is composite?

A 17

B 27

C 37

D 47

11 A whale weighs about 62,400 pounds. A seal weighs about 197 pounds. *About* how many times heavier is the whale?

F 3,000

G 300

H 30

J 3

Name ____________________

Problem Solving Strategy: Draw a Diagram

STANDARD

Sometimes drawing a diagram can help you solve a problem.

When you draw a diagram, you can label it with the information given in the problem.

Problem

A scout group went on a hike. First they walked $\frac{1}{2}$ mile east, then $\frac{3}{4}$ mile south, then 1 mile west, then $\frac{1}{4}$ mile north, then $\frac{1}{2}$ mile east. How far is the scout group from their starting point?

1 Understand As you reread, ask yourself questions.

- What do you know about the distances walked?

  The scout group walked $\frac{1}{2}$ mile east, $\frac{3}{4}$ mile south, 1 mile west, $\frac{1}{4}$ mile north, $\frac{1}{2}$ mile east.

- What information do you need to find?

  ____

2 Decide Choose a method for solving.Try the strategy Draw a Diagram.

- Make a diagram, or map, of the distances and directions walked.

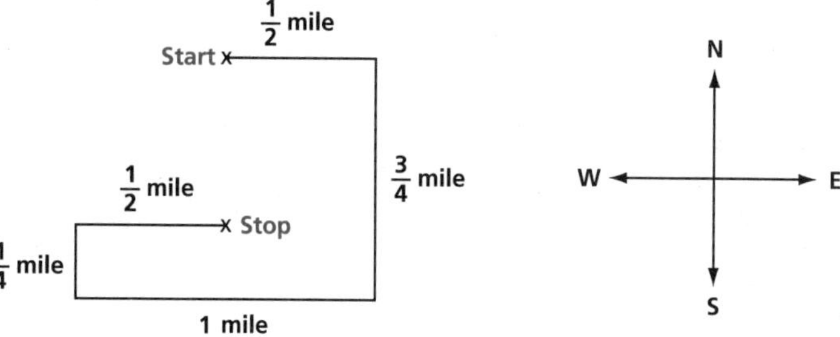

3 Solve Choose the operation for solving.

- What numbers will you use to find the distance between the starting point and where the group stopped hiking? What operation will you use?

  ____

4 Look back Check your answer. Write your answer below.

Answer: ____________________

STANDARD

Use the Draw a Diagram strategy or any other strategy you have learned.

1. A picture frame containing a photograph is **11** inches wide and **14** inches high. A mat around the photograph is $1\frac{1}{2}$ inches wide on all sides. What are the dimensions of the photograph?

Think: Do you want to add to or subtract from each side?

____

Answer ______________________

2. A carpenter used **3** pieces of wood, each $\frac{3}{4}$ inch thick, to make a **2**-shelf bookcase. He spaced the shelves **14** inches apart. What was the height of the bookcase?

Think: How many times do you need to add $\frac{3}{4}$ inch to find the total height?

____

Answer ______________________

3. The Jansons, the Klines, the Littles, the Meegans, and the Nelsons all live on the same straight road. The Littles live in the middle house. The Meegans live in the last house. The Jansons live between the Nelsons and the Littles. Who are the Meegans' next-door neighbors?

____

4. Lisa ordered **3** pizzas for a party. Each had a different topping. There were **8** slices in each pizza. After the party, **2** slices were left in one pie, **3** left in another pie, and none left in the third pie. What fractional part of the pizzas was eaten?

____

5. A log is **9** feet long. Lee wants to cut it into **4** pieces of equal size. How many cuts must he make?

____

6. A corral is in the shape of a square. There are **5** fence posts equally spaced on each side of the corral. How many fence posts are there in all?

____

7. A garden is divided into **3** sections. There are three times as many pepper plants as cucumber plants and twice as many tomato plants as pepper plants. If there are **8** cucumber plants, how many tomato plants are there?

____

8. Five students compared their heights. Rose was the shortest. Stan was **5** feet tall. Pearl was not the tallest. Tyler was taller than Vincent, but not as tall as Pearl. Who is the tallest?

____

Name ______________________________

Least Common Multiple, Least Common Denominator

STANDARD

These two fractions have **unlike denominators.**

$\frac{3}{4}$ $\frac{1}{6}$

To add or subtract the fractions, you first need to find a **common denominator.**

1. Find multiples of each denominator.

The denominator of $\frac{3}{4}$ is **4**.

The denominator of $\frac{1}{6}$ is **6**.

Find multiples of **4** and **6**. Do not list **0**.

Multiples of **4**:
4, 8, 12, 16, 20, 24, . . .

Multiples of **6**:
6, 12, 18, 24, 30, 36, . . .

2. Compare the lists of multiples. Circle the numbers that are the same in both lists. These are **common multiples**.

Multiples of **4**:
4, 8, (12), 16, 20, (24) . . .

Multiples of **6**:
6, (12), 18, (24), 30, 36, . . .

12 is the least number in both lists. It is called the **least common multiple (LCM).**

3. Write equivalent fractions. Use the **LCM** as the **least common denominator (LCD).**

$$\frac{3 \times 3}{4 \times 3} = \frac{9}{12}$$

$$\frac{1 \times 2}{6 \times 2} = \frac{2}{12}$$

Then add or subtract.

$$\frac{9}{12} + \frac{2}{12} = \frac{11}{12}$$

Write two common multiples of each pair of numbers. Then write the least common multiple.

Multiples of **4**: **4, 8, 12, 16, 20, 24, 28, 32, 36, 40, 44, 48, 52, 56, . . .**
Multiples of **5**: **5, 10, 15, 20, 25, 30, 35, 40, 45, 50, 55, 60, 65, 70, 75, 80, . . .**
Multiples of **8**: **8, 16, 24, 32, 40, 48, 56, 64, 72, 80, 88, 96, 104, . . .**
Multiples of **10**: **10, 20, 30, 40, 50, 60, 70, 80, 90, 100, 110, 120, . . .**

1. **4** and **5**
Common multiples: ____________
Least common multiple: ____________

4 and **8**
Common multiples: ____________
Least common multiple: ____________

2. **4** and **10**
Common multiples: ____________
Least common multiple: ____________

5 and **8**
Common multiples: ____________
Least common multiple: ____________

3. **5** and **10**
Common multiples: ____________
Least common multiple: ____________

8 and **10**
Common multiples: ____________
Least common multiple: ____________

STANDARD

Find the least common denominator of two mixed numbers the same way you find the least common denominator of two fractions.

Find the **LCD** of $4\frac{1}{5}$ and $2\frac{5}{6}$.

Multiples of **5**: 5, 10, 15, 20, 25, (30), 35, . . .

Multiples of **6**: 6, 12, 18, 24, (30), 36, . . .

The **LCD** of $4\frac{1}{5}$ and $2\frac{5}{6}$ is 30.

Write multiples of each denominator. Then find the LCD.

4. $2\frac{2}{3}$ ________

$5\frac{1}{4}$ ________

LCD ______

5. $1\frac{2}{5}$ ________

$6\frac{1}{3}$ ________

LCD ______

6. $4\frac{3}{10}$ ________

$4\frac{2}{5}$ ________

LCD ______

Solve.

7. A set of wrenches contains these sizes: $\frac{1}{4}$, $\frac{1}{2}$, $\frac{3}{4}$, and **1** inch. You need wrenches to fit bolts of these sizes: $\frac{1}{8}$, $\frac{2}{8}$, $\frac{3}{8}$, $\frac{4}{8}$, $\frac{5}{8}$, $\frac{6}{8}$, $\frac{7}{8}$, and $\frac{8}{8}$ inch. What size wrenches should you add to the set?

____

Quick Check

Write the answer in simplest form.

Work Space

8. $\frac{5}{8} + \frac{2}{8}$ ______

9. $2\frac{7}{10} + \frac{9}{10}$ ______

10. $1\frac{3}{4} + 4\frac{3}{4}$ ______

11. $\frac{7}{8} - \frac{1}{8}$ ______

12. $7\frac{11}{12} - \frac{5}{12}$ ______

13. $3\frac{5}{9} - 3\frac{2}{9}$ ______

Find the LCD for the fractions or mixed numbers.

14. $\frac{7}{12}$ and $\frac{1}{3}$ ______

15. $1\frac{3}{10}$ and $2\frac{1}{8}$ ______

16. $3\frac{1}{4}$ and $2\frac{2}{5}$ ______

Name ______________________

Adding Fractions with Unlike Denominators

STANDARD

Before you can add fractions with **unlike denominators**, you need to write the fractions as equivalent fractions with like denominators.

$\frac{3}{4} = \frac{9}{12}$

$\frac{1}{6} = \frac{2}{12}$

Find $\frac{3}{4} + \frac{1}{6}$

1. Find the least common denominator (LCD) of **4** and **6**.

$$\begin{array}{rcr} \frac{3}{4} & = & \frac{\quad}{12} \\ +\frac{1}{6} & = & +\frac{\quad}{12} \\ \hline \end{array}$$

The LCM of **4** and **6** is **12**.

2. Write equivalent fractions for $\frac{3}{4}$ and $\frac{1}{6}$. Then add.

$$\begin{array}{rcr} \frac{3}{4} & = & \frac{9}{12} \\ +\frac{1}{6} & = & \frac{2}{12} \\ \hline & & \frac{11}{12} \end{array}$$

Think: **3** × **4** = **12.** Multiply the numerator by 3.

Think: **2** × **6** = **12.** Multiply the numerator by 2.

Add. Write the sum in simplest form.

1. $\frac{1}{2} = \frac{\quad}{4}$, $+\frac{1}{4} = +\frac{1}{4}$ $\qquad$ $\frac{2}{5} = \frac{\quad}{15}$, $+\frac{1}{3} = +\frac{\quad}{15}$ $\qquad$ $\frac{1}{6} = \frac{\quad}{12}$, $+\frac{1}{4} = +\frac{\quad}{12}$ $\qquad$ $\frac{5}{6} = \frac{\quad}{24}$, $+\frac{1}{8} = +\frac{\quad}{24}$

2. $\frac{2}{3} + \frac{1}{9}$ $\qquad$ $\frac{1}{10} + \frac{3}{4}$ $\qquad$ $\frac{1}{9} + \frac{5}{6}$ $\qquad$ $\frac{4}{5} + \frac{2}{3}$

3. $\frac{2}{3} + \frac{1}{4}$ $\qquad$ $\frac{1}{2} + \frac{2}{5}$ $\qquad$ $\frac{3}{5} + \frac{1}{4}$ $\qquad$ $\frac{3}{10} + \frac{1}{2}$

4. $\frac{1}{6} + \frac{7}{10}$ $\qquad$ $\frac{5}{12} + \frac{1}{2}$ $\qquad$ $\frac{3}{10} + \frac{5}{8}$ $\qquad$ $\frac{3}{5} + \frac{2}{9}$

STANDARD

To find the sum of three fractions, you follow the same steps.

$\left(\frac{1}{2} + \frac{1}{3}\right) + \frac{1}{6}$

1. Find the LCD of **2, 3,** and **6.**

$\frac{1}{2} = \frac{}{6}$

$\frac{1}{3} = \frac{}{6}$

$+\frac{1}{6} = \frac{}{6}$

The LCM of **2, 3,** and **6** is **6.**

2. Write equivalent fractions. Add. Write the sum in simplest form.

$\frac{1}{2} = \frac{3}{6}$

$\frac{1}{3} = \frac{2}{6}$

$+\frac{1}{6} = \frac{1}{6}$

$\frac{6}{6} = 1$ ← simplest form

Write the sum in simplest form.

5. $\left(\frac{1}{8} + \frac{3}{8}\right) + \frac{2}{8} =$ ______ $\frac{1}{3} + \left(\frac{2}{3} + \frac{1}{3}\right) =$ ______ $\left(\frac{1}{2} + \frac{3}{4}\right) + \frac{1}{8} =$ ______

6. $\left(\frac{4}{5} + \frac{2}{5}\right) + \frac{3}{5} =$ ______ $\frac{3}{10} + \left(\frac{3}{5} + \frac{1}{2}\right) =$ ______ $\frac{2}{3} + \left(\frac{1}{6} + \frac{2}{9}\right) =$ ______

Problem Solving Reasoning **Solve.**

7. In the Lincoln School, $\frac{1}{6}$ of the students are on the track team and $\frac{1}{4}$ of the students are on the tennis team. No students play on both teams. What fraction of the students are on the two teams altogether? ______

Test Prep ★ Mixed Review

8 **Which expression does not have the value of 6?**

A 600 ÷ (2 + 8)

B (6 ÷ 3) × 2 + 2

C 60 ÷ (2 × 5)

D (6 – 3) + (12 ÷ 4)

9 **Which two numbers have a product of *about* 400?**

F 400 and 3

G 320 and 2

H 26 and 15

J 24 and 30

Name ______________________________

Adding Mixed Numbers with Unlike Denominators

STANDARD

When you add mixed numbers with unlike denominators, you must find a common denominator for the fractions before you add. Write the sum in simplest form.

$$\begin{array}{r} 3\frac{1}{4} = 3\frac{2}{8} \\ +\,1\frac{3}{8} = 1\frac{3}{8} \\ \hline 4\frac{5}{8} \end{array}$$

$$\begin{array}{r} 2\frac{3}{4} = 2\frac{6}{8} \\ +\,4\frac{5}{8} = 4\frac{5}{8} \\ \hline 6\frac{11}{8} = 7\frac{3}{8} \end{array} \leftarrow \text{simplest form}$$

Add. Write the sum in simplest form.

1. $6\frac{2}{3} + 4\frac{1}{6}$ $\qquad 2\frac{3}{4} + 1\frac{1}{2}$ $\qquad 5\frac{1}{6} + 3\frac{3}{4}$

2. $5\frac{7}{8} + 7\frac{3}{4}$ $\qquad 6\frac{5}{9} + 5\frac{5}{6}$ $\qquad 6\frac{7}{8} + 7\frac{1}{2}$

3. $16\frac{11}{12} + 7\frac{1}{4}$ $\qquad 3\frac{2}{3} + 2\frac{1}{4}$ $\qquad 2\frac{3}{4} + 1\frac{2}{3}$

4. $8\frac{5}{18} + 5\frac{5}{9}$ $\qquad 14\frac{11}{24} + 9\frac{1}{3}$ $\qquad 1\frac{7}{10} + 6\frac{3}{4}$

5. $9\frac{3}{4} + 8\frac{2}{3}$ $\qquad 5\frac{2}{3} + 6\frac{1}{5}$ $\qquad 6\frac{7}{8} + 3\frac{5}{6}$

STANDARD

To find the sum of three mixed numbers, follow these steps.

Add $6\frac{1}{2} + 1\frac{3}{4} + 7\frac{2}{3}$

1. Find the LCD. — The LCM of **2**, **4**, and **3** is **12**.

2. Use the LCD and write equivalent fractions. — $\frac{1}{2} = \frac{6}{12}$ $\frac{3}{4} = \frac{9}{12}$ $\frac{2}{3} = \frac{8}{12}$

3. Add the fractions. Then add the whole numbers. Write your answer in simplest form.

$$\begin{array}{rcr} 6\frac{1}{2} & \rightarrow & 6\frac{6}{12} \\ 1\frac{3}{4} & \rightarrow & 1\frac{9}{12} \\ +7\frac{2}{3} & \rightarrow & 7\frac{8}{12} \\ \hline & & 14\frac{23}{12} = 15\frac{11}{12} \end{array}$$

Write the sum in simplest form.

6. $1\frac{1}{3} + 1\frac{2}{3} + 5\frac{1}{3} =$ ______ $3\frac{1}{4} + 1\frac{3}{4} + 2\frac{1}{4} =$ ______

7. $2\frac{5}{6} + 4\frac{1}{2} + 1\frac{5}{12} =$ ______ $5\frac{2}{3} + 8\frac{4}{9} + 4\frac{1}{3} =$ ______

8. $9\frac{3}{8} + 2\frac{1}{4} + 6\frac{2}{3} =$ ______ $3\frac{1}{2} + 1\frac{3}{10} + 6\frac{1}{2} =$ ______

Problem Solving Reasoning **Write the next three numbers in the pattern.**

9. $1, 1\frac{3}{4}, 2\frac{1}{2}, 3\frac{1}{4}, 4,$ ______

10. $2\frac{1}{2}, 2\frac{3}{4}, 3, 3\frac{1}{4}, 3\frac{1}{2},$ ______

11. $4\frac{5}{8}, 5\frac{3}{4}, 6\frac{7}{8}, 8, 9\frac{1}{8},$ ______

12. $3\frac{5}{8}, 6, 8\frac{3}{8}, 10\frac{3}{4}, 13\frac{1}{8},$ ______

Test Prep ★ Mixed Review

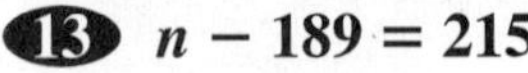

13 $n - 189 = 215$
What is the value of the variable n?

A 26

B 36

C 404

D 414

14 Which number is greatest?

F 4^4

G 3,000

H 3^5

J 20×10^2

Name ___________________________

Subtracting Fractions with Unlike Denominators

STANDARD

Before you can subtract fractions with **unlike denominators,** you need to write the fractions as equivalent fractions with like denominators.

Find $\frac{3}{4} - \frac{1}{6}$

$\frac{3}{4} = \frac{9}{12}$

$\frac{1}{6} = \frac{2}{12}$

1. Find the LCD of **4** and **6.**

$$\begin{array}{r} \frac{3}{4} = \frac{}{12} \leftarrow \\ -\frac{1}{6} = \frac{}{12} \leftarrow \\ \hline \end{array}$$

The LCM of **4** and **6** is **12**.

2. Write equivalent fractions. Subtract. Simplify if necessary.

$$\begin{array}{r} \frac{3}{4} = \frac{9}{12} \\ -\frac{1}{6} = \frac{2}{12} \\ \hline \frac{7}{12} \end{array}$$

Subtract. Write the difference in simplest form.

1. $\begin{array}{r} \frac{3}{4} = \frac{}{4} \\ -\frac{1}{2} = \frac{}{4} \\ \hline \end{array}$ $\begin{array}{r} \frac{5}{8} = \frac{}{8} \\ -\frac{1}{4} = \frac{}{8} \\ \hline \end{array}$ $\begin{array}{r} \frac{3}{4} = \frac{}{16} \\ -\frac{5}{16} = \frac{}{16} \\ \hline \end{array}$ $\begin{array}{r} \frac{8}{15} = \frac{}{30} \\ -\frac{3}{10} = \frac{}{30} \\ \hline \end{array}$

2. $\begin{array}{r} \frac{9}{11} \\ -\frac{1}{2} \\ \hline \end{array}$ $\begin{array}{r} \frac{1}{3} \\ -\frac{1}{7} \\ \hline \end{array}$ $\begin{array}{r} \frac{3}{5} \\ -\frac{1}{2} \\ \hline \end{array}$ $\begin{array}{r} \frac{1}{6} \\ -\frac{1}{15} \\ \hline \end{array}$

3. $\begin{array}{r} \frac{4}{5} \\ -\frac{7}{12} \\ \hline \end{array}$ $\begin{array}{r} \frac{3}{4} \\ -\frac{3}{10} \\ \hline \end{array}$ $\begin{array}{r} \frac{9}{10} \\ -\frac{1}{4} \\ \hline \end{array}$ $\begin{array}{r} \frac{3}{8} \\ -\frac{1}{6} \\ \hline \end{array}$

4. $\begin{array}{r} \frac{4}{5} \\ -\frac{2}{3} \\ \hline \end{array}$ $\begin{array}{r} \frac{7}{10} \\ -\frac{1}{5} \\ \hline \end{array}$ $\begin{array}{r} \frac{3}{4} \\ -\frac{2}{5} \\ \hline \end{array}$ $\begin{array}{r} \frac{1}{2} \\ -\frac{3}{10} \\ \hline \end{array}$

STANDARD

Write the sum or difference in simplest form.

5. $\frac{2}{8} + \frac{1}{4}$ $\frac{1}{8} + \frac{5}{12}$ $\frac{3}{5} + \frac{3}{20}$ $\frac{4}{9} + \frac{3}{10}$

6. $\frac{5}{12} - \frac{1}{3}$ $\frac{3}{8} - \frac{1}{5}$ $\frac{5}{16} + \frac{1}{4}$ $\frac{5}{8} - \frac{1}{2}$

Problem Solving
Reasoning

Solve.

7. A cook estimates that mixing **4** $\frac{3}{4}$ pounds of flour with 2 $\frac{7}{8}$ pounds of flour will create about **8** pounds of flour. Is the cook's estimate reasonable? Explain.

____

Quick Check

Add. Write the sum in simplest form.

Work Space

8. $\frac{2}{8} + \frac{5}{12}$ ______

9. $\frac{5}{16} + \frac{1}{4}$ ______

10. $\frac{2}{3} + \frac{1}{6}$ ______

11. $2\frac{5}{6} + 3\frac{4}{9}$ ______

12. $4\frac{4}{5} + 7\frac{2}{5}$ ______

13. $3\frac{6}{8} + 6\frac{1}{2}$ ______

Subtract. Write the difference in simplest form.

14. $\frac{1}{4} - \frac{1}{6}$ ______

15. $\frac{4}{5} - \frac{1}{2}$ ______

16. $\frac{4}{8} - \frac{1}{6}$ ______

Name ____________________

Subtracting from Whole Numbers

STANDARD

Sometimes when you subtract, you must rename **1** as a fraction. Here are some different ways to rename **1**.

$1 = \frac{2}{2}$ $1 = \frac{3}{3}$ $1 = \frac{4}{4}$ $1 = \frac{5}{5}$ $1 = \frac{6}{6}$ $1 = \frac{7}{7}$ $1 = \frac{8}{8}$

To subtract a fraction or a mixed number from a whole number, rename the whole number as a mixed number, then subtract.

Find $4 - \frac{1}{6}$.

1. Rename the whole number as a mixed number.

$$\begin{array}{rcr} 4 & = & 3\frac{6}{6} \\ -\ \frac{1}{6} & = & -\ \frac{1}{6} \\ \hline \end{array}$$

$4 = 3 + 1$
$= 3 + \frac{6}{6}$
$= 3\frac{6}{6}$

2. Subtract.

$$\begin{array}{rcr} 4 & = & 3\frac{6}{6} \\ -\ \frac{1}{6} & = & -\ \frac{1}{6} \\ \hline & & 3\frac{5}{6} \end{array}$$

Subtract. Write the difference in simplest form.

1. $7 - 1\frac{3}{4}$ $3 - 1\frac{2}{7}$ $7 - 5\frac{1}{4}$ $6 - 2\frac{1}{2}$

2. $8 - \frac{2}{5}$ $4 - \frac{1}{6}$ $1 - \frac{3}{8}$ $2 - \frac{1}{3}$

3. $10 - 4\frac{1}{2}$ $9 - 1\frac{4}{7}$ $6 - 5\frac{1}{3}$ $4 - 1\frac{7}{9}$

4. $3 - \frac{1}{6}$ $6 - \frac{2}{8}$ $8 - \frac{2}{5}$ $7 - \frac{4}{10}$

STANDARD

Add or subtract. Write the sum or difference in simplest form.

5. $6\frac{3}{4} - 1$ = ____ $8 - 5\frac{2}{3}$ = ____ $7\frac{3}{5} + 5$ = ____

6. $6\frac{5}{7} - \frac{3}{7}$ = ____ $8\frac{3}{4} + 7$ = ____ $5 - 2\frac{5}{6}$ = ____

7. $7 - 3\frac{2}{3}$ = ____ $4\frac{5}{8} + 4$ = ____ $9 - 5\frac{7}{8}$ = ____

Problem Solving Reasoning Solve.

8. What number must be subtracted from 9 to have a difference of $4\frac{5}{9}$? ____

9. What number can be added to $3\frac{2}{3}$ to have a sum of about $4\frac{1}{2}$? ____

10. What number must be added to $3\frac{1}{2}$ to have a sum of 7? ____

11. What number can be added to $5\frac{3}{8}$ to get about $9\frac{1}{2}$? ____

Test Prep ★ Mixed Review

12. There are approximately 3500 seats in the community theater. The 12 sections are the same size. About how many seats are in each section?

A 200
B 250
C 275
D 300

13. What is the value of the expression $5^2 - (72 - 6 \times 9)$?

F 594
G 25
H 7
J 5

Name ___________________________

Subtracting Mixed Numbers with Renaming

STANDARD

Sometimes, you need to rename when you subtract mixed numbers.

Find $3\frac{1}{4} - 1\frac{2}{4}$

1. Rename $3\frac{1}{4}$.

$$3\frac{1}{4} = 3 + \frac{1}{4}$$
$$= 2 + 1 + \frac{1}{4}$$
$$= 2 + \left(\frac{4}{4} + \frac{1}{4}\right)$$
$$= 2 + \frac{5}{4}$$

2. Subtract the fractions.

$$\begin{array}{r} 3\frac{1}{4} = 2\frac{5}{4} \\ -\ 1\frac{3}{4} = 1\frac{3}{4} \\ \hline \frac{2}{4} \end{array}$$

3. Subtract the whole numbers. Simplify.

$$\begin{array}{r} 3\frac{1}{4} = 2\frac{5}{4} \\ -\ 1\frac{3}{4} = 1\frac{3}{4} \\ \hline 1\frac{2}{4} = 1\frac{1}{2} \end{array}$$

Rename the mixed number.

1. $5\frac{5}{6} = 4\frac{\ }{6}$ $\quad 8\frac{5}{7} = 7\frac{\ }{7}$ $\quad 6\frac{5}{12} = 5\frac{\ }{12}$ $\quad 9\frac{5}{6} = 8\frac{\ }{6}$

2. $6\frac{2}{5} = 5\frac{\ }{5}$ $\quad 5\frac{2}{9} = 4\frac{\ }{9}$ $\quad 6\frac{2}{8} = 5\frac{\ }{8}$ $\quad 2\frac{4}{5} = 1\frac{\ }{5}$

3. $2\frac{4}{9} =$ ______ $\quad 3\frac{5}{8} =$ ______ $\quad 4\frac{1}{4} =$ ______ $\quad 3\frac{4}{5} =$ ______

Subtract. Write the difference in simplest form.

4. $3\frac{1}{8} - 1\frac{5}{8}$ $\quad 6\frac{2}{9} - 3\frac{7}{9}$ $\quad 5\frac{4}{7} - 2\frac{6}{7}$ $\quad 6\frac{1}{3} - 1\frac{2}{3}$

5. $8\frac{3}{5} - 4\frac{4}{5}$ $\quad 6\frac{3}{9} - 2\frac{5}{9}$ $\quad 7\frac{1}{8} - 2\frac{5}{8}$ $\quad 5\frac{1}{7} - 1\frac{4}{7}$

6. $4\frac{1}{4} - 2\frac{3}{4}$ $\quad 6\frac{1}{5} - 1\frac{4}{5}$ $\quad 3\frac{1}{3} - 1\frac{2}{3}$ $\quad 4\frac{1}{9} - 1\frac{4}{9}$

STANDARD

Subtract. Write the difference in simplest form.

7. $4\frac{3}{8} - 1\frac{5}{8}$ ______ $8\frac{1}{6} - 3\frac{5}{6}$ ______ $7\frac{1}{3} - 2\frac{2}{3}$ ______ $10\frac{4}{5} - 4\frac{3}{5}$ ______

8. $9\frac{3}{10} - 3\frac{7}{10}$ ______ $6\frac{1}{2} - 1\frac{1}{2}$ ______ $6\frac{1}{8} - 4\frac{3}{8}$ ______ $3\frac{1}{10} - 2\frac{3}{10}$ ______

Problem Solving Reasoning Solve.

9. On Saturday Jamie rode her bike $2\frac{7}{10}$ miles from her house to soccer practice. After riding $1\frac{9}{10}$ miles on the way back home, she got a flat tire. How far was Jamie from her house when she got the flat tire? __________

10. How far had Jamie ridden altogether on Saturday before she got the flat tire? __________

11. Jamie's tire was fixed and she rode back home. How far did she ride in all on Saturday? __________

Test Prep ★ Mixed Review

12. At a farm stand, Tanya bought $1\frac{1}{16}$ lb of snow peas, $2\frac{1}{4}$ lb of potatoes, $4\frac{1}{16}$ lb of broccoli, and $2\frac{3}{4}$ lb of carrots. Which two vegetables together weigh about 7 lb?

A snow peas and potatoes

B broccoli and carrots

C snow peas and broccoli

D potatoes and carrots

13. What is the prime factorization of 54 in exponent form?

F $2 \times 3 \times 9$

G 2×3^3

H $2^3 \times 3$

J 2×3^2

Name ______________________________

Subtracting Mixed Numbers with Unlike Denominators

STANDARD

When you subtract mixed numbers with unlike denominators, you must find a common denominator for the fractions before you subtract.

The LCM of **6** and **3** is **6**.

$$\begin{array}{r} 4\frac{5}{6} = 4\frac{5}{6} \\ -1\frac{2}{3} = 1\frac{4}{6} \\ \hline 3\frac{1}{6} \end{array}$$

$$\begin{array}{r} 9\frac{1}{6} = \ 9\frac{1}{6} \rightarrow \ 8\frac{7}{6} \\ -1\frac{2}{3} = -1\frac{4}{6} \rightarrow -1\frac{4}{6} \\ \hline 7\frac{3}{6} = 7\frac{1}{2} \end{array}$$ ← **simplest form**

Not enough to subtract. So, rename the whole number. $\mathbf{9 = 8\frac{6}{6}}$

$9\frac{1}{6} = 8\frac{7}{6}$

Subtract. Write the difference in simplest form.

1. $7\frac{1}{4} - 2\frac{5}{6}$ $\qquad$ $8\frac{1}{2} - 1\frac{2}{3}$ $\qquad$ $9\frac{1}{4} - 5\frac{1}{2}$

2. $6\frac{1}{3} - 5\frac{4}{6}$ $\qquad$ $10\frac{1}{2} - 2\frac{4}{5}$ $\qquad$ $12\frac{2}{3} - 6\frac{3}{4}$

3. $5\frac{1}{2} - 3\frac{3}{4}$ $\qquad$ $15\frac{1}{8} - 7\frac{3}{4}$ $\qquad$ $9\frac{2}{3} - 2\frac{5}{6}$

4. $10\frac{1}{2} - 4\frac{7}{8}$ $\qquad$ $11\frac{1}{4} - 6\frac{5}{8}$ $\qquad$ $12\frac{1}{3} - 4\frac{2}{3}$

Circle the expression that has the greater difference.

5. $4\frac{1}{3} - 2\frac{1}{6}$ or $4\frac{1}{3} - 2\frac{1}{2}$ $\qquad$ $5\frac{2}{5} - 4\frac{1}{2}$ or $5\frac{2}{3} - 4\frac{1}{2}$

6. $3\frac{7}{8} - 3\frac{1}{8}$ or $3\frac{3}{4} - 3\frac{1}{8}$ $\qquad$ $8\frac{1}{4} - 3\frac{3}{5}$ or $8\frac{1}{4} - 3\frac{3}{4}$

STANDARD

Subtract. Write the difference in simplest form.

7. $\begin{array}{r} 4\frac{1}{2} \\ -\ 1\frac{5}{6} \\ \hline \end{array}$ $\qquad$ $\begin{array}{r} 10\frac{3}{4} \\ -\ 5\frac{1}{6} \\ \hline \end{array}$ $\qquad$ $\begin{array}{r} 6\frac{2}{5} \\ -\ 2\frac{5}{6} \\ \hline \end{array}$

8. $\begin{array}{r} 5\frac{3}{4} \\ -\ 2\frac{1}{3} \\ \hline \end{array}$ $\qquad$ $\begin{array}{r} 2\frac{1}{4} \\ -\ 1\frac{5}{8} \\ \hline \end{array}$ $\qquad$ $\begin{array}{r} 9\frac{3}{4} \\ -\ 3\frac{5}{6} \\ \hline \end{array}$

Problem Solving
Reasoning

Solve.

9. Anna has $3\frac{1}{4}$ yd of fabric. She plans to use $2\frac{1}{2}$ yd for curtains. Does she have enough left to make 2 pillows that each use $\frac{5}{8}$ yd of fabric? Explain.

____

Quick Check

Subtract. Write the difference in simplest form.

Work Space

10. $\begin{array}{r} 4 \\ -\ 3\frac{6}{7} \\ \hline \end{array}$ $\qquad$ **11.** $\begin{array}{r} 7 \\ -\ 5\frac{5}{8} \\ \hline \end{array}$ $\qquad$ **12.** $\begin{array}{r} 8 \\ -\ 4\frac{1}{4} \\ \hline \end{array}$

13. $\begin{array}{r} 4\frac{7}{12} \\ -\ 3\frac{11}{12} \\ \hline \end{array}$ $\qquad$ **14.** $\begin{array}{r} 8\frac{1}{5} \\ -\ 2\frac{4}{5} \\ \hline \end{array}$ $\qquad$ **15.** $\begin{array}{r} 10\frac{3}{8} \\ -\ 5\frac{7}{8} \\ \hline \end{array}$

16. $\begin{array}{r} 3\frac{2}{5} \\ -\ 1\frac{1}{4} \\ \hline \end{array}$ $\qquad$ **17.** $\begin{array}{r} 15\frac{1}{3} \\ -\ 2\frac{5}{6} \\ \hline \end{array}$ $\qquad$ **18.** $\begin{array}{r} 12\frac{2}{8} \\ -\ 7\frac{5}{12} \\ \hline \end{array}$

Name ______________________

Problem Solving Application: Use a Diagram

STANDARD

Sometimes it is helpful to use a diagram such as a number line to solve problems.

In this lesson, you will use a number line to help you solve problems involving the comparison, addition, and subtraction of whole numbers, fractions, and mixed numbers.

Tips to Remember

1. Understand 2. Decide 3. Solve 4. Look back

- Ask yourself whether you have solved a problem like this before.
- When you can, make predictions about the answer. Then compare your answer and your prediction.
- When solving the problems, use the number lines to help you find equivalent fractions.
- Check your answer by doing the actual computation.

Solve. Use the number lines.

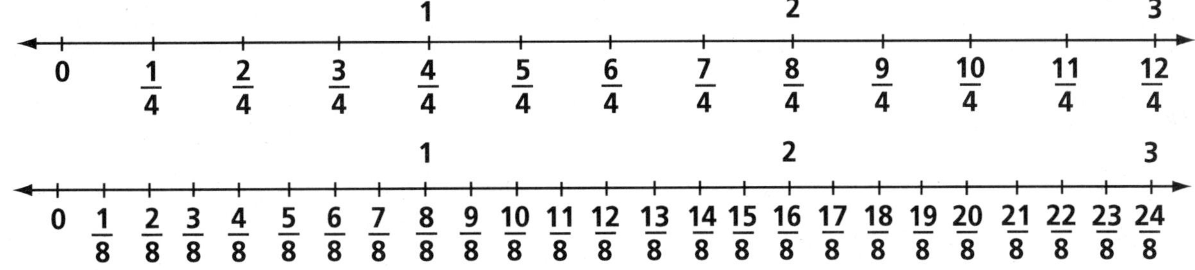

1. Mario and his friends ordered **3** pizzas. Each pizza was sliced into **8** pieces. They ate **21** slices. How much pizza did they eat? Write your answer as a mixed number.

Think: Which number line will you use? Between which two whole numbers is $\frac{21}{8}$?

____

Answer ______________________

2. Alana walked $\frac{3}{4}$ mile to the library. Later she walked $\frac{7}{8}$ mile to the ice cream store. How far did she walk in all?

Think: Which fraction is equivalent to $\frac{3}{4}$? Is the distance walked greater than **1** mile? ______________________

____

Answer ______________________

STANDARD

Solve. Use the number lines.

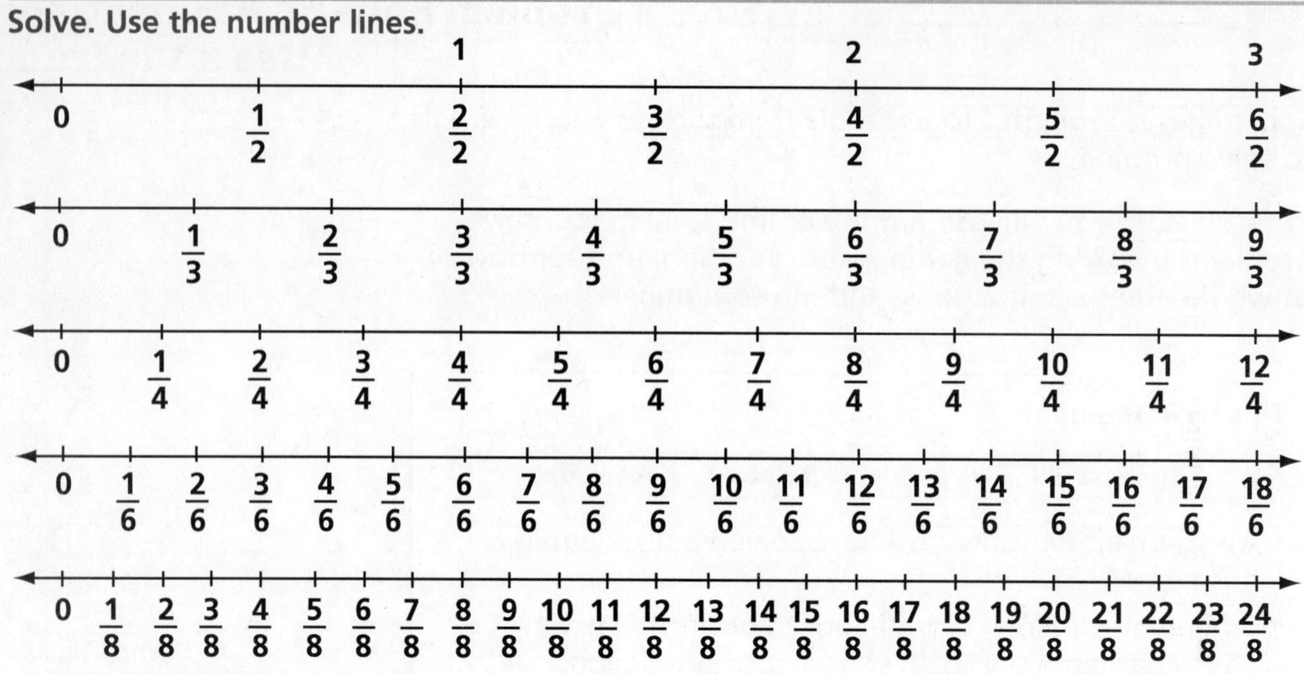

3. Tamika sliced an apple into **8** equal pieces and ate **6** of them. Mary sliced an apple into **4** equal pieces. Mary and Tamika ate the same amount. How many pieces did Mary eat?

____

4. Shira, Tess, and Uri wanted to see who could run the farthest in ten minutes. Shira ran $\frac{5}{8}$ mile, Tess ran $\frac{5}{6}$ mile, and Uri ran $\frac{3}{4}$ mile. Who ran the farthest?

____

5. A cake recipe calls for a total of **3** cups of flour. The baker has already included $1\frac{1}{3}$ cups. How many more cups of flour must be added?

____

6. A math book is $\frac{3}{4}$ inch thick. A social studies book is $1\frac{1}{2}$ inches thick. Will these books fit one on top of the other in a space that is **2** inches high?

____

Extend Your Thinking

7. Look back at problem 4. Explain how you arrived at your answer. Who ran the second farthest? Who ran the least distance?

____

____

____

8. Look back at problem 5. Explain the method you used to solve the problem. Tell which number line you used. What operations did you use to find the answer?

____

____

____

Name ______________________

Unit 4 Review

Use multiplication or division to write three equivalent fractions.

1. $\frac{2}{3}$ ______, ______, ______

2. $\frac{24}{48}$ ______, ______, ______

Write each mixed number as a fraction and each fraction as a mixed number.

3. $1\frac{2}{3} =$ ______

4. $2\frac{4}{5} =$ ______

5. $\frac{11}{8} =$ ______

6. $\frac{20}{9} =$ ______

Write each fraction or mixed number in simplest form.

7. $\frac{8}{32} =$ ______

8. $\frac{12}{15} =$ ______

9. $2\frac{9}{18} =$ ______

10. $4\frac{24}{40} =$ ______

Add or subtract. Write each answer in simplest form.

11. $\frac{3}{5} + \frac{1}{5}$

12. $\frac{5}{8} - \frac{4}{8}$

13. $1\frac{3}{4} + \frac{1}{4}$

14. $2\frac{9}{10} - 1\frac{3}{10}$

15. $\frac{1}{4} + \frac{3}{8}$

16. $\frac{9}{10} - \frac{3}{5}$

17. $2\frac{5}{8} + 3\frac{1}{12}$

18. $5\frac{1}{2} - 4\frac{1}{3}$

19. $6 - \frac{3}{5}$

20. $8 - \frac{5}{8}$

21. $5 + 3\frac{5}{9}$

22. $4\frac{1}{8} + 1$

On another sheet of paper, draw a number line to represent a 12-mile race. Then use the number line to solve each problem.

23. Tina stopped for water after $4\frac{3}{4}$ miles. How far was she from the finish? ______

24. Benny stopped for water after running $10\frac{1}{2}$ miles. How far was Benny from the finish? ______

Name ______________________________

Cumulative Review
★ Test Prep

1 **Which picture shows another name for $\frac{2}{3}$?**

A 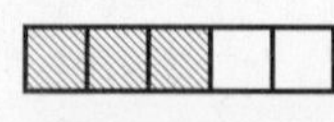

B

C

D

2 **What is the cost of buying 1 ear of corn?**

F 40¢ H 25¢

G 30¢ J 15¢

Use these spools to answer questions 3 and 4.

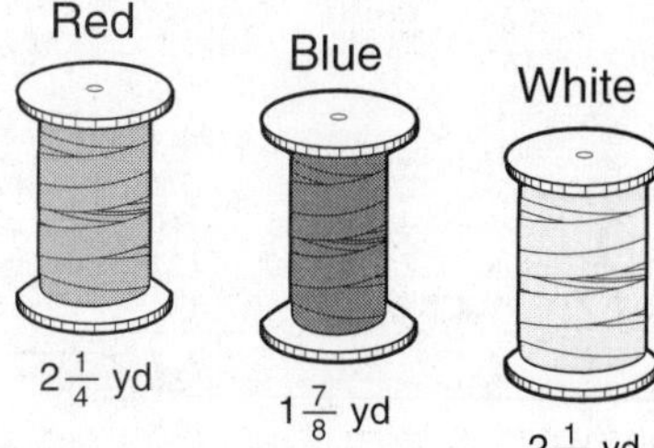

3 **Which list shows the spools of ribbon in greatest to least order?**

A red, blue, white

B red, white, blue

C white, blue, red

D white, red, blue

4 **About how much ribbon is there altogether?**

F Between 6 yards and 7 yards

G Between 5 yards and 6 yards

H Between 4 yards and 5 yards

J Fewer than 4 yards

5 **$16 - 2 \times 3 + 6 =$**

A 4 C 48 E Not here

B 16 D 126

6 **What is the value of the variable n?**
$4 \times (2 \times 9) = (4 \times n) \times 9$

F 72 H 9 K 2

G 36 J 4

7 **Which statement is true about the numbers 5 and 35?**

A Their GCF is 105.

B One is a prime factor of the other.

C Both are prime numbers.

D Both are composite numbers.

E Both are even numbers.

8 **The number of people who came to the hockey game does not round to 30,000 to the nearest ten thousand. How many people came to the hockey game?**

F 24,956 H 26,459 K 29,456

G 25,496 J 26,945

9 **You write two numbers on a piece of paper. Their difference is 2,416. One of the numbers is 5,482. What could the other number be?**

A 2,982 C 7,599 E 7,898

B 2,066 D 7,808

10 **You buy a dozen rolls that cost $.25 each and 4 bagels that cost $.45 each. Which expression below shows your total cost?**

F ($.25) + 4 × $.45

G (12 × $.25) × (4 + $.45)

H (12 × $.25) + (4 × $.45)

J (12 × $25) + (4 × $45)

K Not here

UNIT 5 • TABLE OF CONTENTS

Multiplication and Division of Fractions and Mixed Numbers

We will be using this vocabulary:

reciprocals two numbers whose product is **1**

pictograph a graph in which pictorial symbols are used to represent multiples of a number

bar graph a representation of numbers or numerical facts that uses lengths of bars to show information

Dear Family,

During the next few weeks, our math class will be learning and practicing the multiplication and division of fractions and mixed numbers.

You can expect to see homework that provides practice with multiplying whole numbers and fractions. Here is a sample you may want to keep handy to give help if needed.

Multiplying Whole Numbers and Fractions

Example: Find $8 \times \frac{3}{4}$.

To multiply a whole number and a fraction, first write the whole number as a fraction. To write a whole number as a fraction, write it over **1**.

$$8 \times \frac{3}{4} = \frac{8}{1} \times \frac{3}{4}$$

Then multiply the numerators and multiply the denominators.

$$\frac{8}{1} \times \frac{3}{4} = \frac{24}{4}$$

When working with fractions, write the answer in simplest form. One way to write a fraction in simplest form is to divide. Find the greatest common factor and divide both the numerator and the denominator by it.

$$\frac{24 \div 4}{4 \div 4} = \frac{6}{1} = 6$$

During this unit, students will need to continue practicing multiplication and division facts.

Sincerely,

Name ______________________________

Multiplying Whole Numbers and Fractions

STANDARD

You can write a division equation to show **6** apples separated into **2** groups with **3** apples in each group.

$$6 \div 2 = 3$$

Each of the **2** groups has $\frac{1}{2}$ of the total number of apples. You can write a multiplication sentence to show this.

$$\frac{1}{2} \times 6 = 3$$

Here is how you multiply a whole number and a fraction:

1. Write the whole number as a fraction. Multiply the numerators.

$$\frac{4}{1} \times \frac{2}{5} = \frac{4 \times 2}{?}$$

2. Multiply the denominators.

$$\frac{4}{1} \times \frac{2}{5} = \frac{4 \times 2}{5}$$

$$= \frac{8}{5}$$

3. Write your answer in simplest form.

$$\frac{4}{1} \times \frac{2}{5} = \frac{4 \times 2}{5}$$

$$= \frac{8}{5} \text{ or } 1\frac{3}{5}$$

Multiply. Write each product in simplest form.

1. $\frac{1}{2} \times 8 =$ ______	$\frac{1}{4} \times 12 =$ ______	$6 \times \frac{2}{3} =$ ______
2. $\frac{1}{6} \times 18 =$ ______	$\frac{1}{5} \times 10 =$ ______	$\frac{3}{8} \times 9 =$ ______
3. $\frac{1}{3} \times 15 =$ ______	$20 \times \frac{1}{4} =$ ______	$11 \times \frac{1}{3} =$ ______
4. $\frac{3}{4} \times 8 =$ ______	$14 \times \frac{5}{7} =$ ______	$\frac{2}{5} \times 25 =$ ______
5. $3 \times \frac{4}{7} =$ ______	$\frac{2}{9} \times 4 =$ ______	$\frac{1}{4} \times 24 =$ ______

STANDARD

Multiply. Write each product in simplest form.

6. $5 \times \frac{3}{5} =$ ______ $8 \times \frac{1}{6} =$ ______ $\frac{2}{5} \times 13 =$ ______

7. $\frac{1}{4} \times 16 =$ ______ $\frac{5}{8} \times 4 =$ ______ $24 \times \frac{1}{12} =$ ______

8. $6 \times \frac{3}{4} =$ ______ $\frac{1}{6} \times 20 =$ ______ $42 \times \frac{1}{4} =$ ______

9. $10 \times \frac{3}{5} =$ ______ $3 \times \frac{8}{9} =$ ______ $\frac{1}{8} \times 12 =$ ______

10. $\frac{1}{3} \times 17 =$ ______ $\frac{3}{4} \times 5 =$ ______ $2 \times \frac{3}{10} =$ ______

11. $4 \times \frac{4}{5} =$ ______ $\frac{7}{8} \times 6 =$ ______ $4 \times \frac{3}{16} =$ ______

Problem Solving Reasoning

Solve.

12. Jake spent a $\frac{1}{2}$ hour doing homework. Rosa spent 35 minutes doing homework. Who spent more time doing homework?

Explain. ______

13. The first quarter of a football game lasted 45 minutes. The second quarter lasted $\frac{3}{5}$ of an hour. Which quarter took less time?

Explain. ______

14. Latrice enjoys sewing and has $1\frac{1}{3}$ yards of fabric. If she uses $\frac{2}{3}$ of the fabric to make a pillow, how much fabric will she use?

Explain. ______

Test Prep ★ Mixed Review

15. A shop printed 8^3 posters. What is 8^3 equivalent to?

A 24

B 64

C 512

D 1,000

16. A small car travels 32 miles on a gallon of gas. *About* how much gas will the car use on a trip of 232 miles?

F less than 15 gallons

G between 15 and 20 gallons

H between 25 and 30 gallons

J more than 30 gallons

Name ______________________________

Modeling Multiplication of Fractions

STANDARD

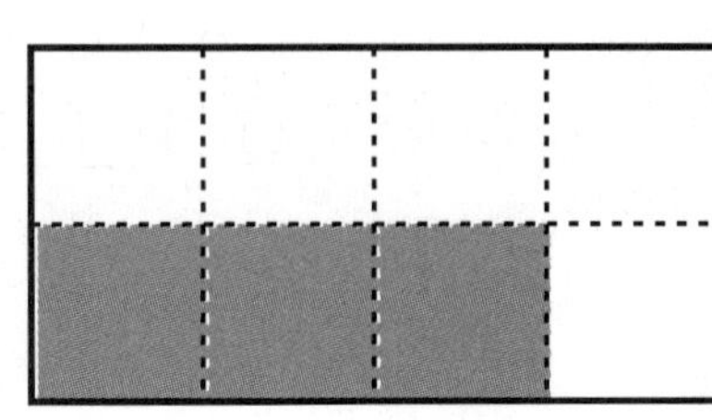

Suppose you ate $\frac{3}{4}$ of $\frac{1}{2}$ of a pan of corn bread.

You actually ate $\frac{3}{8}$ of the whole pan of corn bread.

$$\frac{3}{4} \text{ of } \frac{1}{2} = \frac{3}{8}$$

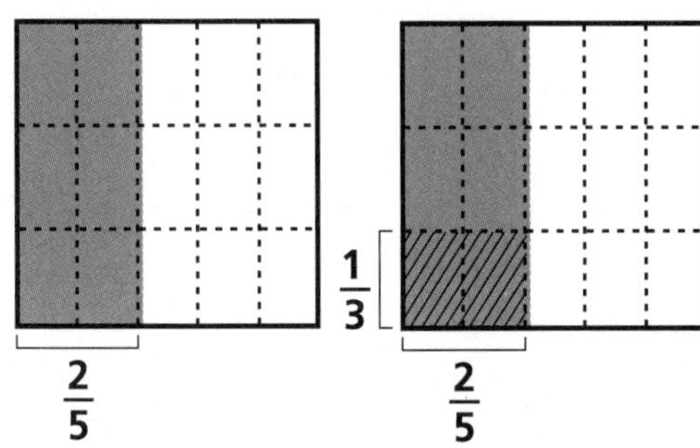

Suppose you cut another whole pan of corn bread into **15** pieces as shown in the model on the left.

What is $\frac{1}{3}$ of $\frac{2}{5}$ of the corn bread?

$$\frac{1}{3} \text{ of } \frac{2}{5} = \frac{2}{15}$$

Finding a fraction of a fraction is the same as multiplying a fraction by a fraction.

Here's how to multiply $\frac{3}{4} \times \frac{1}{2}$.

$$\frac{3}{4} \text{ of } \frac{1}{2} = \frac{3}{4} \times \frac{1}{2}$$

1. Multiply the numerators to find the numerator of the product.

$$\frac{3}{4} \times \frac{1}{2} = \frac{3}{?}$$

2. Multiply the denominators to find the denominator of the product.

$$\frac{3}{4} \times \frac{1}{2} = \frac{3}{8}$$

Multiply. Use the model to check your answer.

1. 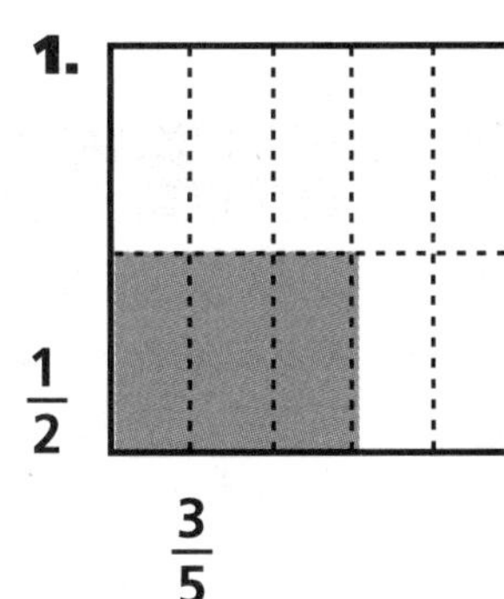

$\frac{1}{2} \times \frac{3}{5} =$ ______

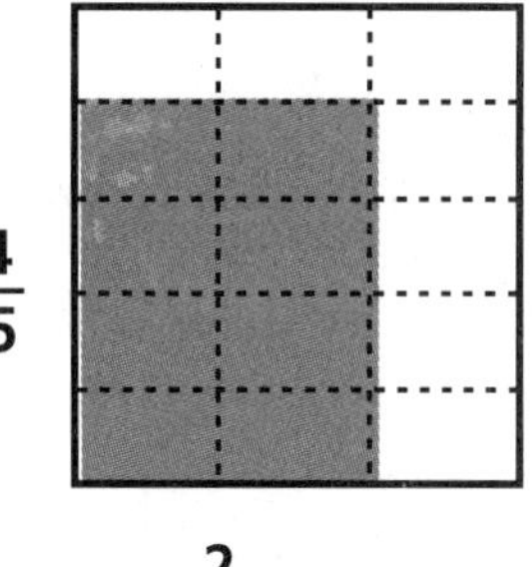

$\frac{4}{5} \times \frac{2}{3} =$ ______

STANDARD

Multiply. Use the model to check your answer.

2. $\frac{1}{2} \times \frac{1}{3} =$ ______

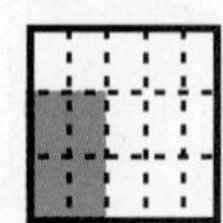

$\frac{2}{3} \times \frac{2}{5} =$ ______

3. 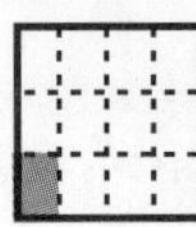

$\frac{1}{3} \times \frac{1}{4} =$ ______

$\frac{2}{3} \times \frac{2}{3} =$ ______

4. 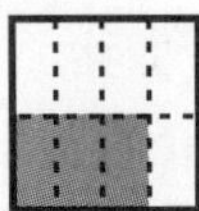

$\frac{1}{2} \times \frac{3}{4} =$ ______

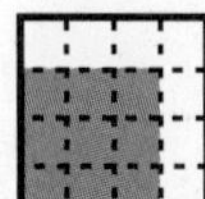

$\frac{3}{4} \times \frac{3}{4} =$ ______

5. 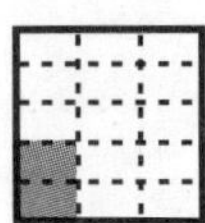

$\frac{2}{5} \times \frac{1}{3} =$ ______

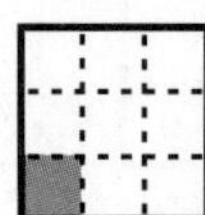

$\frac{1}{3} \times \frac{1}{3} =$ ______

6. 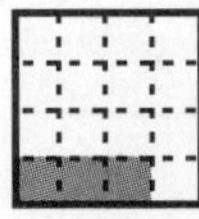

$\frac{1}{4} \times \frac{3}{4} =$ ______

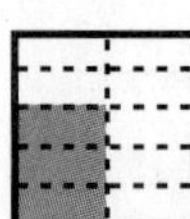

$\frac{3}{5} \times \frac{1}{2} =$ ______

Problem Solving Reasoning **Solve.**

7. When you multiply two whole numbers the product is equal to or greater than either of the factors. Is this true or false? Explain with examples.

______

______

8. When you multiply two fractions, is the product greater than or less than either of the factors? Give an example.

______

______

Test Prep ★ Mixed Review

9 Which number makes the equation true?
$31 - n = 26$

A 2

B 3

C 4

D 5

10 Which number completes the table?

n	3	40	500
$n \times 500$	1,500	20,000	?

F 2,500

G 25,000

H 250,000

J 2,500,000

Name ______________________

Multiplying Fractions

STANDARD

Remember, to multiply fractions:

1. Multiply the numerators to find the numerator of the product.
2. Multiply the denominators to find the denominator of the product.
3. Write your answer in simplest form.

$\frac{5}{6} \times \frac{3}{4} = \frac{15}{24}$ or $\frac{5}{8}$ ← simplest form $\quad \frac{7}{8} \times \frac{4}{3} = \frac{28}{24}$ or $1\frac{1}{6}$ ← simplest form

Multiply.

1. $\frac{5}{8} \times \frac{3}{4} =$ ______ $\quad \frac{2}{9} \times \frac{4}{3} =$ ______ $\quad \frac{7}{6} \times \frac{1}{4} =$ ______

2. $\frac{2}{3} \times \frac{5}{7} =$ ______ $\quad \frac{1}{10} \times \frac{1}{2} =$ ______ $\quad \frac{3}{5} \times \frac{7}{5} =$ ______

Multiply. Write each product in simplest form.

3. $\frac{2}{3} \times \frac{7}{8} =$ ______ $\quad \frac{4}{9} \times \frac{1}{2} =$ ______ $\quad \frac{6}{7} \times \frac{3}{4} =$ ______

4. $\frac{5}{6} \times \frac{2}{3} =$ ______ $\quad \frac{2}{7} \times \frac{1}{3} =$ ______ $\quad \frac{1}{9} \times \frac{3}{7} =$ ______

5. $\frac{3}{5} \times \frac{1}{2} =$ ______ $\quad \frac{4}{7} \times \frac{3}{4} =$ ______ $\quad \frac{8}{9} \times \frac{5}{8} =$ ______

6. $\frac{4}{5} \times \frac{2}{9} =$ ______ $\quad \frac{8}{9} \times \frac{3}{4} =$ ______ $\quad \frac{1}{9} \times \frac{1}{8} =$ ______

7. $\frac{1}{3} \times \frac{8}{9} =$ ______ $\quad \frac{2}{3} \times \frac{7}{9} =$ ______ $\quad \frac{3}{4} \times \frac{2}{5} =$ ______

8. $\frac{4}{5} \times \frac{7}{8} =$ ______ $\quad \frac{3}{4} \times \frac{6}{7} =$ ______ $\quad \frac{7}{8} \times \frac{2}{9} =$ ______

9. $\frac{3}{4} \times \frac{2}{3} =$ ______ $\quad \frac{4}{9} \times \frac{2}{7} =$ ______ $\quad \frac{1}{9} \times \frac{1}{4} =$ ______

STANDARD

Multiply. Write each product in simplest form.

10. $\frac{3}{5} \times 5 =$ ______ $6 \times \frac{2}{3} =$ ______ $\frac{1}{4} \times 10 =$ ______

11. $\frac{1}{6} \times \frac{9}{5} =$ ______ $\frac{6}{5} \times \frac{5}{3} =$ ______ $\frac{5}{8} \times \frac{1}{5} =$ ______

12. $\frac{3}{4} \times \frac{3}{4} =$ ______ $\frac{5}{3} \times \frac{9}{10} =$ ______ $3 \times \frac{3}{2} =$ ______

Problem Solving
Reasoning

Solve.

13. Joseph and his friends baked 48 cookies. They ate $\frac{1}{6}$ of them. How many cookies did Joseph and his friends eat? ______

14. Lisa lives $\frac{3}{5}$ mile from school. She walks $\frac{1}{2}$ of this distance to get to the bus stop. How far is it from her home to the bus stop? ______

Quick Check

Multiply. Write the answer in simplest form.

15. $\frac{1}{2} \times 5$ ______

16. $\frac{2}{3} \times 4$ ______

17. $6 \times \frac{3}{4}$ ______

Use the picture. Multiply.

18. 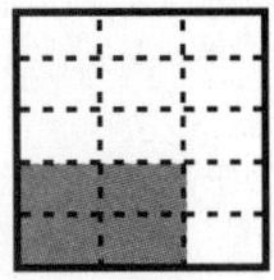

$\frac{2}{5} \times \frac{2}{3}$ ______

19. 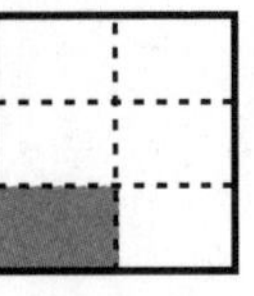

$\frac{1}{2} \times \frac{1}{3}$ ______

20. 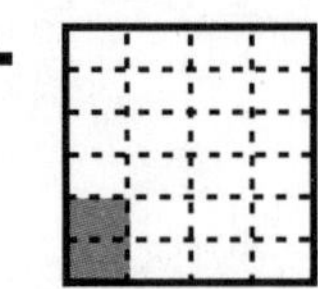

$\frac{2}{3} \times \frac{1}{8}$ ______

Multiply. Write the answer in simplest form.

21. $\frac{1}{3} \times \frac{1}{4}$ ______

22. $\frac{6}{8} \times \frac{2}{3}$ ______

23. $\frac{3}{8} \times \frac{8}{9}$ ______

Work Space

Name ____________________

Multiplying with Mixed Numbers

STANDARD

Here is how you can multiply with a mixed number. Write any mixed numbers or whole numbers as fractions. Then multiply the fractions.

$$6 \times 1\frac{1}{2} = \frac{6}{1} \times \frac{3}{2}$$

$$= \frac{18}{2} \text{ or } 9$$

Here is another way to multiply fractions and mixed numbers:

1. Divide any numerator and any denominator by their GCF.

2. Multiply.

3. Then simplify if possible.

$$6 \times 1\frac{1}{2} = \frac{\overset{3}{\cancel{6}}}{1} \times \frac{3}{\underset{1}{\cancel{2}}}$$

$$= \frac{9}{1} \text{ or } 9$$

The GCF of **6** and **2** is **2.**
6 ÷ 2 = 3 and **2 ÷ 2 = 1.**

$$\frac{3}{8} \times 1\frac{5}{9} = \frac{\overset{1}{\cancel{3}}}{\underset{4}{\cancel{8}}} \times \frac{\overset{7}{\cancel{14}}}{\underset{3}{\cancel{9}}}$$

$$= \frac{7}{12}$$

The GCF of **3** and **9** is **3.**
3 ÷ 3 = 1 and **9 ÷ 3 = 3.**
The GCF of **14** and **8** is **2.**
14 ÷ 2 = 7 and **8 ÷ 2 = 4.**

Write the mixed number as a fraction.

1. $3\frac{5}{9}$ = ______ $2\frac{3}{20}$ = ______ $5\frac{1}{4}$ = ______ $2\frac{5}{12}$ = ______ $2\frac{1}{14}$ = ______

Multiply. Write the product in simplest form.

2. $3 \times 3\frac{5}{9}$ = ______ $5\frac{1}{4} \times 8$ = ______ $1\frac{1}{2} \times 3$ = ______

3. $\frac{7}{8} \times \frac{8}{7}$ = ______ $5\frac{1}{2} \times \frac{1}{4}$ = ______ $4\frac{2}{3} \times \frac{1}{10}$ = ______

4. $5 \times 2\frac{3}{20}$ = ______ $2\frac{5}{12} \times 6$ = ______ $5 \times 1\frac{3}{4}$ = ______

5. $\frac{2}{5} \times 2\frac{1}{2}$ = ______ $3\frac{1}{9} \times \frac{4}{7}$ = ______ $2 \times 2\frac{3}{8}$ = ______

STANDARD

Multiply. Write each product in simplest form.

6. $7 \times 2\frac{3}{21} =$ ______ $5\frac{1}{4} \times \frac{1}{2} =$ ______ $\frac{1}{3} \times 2\frac{1}{6} =$ ______

7. $2\frac{2}{3} \times \frac{3}{4} =$ ______ $3\frac{1}{5} \times \frac{3}{4} =$ ______ $10\frac{1}{2} \times 1\frac{1}{2} =$ ______

8. $6\frac{1}{5} \times \frac{5}{6} =$ ______ $\frac{2}{5} \times 6\frac{1}{4} =$ ______ $4 \times 3\frac{1}{8} =$ ______

9. $5\frac{3}{8} \times 4 =$ ______ $6\frac{3}{4} \times \frac{4}{5} =$ ______ $6\frac{2}{5} \times 5 =$ ______

10. $\frac{1}{5} \times 3\frac{1}{3} =$ ______ $7\frac{3}{4} \times \frac{3}{10} =$ ______ $2 \times 9\frac{5}{6} =$ ______

Problem Solving Reasoning Use the recipe to solve the problems.

11. Write the amount of the ingredients you would need to make **3** dozen muffins.

______

______

______

______

12. How much flour would you need to make $1\frac{1}{2}$ dozen muffins?

______

Muffins
Makes 1 dozen muffins
$1\frac{3}{4}$ *cups flour*
$\frac{1}{3}$ *cup sugar*
2 teaspoons baking powder
1 egg
$\frac{3}{4}$ *cup milk*
$\frac{1}{4}$ *cup cooking oil*
$\frac{3}{4}$ *cup blueberries*

Test Prep ★ Mixed Review

13. **Which expression shows the prime factorization of 60?**

A $2^2 \times 3 \times 5$

B $2 \times 3 \times 5^2$

C 6×10

D $1 \times 2 \times 3 \times 4 \times 5$

14. **You are at the post office. The bank is $\frac{3}{4}$ mile away. The cleaner is $\frac{2}{3}$ mile away. How much closer are you to the cleaner than to the bank?**

F $1\frac{5}{12}$ mile

G $\frac{5}{7}$ mile

H $\frac{1}{6}$ mile

J $\frac{1}{12}$ mile

Name ____________________

Fractions and Properties

STANDARD

The properties of addition and multiplication can help you find sums and products of fractions. Look at the examples below.

Addition Properties	Multiplication Properties
The Commutative Property	**The Commutative Property**
When the order of the addends is changed, the sum remains the same. $\frac{3}{8} + \frac{5}{8} = \frac{5}{8} + \frac{3}{8}$	When the order of the factors is changed, the product remains the same. $\frac{3}{8} \times \frac{5}{8} = \frac{5}{8} \times \frac{3}{8}$
The Associative Property	**The Associative Property**
When the grouping of the addends is changed, the sum remains the same. $\left(\frac{1}{5} + \frac{1}{4}\right) + \frac{1}{2} = \frac{1}{5} + \left(\frac{1}{4} + \frac{1}{2}\right)$	When the grouping of the factors is changed, the product remains the same. $\left(\frac{1}{5} \times \frac{1}{4}\right) \times \frac{1}{2} = \frac{1}{5} \times \left(\frac{1}{4} \times \frac{1}{2}\right)$
The Adding Zero Property	**The Multiplying by One Property**
When you add 0 to any number, the sum is that number. $\frac{1}{2} + 0 = \frac{1}{2}$ $\quad 0 + 1\frac{1}{4} = 1\frac{1}{4}$	When you multiply any number by 1, the product is that number. $\frac{1}{2} \times 1 = \frac{1}{2}$ $\quad 1 \times 2\frac{1}{6} = 2\frac{1}{6}$

Complete the equation. Then circle *C*, *A*, or *Z* to tell which property of addition is being shown. (You may circle more than one letter.)

1. $\left(\frac{2}{3} + \frac{1}{6}\right) + \frac{5}{6} = \frac{2}{3} + \left(\_\_\_\_ + \frac{5}{6}\right)$ C A Z $\qquad 1\frac{2}{5} + \_\_\_\_ = 1\frac{2}{5}$ C A Z

2. $\frac{5}{8} + \frac{1}{4} = \_\_\_\_ + \frac{5}{8}$ C A Z $\qquad 1\frac{1}{4} + \left(\frac{1}{8} + \frac{3}{4}\right) = \left(1\frac{1}{4} + \_\_\_\_\right) + \frac{1}{8}$ C A Z

Complete the equation. Then circle *C*, *A*, or *O* to tell which property of multiplication is being shown. (You may circle more than one letter.)

3. $\frac{1}{3} \times \frac{1}{2} = \frac{1}{2} \times \_\_\_\_$ C A O $\qquad 2 \times \left(1\frac{1}{2} \times \frac{5}{8}\right) = \left(\_\_\_\_ \times 1\frac{1}{2}\right) \times \frac{5}{8}$ C A O

4. $1 \times \_\_\_\_ = 3\frac{2}{3}$ C A O $\qquad \left(\frac{1}{2} \times 1\right) \times \frac{9}{10} = \_\_\_\_ \times \frac{1}{2}$ C A O

STANDARD

You can use the Multiplying by One Property to find equivalent fractions.

Some equivalent fractions for the number **1** are:

$$\frac{1}{1}, \frac{2}{2}, \frac{3}{3}, \frac{4}{4}, \frac{5}{5}, \frac{6}{6}, \frac{7}{7}, \frac{8}{8}$$

You can use any name for **1** and the property will still be true.

Examples: $\frac{1}{4} \times 1 = \frac{1}{4}$ $\frac{1}{4} \times \frac{2}{2} = \frac{2}{8}$

Multiplying $\frac{1}{4}$ by **1** and by $\frac{2}{2}$ does not change the value of $\frac{1}{4}$, because $\frac{1}{4}$ and $\frac{2}{8}$ are equivalent fractions.

Complete the equation with a name for 1.

5. $\frac{1}{2} \times$ ______ $= \frac{2}{4}$ $\frac{6}{7} \times$ ______ $= \frac{12}{14}$ $\frac{3}{4} \times$ ______ $= \frac{9}{12}$ $\frac{5}{8} \times$ ______ $= \frac{20}{32}$

Complete the equation to find an equivalent fraction.

6. $\frac{6}{7} \times \frac{4}{4} = \frac{}{28}$ $\frac{4}{10} \times \frac{}{} = \frac{}{20}$ $\frac{6}{9} \times \frac{}{} = \frac{12}{}$

7. $\frac{1}{5} \times \frac{}{} = \frac{2}{10}$ $\frac{2}{5} \times \frac{}{} = \frac{10}{}$ $\frac{3}{4} \times \frac{}{} = \frac{}{12}$

8. $\frac{3}{4} \times \frac{}{} = \frac{}{16}$ $\frac{3}{5} \times \frac{}{} = \frac{12}{}$ $\frac{5}{6} \times \frac{}{} = \frac{30}{}$

Problem Solving Reasoning Solve using mental math.

9. $\frac{250}{250} \times \frac{37}{90} = a$ $\left(\frac{1}{2} + \frac{47}{56}\right) + \frac{1}{2} = w$ $p + \left(\frac{81}{84} - \frac{81}{84}\right) = \frac{75}{79}$

______ $= a$ ______ $= w$ ______ $= p$

Test Prep ★ Mixed Review

10 Which number makes $1 + 99 = n + 1$ a true equation?

A 101

B 99

C 98

D 97

11 The school nurse measured four students. Taisha is 48 in. tall. Chan is 52 in. tall. Alaina and Mario are each 56 in. tall. What is their average height?

F 48 in.

G 52 in.

H 53 in.

J 56 in.

Name ______________________________

Problem Solving Application: Use a Graph

STANDARD

This pictograph shows the enrollment in the intermediate grades in the Watkins School. Each figure represents a particular number of children.

In this lesson you will need to use the graph to compare and draw conclusions about the data.

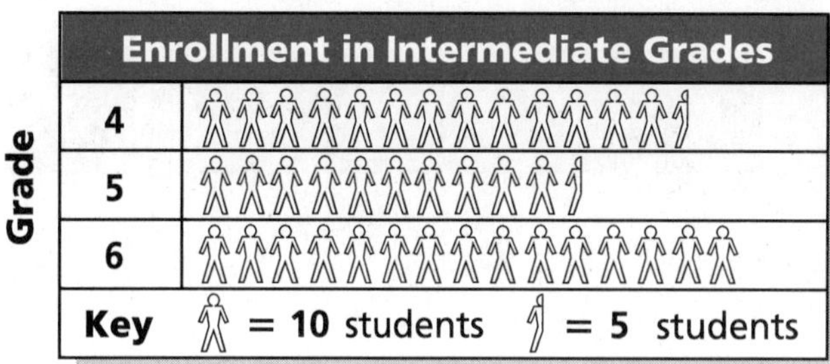

Tips to Remember

1. Understand 2. Decide 3. Solve 4. Look back

- Ask yourself whether you have solved a problem like this before.
- Think about strategies you have learned, and use them to help you solve a problem.
- When using a pictograph, remember to use the key.

Use the pictograph to solve the problem.

1. How many students are in each grade? Explain how you got your answer.

Think: How can the key and multiplication help you find the answer?

____

____

____

____

Answer ______________________________

____

____

2. If the same graph were drawn with each symbol representing **15** students, then how many symbols would be needed to show the grades?

Think: Should you use division or multiplication to find how many symbols are needed?

____

____

Answer ______________________________

____

____

STANDARD

Use the appropriate graph to solve the problem.

Students Who Like Pizza	
Grade 4	
Grade 5	
Grade 6	
Key	= **10** students
	= **5** students

Pizzas Preferences

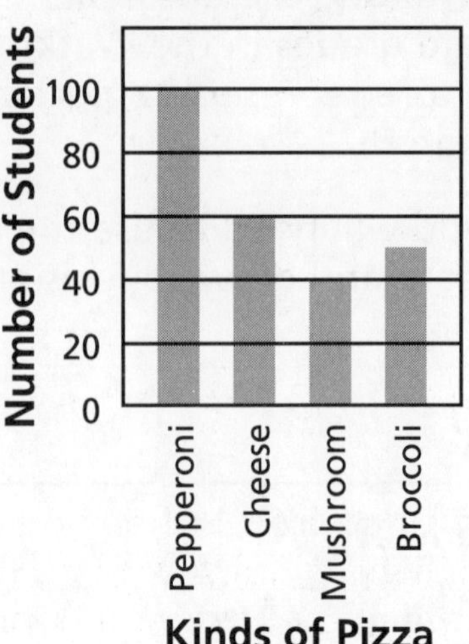

3. What is the total number of students who like pizza? Which graph did you use?

____

____

4. How many students like to eat their pizza with a topping other than cheese?

____

____

5. How many more fifth graders like pizza than fourth graders?

____

6. If you were to draw a pictograph for the bar graph, what symbol would you use and how many students would it represent?

____

____

Extend Your Thinking

7. Write a problem about the bar graph. Solve the problem.

____

____

____

____

8. Look back at the pictograph. Could each whole symbol stand for **15** children? Explain your answer.

____

____

____

Name ______________________

Reciprocals

STANDARD

Two numbers whose product is **1** are called **reciprocals** of each other.

$3 \times \frac{1}{3} = \frac{3 \times 1}{3} = \frac{3}{3} = 1$ — 3 and $\frac{1}{3}$ are reciprocals.

$\frac{3}{5} \times \frac{5}{3} = \frac{3 \times 5}{5 \times 3} = \frac{15}{15} = 1$ — $\frac{3}{5}$ and $\frac{5}{3}$ are reciprocals.

$4\frac{1}{2} \times \frac{2}{9} = \frac{9}{2} \times \frac{2}{9} = \frac{9 \times 2}{2 \times 9} = \frac{18}{18} = 1$ — $4\frac{1}{2}$ and $\frac{2}{9}$ are reciprocals.

You can write the reciprocal of any number.
- First, write any whole number or mixed number as a fraction.
- Then reverse the numerator and denominator.

$\frac{2}{3} \rightarrow \frac{3}{2}$

$\frac{1}{4} \rightarrow \frac{4}{1}$ or 4

$8 = \frac{8}{1} \rightarrow \frac{1}{8}$

$3\frac{1}{5} = \frac{16}{5} \rightarrow \frac{5}{16}$

reciprocals

Write the reciprocal of each number.

1. $\frac{1}{2}$ ______ 7 ______ $4\frac{1}{3}$ ______ $\frac{2}{9}$ ______

2. $\frac{4}{5}$ ______ $2\frac{1}{16}$ ______ $\frac{3}{4}$ ______ $\frac{1}{7}$ ______

3. $5\frac{5}{6}$ ______ $\frac{1}{5}$ ______ $\frac{17}{20}$ ______ 25 ______

4. $\frac{1}{9}$ ______ $\frac{5}{9}$ ______ 2 ______ $4\frac{2}{3}$ ______

5. 9 ______ $1\frac{1}{2}$ ______ $\frac{9}{10}$ ______ $\frac{1}{4}$ ______

6. $\frac{11}{12}$ ______ $\frac{1}{13}$ ______ 15 ______ $6\frac{4}{5}$ ______

STANDARD

Complete the equation. Write your answer in simplest form.

7. $3 \times \frac{1}{3} =$ ______ $2 \times$ ______ $= 1$ ______ $\times \frac{1}{3} = 1$ $4 \times$ ______ $= 1$

8. $5 \times \frac{1}{5} =$ ______ $10 \times$ ______ $= 1$ ______ $\times \frac{1}{6} = 1$ $\frac{1}{8} \times$ ______ $= 1$

9. $7 \times \frac{1}{7} =$ ______ $6 \times$ ______ $= 1$ ______ $\times \frac{1}{9} = 1$ $12 \times$ ______ $= 1$

Problem Solving Reasoning Solve.

10. What number is its own reciprocal?

______

11. What number has no reciprocal?

______

Quick Check

Multiply. Write the answer in simplest form.

Work Space

12. $3 \times 1\frac{5}{6}$ ______

13. $\frac{3}{4} \times 1\frac{4}{9}$ ______

14. $3\frac{1}{8} \times \frac{12}{25}$ ______

Use the properties to find the values.

15. $(11 \times \frac{3}{10}) + (11 \times \frac{7}{10})$ ______

16. $\frac{3}{3} + \frac{2}{2} + \frac{0}{9}$ ______

17. $\frac{2}{3} \times \frac{7}{7}$ ______

Find the reciprocal to complete.

18. $\frac{1}{2} \times$ ______ $= 1$

19. ______ $\times 10 = 1$

20. $2\frac{1}{3} \times$ ______ $= 1$

Name ______________________

Dividing on the Number Line

STANDARD

This number line shows halves.

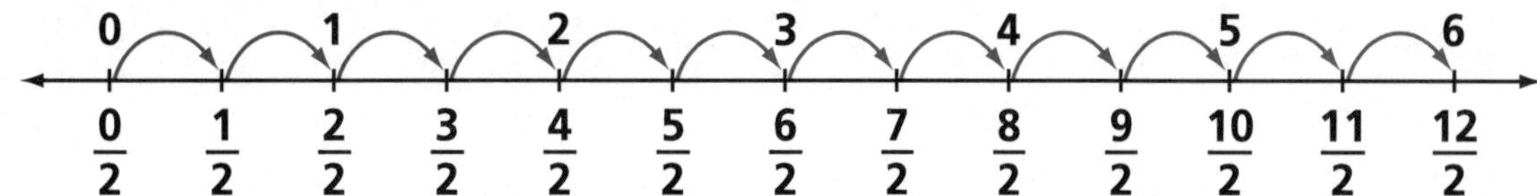

To find the number of halves in **6**, you can count the number of halves on the number line or in **6** objects:

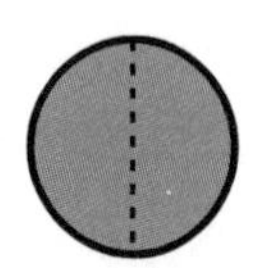
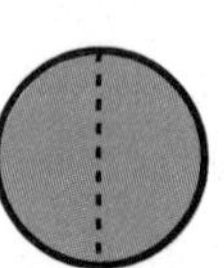
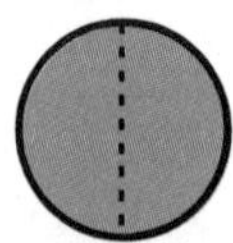
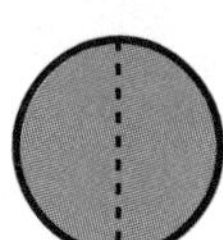
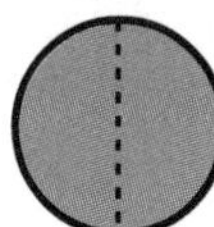
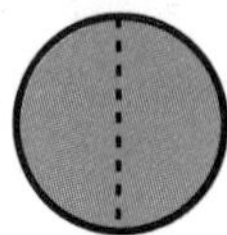

$$6 \div \frac{1}{2} = 12$$

Since there are **2** halves in each whole, you could also multiply by the reciprocal of $\frac{1}{2}$.

$6 \times \frac{2}{1}$ or $6 \times 2 = 12$ So, there are **12** halves in **6**.

Complete the number sentence. Write your answer in simplest form.

1. $3 \div \frac{1}{2} =$ ______
$3 \times 2 =$ ______

2. $5 \div \frac{1}{2} =$ ______
$5 \times 2 =$ ______

3. $4 \div \frac{1}{2} =$ ______
$4 \times 2 =$ ______

4. $7 \div \frac{1}{2} =$ ______
$7 \times 2 =$ ______

Use the number line and the pictures.
Complete the number sentence.

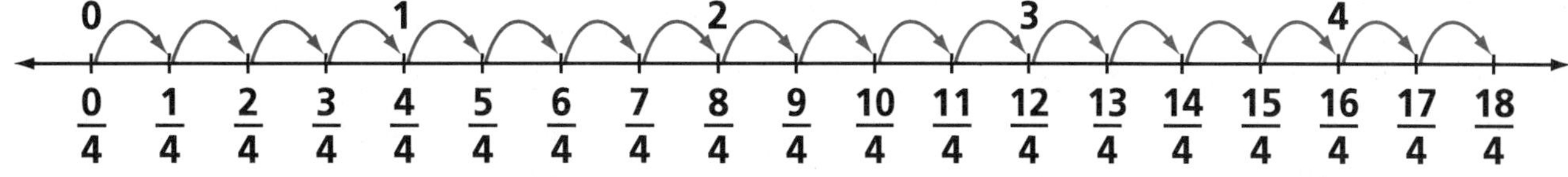

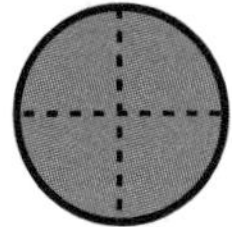
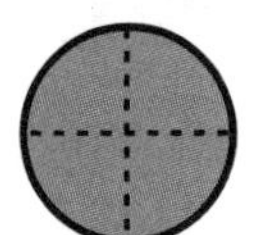
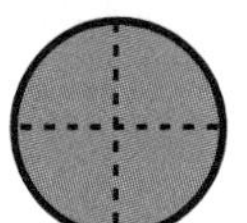
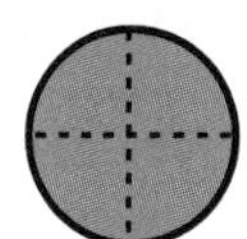
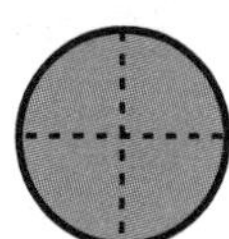

5. $1 \div \frac{1}{4} =$ ______
$1 \times 4 =$ ______

6. $3 \div \frac{1}{4} =$ ______
$3 \times 4 =$ ______

7. $2 \div \frac{1}{4} =$ ______
$2 \times 4 =$ ______

8. $4 \div \frac{1}{4} =$ ______
$4 \times 4 =$ ______

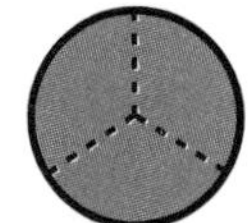

9. $1 \div \frac{1}{3} =$ ______
$4 \div \frac{1}{3} =$ ______

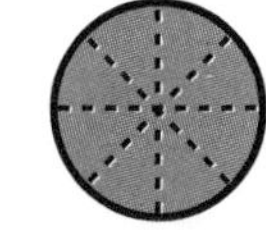

10. $1 \div \frac{1}{8} =$ ______
$3 \div \frac{1}{8} =$ ______

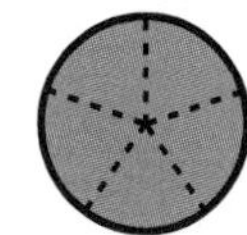

11. $1 \div \frac{1}{5} =$ ______
$4 \div \frac{1}{5} =$ ______

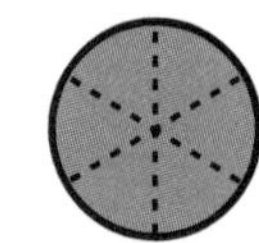

12. $1 \div \frac{1}{6} =$ ______
$3 \div \frac{1}{6} =$ ______

STANDARD

You can use a number line to find how many three-fourths are in $\frac{18}{4}$.

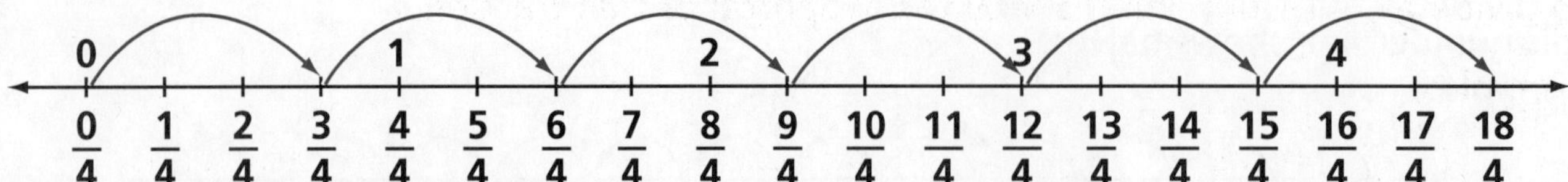

Count the number of three-fourths shown on the number line or in the fraction models.

$$\frac{18}{4} \div \frac{3}{4} = 6$$

You can also multiply by the reciprocal of $\frac{3}{4}$:

$$\frac{\overset{6}{\cancel{18}}}{\underset{1}{\cancel{4}}} \times \frac{\overset{1}{\cancel{4}}}{\underset{1}{\cancel{3}}} = 6$$

So, there are 6 three-fourths in $\frac{18}{4}$.

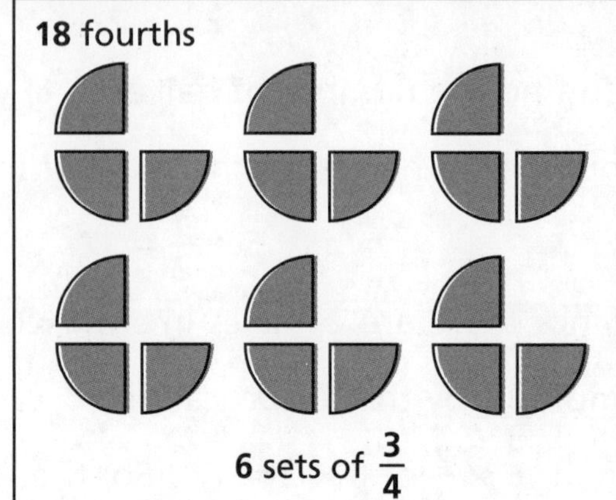

Complete. Write your answer in simplest form.

13. $\frac{6}{4} \div \frac{3}{4} =$ ______

$\frac{6}{4} \times \frac{4}{3} =$ ______

14. $\frac{15}{4} \div \frac{3}{4} =$ ______

$\frac{15}{4} \times \frac{4}{3} =$ ______

15. $3 \div \frac{3}{4} =$ ______

$3 \times \frac{4}{3} =$ ______

16. $6 \div \frac{3}{4} =$ ______

$6 \times \frac{4}{3} =$ ______

Problem Solving
Reasoning

Solve. Draw a number line or a picture to help.

17. A grocer is dividing a **10**-pound block of cheese into pieces weighing $\frac{1}{4}$ pound each. How many pieces will be created from the block?

______

18. At Ryan's school, the school day lasts **6** hours. Each period of the day is $\frac{2}{3}$ hour long. How many periods are in one school day?

______

Test Prep ★ Mixed Review

19 **Marta is 5 years older than Josh. If *a* is Josh's age, which expression shows Marta's age?**

A $a - 5$

B $a + 5$

C $a \div 5$

D $a \times 5$

20 **A flower weighs $6\frac{3}{4}$ ounces. Which point is $6\frac{3}{4}$ on the number line?**

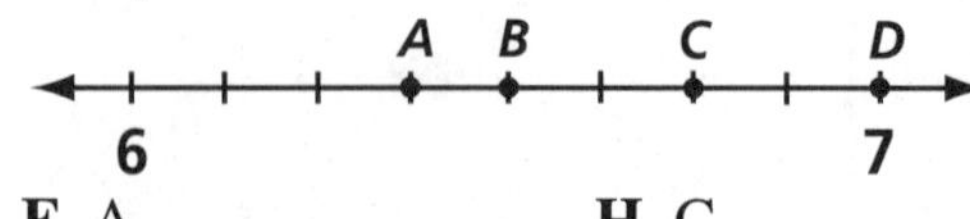

F A **H** C

G B **J** D

Name ______________________

Dividing by a Fraction

STANDARD

To divide by a fraction, multiply by the reciprocal of that fraction.

Examples

reciprocals

$3 \div \frac{1}{2} = 3 \times 2$

$= 6$

reciprocals

$\frac{5}{6} \div \frac{1}{2} = \frac{5}{\cancel{6}_3} \times \frac{\cancel{2}^1}{1}$

$= \frac{5}{3}$ or $1\frac{2}{3}$

reciprocals

$\frac{5}{6} \div \frac{2}{3} = \frac{5}{\cancel{6}_2} \times \frac{\cancel{3}^1}{2}$

$= \frac{5}{4}$ or $1\frac{1}{4}$

Divide. Write each quotient in simplest form.

1. $\frac{2}{3} \div \frac{5}{8} =$ ______ $\frac{1}{3} \div \frac{8}{24} =$ ______ $\frac{4}{15} \div \frac{28}{30} =$ ______

2. $\frac{4}{5} \div \frac{7}{15} =$ ______ $\frac{3}{5} \div \frac{15}{27} =$ ______ $\frac{4}{17} \div \frac{1}{34} =$ ______

3. $\frac{5}{7} \div \frac{3}{5} =$ ______ $\frac{2}{3} \div \frac{3}{4} =$ ______ $\frac{7}{4} \div \frac{1}{3} =$ ______

4. $\frac{2}{3} \div \frac{1}{2} =$ ______ $\frac{8}{9} \div \frac{4}{7} =$ ______ $\frac{5}{3} \div \frac{5}{9} =$ ______

5. $\frac{7}{8} \div \frac{5}{8} =$ ______ $\frac{4}{5} \div \frac{3}{4} =$ ______ $\frac{6}{7} \div \frac{5}{6} =$ ______

6. $\frac{4}{9} \div \frac{2}{3} =$ ______ $\frac{1}{9} \div \frac{2}{5} =$ ______ $\frac{7}{8} \div \frac{4}{7} =$ ______

7. $\frac{5}{2} \div \frac{5}{6} =$ ______ $\frac{1}{6} \div \frac{3}{2} =$ ______ $\frac{3}{7} \div \frac{3}{10} =$ ______

To divide a fraction by a whole number, multiply the fraction by the reciprocal of the whole number.

$$\frac{14}{9} \div 3 = \frac{14}{9} \times \frac{1}{3} \text{ or } \frac{14}{27}$$

Divide. Write each quotient in simplest form.

8. $\frac{3}{8} \div 5 =$ ______ $\frac{8}{9} \div 4 =$ ______ $\frac{1}{3} \div 9 =$ ______

STANDARD

Divide. Write each quotient in simplest form.

9. $\frac{5}{6} \div \frac{7}{8} =$ ______ $\frac{1}{2} \div 7 =$ ______ $4 \div \frac{3}{10} =$ ______

10. $\frac{4}{5} \div \frac{3}{7} =$ ______ $\frac{7}{8} \div 3 =$ ______ $6 \div \frac{2}{5} =$ ______

11. $\frac{2}{3} \div 12 =$ ______ $\frac{4}{9} \div 2 =$ ______ $\frac{7}{3} \div 6 =$ ______

12. $8 \div \frac{4}{5} =$ ______ $10 \div \frac{1}{3} =$ ______ $\frac{1}{4} \div \frac{7}{12} =$ ______

Problem Solving Reasoning Solve.

13. Jill is making a decoration. She cuts an **8**-foot ribbon into pieces that are each $\frac{3}{4}$ foot long. The remaining piece of ribbon is shorter than the others. How long is it? ______

14. Sam has $\frac{2}{3}$ of a piece of poster board. He cuts the poster board into **6** equal-size pieces. What part of the whole poster board is each smaller piece? ______

15. Suppose you are dividing a fraction by a whole number. Will your answer be less than or greater than the dividend? Give an example.

______

Quick Check

Use the number line to complete. Divide. Write each quotient in simplest form.

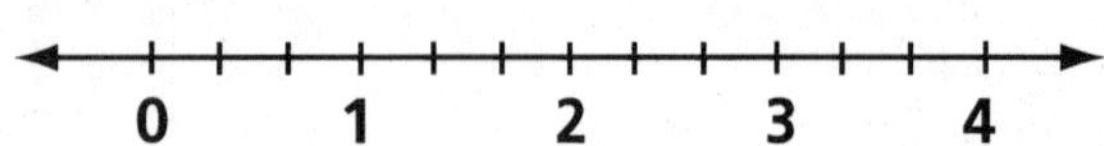

16. $2 \div \frac{1}{3}$ ______ 17. $4 \div \frac{1}{3}$ ______ 18. $3 \div \frac{1}{3}$ ______

Divide. Write each quotient in simplest form.

19. $\frac{1}{2} \div \frac{3}{8}$ ______ 20. $\frac{2}{10} \div 4$ ______ 21. $\frac{10}{12} \div \frac{4}{6}$ ______

Work Space

Name ______________________

Dividing by a Mixed Number

STANDARD

Tom, Carey, Dave, and Kim had $1\frac{1}{2}$ quarts of orange juice to divide equally. How much of the juice will each person get?

To divide mixed numbers and whole numbers:

1. Write any mixed numbers or whole numbers as fractions.

$$1\frac{1}{2} \div 4 = \frac{3}{2} \div \frac{4}{1}$$

2. Divide as you do with fractions.

$$1\frac{1}{2} \div 4 = \frac{3}{2} \div \frac{4}{1}$$
$$= \frac{3}{2} \times \frac{1}{4}$$
$$= \frac{3}{8}$$

Each person will get $\frac{3}{8}$ quart of the juice.

Write the mixed number as a fraction.

1. $1\frac{1}{2} =$ ______ $4\frac{1}{3} =$ ______ $3\frac{2}{3} =$ ______ $2\frac{1}{6} =$ ______

2. $10\frac{1}{4} =$ ______ $8\frac{1}{3} =$ ______ $4\frac{6}{7} =$ ______ $9\frac{1}{8} =$ ______

Divide. Write the quotient in simplest form.

3. $5 \div 4\frac{1}{3} =$ ______ $8 \div 2\frac{2}{3} =$ ______ $7 \div 1\frac{1}{2} =$ ______

4. $4 \div 3\frac{3}{4} =$ ______ $3\frac{1}{7} \div 4 =$ ______ $5\frac{1}{4} \div 3 =$ ______

5. $2\frac{1}{4} \div 8 =$ ______ $4\frac{6}{7} \div 4 =$ ______ $8\frac{2}{3} \div \frac{1}{2} =$ ______

6. $2\frac{1}{4} \div \frac{4}{9} =$ ______ $1\frac{1}{4} \div 1\frac{1}{2} =$ ______ $\frac{10}{3} \div 3\frac{1}{3} =$ ______

7. $9 \div 1\frac{2}{3} =$ ______ $6 \div 4\frac{3}{5} =$ ______ $\frac{1}{8} \div 7 =$ ______

8. $3\frac{5}{8} \div 6 =$ ______ $5\frac{1}{3} \div 1\frac{1}{9} =$ ______ $2\frac{1}{7} \div 1\frac{1}{2} =$ ______

STANDARD

Problem Solving Reasoning Solve.

Waffles Makes 12 small squares
2 eggs
2 cups flour
$\frac{1}{2}$ cup vegetable oil
$1\frac{3}{4}$ cups milk
1 tablespoon sugar
4 teaspoons baking powder
$\frac{1}{4}$ teaspoon salt

Apple Crisp Serves 24
16 cups sliced apples
$2\frac{2}{3}$ cups packed brown sugar
2 cups flour
2 cups oats
$1\frac{1}{3}$ cups margarine
3 teaspoons cinnamon
3 teaspoons nutmeg

9. If one batch of waffles makes **12** small squares, then **2** times each ingredient will make ______ small squares. Using $\frac{1}{2}$ of each ingredient will make ______ small squares. To make **36** small squares, use ______ times each ingredient. To make **8** small squares, use ______ times each ingredient.

10. If one recipe of apple crisp serves **24**, then **2** times each ingredient will serve ______. To serve ______, use $\frac{1}{2}$ of each ingredient. To serve 6, use ______ times each ingredient. To serve 36, use ______ times each ingredient.

Test Prep ★ Mixed Review

11 Davio helped his father $\frac{1}{2}$ hour before lunch and $\frac{9}{10}$ hour after lunch. How long did he help his father?

A $\frac{4}{10}$ hour **C** $1\frac{2}{5}$ hours

B $\frac{5}{11}$ hour **D** $1\frac{1}{2}$ hours

12 Davio sleeps $\frac{3}{8}$ of the 24 hours in a day. How many hours of the day is Davio asleep?

F $23\frac{5}{8}$ **H** 12

G $24\frac{3}{8}$ **J** 9

Name ____________________

Fractions and the Order of Operations

STANDARD

You can simplify an expression that includes fractions and more than one operation. Follow the same order of operations that you follow when you work with whole numbers:

1. Do the operations inside parentheses first. $\frac{1}{4}+\left(\frac{1}{2}\right)^2 \times \left(\frac{1}{6}+\frac{2}{3}\right)$ $\quad \boxed{\frac{1}{6}+\frac{2}{3}=\frac{5}{6}}$

2. Simplify exponents. $\frac{1}{4}+\left(\frac{1}{2}\right)^2 \times \frac{5}{6}$ $\quad \boxed{\left(\frac{1}{2}\right)^2=\frac{1}{2}\times\frac{1}{2} \text{ or } \frac{1}{4}}$

3. Multiply and divide from left to right. $\frac{1}{4}+\frac{1}{4}\times\frac{5}{6}$ $\quad \boxed{\frac{1}{4}\times\frac{5}{6}=\frac{5}{24}}$

4. Add and subtract from left to right. $\frac{1}{4}+\frac{5}{24}$

$\frac{11}{24}$

Complete to simplify each expression.

1. $\frac{3}{8}+\frac{5}{8}\div\frac{1}{2}$

$\frac{3}{8}+$ ______

______

2. $2-\left(\frac{1}{3}\right)^2+\frac{5}{9}$

$2-$ ______ $+\frac{5}{9}$

______ $+\frac{5}{9}=2\frac{4}{9}$

3. $\left(\frac{2}{5}+\frac{3}{5}\right)\times\left(\frac{9}{10}-\frac{1}{5}\right)$

______ $\times$ ______

______

Simplify each expression.

4. $2\times\left(\frac{11}{12}-\frac{7}{12}\right)=$ ______

$\left(\frac{1}{2}\times\frac{1}{3}\right)^2=$ ______

5. $1-\left(\frac{2}{5}\right)^2=$ ______

$\frac{5}{6}\div\frac{1}{6}\times\frac{1}{4}=$ ______

6. $\frac{7}{8}-\frac{1}{4}\div 2=$ ______

$2\frac{1}{2}\div\left(\frac{1}{4}+\frac{1}{8}\right)=$ ______

7. $1\frac{1}{3}+2\times\frac{1}{2}-\frac{1}{4}=$ ______

$\left(\frac{3}{4}\right)^2-\frac{1}{4}\times\frac{3}{4}=$ ______

8. $7\frac{1}{6}-\frac{5}{6}\div\frac{1}{6}+\frac{2}{3}=$ ______

$\frac{1}{2}\times 3+\frac{1}{3}\times\left(\frac{1}{2}\right)^2=$ ______

STANDARD

Problem Solving
Reasoning

Circle the expression that best represents the problem. Then solve.

9. Kara rode her bike $\frac{3}{4}$ mile east from her house to the park. Then she rode $\frac{1}{4}$ mile west to her friend's house. Then she rode $1\frac{1}{4}$ miles east to the library. How far was Kara from her home?

$\frac{3}{4} + \left(\frac{1}{4} + 1\frac{1}{4}\right)$

$\frac{3}{4} - \frac{1}{4} + 1\frac{1}{4}$

$\frac{3}{4} - \left(1\frac{1}{4} + \frac{1}{4}\right)$

______

10. The Ming family lives on **8** acres. Their house, garage, and barn cover $\frac{1}{4}$ acre, and **2** acres are planted with hay. The rest of their property is pasture. How many acres of pasture do the Mings have?

$8 + \frac{1}{4} - 2$

$8 - \frac{1}{4} + 2$

$8 - \left(\frac{1}{4} + 2\right)$

______

Solve.

11. The roof of a birdhouse is made of two square pieces of wood that are $4\frac{1}{2}$ inches long on a side. You are buying cedar shingles to cover the whole roof. What is the area of the roof to be shingled? ______

12. Toya needs $2\frac{1}{2}$ yards of fabric for curtains. She needs $\frac{3}{4}$ yard of the same kind of fabric for each of **3** pillows. How much fabric does she need in all? ______

Quick Check

Divide. Write each quotient in simplest form.

13. $6 \div 3\frac{3}{8}$ ______

14. $\frac{5}{6} \div 2\frac{1}{3}$ ______

15. $3\frac{3}{5} \div 6\frac{3}{4}$ ______

Write the value of each expression.

16. $8 \times \frac{4}{7} + \frac{3}{7}$ ______

17. $\left(\frac{0}{8} \div \frac{8}{8}\right) \times \frac{1}{8}$ ______

18. $\frac{4}{5} \times \left(1 \div \frac{1}{4}\right)$ ______

Work Space

Name ______________________

Problem Solving Strategy: Solve a Simpler Problem

STANDARD

Sometimes problems that seem difficult to solve may be easier to understand using other numbers.

To solve these problems, try substituting simpler numbers. Then use the same method with the actual numbers.

Problem

Martin has $760 to invest in the stock market. How many shares of a stock selling at $\$47\frac{1}{2}$ each can he buy?

1 Understand As you reread, ask yourself questions.

- What do you know?

Martin has $760.
He wants to buy shares of stock that cost $\$47\frac{1}{2}$ each.

What do you need to find?

____

2 Decide Choose a method for solving.

- Try the strategy Solve a Simpler Problem.
- What operation is involved? ______________

Write a problem using simpler numbers.

____

3 Solve Use the numbers from your simpler problem to write an expression

- Solve the simpler problem.

____

- Solve the original problem.

____

4 Look back Think about your answer.

Explain how the estimate helps check the actual answer.

____

STANDARD

Use the Solve a Simpler Problem strategy or any other strategy you may have learned.

1. A shelf is $32\frac{1}{2}$ inches long. If each trophy is $3\frac{3}{4}$ inches wide, how many trophies can be lined up side by side on the shelf?

Think: What simpler problem would help?

____

Answer ______________________

____

2. A cookie recipe calls for $1\frac{2}{3}$ cups of flour for each dozen cookies. How many cups of flour are needed for $7\frac{1}{2}$ dozen cookies?

Think: What simpler number can you use for $1\frac{2}{3}$?

____

Answer ______________________

3. In 1998 the population of the United States was **270,312,000**. The estimated population of the United States for the year 2020 is **322,052,000**. By how much is the population expected to increase?

____

4. Beth bought some **33¢** and some **23¢** stamps. The number of **33¢** stamps was twice the number of **23¢** stamps. She paid **$4.45** in all for the stamps. How many of each did she buy?

____

____

5. In 1997, **86,588,369** people visited zoos and **35,781,485** people visited aquariums. What was the total annual attendance for both zoos and aquariums?

____

6. Peter picked $5\frac{1}{2}$ pecks of pickled peppers. If there are **8** quarts in a peck, how many quarts of pickled peppers did Peter pick?

____

7. During a rainstorm, $3\frac{3}{4}$ inches of rain fell in $2\frac{1}{2}$ hours. What was the average number of inches of rain that fell per hour?

____

8. Gina wants to buy **48** shares of a stock that is selling for $\$14\frac{3}{4}$ each. How much money does she need to buy this stock?

____

Name ______________________

Write each product or quotient in simplest form.

1. $10 \times \frac{2}{5} =$ ______

2. $\frac{5}{9} \times \frac{3}{4} =$ ______

3. $\frac{2}{3} \times \frac{3}{8} =$ ______

4. $2\frac{3}{5} \times \frac{2}{3} =$ ______

5. $2\frac{2}{3} \times 6 =$ ______

6. $1\frac{5}{6} \times 2\frac{1}{2} =$ ______

7. $4 \div \frac{1}{4} =$ ______

8. $\frac{3}{8} \div \frac{1}{9} =$ ______

9. $\frac{4}{5} \div 6 =$ ______

10. $2\frac{3}{4} \div \frac{5}{8} =$ ______

11. $4 \div 1\frac{2}{3} =$ ______

12. $5\frac{1}{2} \div 1\frac{4}{5} =$ ______

Complete each equation.

13. $\frac{2}{3} \times \frac{4}{5} = \frac{4}{5} \times$ ______

14. $\frac{2}{5} + 5\frac{1}{3} =$ ______ $+ \frac{2}{5}$

15. $0 + \frac{5}{6} =$ ______

16. $\frac{1}{2} \times \left(\frac{5}{6} \times 2\right) = \left(\frac{1}{2} \times \right.$ ______ $\left.\right) \times 2$

17. $\frac{2}{3} + \left(\frac{5}{6} + \frac{5}{8}\right) = \left(\right.$ ______ $\left. + \frac{5}{6}\right) + \frac{5}{8}$

Use the graph to answer the question.

18. Two-thirds of the cans collected on Monday came from fifth-grade students. How many cans did fifth-grade students collect on Monday? ______

Number Of Cans Collected	
Mon.	🥫🥫🥫🥫🥫🥫
Tues.	🥫🥫
Wed.	🥫🥫🥫🥫
Thurs.	🥫🥫🥫
Fri.	🥫🥫🥫
Key	🥫 = 10 cans

Solve by using simpler numbers.

19. One-fourth of the **20,000** people in a stadium are in lower-deck seats. How many people are in lower-deck seats? ______

Solve.

20. What number is the reciprocal of $2\frac{1}{2}$? ______

Name ______________________

Cumulative Review

★ Test Prep

A toy store recorded how much time customers played with some toys. Use the results to answer questions 1 and 2.

Toy	Number of Hours
Squeaky Toy	10
Art Chest	12
Giant Ball	19
Spinning Top	8
Walking Doll	7

1 According to the survey, which toy did people seem least interested in?

A Squeaky Toy
C Spinning Top
B Art Chest
D Walking Doll

2 The store manager drew a pictograph of the data.

Total Play Time for Toys	
Squeaky Toy	🕒 🕒 ½🕒
Art Chest	🕒 🕒 🕒
Giant Ball	🕒 🕒 🕒 🕒 ¾🕒
Spinning Top	🕒 🕒
Walking Doll	?
Key 🕒 = 4 hours	

How many 🕒 are needed for the Walking Doll?

F 1
H $1\frac{3}{4}$
G $1\frac{1}{4}$
J 2

3 Which expression is equivalent to $n \cdot (47 + 76)$?

A $47 \cdot n \cdot 76$
B $47 + 76 + n$
C $(n \cdot 47) + (n \cdot 76)$
D $(47 \cdot n) + 76$

4 Which expression equals 80?

F $(2 \times 4) + (2 \times 36)$
G 5×2^3
H $2 \times 2 \times 2 \times 2 \times 10$
J $2 \times 2 \times 2 \times 5$

5 The product of two numbers is $\frac{9}{10}$. One of the numbers is $\frac{5}{6}$. What is the other number?

A $4\frac{1}{2}$
C $\frac{25}{27}$
B $1\frac{2}{25}$
D $\frac{1}{15}$

6 Briana lives $\frac{3}{5}$ mile east of school. Dean lives on the same street $\frac{1}{2}$ mile west of school. Which shows the distance in miles between the students?

F $\frac{4}{10}$
H $\frac{4}{7}$
K Not here
G $\frac{9}{10}$
J $1\frac{1}{10}$

7 Each day a man jogs $\frac{1}{2}$ mile. After 5 days, how many miles will he have jogged?

A $\frac{1}{2}$
C $4\frac{1}{2}$
E $5\frac{1}{2}$
B $2\frac{1}{2}$
D 5

8 A ribbon is $\frac{6}{12}$ foot long. Jason cuts a piece $\frac{4}{12}$ foot long from it. Which fraction shows how much ribbon is left in simplest form?

F $\frac{10}{12}$ foot
H $\frac{2}{12}$ foot
K Not here
G $\frac{1}{6}$ foot
J $\frac{2}{6}$ foot

UNIT 6 • TABLE OF CONTENTS

Decimals

We will be using this vocabulary:

decimal a number such as **0.5** (five tenths) and **3.67** (three and sixty-seven hundredths); a decimal is sometimes called a decimal fraction

factor a number to be multiplied

order to arrange numbers in a certain way, such as from least to greatest or greatest to least

powers of 10 numbers such as $10^1 = 10$, $10^2 = 100$, $10^3 = 1{,}000$, and so on

Dear Family,

During the next few weeks, our math class will be learning about decimals.

You can expect to see homework that provides practice with multiplying decimals. Here is a sample you may use to give help if needed.

Multiplying Decimals by Decimals

Multiply decimals the way you multiply whole numbers. Then show the same number of decimal places in your answer as there are in the factors.

Example: Find **1.4 × 2.9.**

Multiply decimals just as you would multiply whole numbers.

$$\begin{array}{r} 1.4 \\ \times\ 2.9 \\ \hline 126 \\ +\ 280 \\ \hline 406 \end{array}$$

Then show the same number of decimal places in your answer as there are in the factors.

$$\begin{array}{rl} 1.4 & \leftarrow \text{one decimal place} \\ \times\ 2.9 & \leftarrow \text{one decimal place} \\ \hline 126 & \\ +\ 280 & \\ \hline 4.06 & \leftarrow \text{two decimal places} \end{array}$$

Example: Find **0.28 × 0.95.**

$$\begin{array}{rl} 0.28 & \leftarrow \text{two decimal places} \\ \times\ 0.95 & \leftarrow \text{two decimal places} \\ \hline 140 & \\ +\ 2520 & \\ \hline 0.2660 & \leftarrow \text{four decimal places} \end{array}$$

During this unit, students will need to continue practicing multiplication and addition facts.

Sincerely,

Name ____________________

Place Value

STANDARD

In our base ten system, each place in a number is 10 times greater than the value of the place to its right. Each place is also $\frac{1}{10}$ of the value of the place to its left. You can extend a place-value chart to include place values less than **1**.

Thousands	Hundreds	Tens	Ones		Tenths	Hundredths	Thousandths
3	5	7	2	.	6	9	4

A decimal point separates the ones and tenths places.

You can write this number in different ways:

- **Standard Form: 3,572.694**
- **Expanded Form: 3,000 + 500 + 70 + 2 + 0.6 + 0.09 + 0.004**
- **Word Form:**
  three *thousand*, five *hundred* seventy-two **and** six hundred ninety-four *thousandths*
- **Short Word Form: 3** *thousand*, **5** *hundred* **72 and 694** *thousandths*

Decimals that name the same amount are **equivalent decimals.**

0.5 = **0.50** = **0.500**

5 *tenths* | 50 *hundredths* | 500 *thousandths*

Other Examples

3.1 three **and** one *tenth* **4.05** **4** and **5** *hundredths* **4.050** **4** and **50** *thousandths*

Write the word form.

1. 0.3 ____________________ 0.07 ____________________

2. 0.90 ____________________ 4.15 ____________________

Write the short word form.

3. 0.20 ____________________ 0.10 ____________________

4. 0.103 ____________________ 3.017 ____________________

Write each decimal.

5. seven tenths __________ **6** hundredths __________

6. **48** hundredths __________ three thousandths __________

7. fifty-one thousandths __________ eight hundred four thousandths __________

8. **2** and **6** tenths __________ **12** and **25** hundredths __________

STANDARD

To compare decimals, you can use a number line. The decimal farther to the right is greater.

0 0.3 0.6 1.0

You can also compare digits with the same place value.

Think: **1.0 > 0.6**

To compare **0.25** and **0.205,** write a zero in the hundredths place so that both numbers have the same number of decimal places.

0.250 ◯ **0.205**

Compare the digits in each place value from left to right.

5 hundredths > 0 hundredths, so **0.250 > 0.205**

Match each number with a point on the number line.

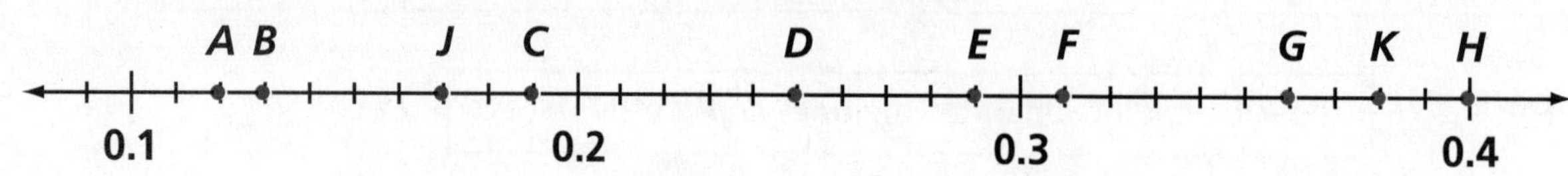

9. 0.25 ______ 0.12 ______ 0.31 ______ 0.13 ______ 0.19 ______

10. 0.29 ______ 0.36 ______ 0.38 ______ 0.40 ______ 0.17 ______

Compare. Write <, >, or =.

11. 0.3 ◯ 0.13 0.12 ◯ 0.012 1.56 ◯ 0.516 0.010 ◯ 0.01

12. 3.28 ◯ 3.820 0.054 ◯ 0.45 1.008 ◯ 0.08 1.25 ◯ 2.95

Write the decimals in order from least to greatest.

13. 0.127, 0.72, 1.270 ______________ 0.71, 0.43, 0.74 ______________

14. 1.295, 2.085, 0.925 ______________ 0.487, 0.58, 0.009 ______________

Problem Solving Reasoning Solve.

15. What is the greatest decimal less than **1** that you can write using the digits **0, 1, 2, 3,** and **4** only once? The least decimal? ______________

Test Prep ★ Mixed Review

16 What is the standard numeral for 8 billion 8 million?

A 8,008,000

B 8,080,000

C 8,008,000,000

D 8,080,000,000

17 What is the value of $400 \times 10 \div a$ when $a = 10$?

F 4

G 40

H 400

J 4000

Name ______________________________

Comparing and Ordering Decimals and Fractions

STANDARD

You can write fractions and mixed numbers as decimals.

$\frac{4}{10} = 0.4 \leftarrow$ 4 tenths $\quad 21\frac{5}{100} = 21.05 \leftarrow$ 21 and 5 hundredths

It is often helpful to know decimal equivalents for common fractions.

$0.5 = \frac{5}{10} \rightarrow \frac{1}{2}$ **Simplest Form** $0.25 = \frac{25}{100} \rightarrow \frac{1}{4}$ $\quad 0.6 = \frac{1}{10} \rightarrow \frac{3}{5}$

To compare a fraction and a decimal, first write them in the same form.

Compare $\frac{1}{2}$ and 0.7.

$\frac{1}{2} = \frac{5}{10} \rightarrow 0.5$

$0.5 < 0.7$, so $\frac{1}{2} < 0.7$

Compare $\frac{3}{100}$ and 0.03.

$\frac{3}{100} = 0.03$

Compare $4\frac{7}{10}$ and 3.2

$4 > 3$, so $4\frac{7}{10} > 3.2$

Use fractions, mixed numbers, and decimals to name points on the number line. Write each missing number.

1.

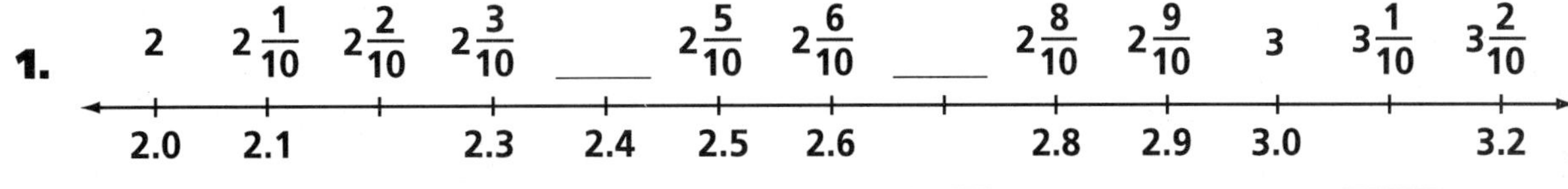

2.

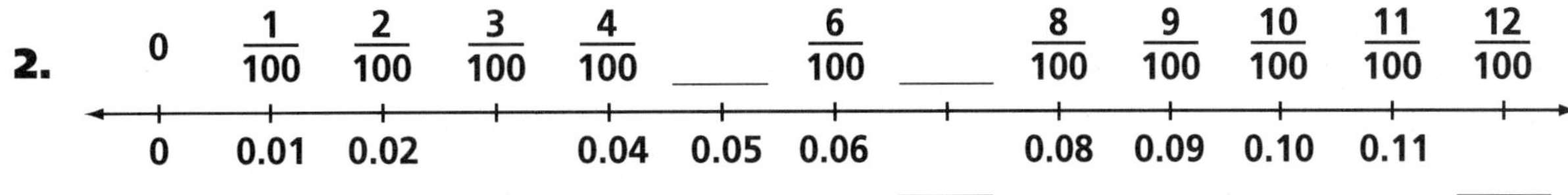

Write each fraction or mixed number as a decimal.

3. $\frac{17}{100} =$ _____ $\quad \frac{83}{100} =$ _____ $\quad 15\frac{30}{100} =$ _____ $\quad 1\frac{52}{100} =$ _____

4. $2\frac{73}{1,000} =$ _____ $\quad \frac{19}{1,000} =$ _____ $\quad 9\frac{142}{1,000} =$ _____ $\quad \frac{1}{1,000} =$ _____

STANDARD

Write each decimal as a fraction or as a mixed number.

5. 0.64 = ______ 0.90 = ______ 3.45 = ______ 0.29 = ______

6. 7.050 = ______ 0.218 = ______ 4.003 = ______ 13.084 = ______

Write each decimal as a fraction in simplest form.

7. 0.1 = ______ 0.500 = ______ 0.25 = ______ 0.75 = ______ 0.8 = ______

8. 0.2 = ______ 0.40 = ______ 2.60 = ______ 4.250 = ______ 10.6 = ______

Compare. Write >, <, or = .

9. 0.75 ◯ 0.08 1.79 ◯ $2\frac{4}{5}$ 36.007 ◯ 36.040 $10\frac{1}{2}$ ◯ 10.5

10. $1\frac{111}{1,000}$ ◯ 1.111 12.9 ◯ $12\frac{85}{100}$ $\frac{3}{5}$ ◯ 0.07 $\frac{1}{4}$ ◯ 0.35

List in order from greatest to least.

11. $\frac{1}{2}$, 0.75, 10.5, 0.40 ______________ $\frac{4}{5}$, $\frac{110}{100}$, $3\frac{1}{2}$, 1.01 ______________

12. 0.33, $\frac{3}{10}$, $\frac{1}{4}$, $\frac{400}{1,000}$ ______________ 0.63, 0.07, $2\frac{3}{4}$, $2\frac{4}{5}$ ______________

Problem Solving Reasoning Solve.

13. Mel bought $2\frac{4}{5}$ lb of fruit. His sister bought more.

Which amount might she have bought, **2.75** lb or $2\frac{9}{10}$ lb? ______

Test Prep ★ Mixed Review

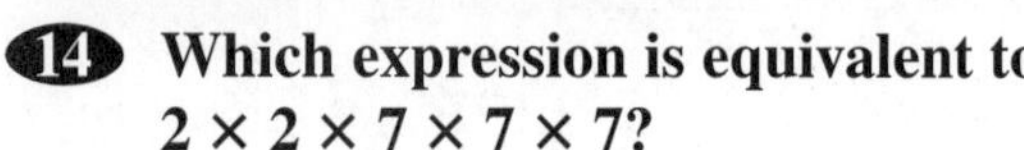

14 Which expression is equivalent to $2 \times 2 \times 7 \times 7 \times 7$?

A 22,777

B $2^2 + 7^3$

C $2^2 \times 7^3$

D $2^2 \div 7^3$

15 A theater has 27 rows with n seats in each row. Which expression shows how many seats there are in all?

F $27 \div n$

G $27 \times n$

H $27 - n$

J $27 + n$

Name ______________________________

Estimating Sums and Differences

STANDARD

You can use what you know about rounding whole numbers to help you round decimals.

Round **4.715** to the nearest hundredth.

- First, look at the digit to the right of the place you are rounding to.
- If the digit is equal to or greater than **5**, *round up.* If the digit is less than **5**, *round down.*

Round to hundredths.

4.715

Look at thousandths. **5 = 5** So, round up.

4.715 rounds to **4.72.**

Other Examples

- Round **76.37** to the nearest whole number. **3 < 5,** so round down to **76.**
- Round **16.87** to the nearest tenth. **7 > 5,** so round up to **16.9**

You can use rounding to estimate decimal sums and differences.

Estimate by rounding.

Round to the nearest whole number.

12.85	→	**13**
+ 16.29	→	**+ 16**
		29

Round to the nearest tenth.

43.657	→	**43.7**
− 11.931	→	**− 11.9**
		31.8

Round each number to the given place.

		Ones	Tenths	Hundredths
1.	1.734	______	______	______
2.	0.005	______	______	______
3.	6.817	______	______	______
4.	9.906	______	______	______
5.	12.522	______	______	______
6.	4.278	______	______	______
7.	25.486	______	______	______
8.	20.111	______	______	______
9.	0.090	______	______	______
10.	5.977	______	______	______
11.	7.771	______	______	______
12.	0.012	______	______	______

STANDARD

Estimate each sum or difference by rounding each number to the given place.

13. nearest whole number	4.38 − 3.91	7.98 −1.05	0.09 + 1.58	14.351 − 12.910
14. nearest tenth	8.057 − 4.138	13.84 + 1.50	38.557 + 9.941	24.010 − 7.284
15. nearest hundredth	0.243 + 0.178	0.677 + 0.475	1.890 − 0.321	2.083 + 0.906
16. nearest tenth	3.00 − 2.19	0.999 + 0.819	4.150 − 4.092	0.05 + 0.09

Problem Solving Reasoning Sometimes an estimate is enough to solve a problem. Sometimes an exact answer is needed. Write *estimate* or *exact* to tell what is needed to solve the problem.

17. Suppose you and two friends go to a movie. How much will you pay for **1** ticket? ______

18. Did the cashier give you the correct change? ______

19. How much money should you bring to pay for **3** tickets and snacks? ______

20. How many people attended the movie? ______

Quick Check

Write each decimal.

21. three hundredths ____ **22.** seven and two tenths ____

23. 7 and 29 thousandths ____

Write <, >, or =.

24. $\frac{6}{10}$ ◯ 0.06 **25.** 2.7 ◯ $2\frac{70}{100}$ **26.** $\frac{452}{1000}$ ◯ 4.52

Use rounding to estimate the sum or difference to the nearest tenth.

27. 4.99 + 3.57 ____ **28.** 24.002 − 1.87 ____

29. 12.643 + 1.24 + 10.17 ____

Work Space

Name ______________________

Adding and Subtracting Decimals

STANDARD

Remember to line up the decimal points when adding or subtracting decimals. Sometimes you may need to write zeros before you add or subtract.

Add: **5.38 + 0.496**

```
   1
  5.380
+ 0.496
  5.876
```

Subtract: **16 − 3.98**

```
  5 9
   10 10
 16.00
− 3.98
 12.02
```

Estimate first. Then add.

1. 1.75 + 2.60 + 3.90 = ____ 5.274 + 0.63 + 0.8 = ____ 2.6 + 0.314 + 4.15 = ____ 8.536 + 0.17 + 0.683 = ____ 21.6 + 7.05 + 0.874 = ____

2. 2.837 + 5.42 = ______ 39.7 + 16.985 = ______

3. 584 + 25.3 = ______ 4.06 + 2.385 + 0.4 = ______

4. 17.2 + 3.5 + 4.73 = ______ 5.55 + 5.5 + 0.5 = ______

5. 16 + 3.80 = ______ 63 + 58.75 = ______

Estimate first. Then subtract.

6. 52.68 − 5.40 6.90 − 5.40 9.36 − 3.42 92.8 − 15.34 32.0 − 25.85

7. 4.385 − 2.63 15.0 − 8.64 9.0 − 3.625 7.425 − 3.8 734.0 − 16.85

8. 5.8 − 4.25 = ______ 15.74 − 3.618 = ______

9. 38 − 3.65 = ______ 74 − 52.80 = ______

10. 49.5 − 37.837 = ______ 74.36 − 36 = ______

STANDARD

Write each missing digit.

11.

0 . 0 4	0 . 4 5	0 . __ __	0 . 0 9	0 . __ __ __
+ 0 . 6 __	+ 0 . __ 6	+ 0 . 0 6	+ 0 . __ __	+ 0 . 2 1 6
0 . __ 1	1 . 2 __	0 . 4 4	0 . 7 5	0 . 2 9 4

Estimate. Write a decimal point in each addend to make the number sentence true.

12. 4 3 3 + 1 3 1 = 1 3 5.3 3 　　6 7 6 + 2 8 = 3 4.7 6

13. 3 8 4 + 2 9 7 = 6 8.1 　　7 2 9 + 5 3 1 = 7 8.2 1

14. 1 8 + 3 9 5 = 4 1.3 　　3 7 8 5 + 2 9 3 = 4 0 7.8

15. 8 0 7 6 + 5 9 9 7 = 8 6 7.5 7 　　1 3 6 + 4 9 8 7 = 1 8.5 8 7

Problem Solving
Reasoning

Solve.

16. The odometer in Mr. Gregory's new car showed **345.6** miles before a trip and **1,400.5** miles after the trip. How many miles long was the trip?

____

17. Janice read a chart at the airport weather station: "Weekly rainfall for the three-week period from March 6 through March 26: **6.4** centimeters, **3.27** centimeters, **4.3** centimeters." Was the total rainfall more or less than **14** centimeters? How much more or less?

____

18. Steve had a temperature of **39°C** in the morning. By evening his temperature had gone down to **37.6°C.** By how many degrees did Steve's temperature change during the day? If normal body temperature is **36.9°C,** did Steve still have a fever?

____

Test Prep ★ Mixed Review

19 **What is the value of the expression $24 \div c - 6$ when $c = 4$?**

A 0

B 8

C 14

D 22

20 **You ate $\frac{1}{4}$ of a pizza. Your sister ate $\frac{1}{6}$ of the pizza. How much of the pizza is left?**

F $\frac{7}{12}$

G $\frac{5}{12}$

H $\frac{7}{10}$

J $\frac{1}{2}$

Name ______________________________

Problem Solving Strategy: Conjecture and Verify

STANDARD

To solve a problem, you may need to begin with a conjecture about the answer.

When you make a conjecture, you make a "first guess" about the answer. Then you verify or check to see if it is correct.

Problem

Mark has some nickels and some dimes. He has 10 coins in all. The total amount of money he has is 80¢. How many nickels does he have? How many dimes does he have?

1 Understand

As you reread, ask yourself questions.

- What do you know about the coins Mark has?

  Mark has 10 coins. Some are nickels. Some are dimes. Together the coins are worth 80¢.

- What information do you already know that is not given in the problem?

  A nickel is worth 5¢. A dime is worth 10¢.

What information do you need to find out?

____

2 Decide

Choose a method for solving.
Try the strategy Conjecture and Verify.

- What will your first guess be? Are there 10 coins?

  Nickels: 5 Dimes: 5 ______

3 Solve

Verify your conjecture. Try again if you need to.

First Guess		**Try Again**
Nickels: 5	**Value: 25¢**	______________
Dimes: 5	**Value: 50¢**	______________
Total: 10	**75¢**	______________

4 Look back

Check your answer. Write the answer below.

Answer: ______________________________

- How did your first guess help you make another try?

____

____

STANDARD

Use the Conjecture and Verify strategy or any other strategy you have learned.

1. Maria and Mike have **$65** between them. Maria has **3** times as much money as Mike. How much money does Mike have? How much does Maria have?

Think: Should you divide **$65** into **3** or **4** parts?

____

Answer ______________________

____

2. Sheryl has **7** more videotapes than Wayne. Together they have **43** videotapes. How many videotapes does Wayne have? How many videotapes does Sheryl have?

Think: Should you add **7** to **43** or subtract **7** from **43**?

____

Answer ______________________

____

3. I'm thinking of two numbers. When I add them, their sum is **25.** When I multiply them, their product is **100.** What are the numbers?

____

4. John drives **3.48** miles each way to and from work. About how far does he drive in two days?

____

5. Anne wants to buy a sweater for **$39.99.** She also wants to buy **2** pairs of gloves costing **$5.99** each. She has **$50.** Does she have enough money?

____

6. Shirley has quarters, nickels, and dimes in her piggy bank. She has **10** quarters, **20** dimes, and **40** nickels. How much money does Shirley have?

____

7. Bob has some pennies, nickels, and dimes. He has **10** coins in all. The total amount of money he has is **40¢.** How many of each coin does he have?

____

8. Jim has some pennies, dimes, and quarters. He has **20** coins in all. The total amount of money is **$2.00.** How many of each coin does he have?

____

9. I'm thinking of two decimals. Their sum is **15.2,** and when the smaller is subtracted from the larger, their difference is **6.4.** What are the two decimals?

____

10. Keiko has **4** pieces of wood with a total length of **19** feet. Three of the pieces are the same length, and one piece is **4** feet long. How long are the other pieces?

____

Name ____________________

Multiplying Whole Numbers and Decimals

STANDARD

Each time Jim rides his bike to and from the store, his odometer increases by **0.7** kilometer. How far does he ride in **3** trips?

To solve the problem, you can write **0.7** as a fraction, multiply, and change the answer to a decimal.

Think:

$$10\overline{)21}\quad \text{quotient } 2\tfrac{1}{10},\ \text{subtract } 20$$

$$3 \times 0.7 = 3 \times \frac{7}{10} = \frac{21}{10} = 2\frac{1}{10} \text{ or } 2.1$$

$3 \times 7 = 21$

You can also multiply using a decimal. Multiply as with whole numbers. Then write the decimal point in the product.

$$\begin{array}{r} 0.7 \\ \times\ 3 \\ \hline 2.1 \end{array}$$

1 decimal place

The product must have as many decimal places as there are in the factors.

Find **3 × 0.82.** Multiply with a fraction.

$$3 \times 0.82 = 3 \times \frac{82}{100} = \frac{246}{100} = 2\frac{46}{100} \text{ or } 2.46$$

$3 \times 82 = 246$

Multiply with a decimal.

$$\begin{array}{r} 0.82 \\ \times\ 3 \\ \hline 2.46 \end{array}$$

2 decimal places

There are a total of **2** decimal places in the factors. So, there are **2** decimal places in the product.

Multiply.

1. 0.3 × 5   0.8 × 9   0.3 × 8   0.2 × 9   0.3 × 9   0.4 × 6   0.5 × 7   0.9 × 7

2. 0.5 × 5   0.1 × 7   0.9 × 6   0.2 × 6   0.4 × 7   0.7 × 7   0.9 × 9   0.6 × 6

Multiply.

3. 0.03 × 5   0.31 × 2   0.11 × 7   0.75 × 5   0.03 × 7   0.33 × 8

4. 0.72 × 3   0.49 × 7   0.38 × 2   0.45 × 8   0.21 × 9   0.14 × 4

Write the number of decimal places the product will have.

5. One factor is a whole number and the other is a decimal in tenths. ______

6. One factor is a whole number and the other is a decimal in hundredths. ______

STANDARD

Find **8 × 0.421**.

Multiply with a fraction.

$$8 \times 0.421 = 8 \times \frac{421}{1{,}000}$$

$$= \frac{3{,}368}{1{,}000}$$

$$= 3\frac{368}{1{,}000} \text{ or } 3.368$$

8 × 421 = 3,368

Multiply with a decimal.

```
 0.421 ┐
 ×   8 ├ 3 decimal places
 3.368 ┘
```

There is a total of **3** decimal places in the factors. So, there are **3** decimal places in the product.

Multiply.

7.

0.695 × 9	0.213 × 8	0.165 × 6	0.982 × 3	0.821 × 5	7.060 × 2

8.

4.70 × 56	0.26 × 89	73 × 7.8	136 × 0.45	4.8 × 96	86 × 0.72

9.

38.07 × 48	7,375 × 0.086	37.7 × 46	4.098 × 89	458 × 0.36	1,004 × 9.5

Problem Solving Reasoning **Solve.**

10. Arnold bought **4** tickets to a play. Each ticket cost **$7.50.**

How much did he spend altogether? _______________

11. Do you think the product of **3 × 8.3** is greater than or equal to **0.3 × 83**? Explain.

Test Prep ★ Mixed Review

12 What is $\frac{2}{3}$ of 6 days?

A 4 days

B $5\frac{1}{3}$ days

C $6\frac{2}{3}$ days

D 9 days

13 One piece of rope is $2\frac{1}{2}$ feet long and the other is $3\frac{3}{8}$ feet long. What is the combined length of the two pieces?

F $5\frac{6}{8}$ ft

G $5\frac{7}{8}$ ft

H $6\frac{1}{8}$ ft

J $6\frac{7}{8}$ ft

Name ____________________

Multiplying Decimals by Decimals

STANDARD

These examples will help you place the decimal point in a product.

$\frac{3}{10} \times \frac{9}{10} = \frac{27}{100}$

↓ ↓ ↓

$0.3 \times 0.9 = 0.27$

Think: *hundredths* means **2** decimal places

$\frac{83}{100} \times \frac{3}{10} = \frac{249}{1,000}$

↓ ↓ ↓

$0.83 \times 0.3 = 0.249$

Think: *thousandths* means **3** decimal places

$\frac{21}{10} \times \frac{7}{10} = \frac{147}{100}$

↓ ↓ ↓

$2.1 \times 0.7 = 1.47$

You can use what you know about whole numbers to multiply decimals.

1. Multiply as you would whole numbers.

$$\begin{array}{r} 1.6 \\ \times\ 0.8 \\ \hline 128 \end{array}$$

2. Find the total number of decimal places in the two factors.

$$\begin{array}{r} \overset{4}{1.6} \\ \times\ 0.8 \\ \hline 128 \end{array} \qquad \begin{array}{r} 1 \text{ place} \\ +\ 1 \text{ place} \\ \hline 2 \text{ places} \end{array}$$

3. Write the decimal point in the product.

$$\begin{array}{r} \overset{4}{1.6} \\ \times\ 0.8 \\ \hline 1.28 \end{array} \leftarrow 2 \text{ places}$$

Complete.

1. If there is one decimal place in each of two factors, then how many decimal places will the product have?

____

2. If there is one decimal place in one factor and two decimal places in the other factor, then how many decimal places will the product have?

____

Sometimes you need to write one or more zeros in the product before you can place the decimal point.

$$\begin{array}{r} 0.4 \\ \times\ 0.2 \\ \hline 0.08 \end{array} \begin{array}{l} 1 \text{ place} \\ 1 \text{ place} \end{array} > 2 \text{ places} \qquad \begin{array}{r} 0.06 \\ \times\ 0.3 \\ \hline 0.018 \end{array} \begin{array}{l} 2 \text{ places} \\ 1 \text{ place} \end{array} > 3 \text{ places}$$

Multiply.

3. $\begin{array}{r} 3.74 \\ \times\ 0.8 \\ \hline \end{array}$ $\begin{array}{r} 8.29 \\ \times\ 0.9 \\ \hline \end{array}$ $\begin{array}{r} 65.3 \\ \times\ 0.7 \\ \hline \end{array}$ $\begin{array}{r} 4.28 \\ \times\ 1.2 \\ \hline \end{array}$ $\begin{array}{r} 93.1 \\ \times\ 2.9 \\ \hline \end{array}$

4. $\begin{array}{r} 72.9 \\ \times\ 3.8 \\ \hline \end{array}$ $\begin{array}{r} 8.34 \\ \times\ 4.7 \\ \hline \end{array}$ $\begin{array}{r} 67.5 \\ \times\ 5.3 \\ \hline \end{array}$ $\begin{array}{r} 5.83 \\ \times\ 0.93 \\ \hline \end{array}$ $\begin{array}{r} 96.2 \\ \times\ 0.89 \\ \hline \end{array}$

5. $\begin{array}{r} 0.02 \\ \times\ 0.4 \\ \hline \end{array}$ $\begin{array}{r} 0.6 \\ \times\ 0.1 \\ \hline \end{array}$ $\begin{array}{r} 0.4 \\ \times\ 0.6 \\ \hline \end{array}$ $\begin{array}{r} 0.03 \\ \times\ 0.5 \\ \hline \end{array}$ $\begin{array}{r} 0.02 \\ \times\ 3 \\ \hline \end{array}$ $\begin{array}{r} 0.01 \\ \times\ 0.3 \\ \hline \end{array}$

STANDARD

If you estimate before you multiply, you will know whether your answer makes sense. Estimating the product will also help you place the decimal point correctly. Find each product. Estimate first.

6. 67.3 × 0.4

Estimate: 70.0 × 0.4 = 28.00 (2 decimal places)

96.7 × 0.2   831.4 × 0.9   172.9 × 0.1   719.2 × 0.6

7. 23.9 × 1.6   63.1 × 1.5   95.7 × 2.7   2.6 × 0.82   3.3 × 2.02   4.1 × 8.01

Problem Solving
Reasoning

Solve.

8. Mary bought some bagels and some rolls. The bagels cost **$.40** each and the rolls cost **$.25**. If she spent **$3.90** in all for **12** items, how many of each did she buy?

____

9. One recipe for bagels uses **0.45** bag of flour. A recipe for rolls uses **1.5** times as much. Does the recipe for rolls use more or less than $\frac{3}{4}$ bag of flour?

____

Quick Check

Add or subtract.

Work Space

10. 0.06 + 0.95 ________

11. 13.904 + 9.88 ________

12. 55 − 16.75 ________

13. 10.16 + 25.071 + 9.5

14. $20.56 − 11.19

15. 57.083 − 39.17 ________

Multiply.

16. 65 × 0.09

17. 9.16 × 42

18. 9.50 × 116

Multiply. Be sure to place the decimal point in each answer.

19. 0.07 × 0.06

20. 6.98 × 0.25

21. 1.17 × 9.9

Name ______________________________

Multiplying and Dividing by Powers of Ten

STANDARD

When you multiply **10** by itself any number of times, the product is called a **power of 10.** You can write a power of **10** using an exponent.

$10 = 10^1$ **$10 \times 10 = 10^2$ or 100** **$10 \times 10 \times 10 = 10^3$ or 1,000**

Write each power of 10 using an exponent and in standard form.

1. $10 \times 10 \times 10 \times 10 =$ ________ ________

2. $10 \times 10 \times 10 \times 10 \times 10 =$ ________ ________

3. $10 \times 10 \times 10 \times 10 \times 10 \times 10 =$ ________ ________

You can use patterns to help you find the product of a number and a power of **10**.

$63 \times 10 = 630$	**$0.75 \times 10 = 7.5$**	**$0.059 \times 10 = 0.59$**
$63 \times 100 = 6{,}300$	**$0.75 \times 100 = 75$**	**$0.059 \times 100 = 5.9$**
$63 \times 1{,}000 = 63{,}000$	**$0.75 \times 1{,}000 = 750$**	**$0.059 \times 1{,}000 = 59$**

Write *2* or *3* to complete each statement.

4. The exponent ______ tells you how many zeros to write when you find the product of a whole number and **10** to the third power.

5. You can multiply a number by **100** mentally. Just move the decimal point in the number to the right ______ places.

Multiply using patterns.

6. $73 \times 10 =$ __________ $31 \times 100 =$ __________ $5.21 \times 10 =$ __________

7. $0.43 \times 1{,}000 =$ __________ $0.107 \times 10^3 =$ __________ $0.006 \times 10^2 =$ __________

8. $17.28 \times 10 =$ __________ $0.093 \times 1{,}000 =$ __________ $42.178 \times 10^2 =$ __________

9. $0.037 \times 1{,}000 =$ __________ $5.401 \times 100 =$ __________ $400{,}000 \times 10 =$ __________

STANDARD

You can also use patterns to divide by powers of **10**.

290 ÷ 10 = 29	**65,000 ÷ 10 = 6,500**	**4.3 ÷ 10 = 0.43**
290 ÷ 100 = 2.9	**65,000 ÷ 100 = 650**	**4.3 ÷ 100 = 0.043**
290 ÷ 1,000 = 0.29	**65,000 ÷ 1,000 = 65**	**4.3 ÷ 1,000 = 0.0043**

Divide. Use patterns to help you.

10. 63 ÷ 10 = ________ 0.59 ÷ 10^1 ________ 4.71 ÷ 10 = ________

11. 0.01 ÷1,000 = ________ 34.8 ÷10^3 = ________ 0.651 ÷ 100 = ________

12. 500,000 ÷ 1,000 = ________ 3,240.27 ÷ 10^2 = ________ 77 ÷ 10^3 = ________

Write *true* or *false* for each statement.

13. When you divide a number by a power of **10,** the decimal point in the number moves to the right. ________

14. The exponent tells how many places to move the decimal point when multiplying or dividing by a power of **10.** ________

Problem Solving Reasoning **Solve.**

15. The highest point in Louisiana is Driskill Mountain. It is about **530** ft high. The highest point in New York, Mount Marcy, is about **10** times as high. About how high is Mount Marcy?

____

16. True or false? **43 × 10^2 = 430,000 ÷ 10^2**. Explain.

____

Test Prep ★ Mixed Review

17 **A carton of books weighed $7\frac{1}{2}$ pounds. What is the total weight of 10 identical cartons?**

A $17\frac{1}{2}$ lb

B 75 lb

C 77 lb

D 150 lb

18 **If 1 centimeter is about $\frac{2}{5}$ inches, then how many centimeters are there in 1 foot (12 inches)?**

F $\frac{2}{5}$

G $2\frac{1}{2}$

H $4\frac{4}{5}$

J 30

Name ______________________

Dividing by Whole Numbers

STANDARD

To divide a decimal by a whole number:

1. Divide as you would with whole numbers.
2. Then place the decimal point in the quotient directly above the decimal point in the dividend. Write zeros as placeholders as necessary.
3. Multiply to check, since multiplication is the inverse of division.

Examples

$$\begin{array}{r} 8.3 \\ 7\overline{)58.1} \\ -56 \\ \hline 2\,1 \\ -2\,1 \\ \hline 0 \end{array}$$

Check:

$$\begin{array}{r} 8.3 \\ \times\ 7 \\ \hline 58.1 \end{array}$$

Write zeros as placeholders

$$\begin{array}{r} 0.08 \\ 4\overline{)0.32} \\ -32 \\ \hline 0 \end{array}$$

Check:

$$\begin{array}{r} 0.08 \\ \times\ 4 \\ \hline 0.32 \end{array}$$

$$\begin{array}{r} 1.402 \\ 6\overline{)8.412} \\ -6 \\ \hline 2\,4 \\ -2\,4 \\ \hline 012 \\ -12 \\ \hline 0 \end{array}$$

Check:

$$\begin{array}{r} 1.402 \\ \times\ 6 \\ \hline 8.412 \end{array}$$

Divide and check.

1. $6\overline{)5.4}$	$7\overline{)41.3}$	$8\overline{)6.32}$	$5\overline{)9.75}$	$9\overline{)3.843}$
2. $2\overline{)0.342}$	$3\overline{)2.88}$	$4\overline{)8.44}$	$6\overline{)1.44}$	$3\overline{)0.639}$
3. $2\overline{)0.846}$	$7\overline{)0.266}$	$4\overline{)0.852}$	$2\overline{)0.684}$	$7\overline{)0.889}$

STANDARD

Place the decimal point in the quotient to make each equation true. Use estimation to help you.

4. 17.5 ÷ 5 = 3 5   27.2 ÷ 8 = 3 4   205.2 ÷ 6 = 3 4 2

Divide and check.

5. $6\overline{)2.46}$ $2\overline{)0.258}$ $3\overline{)5.49}$ $8\overline{)7.76}$ $5\overline{)1.730}$

6. $2\overline{)1.92}$ $9\overline{)1.134}$ $7\overline{)6.216}$ $3\overline{)7.743}$ $6\overline{)0.222}$

Problem Solving Reasoning Solve.

7. The grams of fat in **1** tbs of salad dressings are: Blue cheese **1.5** g, French **1.4** g, Italian **1.3** g, mayonnaise **1.7** g, thousand island **1.0** g. What is the average amount of fat in **1** tbs of each of these salad dressings?

______

8. The Cheese Shop sells **5** pounds of Italian cheese for **$14.50.** At that rate, what is the cost of **1** pound?

______

9. Shaun mailed **100** letters for a charity. The cost of the mailing was **$40.** How much did it cost to mail each envelope?

______

10. Barbara spent **$80.78** for groceries one week. What was her average cost per day for the groceries?

______

Test Prep ★ Mixed Review

11 Your cousin worked for $2\frac{3}{4}$ hours on Monday and $2\frac{2}{3}$ hours on Tuesday. How many hours is that in all?

A $4\frac{5}{7}$

B $4\frac{7}{12}$

C $5\frac{1}{12}$

D $5\frac{5}{12}$

12 Gina bought a used bicycle for $139. She made a down payment of $40. At $11 a week, how long will it take her to pay the rest?

F 11 weeks

G 10 weeks

H 9 weeks

J 8 weeks

Name ____________________

Writing Zeros in the Dividend

STANDARD

Sometimes you must write one or more zeros in the dividend to continue dividing.

Divide: $4\overline{)2.7}$

1. Divide. Write a zero in the hundredths place in the dividend.

Think: **27** ÷ **4** is about **6.**

$$\begin{array}{r} 0.6 \\ 4\overline{)2.70} \\ -\,24 \\ \hline 30 \end{array}$$

2. Divide again. Write a zero in the thousandths place in the dividend.

Think: **30** ÷ **4** is about **7.**

$$\begin{array}{r} 0.67 \\ 4\overline{)2.700} \\ -\,2\,4 \\ \hline 30 \\ -\,28 \\ \hline 20 \end{array}$$

3. Divide a third time.

$$\begin{array}{r} 0.675 \\ 4\overline{)2.700} \\ -\,2\,4 \\ \hline 30 \\ -\,28 \\ \hline 20 \\ -\,20 \\ \hline 0 \end{array}$$

Check:

$$\begin{array}{r} 0.675 \\ \times\ \ \ 4 \\ \hline 2.700 \end{array}$$

Here is another example: $2 \div 5 =$ $\begin{array}{r} 0.4 \\ 5\overline{)2.0} \\ -\,2\,0 \\ \hline 0 \end{array}$

Divide. Write zeros in the dividend if necessary.

1. $5\overline{)2.7}$ $\quad$ $4\overline{)3.5}$ $\quad$ $2\overline{)9.1}$ $\quad$ $8\overline{)5.2}$

2. $8\overline{)19}$ $\quad$ $5\overline{)24}$ $\quad$ $2\overline{)27}$ $\quad$ $4\overline{)19}$

3. $24\overline{)9}$ $\quad$ $24\overline{)15}$ $\quad$ $10\overline{)62.4}$ $\quad$ $16\overline{)12.4}$

STANDARD

Problem Solving Reasoning **Solve.**

4. June has **38** friends coming to a party. She expects to seat her friends at tables with **4** at each table. How many tables does she need?

______

5. June and her sister share the expenses equally. The party costs **$63.** How much does each sister pay?

______

6. Favors for the party can be purchased in packages of **4** or **8.** A package of **4** costs **$9.60** and a package of **8** costs **$22.** Which package is the better buy?

______

7. Juice for the party costs **$3.12** for **8** cartons. How much will one more carton cost?

______

Quick Check

Multiply or divide.

8. 9.53×10 ______

9. 0.8742×10^3 ______

10. 100×0.039 ______

11. $3.7 \div 10^2$ ______

12. $10\overline{)0.98}$

13. $100\overline{)56}$

14. $5\overline{)29.5}$

15. $9\overline{)610.2}$

16. $6\overline{)0.804}$

Divide. Write zeros in the dividend if necessary.

17. $4\overline{)9.6}$

18. $8\overline{)23}$

19. $36\overline{)86.4}$

Work Space

Name ______________________________

Dividing a Decimal by a Decimal

STANDARD

You can use what you know about dividing by a whole number to divide by a decimal.

Multiplying the **divisor** and the **dividend** by the same number does not change the quotient.

Multiply the divisor and dividend by **10.**

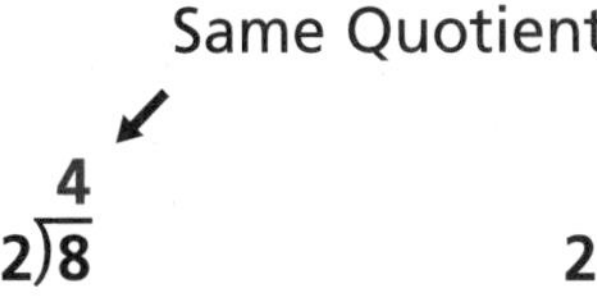

Multiply the divisor and dividend by **100.**

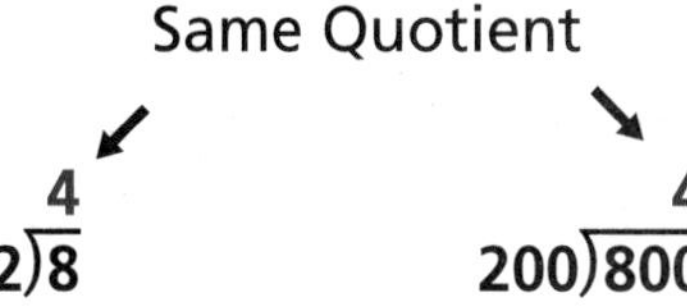

Find the quotient: **2.6)8.06**

1. Change the divisor to a whole number. Multiply by **10.**

   2.6.)8.06

   10 × 2.6 = 26

2. Multiply the dividend by the same number, **10.**

   2.6.)8.0.6

   10 × 8.06 = 80.6

3. Divide and place the decimal point in the quotient.

   3.1
   26)80.6
   −78
   2 6
   −2 6
   0

Rewrite each. Multiply the divisor and dividend by 10, 100, or 1,000.

1. 0.34)42.5 ______ 0.003)2.61 ______ 1.5)4.87 ______ 0.2)1.32 ______

2. 0.009)0.15 ______ 16.2)31 ______ 4.28)2.7 ______ 0.8)15 ______

Find the quotient.

3. 0.3)1.44 0.5)0.385 0.2)1.78 0.4)1.84

4. 0.21)5.46 3.5)17.5 6.1)32.33 1.24)0.4712

STANDARD

Divide. Remember to place the decimal point in the quotient.

5. $0.8\overline{)1.12}$ $0.5\overline{)16.55}$ $0.9\overline{)4.86}$ $0.21\overline{)5.46}$

6. $0.039\overline{)0.2496}$ $0.047\overline{)2.632}$ $0.005\overline{)0.515}$ $0.07\overline{)4.62}$

7. $0.252\overline{)47.88}$ $0.2\overline{)0.13}$ $0.36\overline{)1.872}$ $0.007\overline{)7.28}$

Problem Solving Reasoning Solve.

8. Moira is measuring yarn for the hair on a puppet. Each piece must be **0.5** in. long. How many pieces can she cut from a length of yarn that measures **26** in.?

____

9. A bicycle club rode **38.7** kilometers in **4.5** hours. What was the average number of kilometers they rode each hour?

____

10. Karen bought **10** stamps. Some cost **$.32** and some cost **$.20.** She spent **$2.84.** How many of each did she buy?

____

Test Prep ★ Mixed Review

11 A pencil is $\frac{18}{8}$ inches long. What is another way to write $\frac{18}{8}$ in.?

A $\frac{6}{4}$ in.

B $1\frac{1}{2}$ in.

C $2\frac{1}{8}$ in.

D $2\frac{1}{4}$ in.

12 Which number has a 6 in the hundredths place, a 5 in the tenths place, and a 7 in the thousandths?

F 0.567

G 0.576

H 0.657

J 0.675

Name ______________________

Interpreting Remainders

STANDARD

Sometimes you will need to decide whether to write a remainder as a whole number, fraction, or decimal.

Whole Number Remainder	**Divide.**	**Write the answer.**
A baker is putting **43** muffins in boxes. She puts **4** muffins in one box. How many boxes will she use?	10 R3 4)43 4↓ 03 ← remainder	There will be **10** boxes of **4** muffins, with **3** muffins left over. She needs 11 boxes. Write the remainder as a whole number.

Fraction Remainder	**Divide.**	**Write the answer.**
You need to cut a **43**-inch board into **4** equal-size pieces. How long will each piece be?	$10\frac{3}{4}$ 4)43 4↓ 03 ← remainder	Each piece will be $\mathbf{10\frac{3}{4}}$ inches long. Write the remainder as a fraction.

Decimal Remainder	**Divide.**	**Write the answer.**
Four friends divide the cost of dinner. The bill was **$43.00**. How much did each friend pay?	10.75 4)43.00 4 03 0 2 8 20 20 0 Write zeros in the dividend to continue dividing.	Each friend paid **$10.75.** Write the remainder as a decimal.

Divide. Explain how the quotient should be written.

1. A piece of ribbon **39** feet long is cut into **6** equal pieces. How long is each piece?

____

2. Each dress requires **2** yards of fabric. How many dresses can be made from **7** yards of material?

____

3. Three children are to share **$5.00** equally. How much does each child get?

____

4. There are **14** students going on a field trip. Each car can carry **4** students and an adult driver. How many cars are needed?

____

STANDARD

Problem Solving Reasoning

Solve. Explain how the quotient should be written.

5. Maurice made this chart to record what he spent each day last week in the cafeteria.

Monday	**$7.05**
Tuesday	**$4.28**
Wednesday	**$5.26**
Thursday	**$3.99**
Friday	**$6.21**

What was the average amount he spent per day?

____

6. Six friends spent **$99** for lunch one day. What is each person's share of the bill?

____

7. Kate is making a bookcase with shelves **3** feet long. She has a board **7** feet long. How many shelves can she cut from the board?

____

8. You bring **12** apples for **36** members of the band. How should you cut the apples so each member gets one piece?

____

9. Doug is using yarn to tie packages. He has **15** feet of yarn and **12** packages. He wants to use the same length for each package.How long should he make each piece?

____

10. Mr. Jefferson is delivering pies to a bake sale. He can fit **3** pies in each box. How many boxes does he need for 17 pies?

____

Test Prep ★ Mixed Review

11 A pickup truck is 19 feet long. A sports car is only 13.7 feet long. About how much shorter is the sports car?

A 35 ft

B 25 ft

C 15 ft

D 5 ft

12 Which decimal is equivalent to the fraction $\frac{3}{100}$?

F 300

G 3

H 0.30

J 0.03

Name ______________________

Algebra and Decimals

STANDARD

Simplify: **0.8 × (6.1 + 4.7) + 0.2**

Remember the Order of Operations:

- Work inside parentheses first.
- Multiply and divide from left to right.
- Add and subtract from left to right.

0.8 × (6.1 + 4.7) + 0.2

0.8 × 10.8 + 0.2

8.64 + 0.2

8.84

Simplify. Tell whether the answer would change if the parentheses were removed.

1. (3.9 × 2.8) + 4.2 = ______ 3.9 × (2.8 + 4.2) = ______
2. (19.7 − 3.1) × 2.8 = ______ 19.7 − (3.1 × 2.8) = ______
3. (6.24 ÷ 3) × *k* = ______ 6.24 ÷ (3 × *k*) = ______

Write decimal points as needed to make the equation true. Estimate first to help you place the decimal point.

4. (4 1 × 2 0 2) ÷ 2 = 4 1 . 4 1 4 1 × (2 0 2 ÷ 2) = 4 . 1 4 1
5. (2 5 2 × 3 9) − 2 0 3 = 9 6 . 2 5 2 5 2 × (3 9 − 2 0 3) = 4 7 . 1 2 4
6. (4 3 6 + 1 8 9) × 4 1 7 = 2 6 0 . 6 2 5 4 3 6 + (1 8 9 × 4 1 7) = 5 1 4 . 8 1 3

Remember that the properties and rules for whole numbers are the same for decimals. Name the property shown.

7. (1.5 + 6.9) + 28 = (6.9 + 1.5) + 28 ______
8. 5.37 × 0 = 0 ______ 0 + 14.38 = 14.38 ______
9. (73.4 + *r*) × 3.1 = (73.4 × 3.1) + (*r* × 3.1) ______
10. (28.115 + 79) × 0 = 0 ______
11. 0.032 × 1 = 0.032 ______

STANDARD

Complete each equation. Name the property you used.

11. $12 \times (z + 1.8) = (12 \times$ ______ $) + (12 \times 1.8)$ ____________

12. $1.53 \times (10 \times 2.4) = (2.4 \times 1.53) \times$ ______ ____________

13. $50 + 2.37 + 0 = 2.37 +$ ______ $+ 50$ ____________

14. $8 + (9.3 +$ ______ $) = 17.3$ ____________

Problem Solving
Reasoning

Solve. Evaluate each expression to find the total cost.
Use the distributive property when you can.

15. $3a + 3d$ ______

16. $2a + c$ ______

17. $2b + 2a$ ______

18. $c + 3d$ ______

School Supplies		
a	$2.50	notebook
b	$.55	marker
c	$1.49	package of pencils
d	$.79	pad of paper

Variables

Quick Check

First multiply to make the divisor a whole number.
Then find the quotient.

Work Space

19. $6.1\overline{)32.33}$ **20.** $0.36\overline{)1.872}$ **21.** $0.039\overline{)0.2496}$

Write the remainder as a whole number, a fraction, and a decimal rounded to the nearest hundredth.

22. $3\overline{)89}$ **23.** $8\overline{)413}$ **24.** $4\overline{)301}$

______ ______ ______

Simplify.

25. $0.7 \times (0.8 + 1.2)$ ______

26. $3.2 \div 4 + 3 \times 0.5$ ______

27. $(16.8 - 8.1) - 2.9$ ______

28. What number makes the equation true?

$3 \times 6.2 = (3 \times 6.0) + (n \times 0.2)$ ______

Name ____________________

Problem Solving Application: Solve Multi-Step Problems

STANDARD

Sometimes you need to do more than one step to solve a problem.

In this lesson, you will use the price list to solve multi-step problems.

Menu	
Lemonade	$.85
Hamburger	$2.49
Hot dog	$1.69
Salad	$.99

Tips to Remember

1. Understand 2. Decide 3. Solve 4. Look back

- Think about the action in the problem. Is there more than one action? Which operation best represents each action—addition, subtraction, multiplication, or division?
- Try to break the problem into parts.
- Think about strategies you have learned, and use them to help solve a problem.

Solve. Use the price list above.

1. You had **$5.** You bought a hamburger and a lemonade. How much money did you have left?

Think: Should you add or subtract the prices of the lemonade and hamburger?

____

Answer ____________________

2. You want to buy **1** hot dog, **1** salad, and **1** lemonade. You have **$3.25** in your pocket. Do you have enough money?

Think: Do you need to find an exact answer or is an estimate enough to answer the question?

____

Answer ____________________

3. Mr. Lee bought lunch for his family. He bought **4** lemonade drinks, **2** hamburgers, **2** hot dogs, and **2** salads. How much change did he receive from **$15.00?**

____

4. Mrs. Washington purchased **4** hot dogs and **2** lemonade drinks. Would **2** hamburgers and **2** lemonades have been cheaper?

____

STANDARD

Solve. Use the price list.

The Snack Bar			
Hamburger	$2.49	Salad	$0.99
Superburger	$2.99	Frosty Shake	$1.29
Hot dog	$1.69	Lemonade	$0.85

5. You want to buy **2** frosty shakes. You have only **$1.75** in your pocket. How much more do you need?

____

6. How much more does it cost to buy a superburger and a frosty shake than a hamburger and a lemonade?

____

7. There is **0.25** lb of ground beef in a hamburger and **0.35** lb of ground beef in a superburger. How many pounds of ground beef are needed to make **16** hamburgers and **20** superburgers?

____

8. The Snack Bar bought a package of **48** hot dogs for **$24**, and two packages of **24** rolls for **$7.20** each. One day all the hot dogs were sold. How much profit did The Snack Bar make on hot dogs?

____

9. The Green family stopped at The Snack Bar for lunch. They bought **2** salads, a superburger, and **3** of the same drink. The bill came to **$7.52**. Which drink did they buy?

____

10. Yuko ordered a superburger, a salad, and a frosty shake. When she paid the cashier, she received **2** quarters, **2** dimes, and **3** pennies. How much money had she given the cashier?

____

Extend Your Thinking

11. Look back at problem **8**. What is The Snack Bar's cost of buying a hot dog and a roll? Explain how you found your answer.

____

____

____

12. Look back at problem **9**. Explain how you found your answer.

____

____

____

Name ____________________

Unit 6 Review

Identify the place value of each underlined digit.

1. 5.<u>4</u> ____________

2. 341.6<u>4</u> ____________

3. 700.00<u>9</u> ____________

Compare. Write <, > or =.

4. 1.9 ○ 1.09

5. 13.5 ○ 13.55

6. 476.99 ○ 476.990

Write each fraction or mixed number as a decimal. Write each decimal as a fraction or mixed number.

7. $\frac{5}{100}$ ________

8. $1\frac{43}{100}$ ________

9. 0.3 ________

10. 2.035 ________

Estimate each sum or difference by rounding each number to the given place.

11. one $\begin{array}{r} 46.49 \\ +\ 3.6 \\ \hline \end{array}$

12. hundredth $\begin{array}{r} 8.455 \\ -\ 0.384 \\ \hline \end{array}$

13. tenth $\begin{array}{r} 36.071 \\ -\ 3.04 \\ \hline \end{array}$

Estimate each sum or difference. Then add or subtract.

14. $\begin{array}{r} 4.7 \\ -\ 0.8 \\ \hline \end{array}$

15. $\begin{array}{r} 3.06 \\ +\ 4.7 \\ \hline \end{array}$

16. $\begin{array}{r} 50.56 \\ +\ 29.6 \\ \hline \end{array}$

17. $\begin{array}{r} 650.10 \\ -\ 3.04 \\ \hline \end{array}$

18. $\begin{array}{r} 58.005 \\ +\ 4.77 \\ \hline \end{array}$

Multiply.

19. $\begin{array}{r} 0.8 \\ \times\ 8 \\ \hline \end{array}$

20. $\begin{array}{r} 0.53 \\ \times\ 61 \\ \hline \end{array}$

21. $\begin{array}{r} 6.55 \\ \times\ 0.54 \\ \hline \end{array}$

22. $\begin{array}{r} 10.05 \\ \times\ 0.7 \\ \hline \end{array}$

23. $\begin{array}{r} 0.46 \\ \times\ 100 \\ \hline \end{array}$

Divide and check.

24. $7\overline{)45.5}$

25. $6\overline{)2.7}$

26. $25\overline{)0.3}$

27. $100\overline{)40.6}$

28. $3.7\overline{)8.51}$

Use the Guess and Check strategy. Solve.

29. The total weight of the Sarah's packages is **3.69** kg. One package weighs twice as much as the other. How much does each package weigh? ____________

Name ______________________

Cumulative Review

★ Test Prep

1 **Tan spent $4.80 on stamps. Each stamp cost $0.32. How many stamps did he buy?**

A 13
B 15
C 32
D 48
E Not here

2 **The movie is shown every 3 hours. It is $2\frac{1}{3}$ hours long. What part of an hour is the movie not being shown?**

F $\frac{3}{4}$ h
G $\frac{1}{3}$ h
H $\frac{2}{3}$ h
J $\frac{1}{2}$ h
K $\frac{1}{4}$ h

3 **Nancy earned $38,790.65 last year. Which shows the amount written in words?**

A Three million eight thousand seven hundred ninety dollars and sixty-five cents

B Thirty-eight million seven hundred ninety thousand dollars and sixty-five cents

C Thirty-eight thousand seven hundred dollars and sixty-five cents

D Thirty-eight thousand seven hundred ninety dollars and sixty-five cents

4 **Bobby scored 35 points on each of his spelling tests. He has a total of 385 points. Which equation could be used to find the number of spelling tests Bobby has taken?**

F $385 \times 35 = n$

G $35 \div n = 385$

H $35 \times 385 = n$

J $385 \div 35 = n$

5 **Hannah has saved $8.58 to buy a hat that costs $13.99. Which is a reasonable estimate of how much money she still needs to save in order to buy the hat?**

A $6.00
B $8.58
C $13.99
D $15.00

6 **Ian read that the moon is about 250,000 miles from Earth. Which expression is equivalent to 250,000?**

A 2.5×10^6

B 2.5×10^5

C 2.5×10^4

D 2.5×10^3

The table shows the normal precipitation for a city in California during the first six months of the year. Use the table to answer questions 7–10.

Normal Precipitation in Inches

Jan.	Feb.	Mar.	Apr.	May	June
3.1	3.3	2.3	1.2	0.2	0.1

7 **Which measurement gives the average normal precipitation in inches for the six months?**

A 0.1
B 1.1
C 1.7
D 3.3

8 **What would the average normal precipitation be if the measurement for Jan. was 3.7 inches instead of 3.1 inches?**

F 1.8 inches
G 1.7 inches
H 1.6 inches
J 1.5 inches

9 **Which point on the number line shows the normal precipitation for March?**

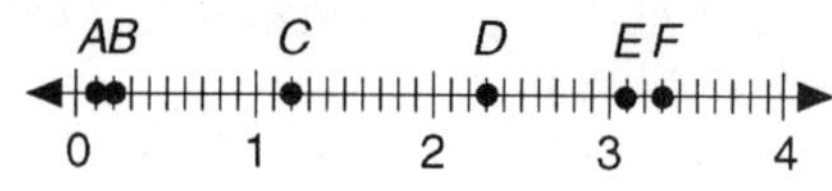

A *A*
B *B*
C *C*
D *D*

10 **Which two months each have normal precipitation of less than $\frac{1}{2}$ inch?**

F May and June
G April and May
H January and June
J February and March

UNIT 7 • TABLE OF CONTENTS

Measurement

We will be using this vocabulary:

metric system an international system of measurement that uses meter, liter, gram, and degrees Celsius as its basic units

customary system a system of measurement currently used in the United States

Dear Family,

During the next few weeks, our math class will be learning about measurement.

You can expect to see homework that provides practice with changing from one unit of measure to another. Here is a sample you may want to keep handy to give help if needed.

Customary Units of Length

The inch (in.), foot (ft), yard (yd), and mile (mi) are customary units of length.

Example 19 in. = ___?___ ft ______ in.

Refer to the chart to find **1** ft = **12** in.

Then divide **19** by **12**.

1 ft = 12 in.
3 ft = 1 yd
1 mi = 5,280 ft

$$12\overline{)19}\quad 1\text{ R}7$$

So, **19** in. = **1** ft **7** in.

Example 5,280 ft = ___?___ yd

Refer to the chart to find **3** ft = **1** yd.

Then divide **5,280** by **3**.

1 ft = 12 in.
3 ft = 1 yd
1 mi = 5,280 ft

$$3\overline{)5,280}\quad 1,760$$

So, **5,280** ft = **1,760** yd.

During this unit, students will need to continue practicing addition, subtraction, multiplication, and division facts.

Sincerely,

Name ______________________________

Metric Units of Length

STANDARD

The basic unit of length in the metric system is the **meter (m).**

10 millimeters (mm) = 1 centimeter (cm)
10 centimeters (cm) = 1 decimeter (dm)
10 decimeters (dm) = 1 meter (m)

The length of a baseball bat is about **1** meter.
The diameter of a baseball is about **1** decimeter.
The width of your fingernail is about **1** centimeter.
The thickness of a dime is about **1** millimeter.

The metric system is based on **10**. To change from one unit to another, multiply or divide by **10, 100,** or **1,000**.

- To change from a longer unit to a shorter unit, multiply.
  5 m = ? cm
  5 m = 500 cm
  Think: **1** m = **100** cm
  5 × **100** = **500**

- To change from a shorter unit to a longer unit, divide.
  50 mm = ? cm
  50 mm = 5 cm
  Think: **10** mm = **1** cm
  50 ÷ **10** = **5**

- Remember to add all the like units together.
  8 m 5 dm = ? dm
  8 m 5 dm = 85 dm
  Think: **1** m = **10** dm
  (**8** × **10**) + **5** = **85**
  Think: **80** dm + **5** dm

Choose the best unit for measuring.
Write *mm, dm, cm,* or *m*.

1. length of pencil ______ thickness of coin ______

2. height of adult ______ width of this page ______

3. thickness of paper clip ______ height of school building ______

Complete.

4. 3 m = ______ cm | 60 mm = ______ cm | 7 m 3 dm = ______ dm

5. 7 dm = ______ cm | 4,000 mm = ______ m | 4 dm 9 cm = ______ cm

6. 5,000 mm = ______ dm | 8 m = ______ mm | 3 cm 4 mm = ______ mm

7. 300 cm = ______ m | 4 dm = ______ mm | 3 dm 8 cm = ______ cm

8. 20 cm = ______ mm | 200 mm = ______ cm | 5 m 2 dm = ______ dm

9. 20 dm = ______ m | 5 m = ______ mm | 4 cm 7 mm = ______ mm

STANDARD

In the metric system, **kilometers (km)** are used to measure greater distances. A kilometer is about the length of **9** football fields.

1 kilometer (km) = 1,000 meters.

Solve.

10. About how many times do you need to walk around your schoolyard to walk **1** km? ______

11. About how many minutes does it take to walk **1** km? ______

12. Estimate each distance.

a. from your home to your school ______ km

b. from your school to the nearest grocery store ______ km

13. Name a place that is about **1** kilometer from your school. ______

Complete.

14. **2** km = ______ m　　**3** km = ______ m　　**5** km **175** m = ______ m

15. **5,000** m = ______ km　　**4,000** m = ______ km　　**8** km **9** m = ______ m

Problem Solving Reasoning

Solve.

16. The wingspan of a butterfly is **77** mm. Its height is **7** cm. Which is greater, its wingspan or its height? ______

17. Mario is **140** cm tall. His brother is **1** m **62** cm tall. His sister is **1,090** mm tall. Who is the tallest? ______

18. The prefixes *deci*, *centi*, *milli*, and *kilo* are used to form other metric units of length. Predict what each prefix means. Then use a dictionary to verify your prediction. ______

Test Prep ★ Mixed Review

19 A watch regularly sells for $47.99. In a sale, the price of the watch has been reduced by $\frac{1}{3}$. *About* how much money do you save if you buy the watch on sale?

A $15　　**C** $25

B $20　　**D** $30

20 When you take money out of an ATM you need to enter a secret number. Suppose the last 3 digits of your code number are divisible by 4, 6, and 8. Which code number could you have?

F 457-621　　**H** 457-216

G 457-612　　**J** 457-126

Name ______________________

Metric Units of Capacity and Mass

STANDARD

Capacity is the amount a container will hold. The basic unit of capacity in the metric system is the liter (**L**). It is about the size of a quart. A smaller unit of capacity is the **milliliter** (**mL**).

1 liter (L) = 1,000 milliliters (mL)

The basic unit of **mass** in the metric system is the **gram (g)**. It is about the weight of a paper clip.

To measure the mass of very light objects, use **milligrams (mg)**.

To measure the mass of heavy objects, use **kilograms (kg)**.

To measure very great masses, use **metric tons (T)**.

1,000 milligrams (mg) = 1 gram (g)
1,000 grams (g) = 1 kilogram (kg)
1,000 kilograms (kg) = 1 metric ton (T)

Choose the most reasonable estimate of capacity.

1. a glass of water	**25** mL	**250** mL	**25** L
2. a sink	**30** L	**300** mL	**300** L
3. a spoon	**100** mL	**10** L	**10** mL
4. a soup bowl	**20** L	**200** mL	**200** L

Choose the best unit for measuring the mass. Write *mg, g, kg,* or *T.*

5. pine needle ________ school bus ________

6. dime ________ person ________

7. book ________ key ________

8. pencil ________ car ________

9. seed ________ basketball ________

STANDARD

Complete.

10. 3 L = _______ mL   2,000 mL = _______ L   1 L 400 mL = _______ mL

11. 5,000 mL = _______ L   15 L = _______ mL   4 L 25 mL = _______ mL

12. 5,000 g = _______ kg   8,000 kg = _______ T   2 g = _______ mg

13. 2 T = _______ kg   1 T = _______ g   42,000 mg = _______ g

Compare. Write > or <.

14. 400 L ◯ 5,000 mL   1,500 mL ◯ 2 L   1 L ◯ 580 mL

15. 4,390 g ◯ 2 kg   8,976 kg ◯ 8 T   30,000 mg ◯ 3 kg

Problem Solving Reasoning **Solve.**

16. Which has a greater mass, a **3**-kilogram box or a **300**-milligram box? Explain. _______________

____

17. How many **200**-milliliter paper cups can be filled from a **2**-liter pitcher of lemonade?

____

18. A recipe for fruit punch requires **1** L of ginger ale, **750** mL of lemonade, and **500** mL of pineapple juice. Jon made twice this amount. How much punch did he make?

____

19. Sarah is using **800**-g bags of sand to fill a sandbox that can hold **5** kg of sand. How many bags will she need to completely fill the sandbox?

____

Test Prep ★ Mixed Review

20 When Arnie was asked how long he spent on his project, he answered that he spent the reciprocal of $\frac{4}{7}$ hour. How long did he spend on the project?

A $\frac{4}{7}$ h   C $1\frac{4}{7}$ h

B $\frac{3}{4}$ h   D $1\frac{3}{4}$ h

21 In the morning, 3,151 people got on the train at Dover. In the afternoon, 19 more people got off the train at Dover than had gotten on in the morning. How many people got off the train in Dover?

F 3,032   H 3,232

G 3,170   J 3,270

Name ______________________________

Decimals and the Metric System

STANDARD

You can use decimals to write measures in the metric system.
The line segment below is **108** mm or **10.8** cm long.

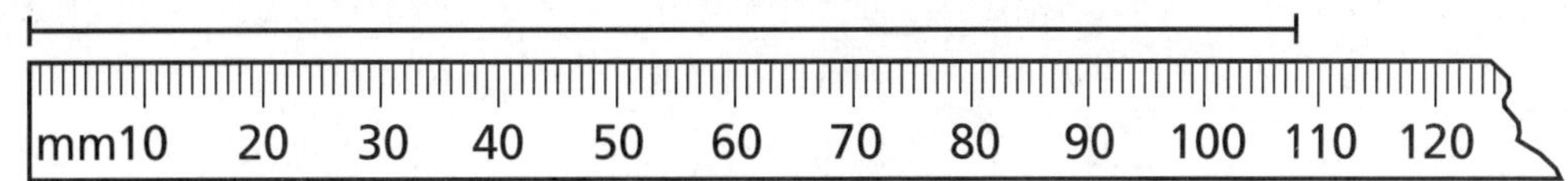

You can use what you know about multiplying and dividing by **10**, **100**, or **1,000** to change from one unit to another.

Longer to shorter unit, multiply. → **10.8** cm = ? mm
10.8 cm = **108** mm

> **Think: 1** cm = **10** mm
> To multiply a decimal by **10**, move the decimal point one place to the right.

Shorter to longer unit, divide. → **10.8** cm = ? m
10.8 cm = **0.108** m

> **Think: 1** m = **100** cm
> To divide a decimal by **100**, move the decimal point two places to the left.

Complete to change units.

1. **4.35** m	**2.** **2.36** m	**3.** ______ m	**4.** ______ m
______ dm	______ dm	**5.725** dm	______ dm
______ cm	______ cm	______ cm	**890** cm
______ mm	______ mm	______ mm	______ mm

Complete.

5.	**15.6** m = ______ dm	**250** mL = ______ L	**7** g = ______ kg
6.	**4.2** kg = ______ T	**6.83** m = ______ mm	**1.8** dm = ______ mm
7.	**53** cm = ______ dm	**9.1** kg = ______ g	**6.4** cm = ______ m
8.	**0.8** L = ______ mL	**0.74** g = ______ mg	**2.09** m = ______ cm
9.	**0.06** T = ______ kg	**402** mm = ______ m	**67** m = ______ km

Write a decimal point to make each statement reasonable.

10. The speed of a jet plane averaged **9 6 8 4 5** kilometers per hour.

11. Some children are **1 2 5** meters tall.

12. The weight of an **11**-year-old student is about **3 7 6** kilograms.

13. The height of a classroom door is **2 0 0 0** decimeters.

14. A baseball player threw a ball a distance of **4 5 6 7 8** meters.

STANDARD

Compare. Write > or <.

15. 0.27 dm ○ 27 cm   3.4 kg ○ 3,004 g   5,620 mL ○ 6 L

16. 420 mg ○ 4.2 g   2,500 m ○ 0.25 km   7.8 cm ○ 70 mm

17. 1.1 L ○ 926 mL   0.8 g ○ 9,000 mg   100.5 dm ○ 10.5 m

Problem Solving
Reasoning

Use the information in the box to solve.

A **$1** bill has a mass of **1** gram.
A **$1** bill is **0.1** millimeter thick.

18. A new car costs **$15,000**. How many kilograms of **$1** bills would it take to buy this car? If the **$1** bills are stacked one on top of another, how many centimeters tall would the stack be?

____

19. Suppose you saved a **$1** bill each day for **10** years, except for February 29. What would be the mass of your savings in grams? How many meters tall would the stack of your savings be?

____

Quick Check

Complete.

20. 3,000 mm = ______ m

21. 4 dm 5 cm = ______ cm

22. 6 km 25 m = ______ m

Compare. Write > or <.

23. 430 g ○ 1 kg

24. 2,500 mL ○ 2 L

25. 1,800 mg ○ 9 g

Complete.

26. 0.6 L = ______ mL

27. 3.2 kg = ______ mg

28. 0.25 cm = ______ m

Work Space

Name ______________________

Problem Solving Application: Use Tables and Graphs

STANDARD

The airline time table shows 4 daily nonstop flights from New York City to Lake Placid, New York.

In this lesson, you will solve problems by reading a time table or a graph.

Flight #	From: NYC	To: Lake Placid
23	8:41 A.M.	10:00 A.M.
55	10:35 A.M.	11:59 A.M.
79	2:59 P.M.	4:15 P.M.
92	6:35 P.M.	8:05 P.M.

Tips to Remember

1. Understand 2. Decide 3. Solve 4. Look back

- Compare the labels on the table or graph with the words and numbers in the problem.
- Use a list to organize the facts you need from the table or graph.
- Reread the problem carefully. Ask yourself questions about any part that you do not understand. Reread to find answers.

Use the airline time table to solve the problems.

1. How much time is there between the departures of Flight 55 and Flight 79?

Think: How much time is there between 10:35 A.M. and 12:00 noon? Between 12:00 noon and 2:59 P.M.?

____

Answer: ______________________

2. How much longer does Flight 92 take than Flight 23?

Think: How can you rewrite **10:00** so that you will be able to subtract the minutes?

____

____

Answer: ______________________

3. How long does Flight 79 take?

____

____

4. Jane arrived at the airport **2** hours and **15** minutes early for Flight 55. Did she get there before the earlier flight departed? Explain how you know.

____

____

STANDARD

Solve. Use the graph.

Students in a class in Canada made this **double-line graph** to show the high and low temperatures in their town.

The double-line graph allows you to compare the two sets of data on one graph. Use the key to find the high and low temperatures.

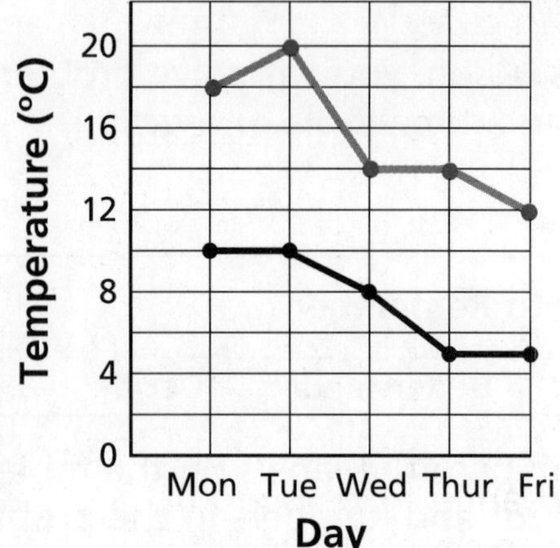

Key
High
Low

5. On which day was the difference between the high and low temperature the greatest? How much was this difference?

6. The class calculated the average temperature for the week. What was the average?

7. The high temperature of the day on Monday occurred at **11:39** A.M. The low temperature occurred at **10:51** P.M. How much time passed between the high and the low temperatures of the day?

8. The low temperature of the day on Friday occurred at **2:15** A.M. The high temperature occurred **10** hours and **30** minutes later. At what time did the high temperature occur?

Extend Your Thinking

9. Describe the **trend** or direction that the temperatures are moving for both the highs and the lows for the **5** days. What season do you think comes next?

10. Look back at problem **6**. Explain the method you used to solve the problem. Describe another method you might have used.

Name ______________________

Customary Units of Length

STANDARD

Standard units of length in the customary system are the **inch (in.), foot (ft), yard (yd),** and **mile (mi).**

You can change from one unit to another by using this information.

12 inches (in.) = **1** foot (ft)
3 feet = **1** yard (yd)
36 inches = **1** yard
5,280 feet = **1** mile (mi)
1,760 yards = **1** mile

- To change from a longer unit to shorter, multiply.
  3 ft = ? in.
  3 ft = **36** in.
  Think: **1** ft = **12** in.
  3 × **12** = **36**
- To change from a shorter unit to longer, divide.
  12 ft = ? yd
  12 ft = **4** yd
  Think: **3** ft = **1** yd
  12 ÷ **3** = **4**
- You may need to write a remainder using the smaller unit.
  42 in. = ? ft ? in.
  42 in. = **3** ft **6** in.
  Think: **12** in. = **1** ft
  42 ÷ **12** = **3 R6**

Choose the best unit for measuring. Write *in., ft, yd,* or *mi.*

1. length of your finger ______ width of a sidewalk ______

2. height of classroom ______ width of a $**1** bill ______

3. distance from school to home ______ length of a soccer field ______

Complete.

4. **7** ft = ______ in. **24** ft = ______ yd **72** in. = ______ yd

5. **60** in. = ______ ft **2** mi = ______ ft **15** yd = ______ ft

6. **108** in. = ______ yd **5** ft = ______ in. **36** ft = ______ yd

7. **5** yd = ______ ft **144** in. = ______ ft **15,840** ft = ______ mi

8. **30** in. = ______ ft ______ in. **10** ft = ______ yd ______ ft

9. **6,000** ft = ______ mi ______ ft **125** in.= ______ ft ______ in.

STANDARD

You may need to regroup when you add customary units.

1. Add inches.

```
  4 ft  7 in.
+ 3 ft  8 in.
       15 in.
```

Think: 7 + 8 = 15

2. Regroup. 15 in. = 1 ft 3 in.

```
  1
  4 ft  7 in.
+ 3 ft  8 in.
        3 in.
```

3. Add feet.

```
  1
  4 ft  7 in.
+ 3 ft  8 in.
  8 ft  3 in.
```

You may also need to regroup when you subtract customary units.

1. Regroup. 6 yd = 5 yd 3 ft

```
  5     4
  6̸ yd  1̸ ft
− 2 yd  2 ft
```

2. Subtract feet.

```
  5     4
  6̸ yd  1̸ ft
− 2 yd  2 ft
        2 ft
```

3. Subtract yards.

```
  5     4
  6̸ yd  1̸ ft
− 2 yd  2 ft
  3 yd  2 ft
```

Add.

10. 4 ft 7 in. + 3 ft 7 in.   6 ft 10 in. + 2 ft 4 in.   5 ft 9 in. + 3 ft 9 in.   7 ft 8 in. + 4 ft 9 in.

Subtract.

11. 3 yd 1 ft − 1 yd 2 ft   8 yd 1 ft − 2 yd 2 ft   5 yd − 2 yd 2 ft   6 yd − 3 yd 1 ft

Problem Solving
Reasoning

Solve.

12. Justin has a piece of wood 4 ft 3 in. long. If he uses 1 ft 5 in. for a project, will he have 1 yd left for another project? Explain.

____

____

13. Lindsey needs 3 ft 8 in. of ribbon for a project and 2 ft 7 in. of ribbon for another project. If she buys 2 yd of ribbon, will she have enough? Explain.

____

____

Test Prep ★ Mixed Review

14 Which measure will make this number sentence true? 0.009 km > □ ?

A 82.4 dm

B 8.24 m

C 8,240 cm

D 82,400 mm

15 The coach treated the team to pizza and punch. She bought 3 pizzas at $8.75 each and punch for $4.99. *About* what was her change from two $20 bills?

F more than $15

G between $10 and $15

H between $5 and $10

J less than $5

Name ______________________

Measuring to the Nearest Inch

STANDARD

To measure the length of small objects in the customary system, you can use fractional parts of an inch.

This ruler measures to the **nearest inch.**

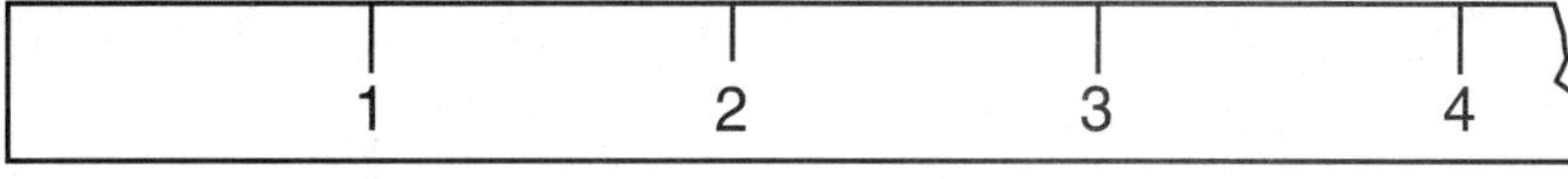

This ruler measures to the **nearest half-inch.**

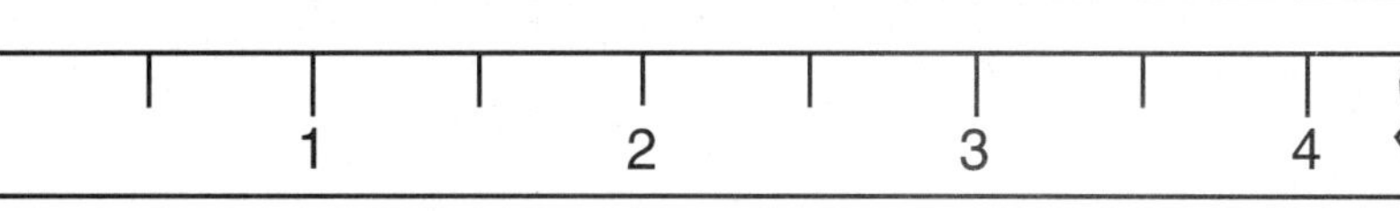

This ruler measures to the **nearest quarter-inch.**

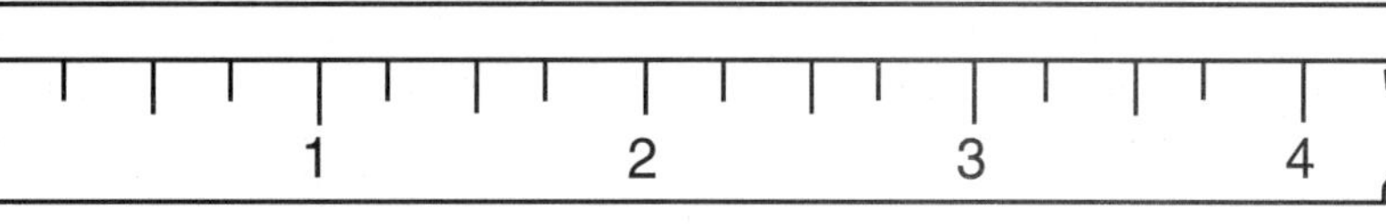

This ruler measures to the **nearest eighth-inch.**

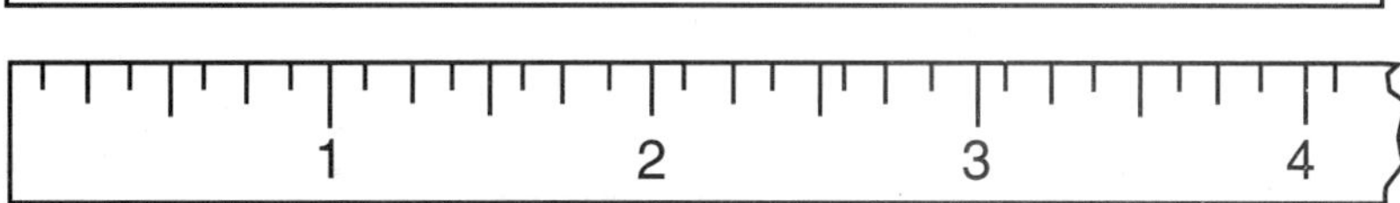

The length of the crayon is: **4** inches to the nearest inch,

3 $\frac{1}{2}$ inches to the nearest half-inch,

3 $\frac{3}{4}$ inches to the nearest quarter-inch,

3 $\frac{5}{8}$ inches to the nearest eighth-inch.

Use a ruler to measure each to the nearest inch, half-inch, quarter-inch, and eighth-inch.

1. ________________________

2. ______________

3. ________________________________

4. ____________________________

A ruler is a kind of number line. Use the number line to draw and label each point.

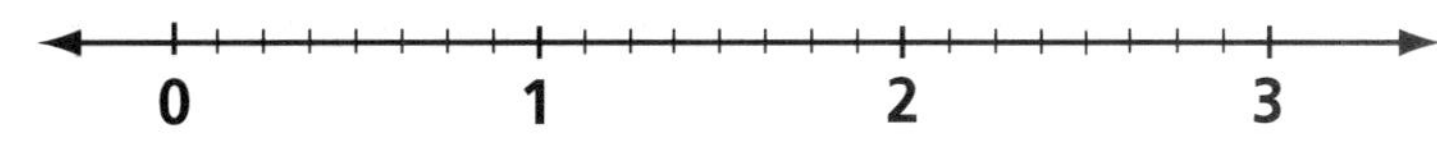

5. Draw *A* at $\frac{3}{4}$. Draw *B* at 1 $\frac{5}{8}$. Draw *C* at 2 $\frac{3}{8}$.

STANDARD

For each figure, measure the length of each side to the nearest eighth-inch. Then write the total distance around the figure.

6.  ______

7. 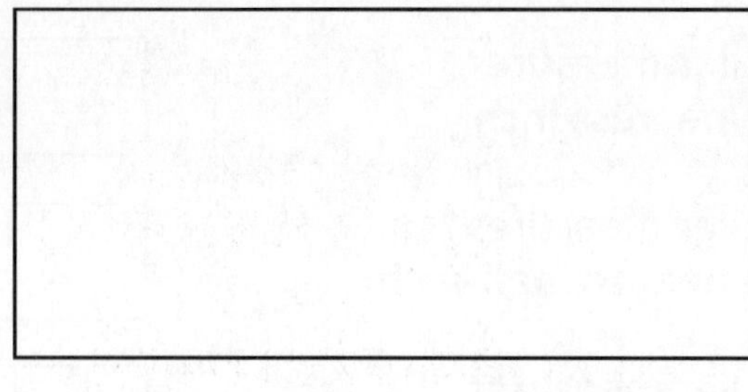 ______

8. 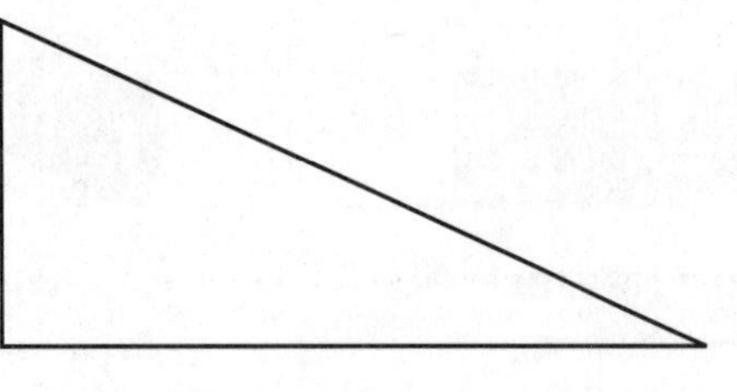 ______

9. 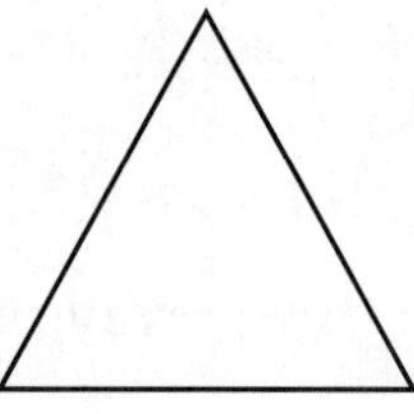 ______

Problem Solving
Reasoning

Use the picture to solve.

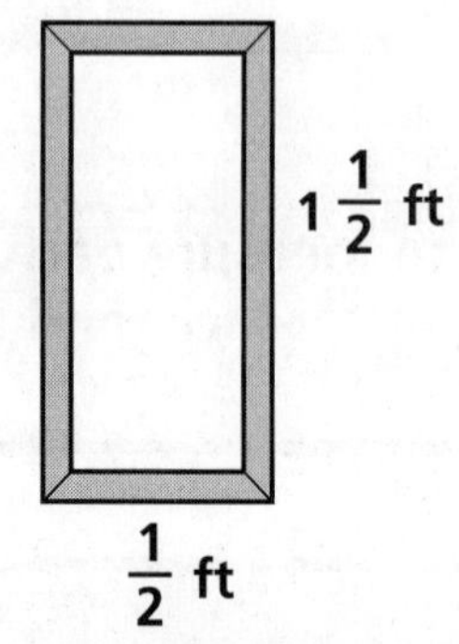

10. If you make a ribbon border for this picture frame, how much ribbon would you need? ______

11. Suppose you already have a **1** yard piece of ribbon. How much more ribbon do you need? ______

Test Prep ★ Mixed Review

12 **In a picture, the length of a pendant is 3.6 cm. The actual pendant is between 1.4 and 1.5 times longer. What is a reasonable estimate for the length of the actual pendant?**

A 9 cm
B 7 cm
C 5 cm
D 3 cm

13 **A lamb chop has 15.8 grams of protein, a frankfurter has 6.9 grams, and a piece of chicken has 21.2 grams. Which of these lists the foods from greatest to least grams of protein?**

F chicken, lamb chop, frankfurter
G chicken, frankfurter, lamb chop
H lamb chop, frankfurter, chicken
J frankfurter, lamb chop, chicken

Name ______________________

Customary Units of Weight and Capacity

STANDARD

In the customary system, weight is measured in **ounces, pounds,** or **tons.**

Weight

16 ounces (oz) = **1** pound (lb)
2,000 pounds = **1** ton (T)

Capacity is the amount of liquid a container can hold.

Capacity

8 fluid ounces = **1** cup (c)
2 cups = **1** pint (pt)
16 fluid ounces = **1** pint
2 pints = **1** quart (qt)
4 quarts = **1** gallon (gal)

= 

4 quarts **1** gallon

Complete.

1. **16** oz = **1** ______ ______ lb = **1** T **4** T = ______ lb

2. **5** T = ______ lb ______ lb = 176 oz **2** T = ______ lb

3. ______ oz = 7 lb 10 lb = ______ oz ______ oz = 9 lb

4. **9,000** lb = ______ T ______ lb 31 oz = ______ lb ______ oz

5. **15,000** lb = ______ T ______ lb 27 oz = ______ lb ______ oz

6. **2,003** lb = ______ T ______ lb 35 oz = ______ lb ______ oz

Complete.

7. **2** c = **1** ______ **12** c = ______ pt **13** pt = ______ c

8. **2** pt = **1** ______ **7** qt = ______ pt **25** qt = ______ pt

9. **4** qt = **1** ______ ______ gal = **52** qt ______ gal = **48** pt

10. **2** qt = **1** half ______ ______ pt = **7** gal **28** c = ______ pt

11. **1** c = **1** half ______ **40** pt = ______ gal ______ c = **3** qt

12. **8** pt = 1 ______ **76** qt = ______ gal ______ c = **1** gal

STANDARD

Problem Solving Reasoning Solve. Use the graph.

13. Was Hector's weight gain between **9** and **10** years old greater than, less than, or equal to his weight gain between **5** and **6** years old?

____

14. How much did Hector weigh when he was **6** years old?

____

15. Between which two years did Hector weigh **55** pounds?

____

16. Between which two years did Hector gain the most weight?

____

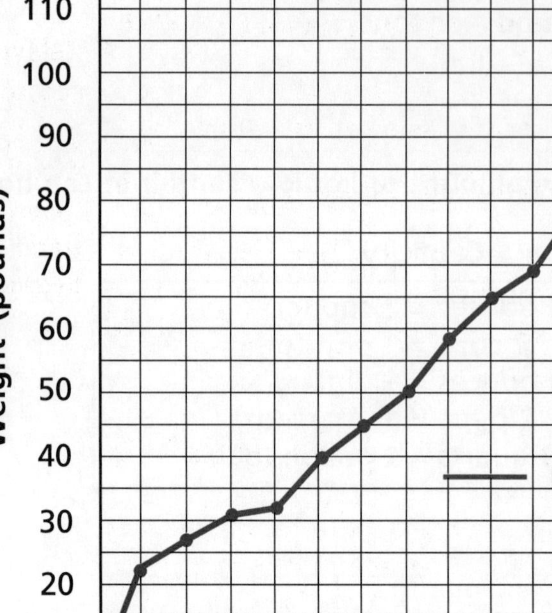

Quick Check

Complete.

17. 10,000 ft = ______ mi ______ ft

18. 90 in. = ______ yd ______ ft ______ in.

19. 3 ft **7** in. + **2** ft **8** in. = ______ ft ______ in.

20. 8 yd – (6 yd 2 ft) = ______ yd ______ ft

21. Use a ruler to measure the segment below to the nearest inch, half inch, quarter inch, and eighth inch.

____

Complete.

22. 7,150 lb = ______ T ______ lb

23. 48 pt = ______ gal

24. 60 oz = ______ lb ______ oz

25. ______ pt = **80** fl oz

Work Space

Name ____________________

Problem Solving Strategy: Draw a Graph

STANDARD

Sometimes you need to draw a graph to solve a problem. First decide what type of graph to draw.

Line graph – shows changes over time

Bar graph – compares numbers

Pictograph – shows data expressed in multiples

Problem

Below are the highest monthly temperatures recorded in a town for nine months. How can you display the data to show the change from month to month?

September: 71°F	February: 27°F	October: 59°F
March: 39°F	November: 41°F	April: 57°F
December: 26°F	May: 69°F	January: 21°F

1 Understand As you reread, ask yourself questions.

What type of data is shown? ____________________

What does the problem ask you to do? ____________________

Decide Choose a method for solving.

Try the Draw a Graph strategy.

Since the data shows the change, what type of graph should you draw?

____

3 Solve Label the horizontal scale with the months. You may abbreviate.

Look at the temperatures.
What is the least value? ______

What is the greatest? ______

Use intervals of 10 for the vertical axis. Start at 0. Then draw a point on the graph for each temperature. Connect the points.

Look back Check your graph.

Does the graph show a trend?

Answer: ____________________

____

STANDARD

Make a graph on another paper for problems 1–4. Use any other strategy for problems 5 and 6.

1. This is a table of Gail's height from age **1** to age **5.** How can you display the data to show the difference from year to year?

Age	Height in Inches
1	29
2	33
3	37
4	43
5	46

Think: What type of graph shows changes over time?

____

Answer ______________________

2. How can you display this data in a graph so you can tell which lake is longest without comparing the numbers?

Great Lake	Length in Miles
Superior	350
Michigan	307
Huron	206
Erie	241
Ontario	193

Think: What type of graph allows you to compare length or distance?

____

Answer ______________________

3. The table below shows the number of immigrants who came to the United States from 1930–1990.

Years	Number of Immigrants
1931-1940	528,431
1941-1950	1,035,039
1951-1960	2,515,479
1961-1970	3,321,677
1971-1980	4,493,314
1981-1990	7,338,062

a. How would you round the data so you can display it in a pictograph?

____

____

b. How many people would each symbol in the graph represent?

____

4. A baseball fan made a graph showing how many players hit the most home runs in a single season. What did the graph look like?

Player	Number of Home Runs
Mark McGwire	70
Sammy Sosa	66
Roger Maris	61
Babe Ruth	60
Hank Greenberg	58
Jimmie Fox	58
Ken Griffey, Jr.	56

5. In degrees Fahrenheit, the freezing point of water is **32**°F. If the boiling point of water is **180**° higher, what is the boiling point of water?

____

6. Each week Dan walks $\frac{1}{2}$ mile farther than the previous week. If he walks **2** miles the first week, how many miles does he walk the fifth week?

____

Name ______________________________

Unit 7 Review

Use a ruler to measure the length of this segment to the nearest inch and to the nearest centimeter.

1. ______ in.

2. ______ cm

Complete each equation.

3. 8 m = ______cm	**4.** 5 km = ______ m	**5.** 15 L = ______mL
6. 50 mL = ______ L	**7.** 3.8 m = ______ dm	**8.** 0.4 kg = ______ g
9. 48 in. =______ ft	**10.** 6 yd = ______ ft	**11.** 3 lb = ______ oz
12. 16,000 lb = _____ T	**13.** 3 pt = ______ c	**14.** 7 gal = ______ qt

This graph shows the Saturday and Sunday temperatures at different times of the day. Use the graph to help answer the questions that follow.

15. Was the temperature at **9** A.M. greater on Saturday or Sunday? By how many degrees was it greater? __________

16. At about what time was the temperature each day the same? ______

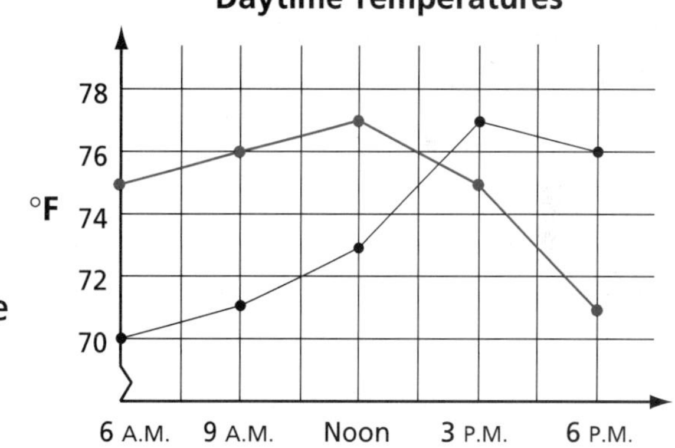

17. The temperature at **9** P.M. on Saturday was **70**°F and the temperature at **9** P.M. Sunday was **73**°F. Extend the graph and plot these times and temperatures.

Solve. Use the information in the table.

18. On the first day of a driving vacation, the Ramirez family drove from **7** A.M. to **11** A.M. at the rates shown in the table. How far from home were they when they stopped driving at **11** A.M.? __________

Time	Distance from Home
7 A.M.	0 mi
8 A.M.	40 mi
9 A.M.	90 mi
10 A.M.	150 mi
11 A.M.	

Name ______________________________

Cumulative Review
★ Test Prep

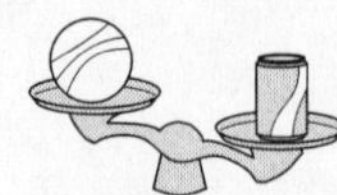 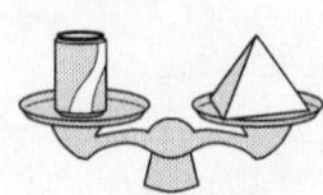 

Which weighs the most?

A 

B

C

D

2 **How many yards is it from the rock to the tree?**

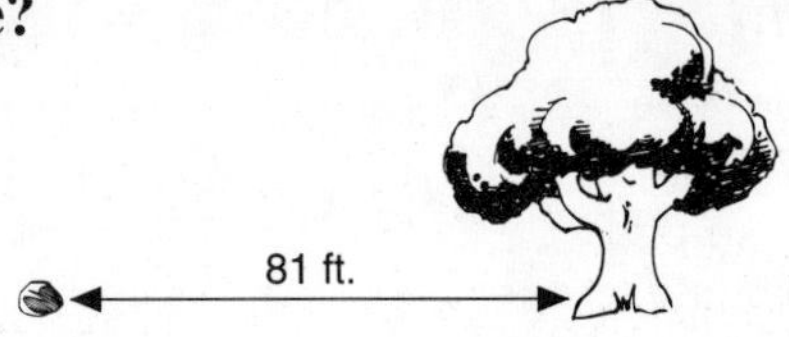

F 972

G 243

H 27

J $6\frac{3}{4}$

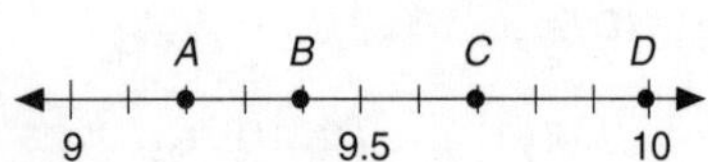

Which point on the number line is closest to $9\frac{15}{100}$?

A *A*

B *B*

C *C*

D *D*

4 **A bag of oranges at a farm stand was on sale for $3.87. *About* how many bags did you buy if you spent about $50.00?**

F 8

G 12

H 16

J 20

5 **Which expression has the greatest value?**

A $(2 \times 3^2) + 4^2$

B $2 \times (3^2 + 4^2)$

C $2 \times (3^2 \times 4^2)$

D $(2 + 3^2) + 4^2$

6 **Nicky skied 0.35 second slower than his sister. If his time was 46.23 seconds, what was her time?**

F 42.73 s

G 45.88 s

H 46.58 s

J 49.73 s

K Not here

7 **A bag of dog food weighs 25 pounds. How much will 15 bags weigh?**

A 40 lb

B 145 lb

C 275 lb

D 350 lb

E Not here

8 **A pizza is cut into 12 slices. Four slices have mushrooms on them. Which number sentence could be used to show the fraction of slices that do not have mushrooms?**

F $\frac{12}{12} - \frac{4}{12} = n$

G $\frac{12}{12} + \frac{4}{12} = n$

H $\frac{12}{12} - \frac{1}{12} = n$

J $\frac{12}{12} + \frac{1}{12} = n$

K $\frac{8}{12} + \frac{4}{12} = n$

UNIT 8 • TABLE OF CONTENTS

Geometry and Measurement

We will be using this vocabulary:

right triangle a triangle with a right, or 90°, angle

area a measure in square units of a region or a surface

perimeter the sum of the measures of the sides of a polygon

surface area the total area of the faces of a space figure

congruent figures figures that have the same size and shape

Dear Family,

During the next few weeks, our math class will be learning about geometry and measurement.

You can expect to see homework that provides practice in finding the areas of rectangles and right triangles. Here is a sample you may want to keep handy to give help if needed.

Areas of Rectangles and of Right Triangles

Area (A) is a measure in square units of a region or a surface.

The area of a rectangle is found by multiplying its length (l) by its width (w).

$$A = l \times w$$
$$A = 6 \times 3 \text{ or } 18 \text{ in.}^2$$

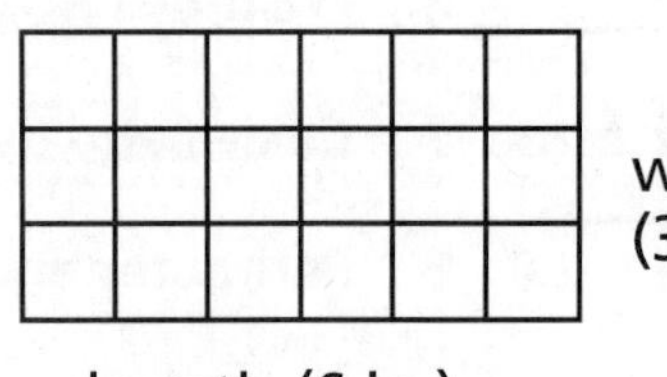
width (3 in.)

length (6 in.)

The area of a right triangle is $\frac{1}{2}$ the area of a rectangle. To find the area of a right triangle, first multiply its base by its height. Then multiply by $\frac{1}{2}$.

$$A = \frac{1}{2}(b \times h)$$

height (3 in.)

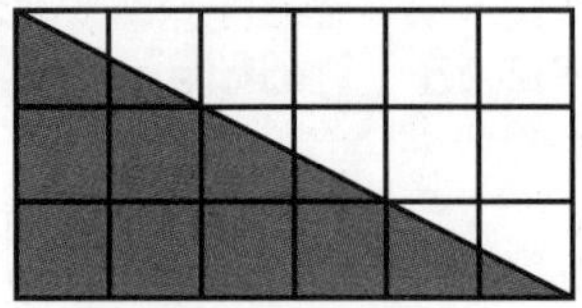

base (6 in.)

$$A = \frac{1}{2}(6 \times 3) \rightarrow \frac{1}{2} \times 18 \text{ or } 9 \text{ in.}^2$$

During this unit, students will need to continue practicing multiplication, addition, and subtraction facts.

Sincerely,

Name ____________________

Points, Lines, Line Segments, and Rays

A **point** is a location in space. • C **Read**: point *C*

A **line** is a set of points in a straight path that extends in two directions without end.

Read: line *CD* or line *DC* **Write**: $\overleftrightarrow{CD}$ or $\overleftrightarrow{DC}$

A **line segment** is part of a line that has two endpoints.

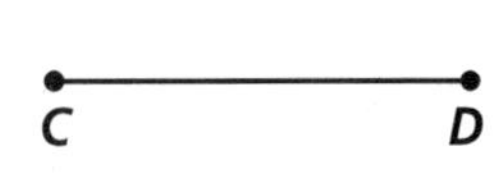

Read: line segment *CD* or line segment DC **Write**: $\overline{CD}$ or $\overline{DC}$

Complete.

1. What is the name of this line? ________
2. Mark point ***L*** between points ***E*** and ***F***. Is $\overleftrightarrow{EF}$ the same as $\overleftrightarrow{LF}$? ____________

Use these two points to complete.

• •

3. Label the two points ***A*** and ***B***.
4. Use your ruler as a straightedge and connect the points.
5. You have drawn a line ________.
6. The endpoints of the figure are _____ and _____. Its name is ________.

Name all the line segments that are a part of each line.

7.

____

8.

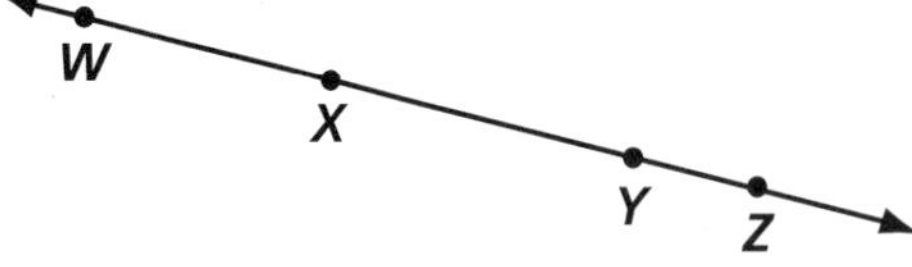

____

STANDARD

A **ray** is a part of a line with only one endpoint. When you name a ray, always write its endpoint first.

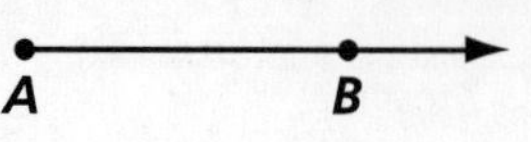

Read: ray ***AB***
Write: $\overrightarrow{AB}$

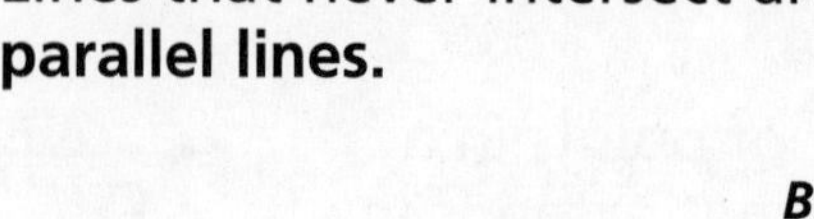

Lines that meet or cross each other are **intersecting lines.**

Read: $\overleftrightarrow{AB}$ intersects $\overleftrightarrow{CD}$

Lines that never intersect are **parallel lines.**

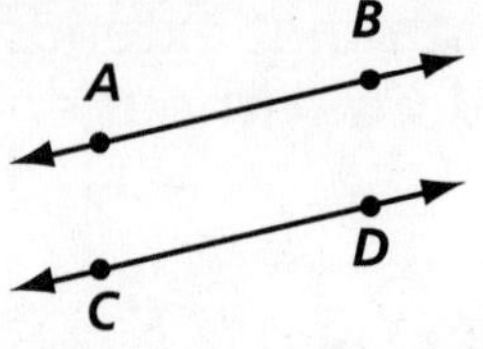

Read: $\overleftrightarrow{AB}$ is parallel to $\overleftrightarrow{CD}$.

Write: $\overleftrightarrow{AB} \parallel \overleftrightarrow{CD}$

Two intersecting lines that form right angles are **perpendicular lines.**

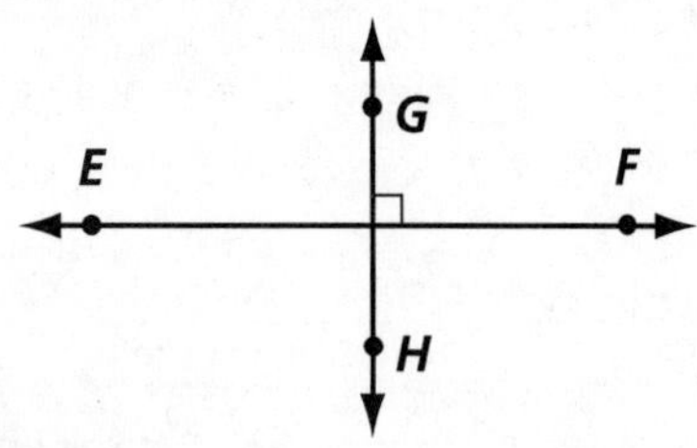

Read: $\overleftrightarrow{EF}$ is perpendicular to $\overleftrightarrow{GH}$.

Write: $\overleftrightarrow{EF} \perp \overleftrightarrow{GH}$

Name each ray.

9.

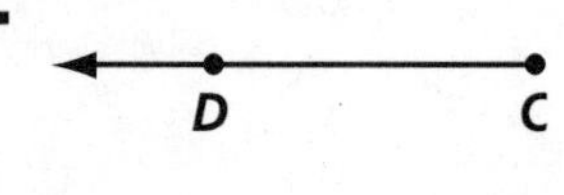

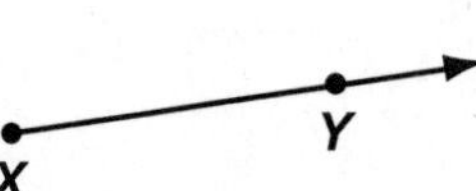

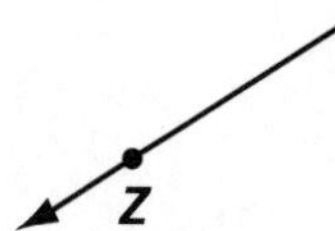

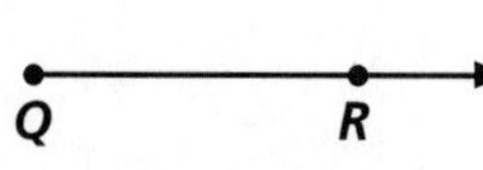

______ ______ ______ ______

Write *intersecting, perpendicular,* or *parallel* to describe each pair of lines.

10.

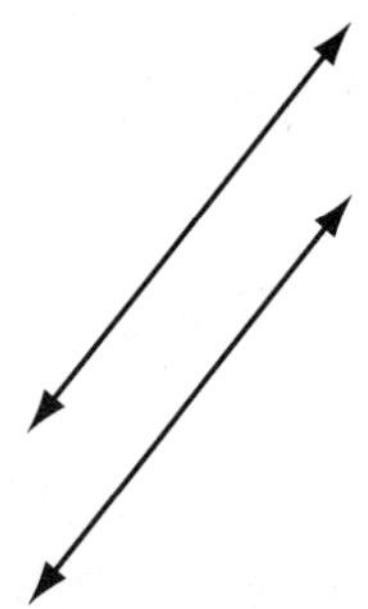

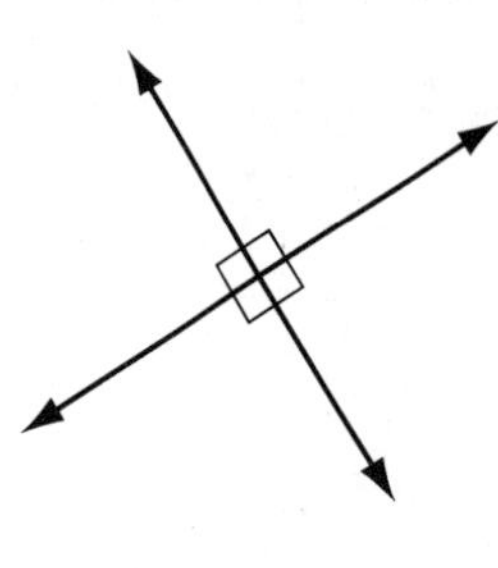

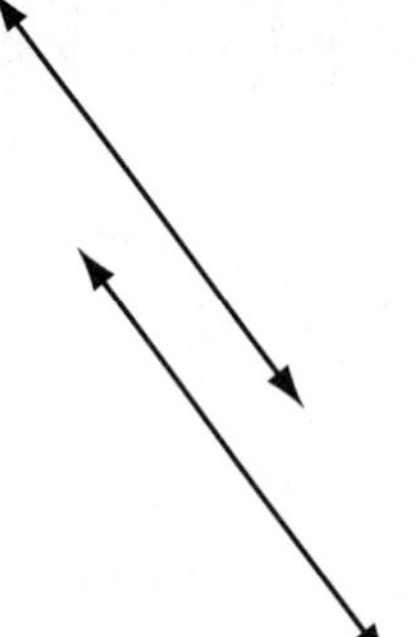

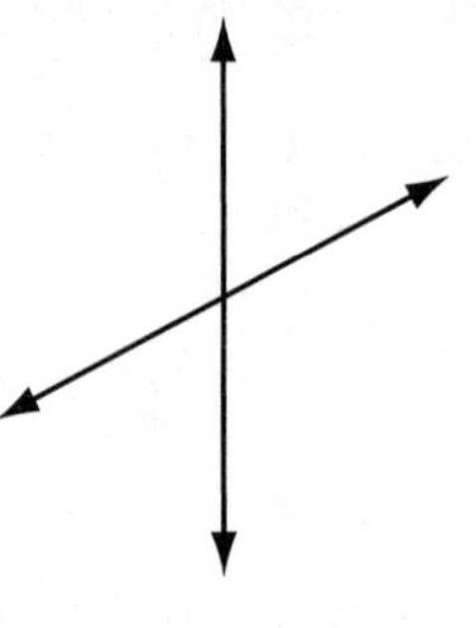

______ ______ ______ ______

Name ____________________

STANDARD

Use a straightedge. Draw and label each figure.

11. line *PQ*

12. point *R*

13. line segment *ST*

14. ray *GH*

15. parallel lines *IJ* and *KL*

16. intersecting lines *MN* and *RS*

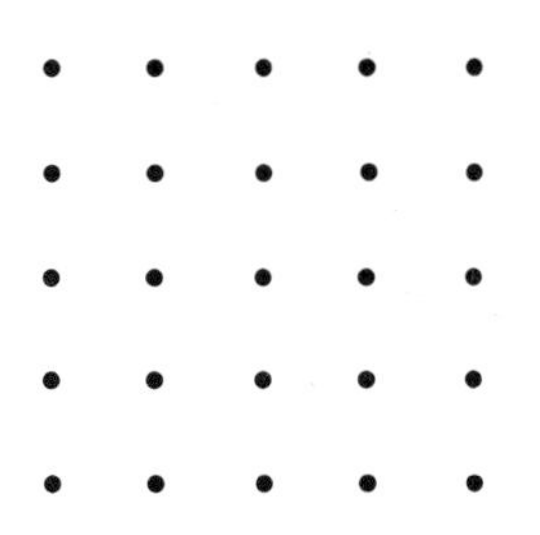

17. perpendicular lines *TU* and *VW*

Problem Solving Reasoning

How many line segments can you draw using the given points as endpoints?

18.

______ line segments

19.

______ line segments

Test Prep ★ Mixed Review

20 **Dana bought a 19.8-pound turkey. What is its weight in ounces?**

A 1.2

B 198

C 316.8

D 633.6

21 **What number is equivalent to $2^3 \times 3^2$?**

F 24

G 36

H 54

J 72

STANDARD

Name ______________________

Naming and Measuring Angles

An **angle** is formed by two rays that share a common endpoint. The common endpoint is called the **vertex.**

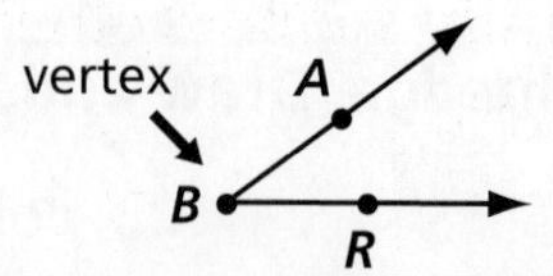

You name an angle using a point on each side and the vertex.

The name of the vertex is always in the *middle.* You can also name an angle by its vertex.

Read: angle ***ABR***, angle ***RBA***, or angle ***B***
Write: $\angle ABR$, $\angle RBA$, or $\angle B$

You can use a **protractor** to measure an angle in **degrees.**

1. Place the center mark of the protractor on the vertex, ***D***.
2. Align the **0°** mark of the scale of the protractor with $\overrightarrow{DF}$ of the angle.
3. To read the measure of the angle, find the place where $\overrightarrow{DE}$ passes through the scale on the protractor. Read the inner scale if the angle opening is on the right. Read the outer scale if the angle opening is on the left.

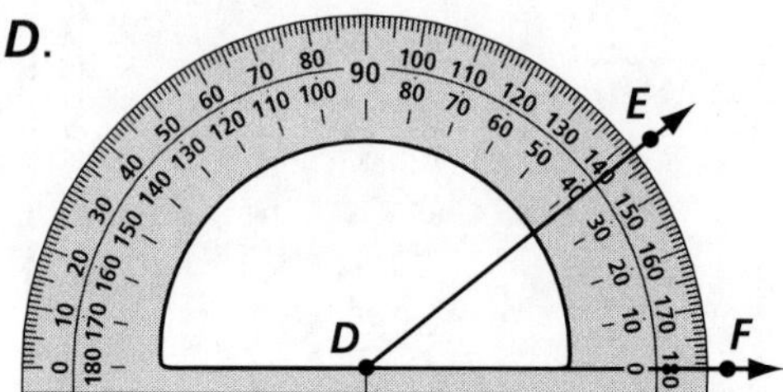

Read: $\angle DEF$ measures 38°.

Name each angle in three ways.

1.

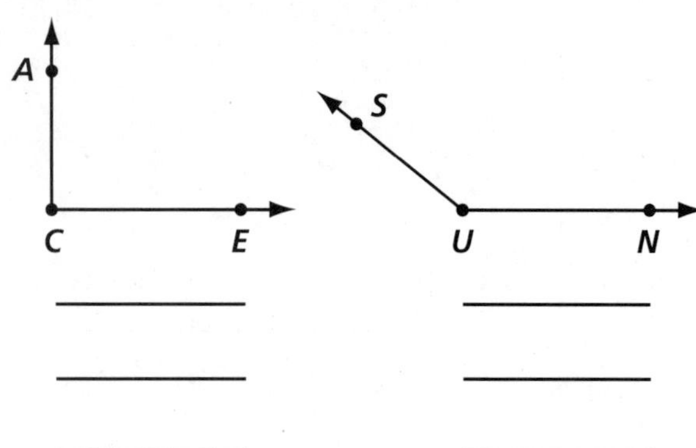

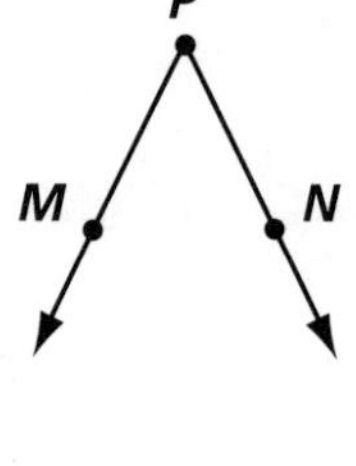

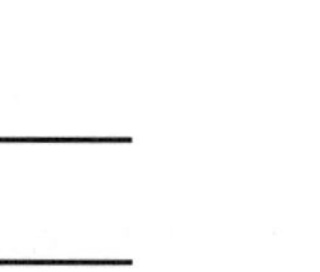

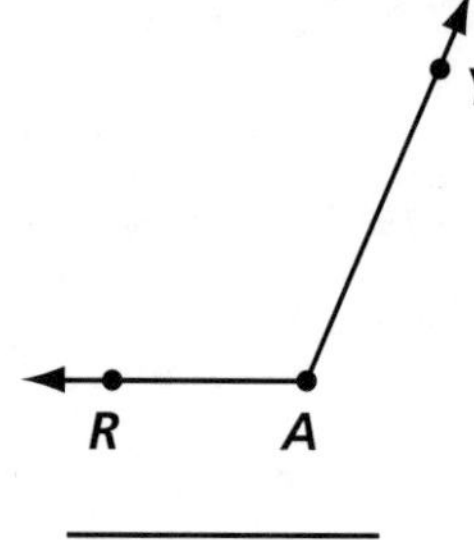

Measure each angle.

2.

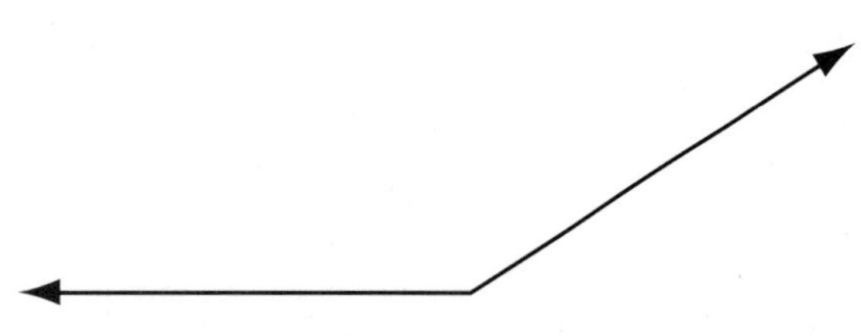

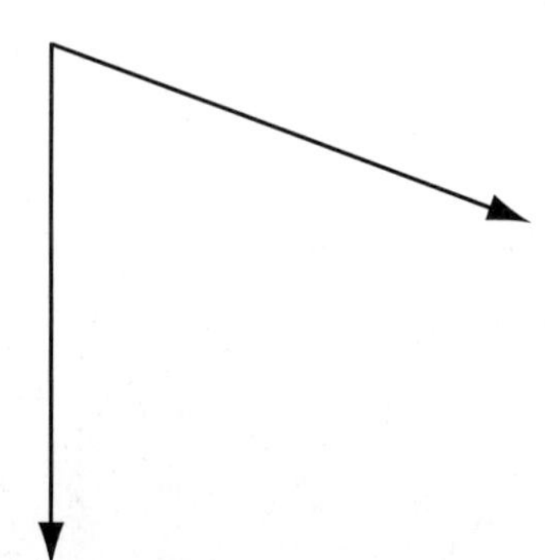

Name ______________________________

STANDARD

You can classify angles by their measures.

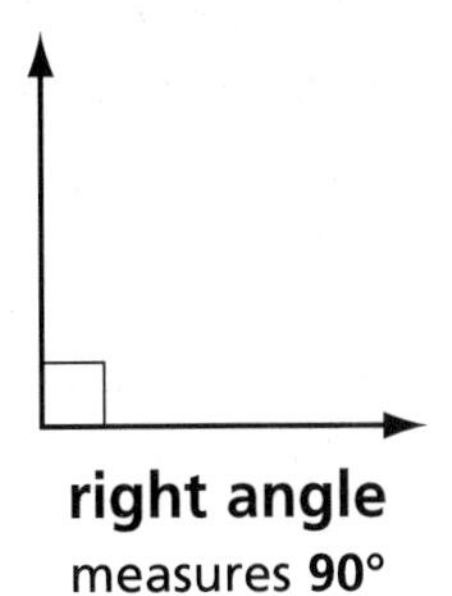

right angle
measures **90°**

acute angle
measures less than **90°**

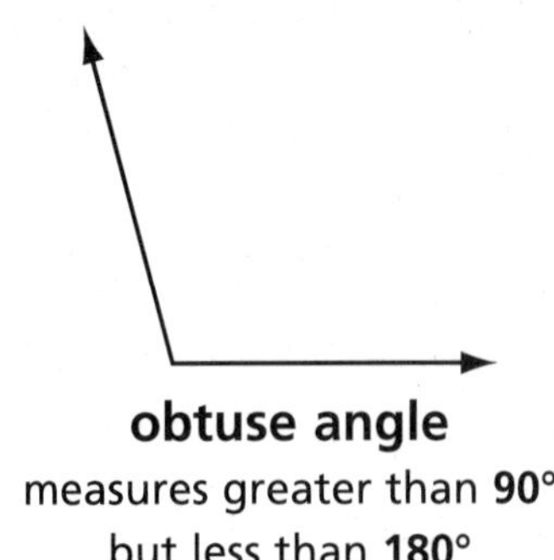

obtuse angle
measures greater than **90°** but less than **180°**

Classify each angle as *right, acute,* or *obtuse.* Then measure each angle with a protractor to check.

3.

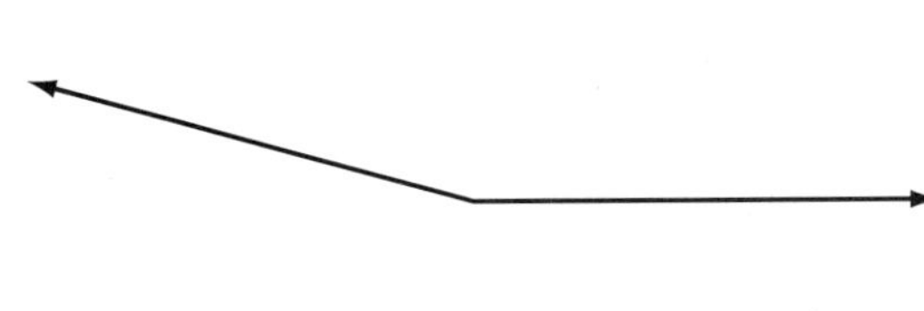

______________ ______________

4.

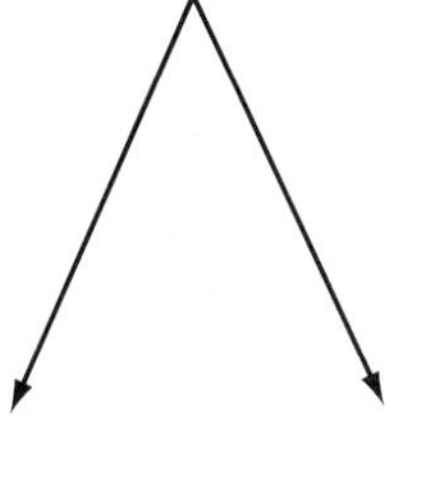

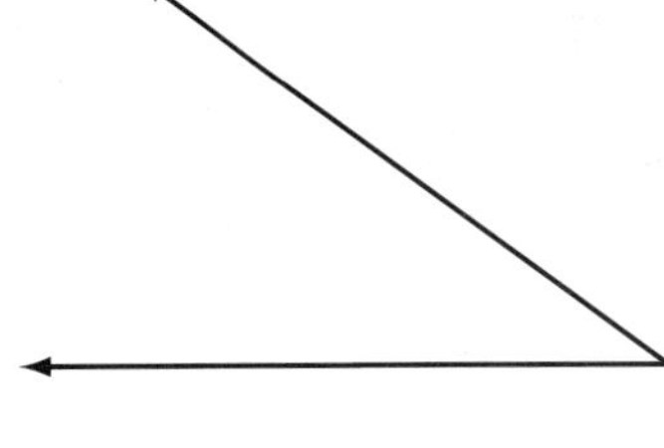

______________ ______________

5.

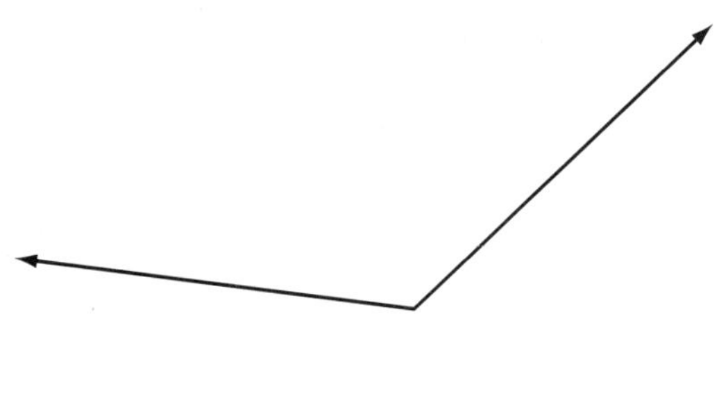

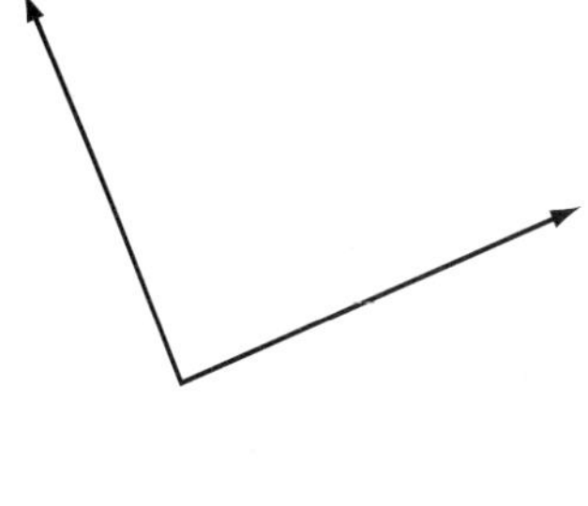

______________ ______________

STANDARD

You can use a protractor to draw an angle:

1. Draw a ray and label it.
2. Place the center mark of the protractor on the endpoint, or vertex. Align the **0°** mark with the ray.
3. Find **75°** on the scale. Mark a point.
4. Draw a ray from the vertex through the point you marked.

Draw ∠***XYZ*** that measures **75°**.

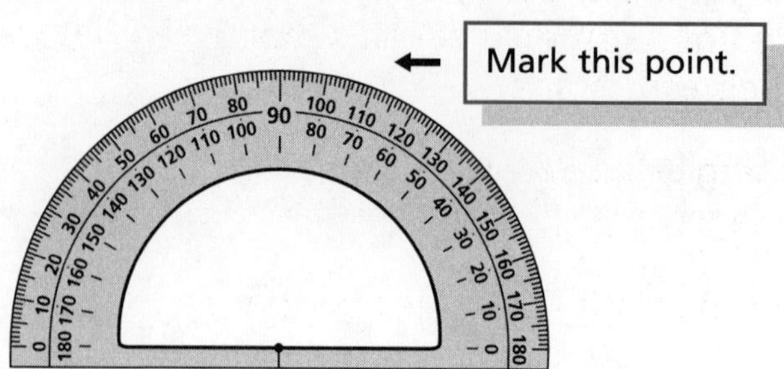

Draw an angle with each measure. Classify the angle as right, acute, or obtuse.

6. 40° ____________

7. 90° ____________

Problem Solving
Reasoning

Solve.

8. Draw a kite having four straight sides. Measure each angle in your drawing. Classify each angle as right, acute, or obtuse.

Test Prep ★ Mixed Review

9 A clerk has $10\frac{1}{2}$ pounds of grapes. How many $\frac{1}{2}$-pound bags of grapes can she make?

A 21

B 11

C 10

D $5\frac{1}{4}$

10 A can of stew contains about $3\frac{1}{2}$ servings. If a serving is $6\frac{1}{4}$ ounces, about how many ounces of stew are in a can?

F 40

G 22

H 10

J 3

Name ______________________

Triangles

STANDARD

A **polygon** is a closed figure made up of three or more line segments called **sides.** The sides meet only at their end points.

A **triangle** is a polygon made up of three line segments.

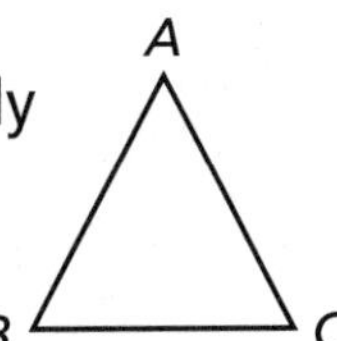

Read: triangle *ABC*
Write: △ *ABC*

You can classify triangles by the lengths of their sides.

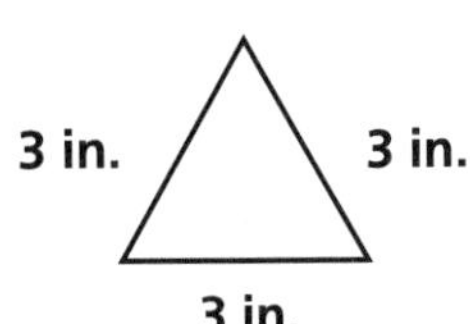

equilateral triangle
all sides of the same length

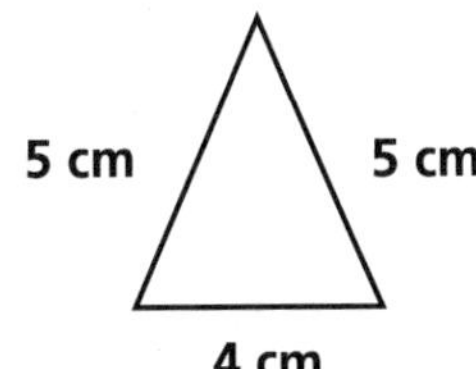

isosceles triangle
at least two sides of the same length

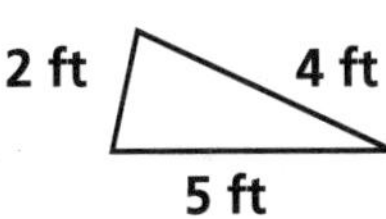

scalene triangle
no sides of the same length

You can also classify triangles by their angle measures.

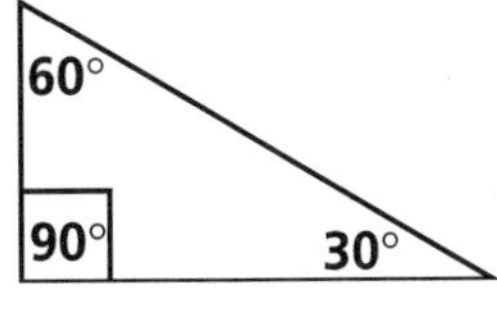

right triangle
one right angle

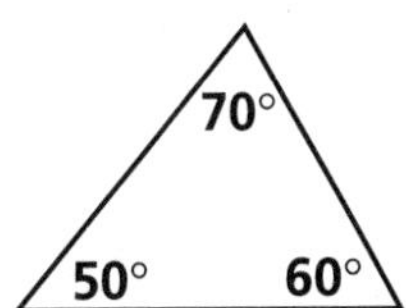

acute triangle
all acute angles

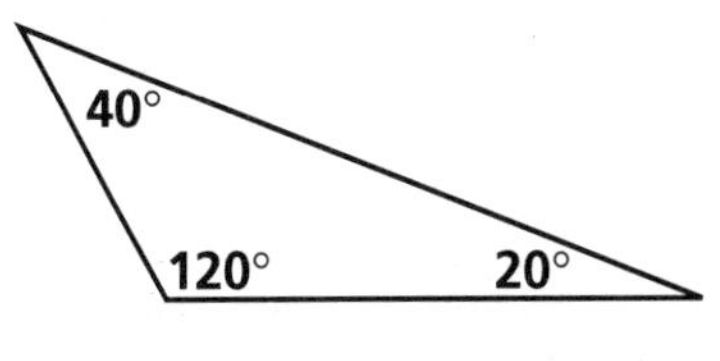

obtuse triangle
one obtuse angle

Classify each triangle as equilateral, isosceles, or scalene. Then classify each as right, acute, or obtuse.

1. 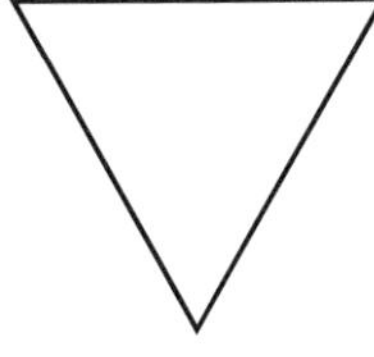 ______ 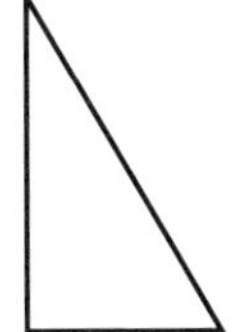 ______ 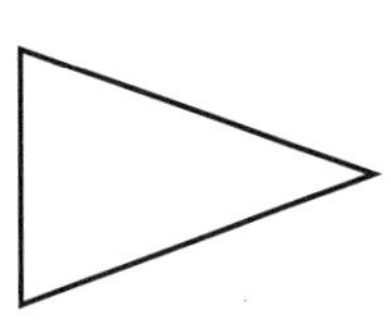 ______ 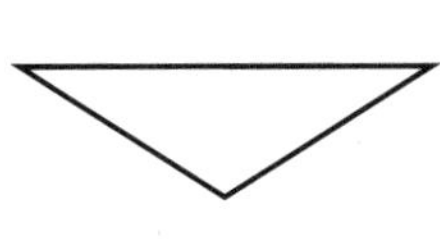 ______

Use the information above about classifying triangles.

2. What is the sum of the measures of the angles of each triangle? right ______ acute ______ obtuse ______

3. What is the sum of the measures of the angles of any triangle? ______

STANDARD

Find the measure of each angle labeled with a question mark.

4.

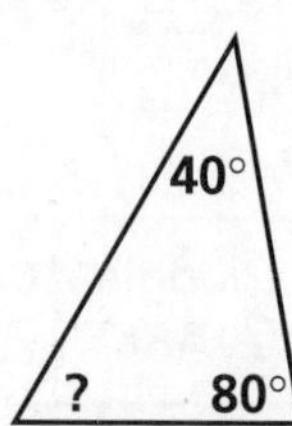

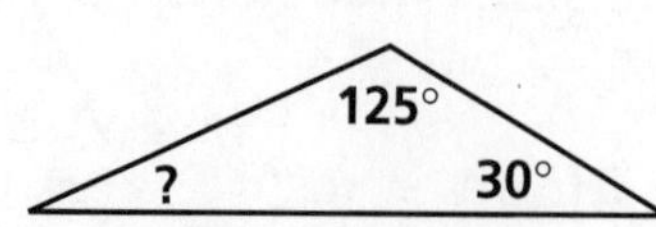

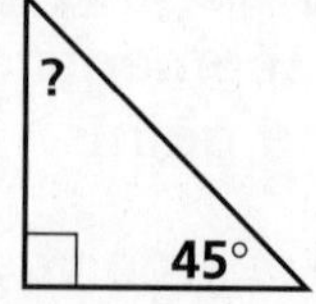

______ ______ ______

Solve.

5. Cut out a triangle. Then, tear off the three angles of the triangle as shown in the picture. Tape them side by side at one vertex.

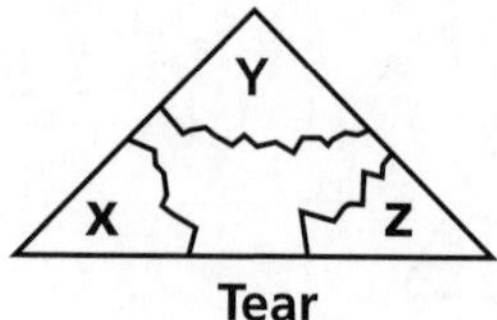

a. What do you observe?

______

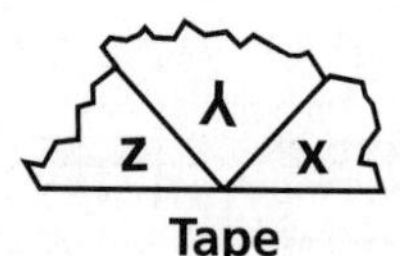

b. Another name for the figure you formed with the angles of a triangle is a **straight angle.** What is the measure of a straight angle? ______

Quick Check

Draw and label each figure on a separate piece of paper.

Work Space

6. ray ***PR*** intersecting ray ***ST*** at point ***V***

7. line segment ***BD*** perpendicular to line ***XY***

8. 25° angle **9.** **110°** angle

10. Classify the angles in exercise 8 and 9 as acute, obtuse or right. ______

Complete.

11. What are the measures of the acute angles in an isosceles right triangle? ______

12. Two angles of a triangle are **15°** and **40°**. What is the measure of the third angle? What kind of triangle has these angle measures? ______

Name ____________________

Congruent figures are figures that have the same size and shape.

These two triangles are congruent.
If you trace figure *A* and put it on top of figure *B*, they will match.

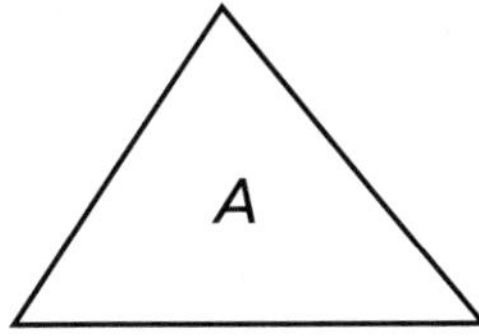

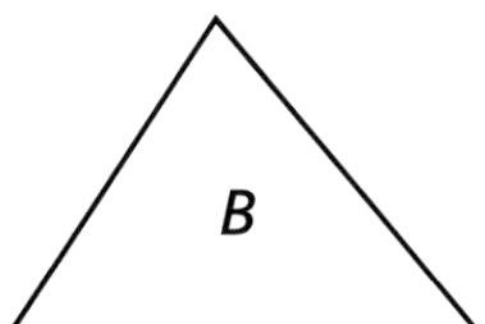

These two squares are not congruent.
They are not the same size.

Sometimes a figure has sides or angles that are congruent to each other.

An equilateral triangle has three congruent sides and three congruent angles. The marks indicate congruent sides and congruent angles.

You measure the angles with a protractor to tell if they are congruent. They are congruent if their measures are equal.

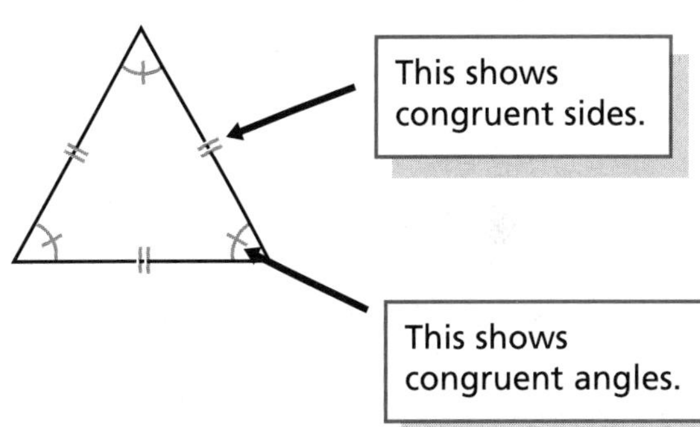

Match each pair of congruent figures.

1.

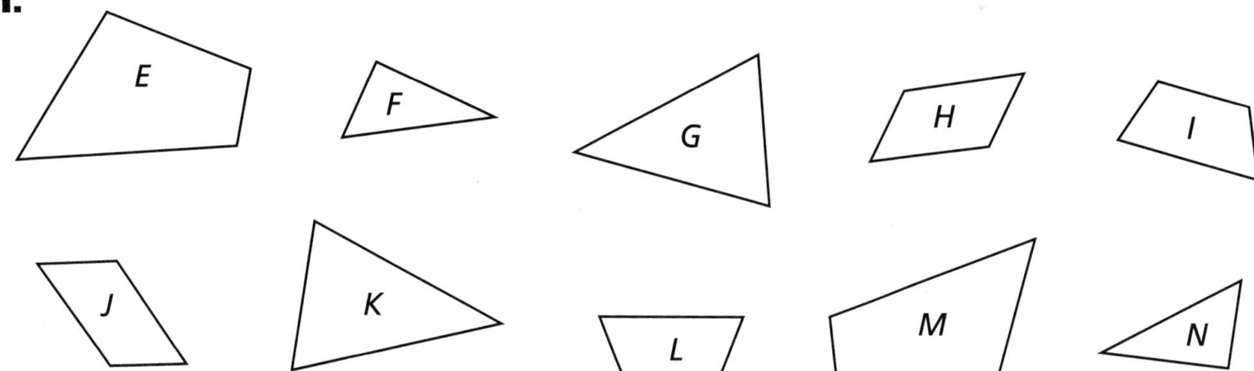

Mark the sides and angles that appear to be congruent. Use a protractor to measure angles.

2.

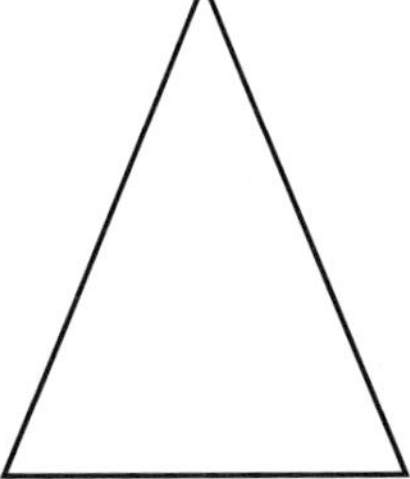

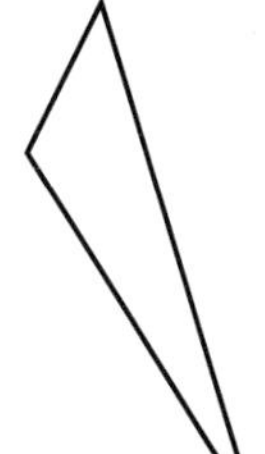

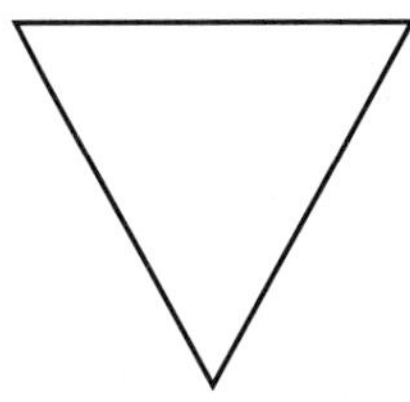

STANDARD

Name the angles and the sides that are congruent in each figure.

	Figure	Any Congruent Sides? Name them.	Any Congruent Angles? Name them.
3.	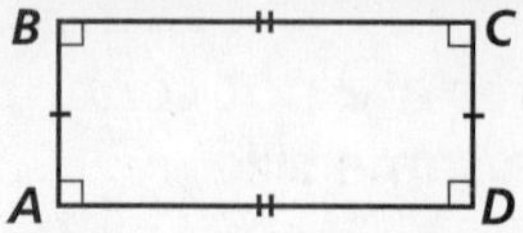 B C A D		
4.	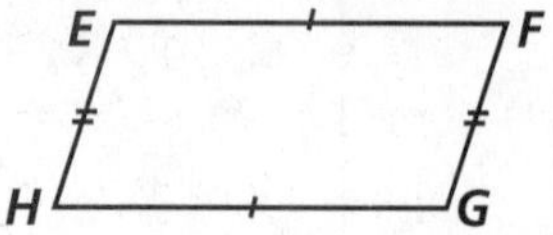 E F H G		
5.	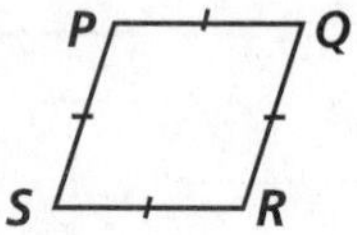 P Q S R		
6.	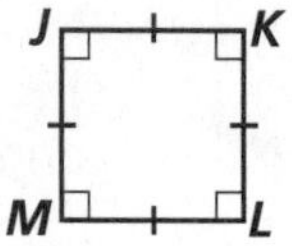 J K M L		
7.	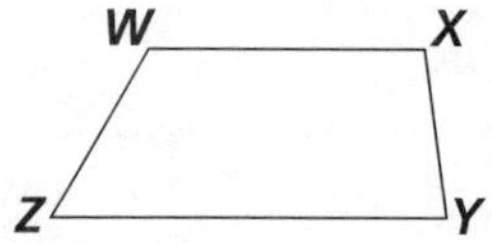 W X Z Y		

Problem Solving Reasoning Use the figures in the table above to solve.

8. Look at the polygon in exercise 3. If the length of $\overline{AB}$ is 4 in. and the length of $\overline{BC}$ is 7 in., what is the total distance around polygon *ABCD*? ______________

9. Look at the polygon in exercise 5. If the length of $\overline{PQ}$ is 6 cm, what is the total distance around polygon *PQRS*? ______________

Test Prep ★ Mixed Review

10 Which two numbers have a difference of about 2,800?

A 821 and 3,036

B 3,036 and 7,385

C 3,036 and 248

D 7,385 and 9,162

11 A carpenter nailed two boards together. One board was $\frac{3}{4}$ in. thick and the other was $\frac{1}{8}$ in. thick. What is the total thickness of the boards?

F $\frac{7}{8}$ in.

H $\frac{4}{12}$ in.

G $\frac{7}{32}$ in.

J $\frac{5}{8}$ in.

Name ______________________________

Quadrilaterals and Other Polygons

STANDARD

A quadrilateral is a four-sided polygon.

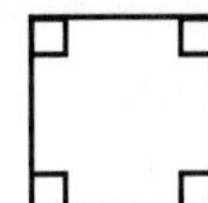

square
four congruent sides
four right angles

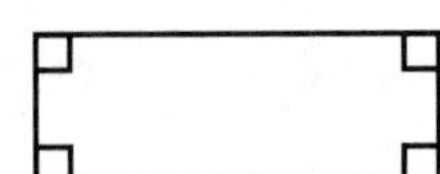

rectangle
opposite sides congruent
four right angles

parallelogram
opposite sides congruent
opposite sides parallel

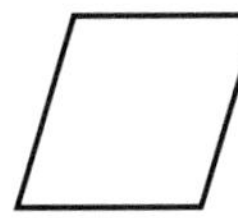

rhombus
four congruent sides
opposite sides parallel

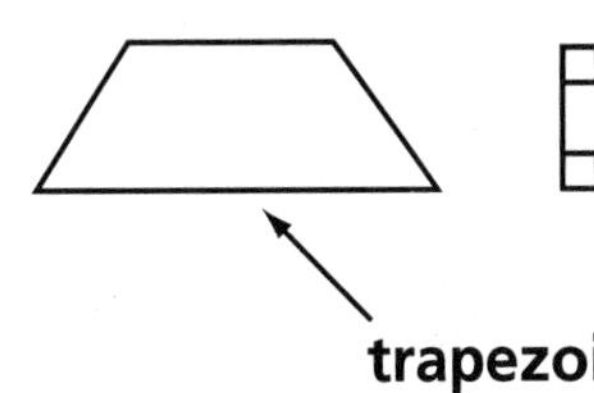

trapezoid
only one pair of
parallel sides

Write the name that best describes each quadritaleral.

1.

____

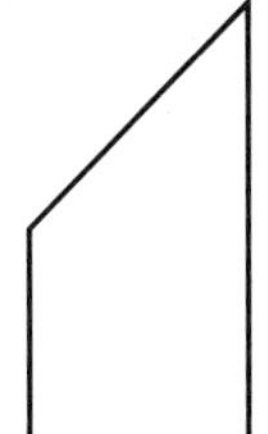

____

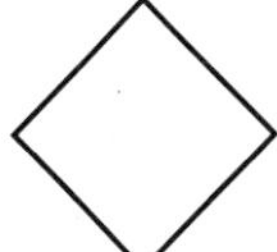

____

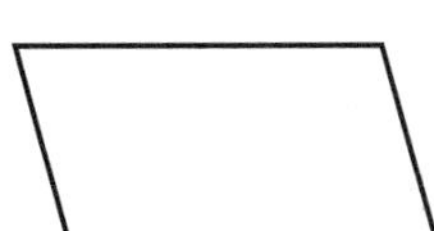

____

Use a straightedge. Draw each quadrilateral. Tell what kind of figure you have drawn.

2. A rectangle that is a rhombus

____

3. A quadrilateral with opposite sides parallel and congruent

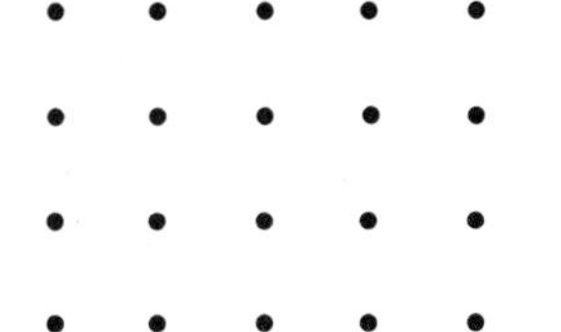

____

4. A quadrilateral with all sides congruent but not all angles congruent

____

STANDARD

Complete the chart.

5.

	Triangle	Quadrilateral	Pentagon	Hexagon	Heptagon	Octagon
Sides	3	4				
Vertices	3					
Angles	3					

Write *true* or *false*.

6. All squares are rectangles. ____________

7. It is possible to have a polygon with fewer sides than a triangle. ____________

Name as many triangles, rectangles, and trapezoids as you can find in the figure at the right.

8. triangles ____________

____

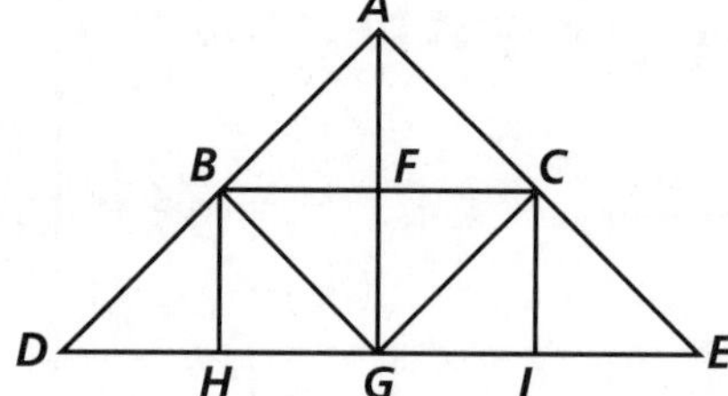

9. rectangles ____________

____

10. trapezoids ____________

____

Problem Solving Reasoning Use a straightedge. Solve.

11. Draw a quadrilateral. Divide it into two triangles. Use the figure to find the sum of the measures of the angles of the quadrilateral.

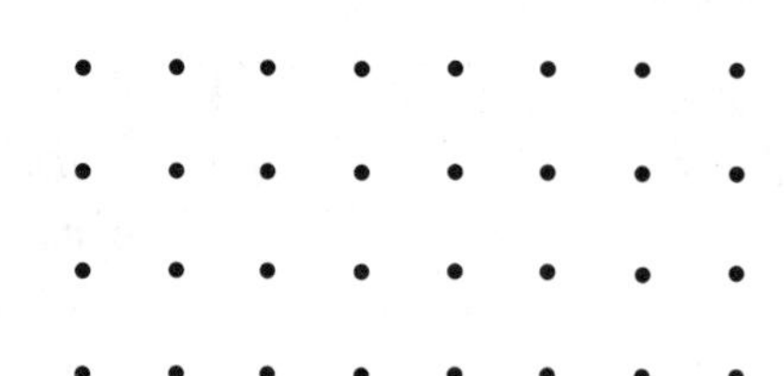

____

Test Prep ★ Mixed Review

12 Which expression could you use to find the value in cents of d dimes?

A $d \div 10$

B $10 + d$

C $d - 10$

D $10 \times d$

13 Selma spent \$.99 for 2 pencils and an eraser. Each pencil cost \$.27. How much more than the pencil was the eraser?

F \$2.25

G \$.45

H \$.18

J \$.09

Name ______________________________

Problem Solving Strategy: Find a Pattern

STANDARD

Sometimes finding a pattern in a diagram or table helps you solve a problem.

Problem

Mr. Higgins arranges 3 pennies in the form of a triangle with 2 pennies in the bottom row and 1 on top. How many pennies will he need to make a triangle with 6 rows?

1 Understand

As you reread, ask yourself questions.

- What do you know about the pennies that Mr. Higgins has?

Mr. Higgins has 3 pennies.
They are arranged in a triangle with 2 rows.

What do you need to find?

____

2 Decide

Choose a method for solving.

- Try the strategy Find a Pattern.

First, draw a diagram of the 3 pennies.

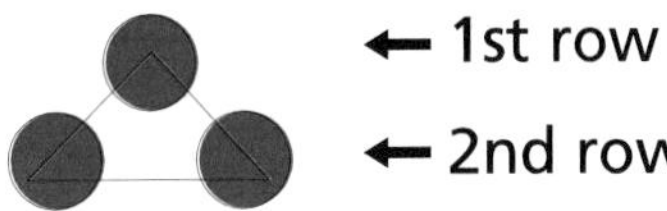

3 Solve

Make a table to find the pattern.

Rows	2	3	4	5	6
Pennies	3				

4 Look back

Describe the pattern. Draw a diagram if you wish.

____

____

____

____

____

STANDARD

Use the Find a Pattern strategy or any other strategy you have learned.

1. A diagonal of a polygon connects **2** opposite vertices. In a quadrilateral, a diagonal forms **2** triangles. How many triangles are formed by the diagonals from **1** vertex in a hexagon?

Think: Can you connect vertices next to one another and form a triangle?

____

Answer: _______________

2. A triangle has no diagonals. A quadrilateral has **2** diagonals. A pentagon has **5** diagonals. How many diagonals does a hexagon have?

Think: If you set up a table to solve the problem, what would the first entries be?

____

Answer: _______________

3. Look at this pattern.
angleangleangle
What letter will be in the thirty-eighth position?

____

4. The first **4** square numbers are **1**, **4**, **9**, and **16**. What are the next four square numbers?

____

5. Erin made this list of numbers.
2, 3, 5, 7, 11, 13, 17.
Jamal added the next three numbers to the list. What numbers did Jamal add to the list?

____

6. On Sunday Andrew spent **$48**. On Monday he spent **$24**. On Tuesday he spent **$12**. If he continues the pattern, how much will he spend on Saturday?

____

7. A bell rings in the Allen Middle School to signify the end of the class. The first three bells ring at **8:20**, **9:05**, and **9:50**. What time is the next bell?

____

8. Caitlin practices the piano for **30** minutes every day after school and for **45** minutes on both Saturday and Sunday. How long does she practice each week?

____

Name ______________________________

STANDARD

A **circle** is the set of all points that are the same distance from a given point called the **center.** The center of the circle at the right is point ***O.***

A **radius** is a line segment joining any point on the circle with its center. $\overline{OT}$ is one radius in this circle.

A **chord** is a line segment joining any two points on a circle. $\overline{SV}$ is a chord in this circle.

A **diameter** is a chord that passes through the center of a circle. $\overline{TU}$ is a diameter of this circle.

A **central angle** is an angle formed by two radii. ∠***ROU*** is a central angle.

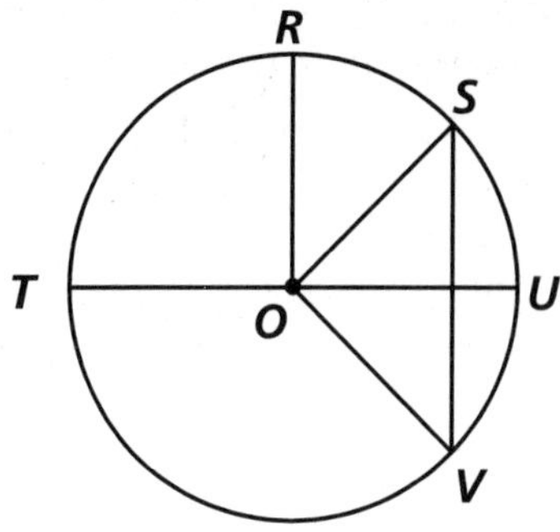

There are 360° in a circle. Use this information to write the measure of each central angle.

1. ∠*ABC* ______ ∠*ABD* ______

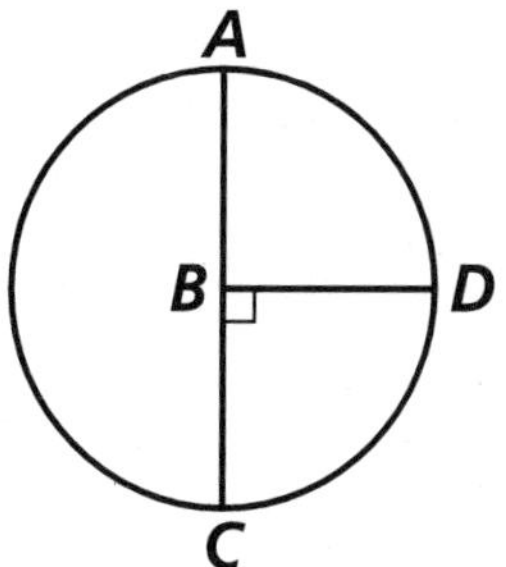

Use a compass.

2. Draw a circle.

a. Draw a point for the center of the circle. Place the compass point on the center of the circle.

b. Set the compass for a radius of **1** inch.

c. Turn the compass completely around.

d. Draw and label these parts of the circle:

center ***P***
radius $\overline{AP}$
chord $\overline{BC}$
diameter $\overline{CD}$ through the center ***P***
central angle ***EPF***

STANDARD

When a figure can be folded along a line, so that one half matches the other half, the figure has **line symmetry.**

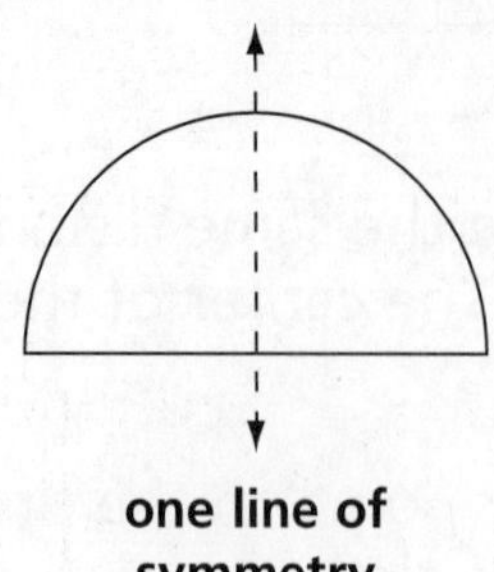

one line of symmetry

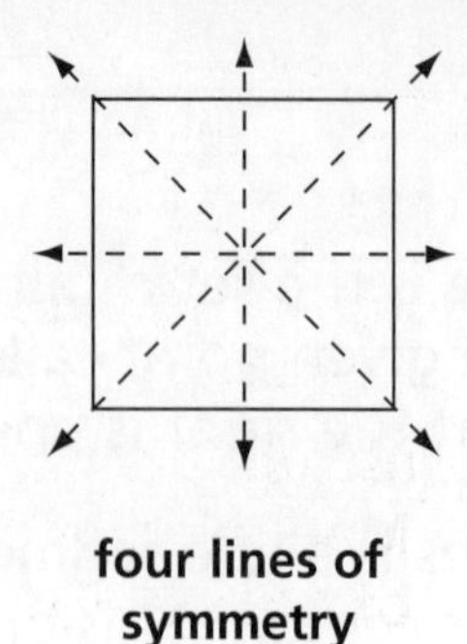

four lines of symmetry

Does each figure have line symmetry? Write *Yes* or *No.* If it does, draw all the lines of symmetry.

3.

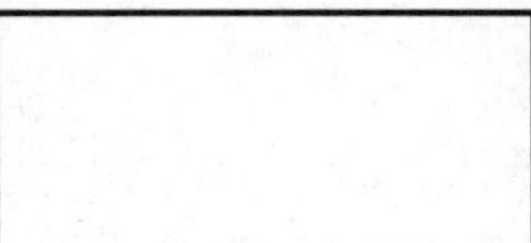

____

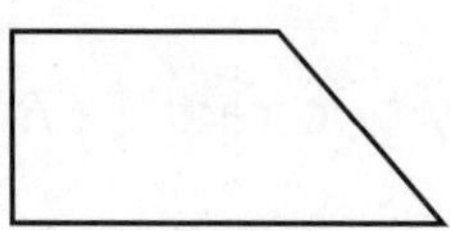

____

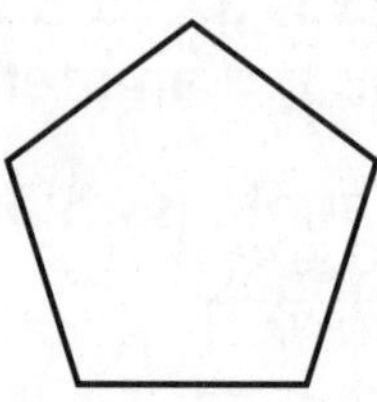

____

Some figures have **rotational symmetry.** This means that you can turn a figure
a quarter turn (or **90°**),
a half turn (or **180°**), or
a three-quarter turn (or **270°**),
and it will match the way it looked before the turn.

Figure *A* will match itself after a half turn, or **180°** turn.

- Try it. Trace Figure *A*. Align the point on the figure with the center point of the circle above.
- With one hand, hold the figure at the center point. With the other hand, slowly turn the figure **180°** to verify that it matches the original image.

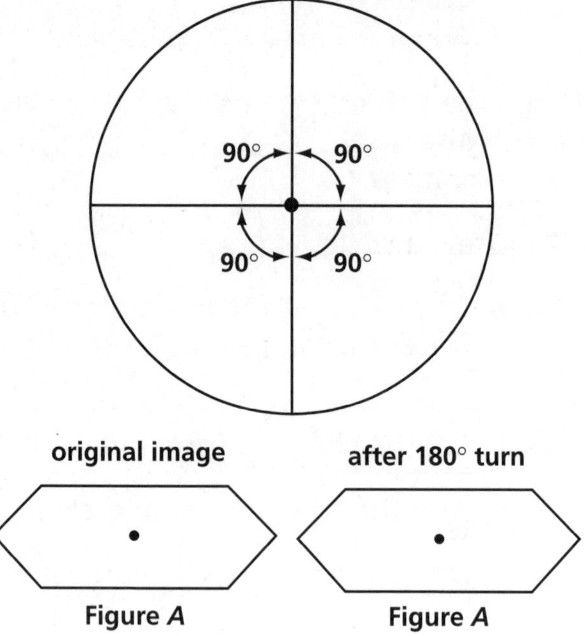

Trace the figure. Turn it. Write *Yes* or *No* to tell if it has rotational symmetry. If it does, tell how many degrees it was turned.

4.

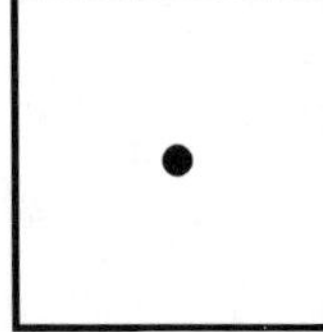

____

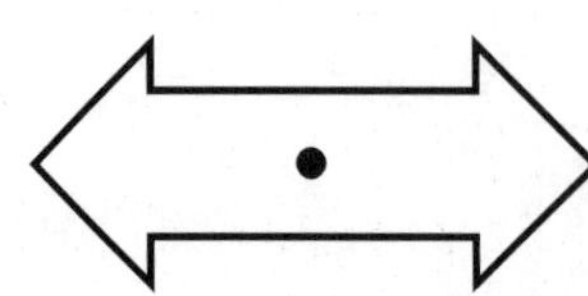

____

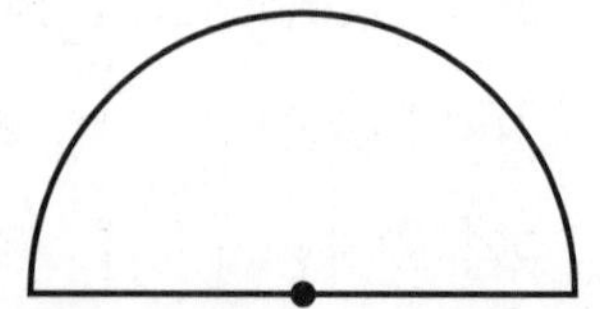

____

Name ______________________

STANDARD

Use a compass to construct figures inside circles.

5. Construct a square inside a circle.
a. Mark a point for the center of a circle. Use the compass to draw a circle.

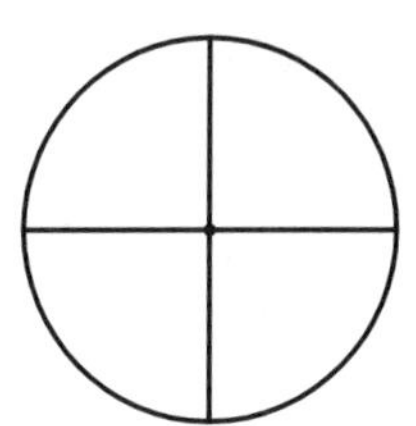

b. Draw a diameter. Use a protractor to draw a second diameter perpendicular to the first.

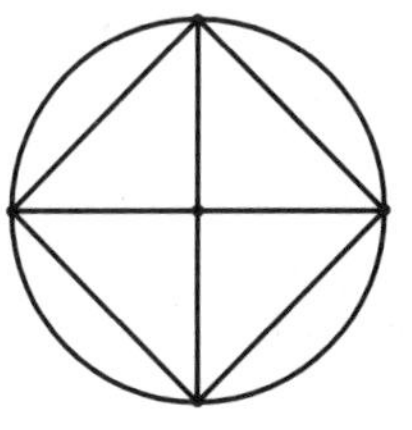

c. Draw chords that connect the endpoints of the diameters to make a square.

6. Construct an equilateral triangle.
a. Draw a circle with a radius of 2 cm.
b. Use the same compass setting. Make 6 marks as shown. Connect the 6 marks with chords.

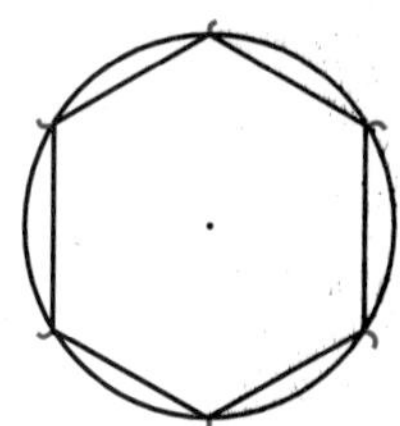

c. Use the hexagon to make an equilateral triangle. Choose any vertex of the hexagon. Connect every second vertex.

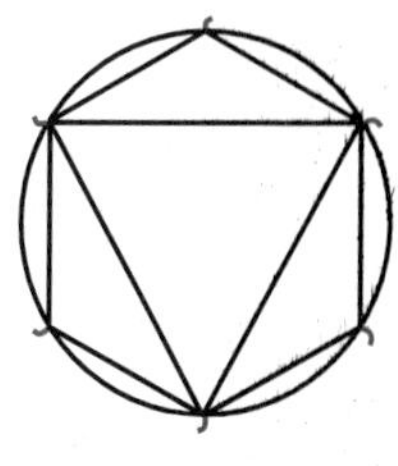

Quick Check

Name the angles and the sides that are congruent in each figure.

7.

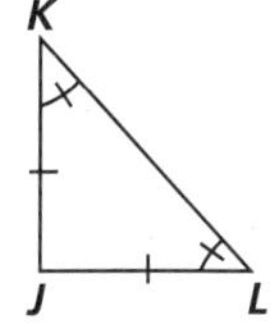

____

____

8.

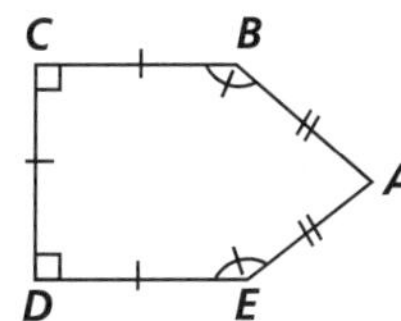

____

____

9.

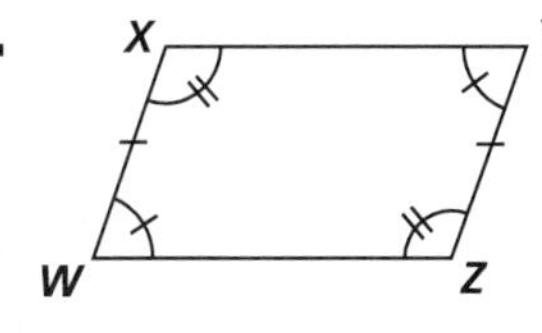

____

____

Complete.

10. Name the quadrilateral in exercise 9. ______________

11. Name the polygon in exercise 8. ______________

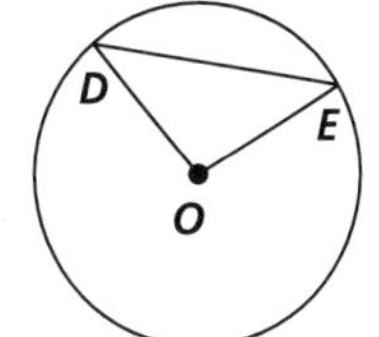

12. Which segments in circle *O* are congruent?

Explain. ______________________

13. Name a central angle in the circle. ______________

14. Which segment is a chord? ______________

15. Does triangle *DOE* have a line of symmetry? Explain.

____

Work Space

Name ______________________

Perimeter and Area

The **perimeter** of a figure is the distance around it. The perimeter is measured in *linear units.*

The **area** of a figure is the amount of surface it covers. The area is measured in *square units.*

Formulas for Rectangle and Square

$P = 2(l + w)$ ← rectangle
$P = 4s$ ← square

$A = l \times w$ ← rectangle
$A = s^2$ ← square

This figure is made up of more than one geometric shape.

To find the perimeter of the figure, add the lengths of all its sides.

To find its area:
- Divide the figure into rectangles.
- Find any missing lengths.
- Find the area of each rectangle.
- Find the sum of the areas.

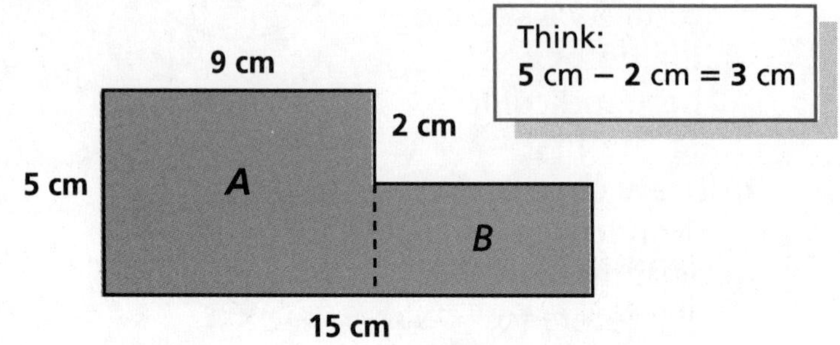

Perimeter

9 + 2 + 6 + 3 + 15 + 5 = 40 cm

Area of rectangle *A*

$9 \times 5 = 45$ cm^2

Area of rectangle *B*

$6 \times 3 = 18$ cm^2

Total Area → $45 + 18 = 63$ cm^2

Find the perimeter and area of each figure.

1.

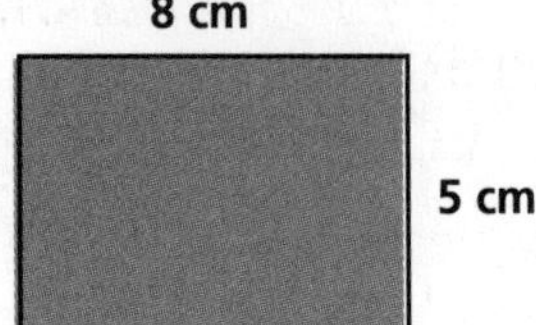

P = ______ *A* = ______

2.

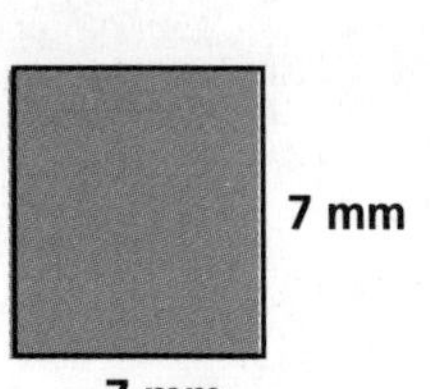

P = ______ *A* = ______

3.

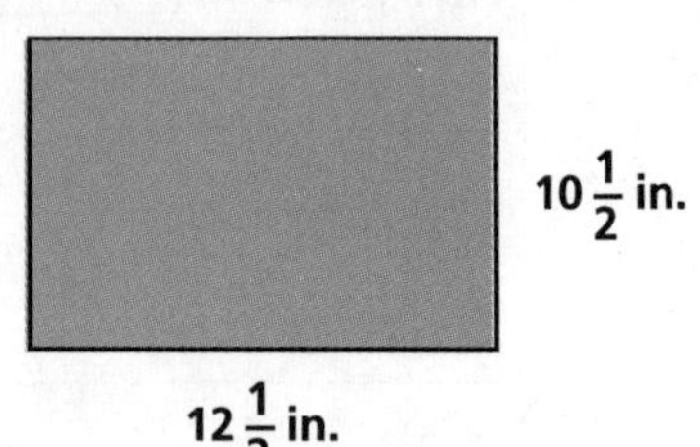

P = ______ *A* = ______

4.

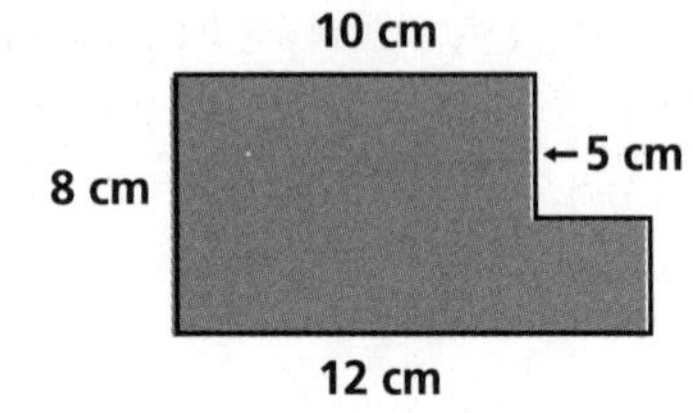

P = ______ *A* = ______

5.

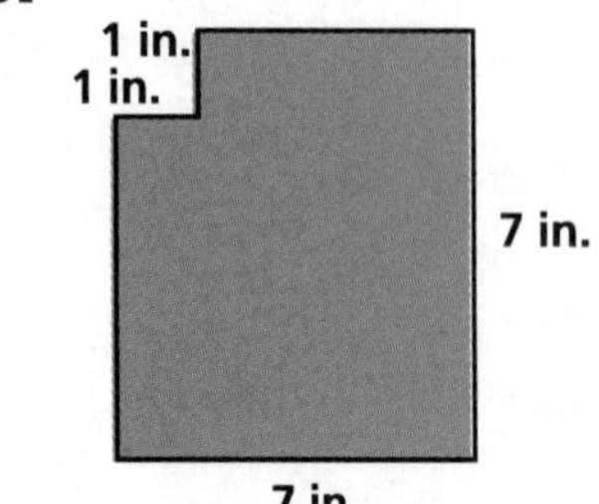

P = ______ *A* = ______

6.

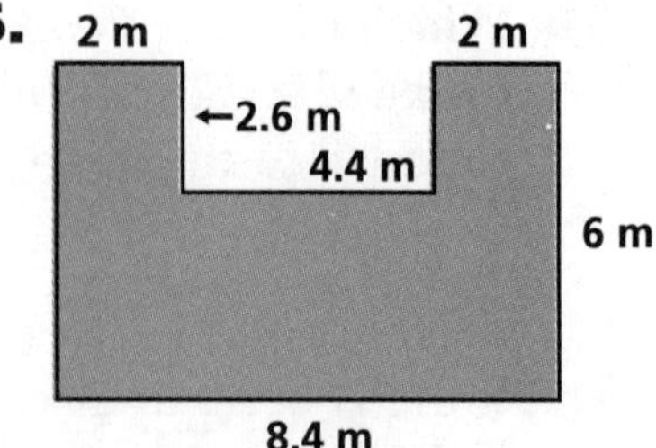

P = ______ *A* = ______

Name ______________________

STANDARD

Find the perimeter and area of each figure.

7.

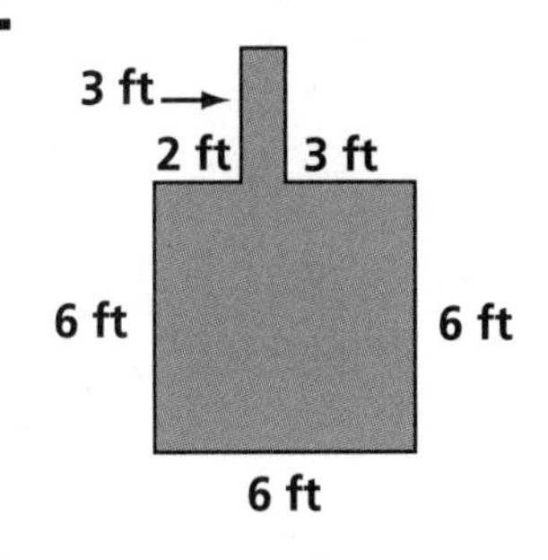

$P =$ ______ $A =$ ______

8.

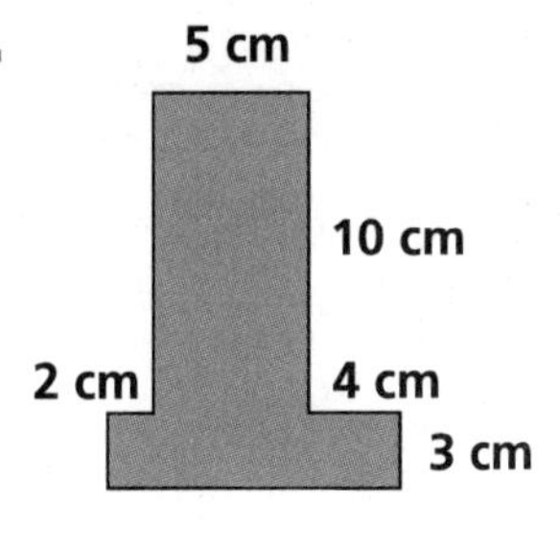

$P =$ ______ $A =$ ______

9.

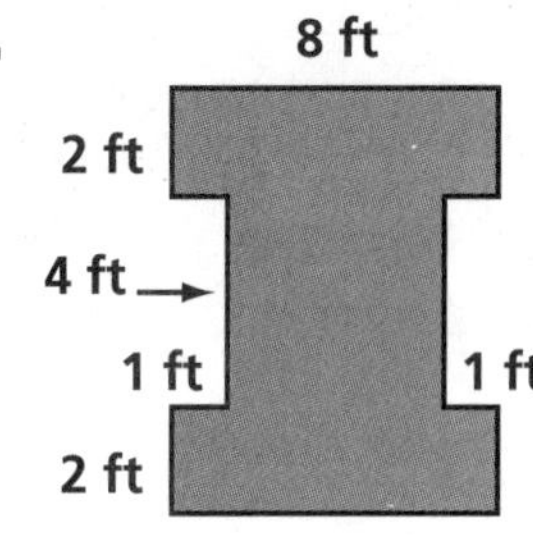

$P =$ ______ $A =$ ______

Find the rectangle with the greater perimeter. Write *a* or *b*.

10. a. length, **23** cm; width, **12** cm
b. length, **29** cm; width, **5** cm

______

11. a. length, **8** in.; width, **16** in.
b. length, **10** in.; width, **15** in.

______

Problem Solving Reasoning Solve.

12. Give the length and width in whole inches of three different rectangles that each have an area of **48 in.^{2}**.

______

______

______

13. Melissa has **60** ft. of fencing for a garden. She wants a rectangular garden with the greatest possible area for planting. What is the length, width, and area of the garden she should make? (Use only whole units for the length and width.)

______

Test Prep ★ Mixed Review

14 Which of these numbers is 7.5 when rounded to the nearest tenth and 7 when rounded to the nearest whole number?

A 7.499

B 7.39

C 7.2

D 7.009

15 A student's test grades were 86, 79, 83, and 72. What grade does she need to get on the fifth test so that her average is 83?

F 80

G 86

H 90

J 95

Name ______________________

Area of a Triangle and a Parallelogram

STANDARD

You can use what you know about the area of a rectangle to find the area of a triangle.

The length of the rectangle below and the **base** of the triangle below are the same.
The width of the rectangle and the **height** of the triangle are the same.

The triangle covers half the area that the rectangle covers.

So the area of a triangle is $\frac{1}{2}$ of the area of the rectangle.

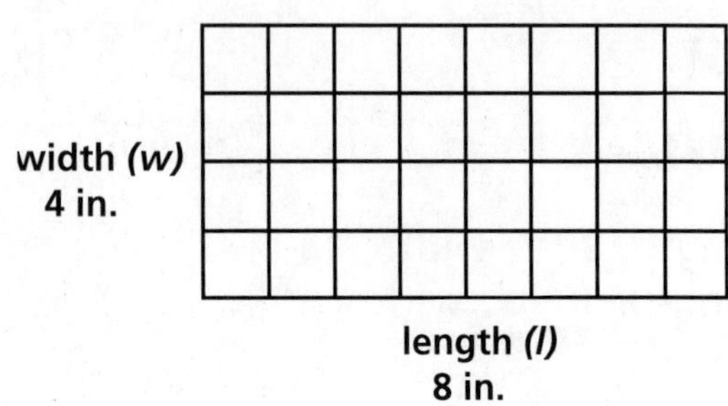

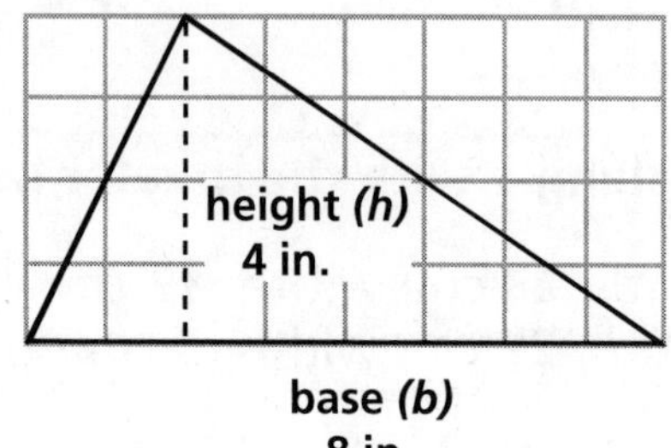

Area of rectangle $= l \times w$

$= 8 \times 4$

$= 32 \text{ in.}^2$

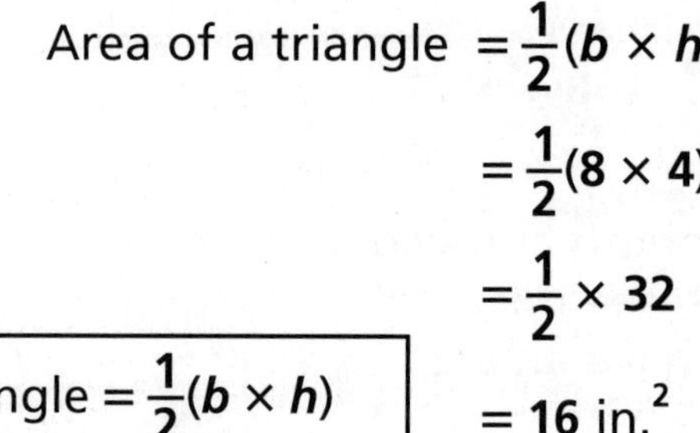

Area of a triangle $= \frac{1}{2}(b \times h)$

$= \frac{1}{2}(8 \times 4)$

$= \frac{1}{2} \times 32$

$= 16 \text{ in.}^2$

Area of a triangle $= \frac{1}{2}(b \times h)$

Find the area of each triangle.

1.

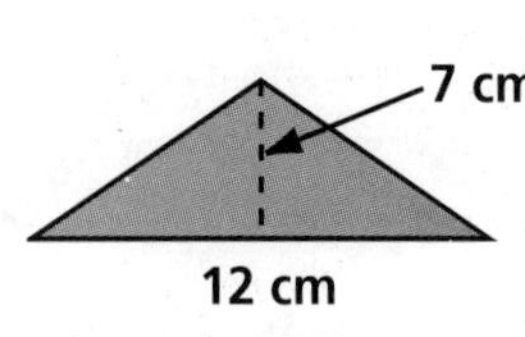

$A =$ ______

2.

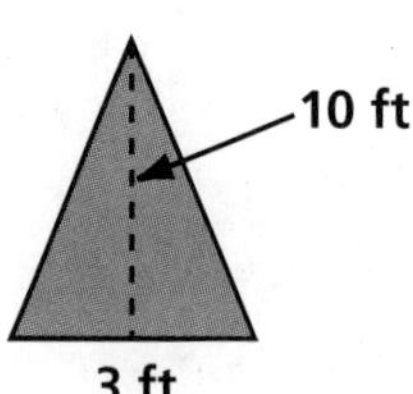

$A =$ ______

3.

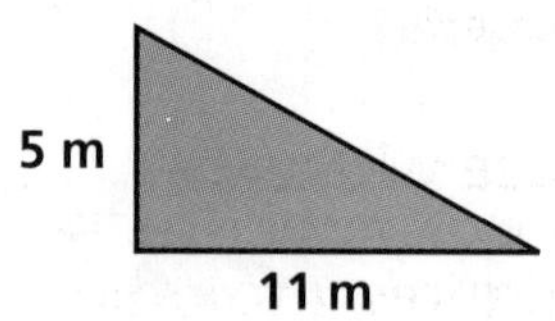

$A =$ ______

4.

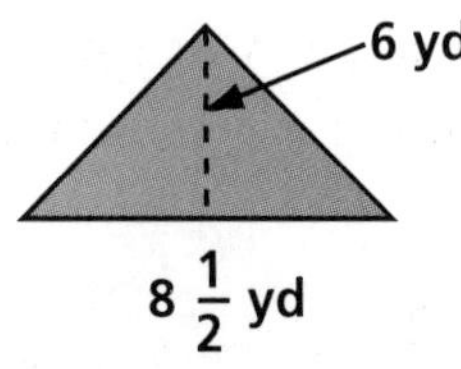

$A =$ ______

5.

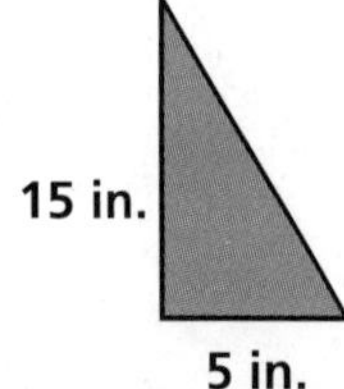

$A =$ ______

6.

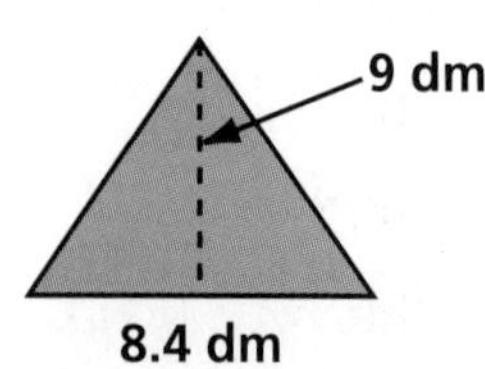

$A =$ ______

Name ______________________________

STANDARD

You can use what you know about the area of triangles to find the area of a **parallelogram**. Note that a diagonal divides the parallelogram into **2** congruent triangles.

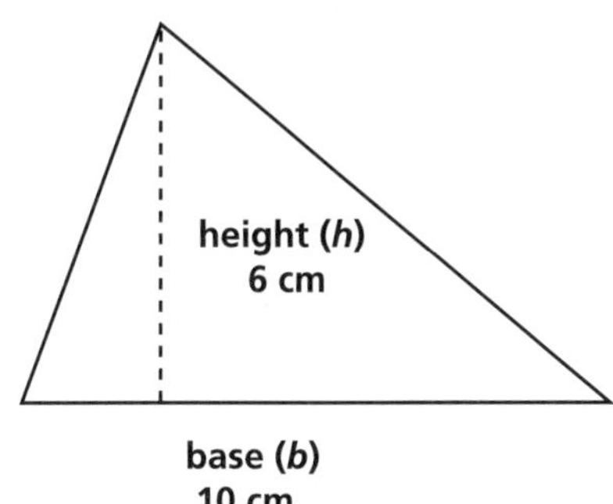

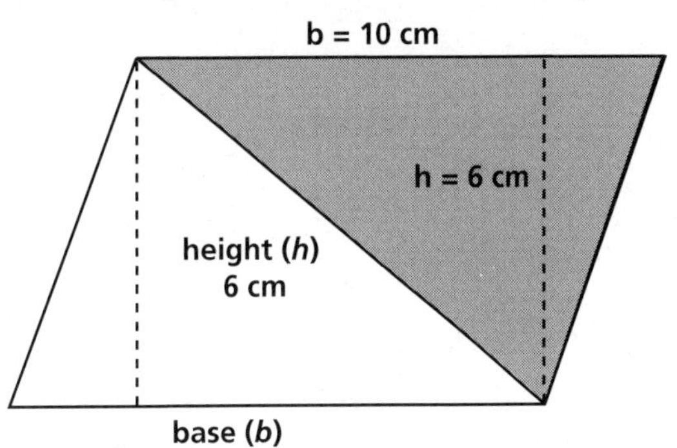

Area of a triangle $= \frac{1}{2}(b \times h)$

$= \frac{1}{2}(10 \times 6)$

$= \frac{1}{2} \times 60$

$= 30 \text{ in.}^2$

Area of a parallelogram $= \frac{1}{2}(b \times h) + \frac{1}{2}(b \times h)$

$= 1\ (b \times h)$

$= 10 \times 6$

$= 60 \text{ cm}^2$

Area of a parallelogram $= b \times h$

Find the area of each parallelogram.

7. 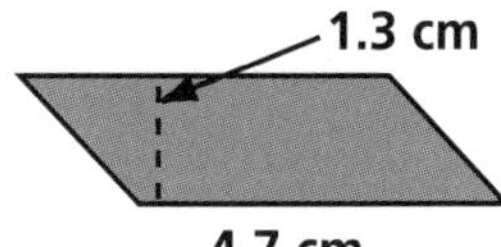

A = ______

8. 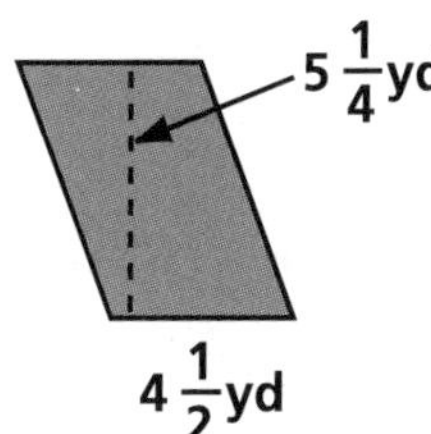

A = ______

9. 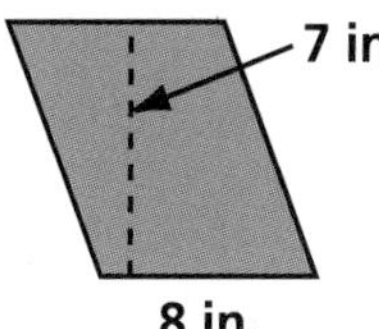

A = ______

Problem Solving Reasoning Solve.

10. Use what you know about area and dividing figures into other figures to find the area. ______

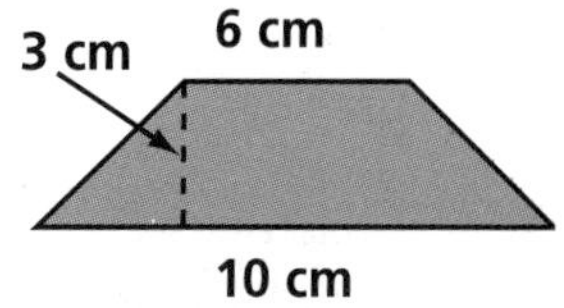

Test Prep ★ Mixed Review

11 **In the number 38,649,254 the 8 is in what place?**

A billions

B millions

C hundred thousands

D thousands

12 **On the average, between 25 and 30 people visit the museum each hour. What is a reasonable total number of people who will visit the museum in a 9-hour day?**

F Less than 200

G Between 240 and 250

H About 300

J More than 300

Name ______________________________

Space Figures

STANDARD

Three-dimensional geometric figures are called **space figures** or **solids.**

Prisms have two congruent bases.

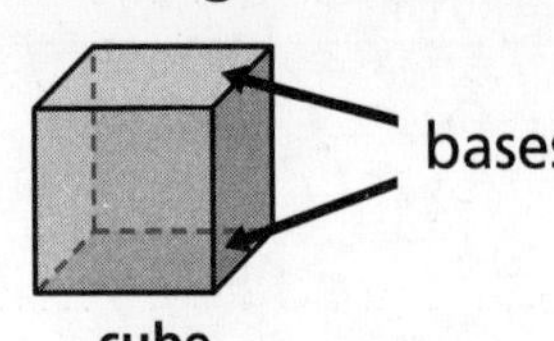

cube

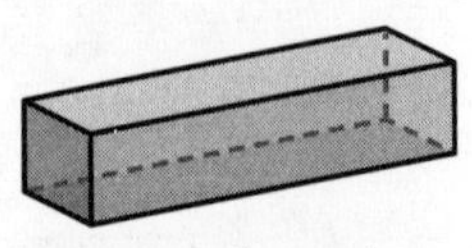

rectangular prism

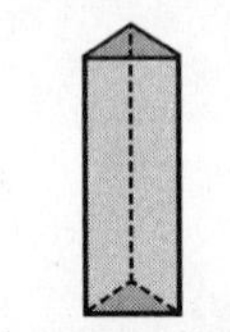

triangular prism

Pyramids have only one base.

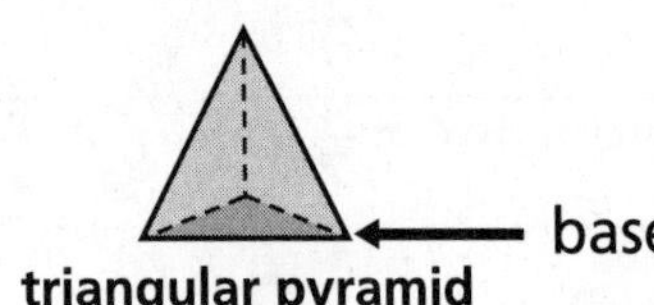

triangular pyramid

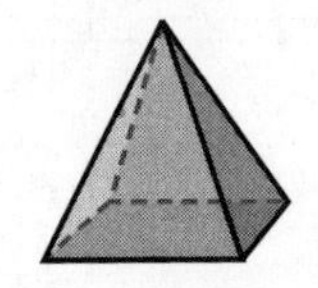

square pyramid

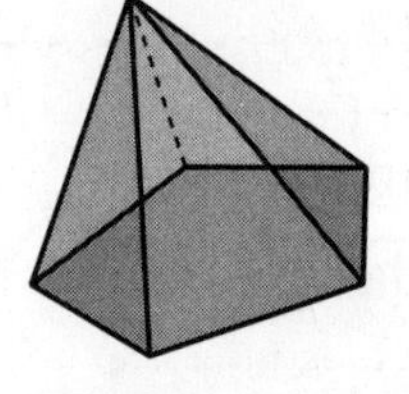

pentagonal pyramid

Some other space figures or solids have curved surfaces.

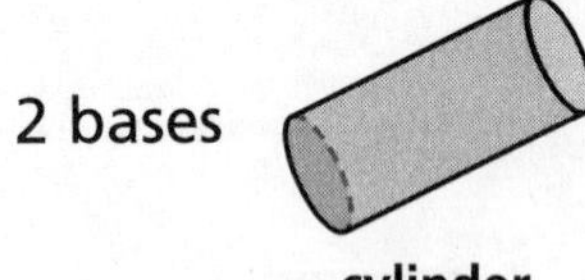

cylinder

1 base

cone

no base

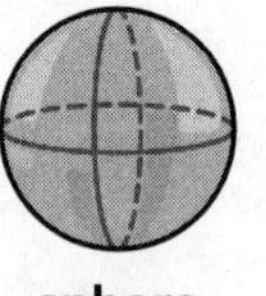

sphere

Circle the kind of space figure you make if you fold each net.

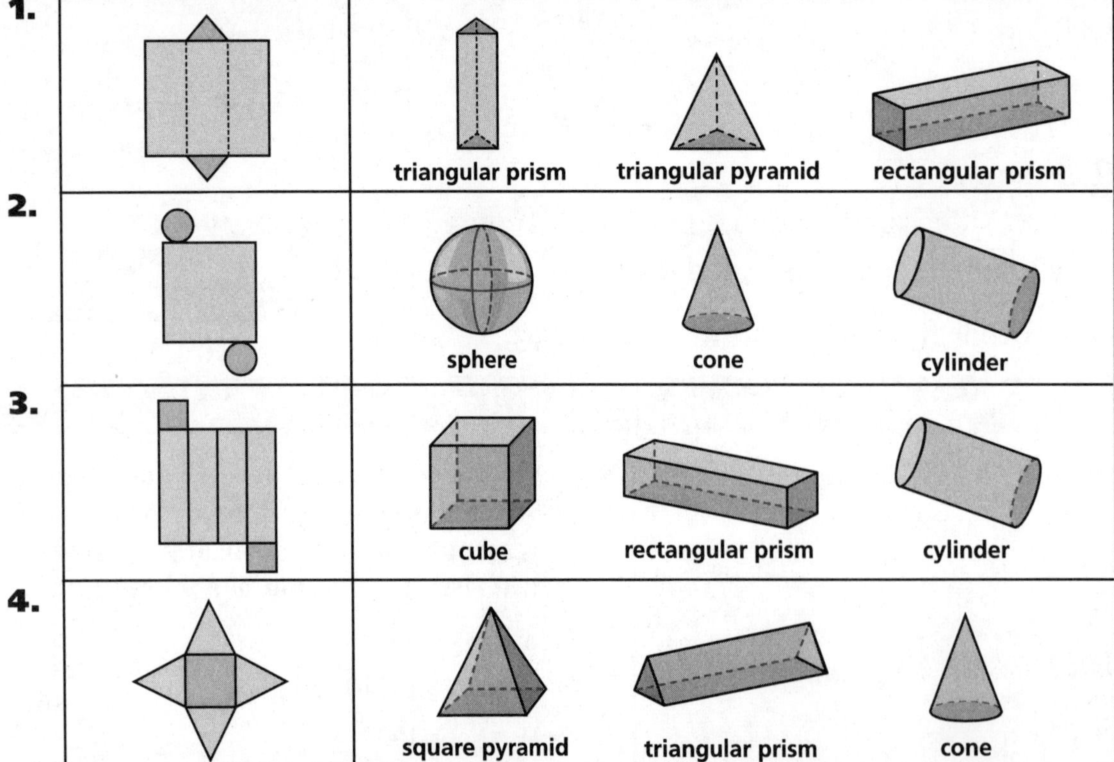

	Net	Choices		
1.		triangular prism	triangular pyramid	rectangular prism
2.		sphere	cone	cylinder
3.		cube	rectangular prism	cylinder
4.		square pyramid	triangular prism	cone

Name ______________________________

STANDARD

The flat surface of a space figure is a **face**. The line segment where two faces meet is an **edge**. The point where several edges meet is a **vertex**.

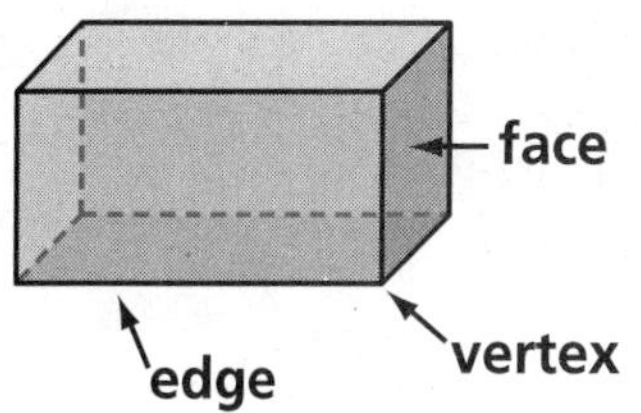

Complete this table.

	Figure	Number of faces	Number of edges	Number of vertices
5.	rectangular prism			
6.	triangular pyramid			
7.	triangular prism			
8.	square pyramid			

Write whether each statement is *always*, *sometimes*, or *never* true.

9. All the faces of a prism are congruent. __________

10. A pyramid can have two square faces. __________

11. A face of a triangular prism is a triangle or a rectangle. __________

12. A cone has two circular faces. __________

13. A space figure can have exactly one vertex. __________

Look at the space figures on page 218. Name the figure whose top and side views are shown.

A space figure looks different when you look at it from above or from a side.

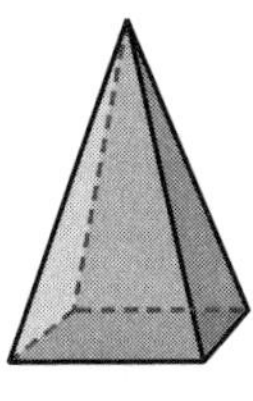
Square pyramid

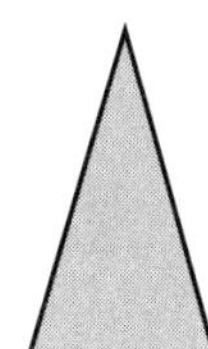
Front view

Top view

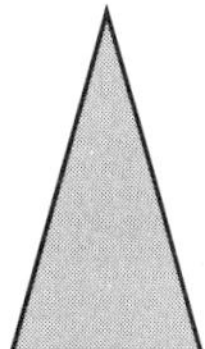
Side view

14.

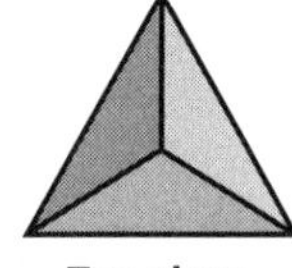
Top view

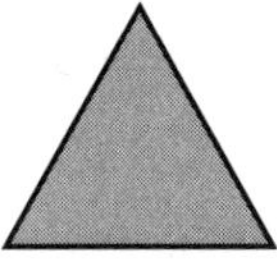
Side view

____

15.

Top view

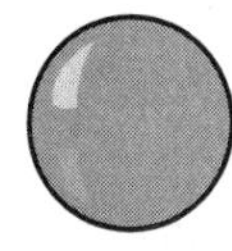
Side view

____

16.

Top view

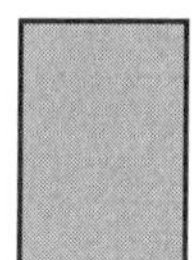
Side view

____

STANDARD

The space figures below are made from cubes. Circle the figure whose views are shown.

17.

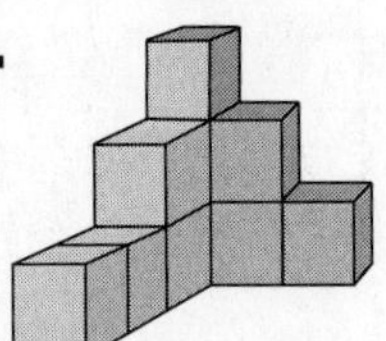

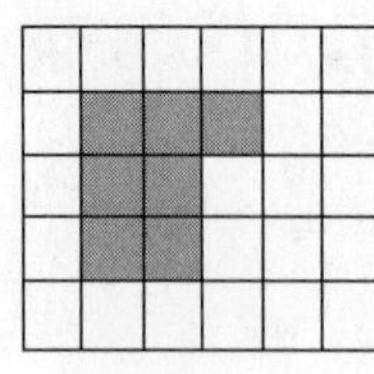

Top view

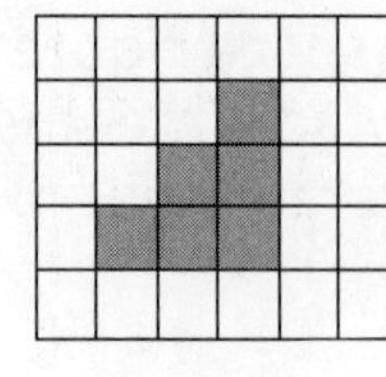

Side view

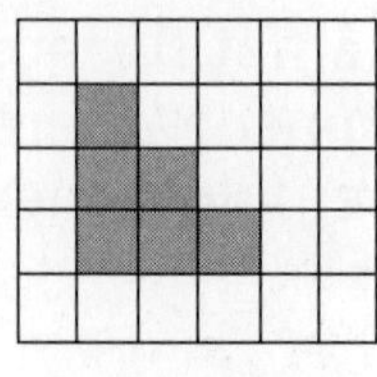

Front view

Problem Solving Reasoning **Solve.**

18. On grid paper, draw and label the front, side, and top views of the other figure above. (Hint: You may want to use cubes to model the figure first.)

Quick Check

Find the area of these figures.

Work Space

19.

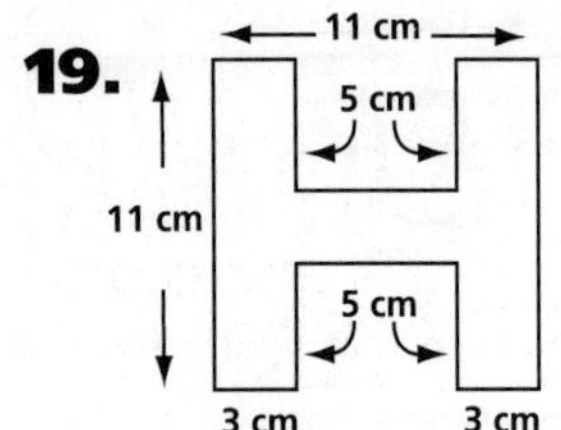

______

20.

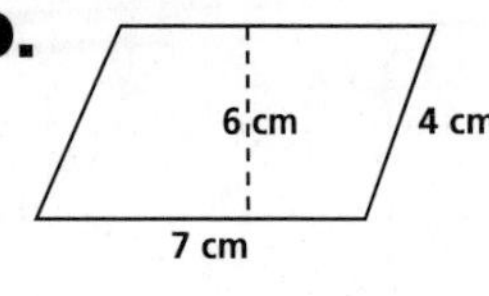

______

21.

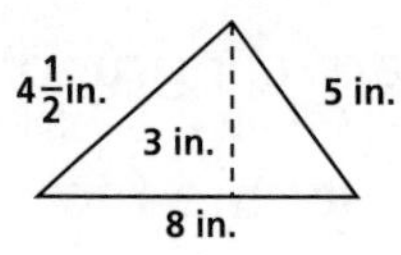

______

22. Find the perimeter of the figure in exercise 19. ______

Complete.

23. Circle the kind of space figure you could make if you fold the net.

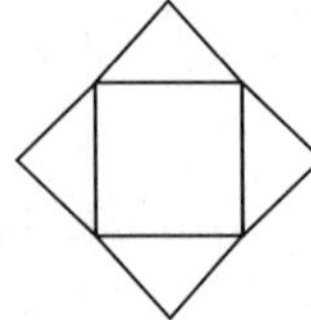

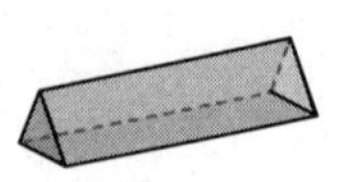

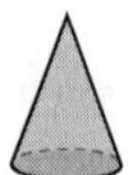

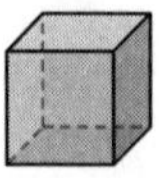

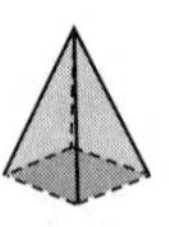

24. Name the space figure you could make. ______

25. How many faces, edges, and vertices does the figure have? ______

26. Name the other figures in exercise 22. ______

Name ______________________

Surface Area

STANDARD

What is the total area of the cardboard needed to form this box if no cardboard overlaps? The total area of all the faces of a space figure is called its **surface area**. In a rectangular prism, the top and bottom are congruent, the two sides are congruent, and the front and back are congruent. The pattern, or **net**, formed by unfolding the faces of this prism is shown below.

Top
Side
Front
1 ft^2

To find the surface area of a rectangular prism:
Find the areas of its top, one side, and front. Find the sum of those areas. Then multiply the sum by **2**.

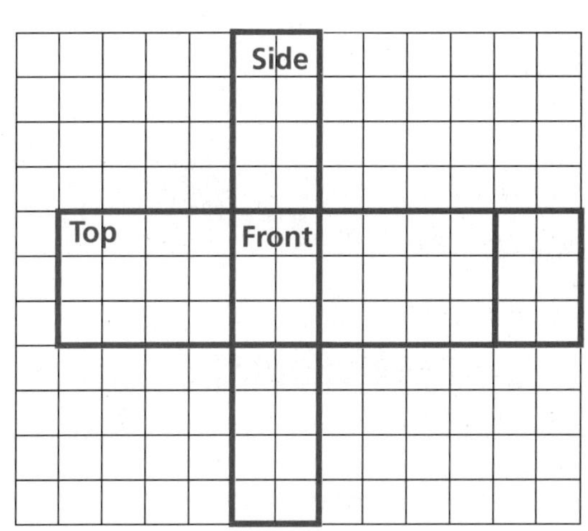

Top: $A = \mathbf{3}$ ft $\times$ $\mathbf{4}$ ft $\rightarrow$ $\mathbf{12}$ ft^2

Side: $A = \mathbf{4}$ ft $\times$ $\mathbf{2}$ ft $\rightarrow$ $\mathbf{8}$ ft^2

Front: $A = \mathbf{3}$ ft $\times$ $\mathbf{2}$ ft $\rightarrow$ $\mathbf{6}$ ft^2

Surface Area $= \mathbf{2} \times (\mathbf{12}\text{ ft}^2 + \mathbf{8}\text{ ft}^2 + \mathbf{6}\text{ ft}^2)$

$= \mathbf{2} \times \mathbf{26}\text{ ft}^2$

$= \mathbf{52}\text{ ft}^2$

So, **52** ft^2 of cardboard is needed for this box.

Find the surface area of each rectangular prism.

1.

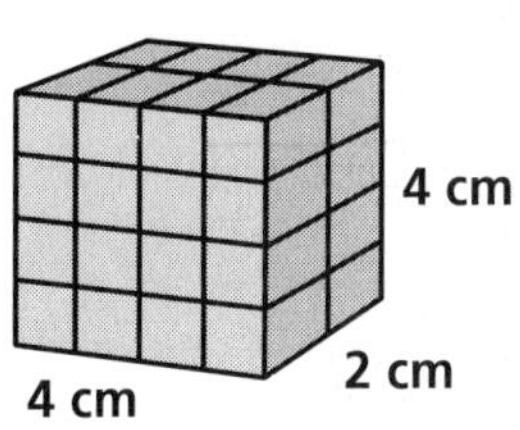

Surface Area = ______

2.

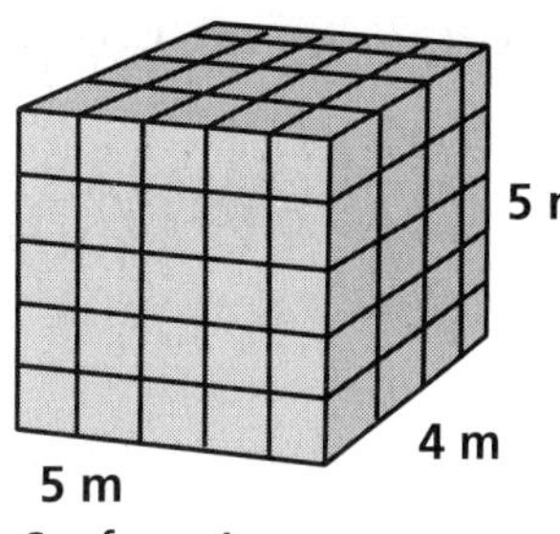

Surface Area = ______

3.

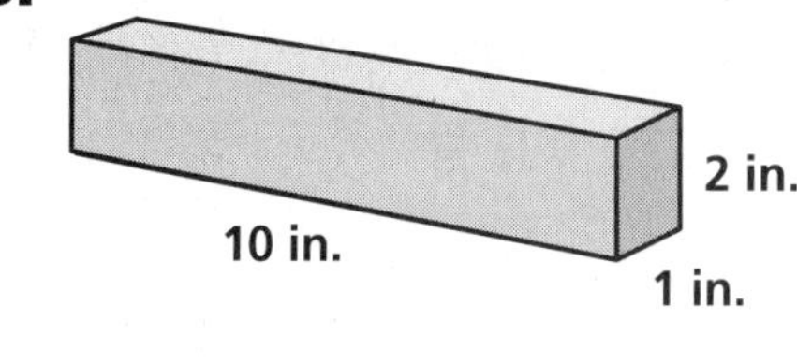

Surface Area = ______

Draw the net formed by unfolding the faces of each prism. Use a grid.

4.

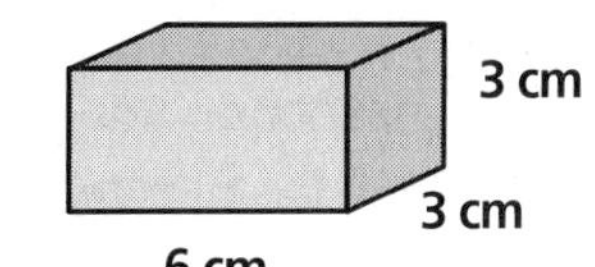

5.

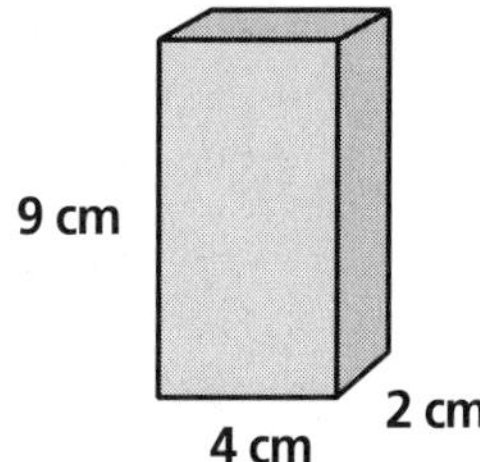

6.

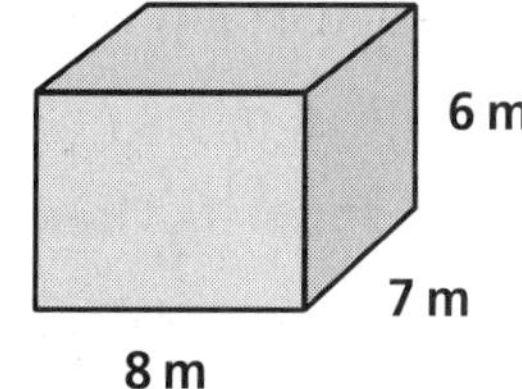

STANDARD

Problem Solving Reasoning Solve.

7. Find the surface area of each cube at the right. How can you find the surface area of a cube using multiplication?

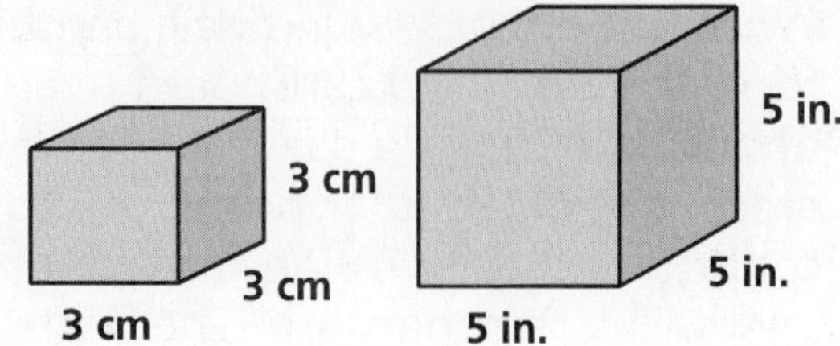

____

____

8. Suppose you cut the block of wood at the right in half. You need to cover the pieces with adhesive paper. Did you need more or less paper before the block was cut? Explain.

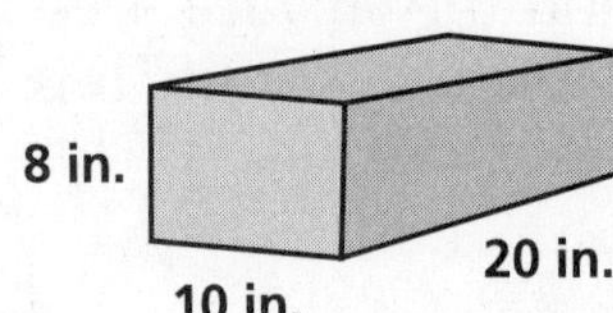

____

____

Each space figure is made up of centimeter cubes. Find each surface area by counting faces. Remember that some cubes cannot be seen.

9.

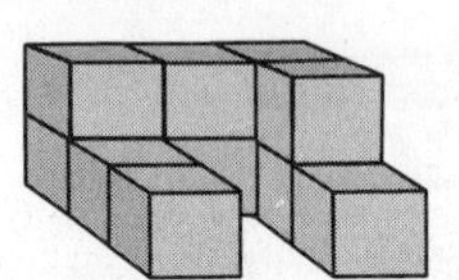

10.

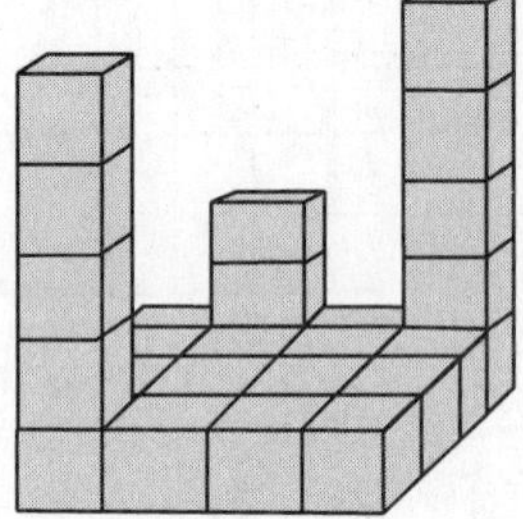

11.

12.

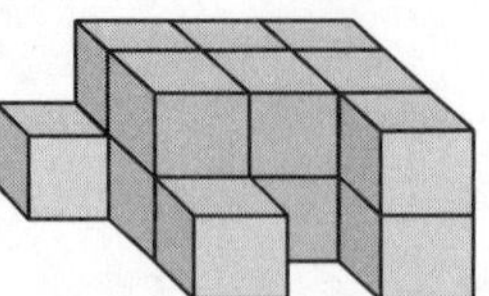

Test Prep ★ Mixed Review

13 The speed of ships is measured in *knots*, or nautical miles per hour. A nautical mile is about $1\frac{1}{6}$ land miles. How many feet are in a nautical mile?

A 4,526 **C** 6,160

B 5,900 **D** 6,610

14 Marla's and Jolene's times in the 200-meter dash were 26.03 seconds and 29.58 seconds. Katy's time was 0.45 seconds slower than the winning time. What was Katy's time?

F 25.58 s **H** 29.13 s

G 26.48 s **J** 30.03 s

Name ______________________

Volume

STANDARD

You measure volume in **cubic units.**

Volume is the number of cubic units that a space figure can hold. To find how many cubic feet this cardboard box can hold, you can use a formula.

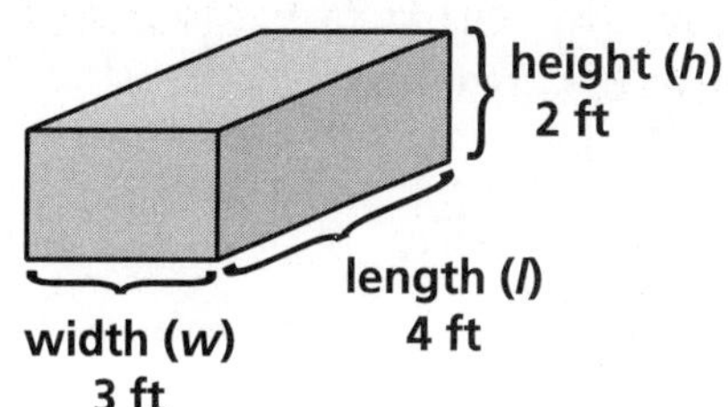

Volume of a rectangular prism: $V = l \times w \times h$

$$V = l \times w \times h$$
$$= 4 \times 3 \times 2$$
$$= 24 \text{ ft}^3$$

To find the volume of a cube, you can also use a formula.

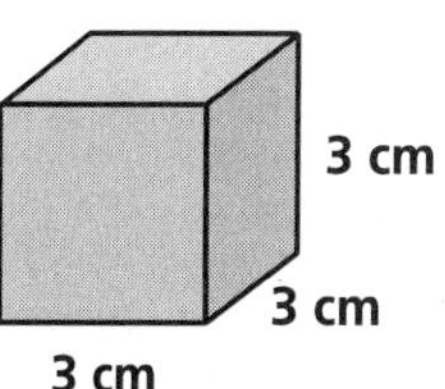

Think: s = length of a side

Volume of a cube: $V = s^3$

$$V = s^3$$
$$= 3^3$$
$$= 27 \text{ cm}^3$$

Find the volume of each prism.

1.

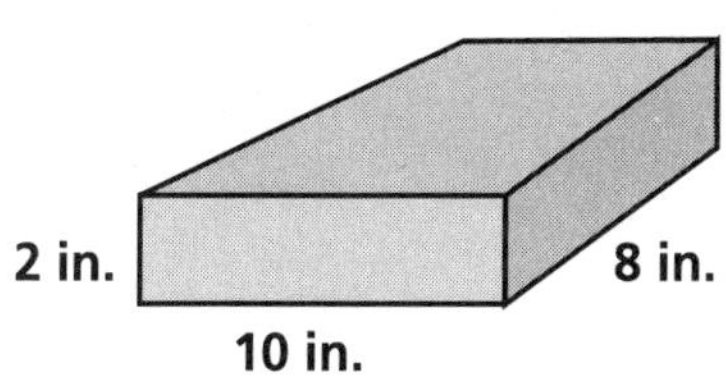

$V =$ ________

2.

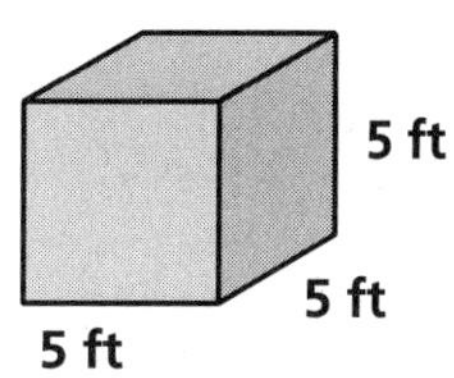

$V =$ ________

3.

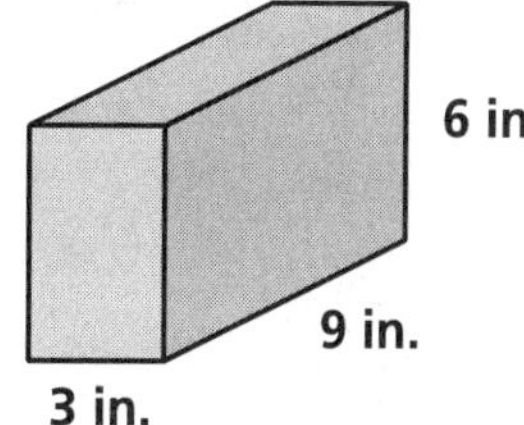

$V =$ ________

4.

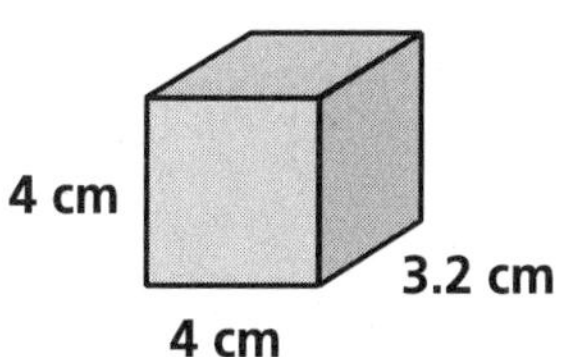

$V =$ ________

5.

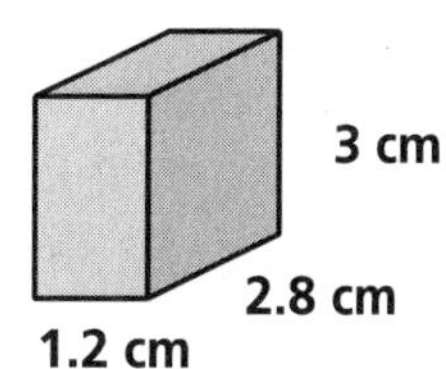

$V =$ ________

6.

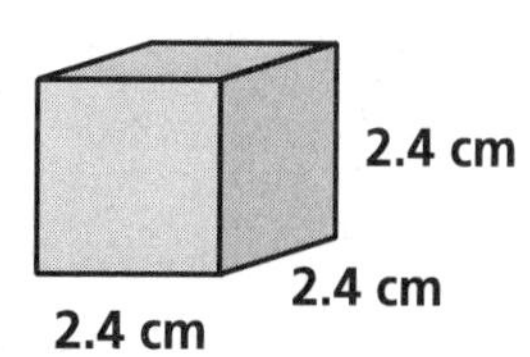

$V =$ ________

STANDARD

Would you find perimeter, area, or volume to answer each question? Write *perimeter, area,* or *volume.*

7. How much wrapping paper is needed to cover a box? ____________

8. How much ribbon is needed to go around a box? ____________

9. How much packing material is needed to fill a box? ____________

10. How much air can a room hold? ____________

11. How much carpeting is needed to carpet a room? ____________

12. How much wallpaper border is needed for a room? ____________

Problem Solving Reasoning **Solve.**

13. The surface area of a cube is **96** cm^2.
What is the volume of the cube?

____

14. A rectangular prism is **4** in. long and **2** in. high.
Its volume is **40** $in.^3$ What is its width?

____

15. A rectangular prism is **6** cm long and **3** cm wide.
Its volume is **90** cm^3. What is its surface area?

____

Quick Check

Find the surface area.

16.
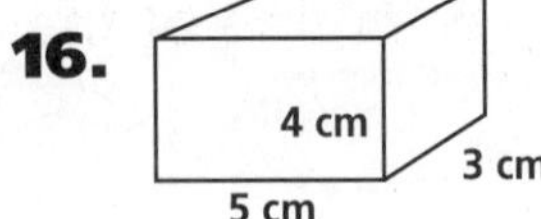

17.
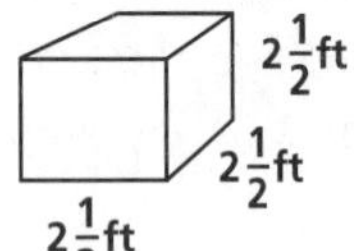

18.
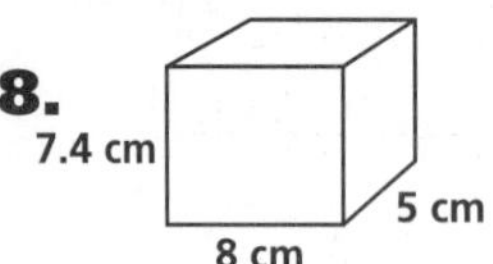

____________ ____________ ____________

Find the volume of each figure in exercises 16–18.

19. ____________ **20.** ____________ **21.** ____________

Work Space

Name ______________________

Problem Solving Application: Use Formulas

STANDARD

In order to solve some problems, you need to know and use formulas.

In this lesson, you will use perimeter, area, and volume formulas. Sometimes you will have to decide which formula is the correct one to use.

Tips to Remember

1. Understand 2. Decide 3. Solve 4. Look back

- Ask yourself whether you have solved a problem like this before.
- Make a rough sketch of the figure. Then write the correct formula.
- Think about what the problem is asking you to do. What information does the problem give you? What do you need to find out?

Solve.

1. Roger's garden is **9** ft long and **4** ft wide. He wants to put fencing around the entire garden to keep the rabbits out. How much fencing must he buy?

Think: Does Roger need to find the perimeter or the area of the garden? What formula will you use?

____

____

Answer ______________________

2. Judy covered a jewelry box with paper to match her wall decorations. The box measured **6** in. long, **2** in. wide, and **3** in. high. How much paper did she use?

Think: How many sides does the box have? Do you have to find the perimeter or area of each side of the box?

____

____

Answer ______________________

3. An aquarium measures **20** in. by **12** in. by **10** in. What is the volume of the aquarium?

____

4. A bedroom measures **12** ft by **15** ft. How many square feet of carpeting are needed for this bedroom?

____

STANDARD

Solve.

5. The cheerleaders used ribbon to form a rectangle. The rectangle was **15** feet long and **10** feet wide. How long was the piece of ribbon?

6. Bethany's kitchen is **10** ft by **12** ft. She wants to tile half of its floor. Tiles are one square foot. How many tiles does she need?

7. The Pentagon building in Arlington, Virginia is in the shape of a regular pentagon. Its perimeter is about **1,640** yd. What is the length of each side of the Pentagon?

8. The Washington Monument in Washington, D.C. has a square base, **55** ft on each side. What is the area of the base of the monument?

9. Coretta hit a home run during the schoolyard baseball game. How many yards did she run if one side of the baseball diamond measures **14** yd?

10. One wall in Tony's bedroom measures **11.5** ft by **8** ft. Tony hung a poster measuring **2** ft by **3** ft on the wall. How much wall space is not covered?

11. Mandy is wrapping a box **1** ft on each side. The wrapping paper is **26** in. by **60** in. What size piece should she cut to wrap the box?

12. Leon is tiling part of the floor in his room. The room is **16** ft by **20** ft. He bought **80** tiles. Each tile is one square foot. What fractional part of the room is he tiling?

Extend Your Thinking

13. Look back at problem 3. One cubic in. of water weighs **0.036** lb. If the aquarium is totally filled, what is the weight of the water in the aquarium?

14. Look back at problem 4. Carpeting is sold by the square yard. Describe how you could find the number of square yards of carpeting needed.

Name ______________________________

Unit 8 Review

Draw and label each figure.

1. line segment *RS* **2.** point *H* **3.** ray *AB* **4.** line *PQ*

Classify each angle. Write *acute, obtuse,* or *right*.

5.

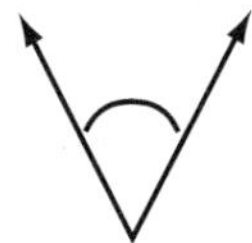

____

6.

____

7.

____

Draw an angle with each measure.

8.

45°

9.

110°

Find the measure of $\angle A$.

10.

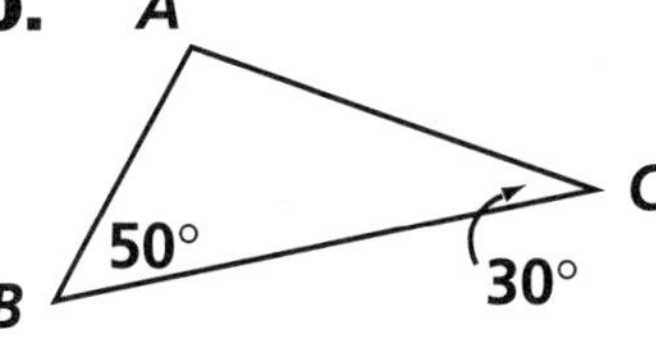

____

11.

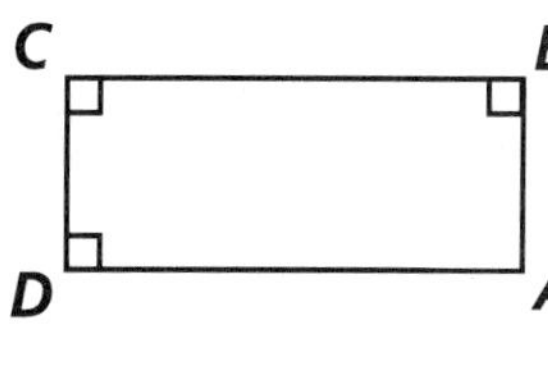

____

Are each pair of figures congruent? Write *yes* or *no*.

12.

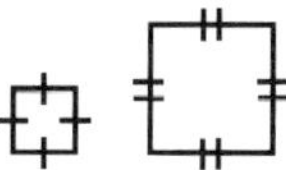

____

13.

____

14.

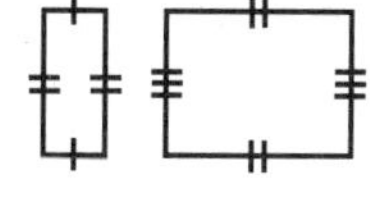

____

Solve.

15. How many lines of symmetry does rectangle ***WXYZ*** have? ______ Draw the lines.

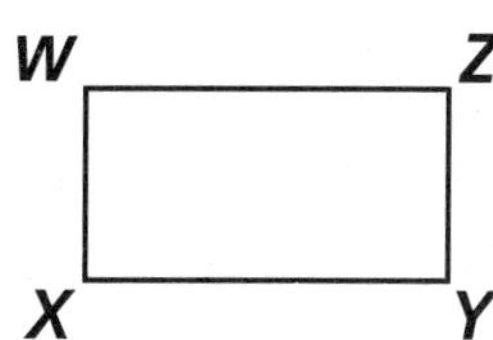

16. Draw a circle with center ***D*** and a diameter of **3** cm. Label the diameter $\overline{EF}$.

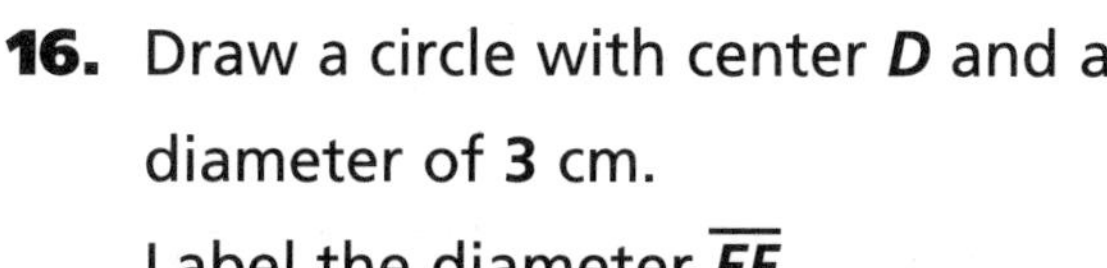

Find the perimeter or area of each figure. Use the formula if you need to.

17.

3 cm
5 cm
4 cm

$A = \frac{1}{2}(b \times h)$

$A =$ ________

18.

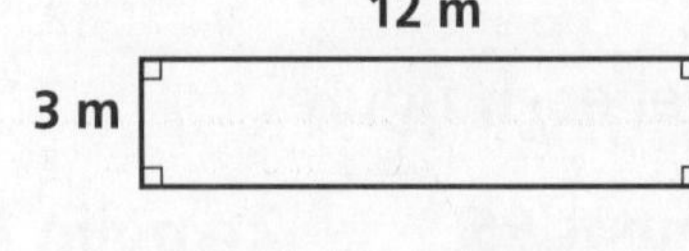

$P = 2(l + w)$

$P =$ ________

19. $P =$ ________ units

$A =$ ________ sq. units

3
2
3
2
1
9

20. Name the space figure you could form if you folded this pattern.

____

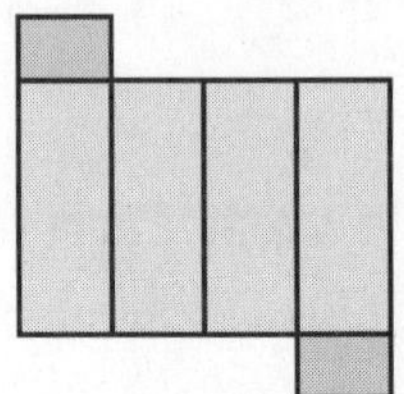

21. Find the volume (V) and surface area (SA) of this figure.

$V =$ ________ $SA =$ ________

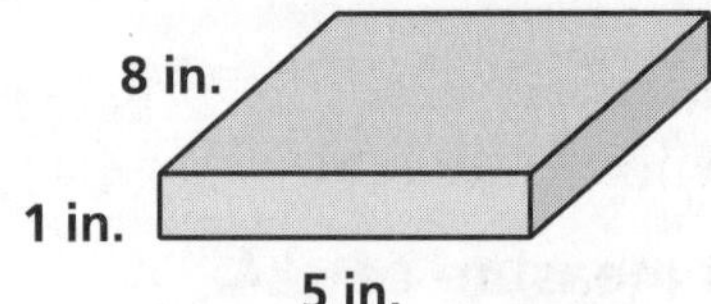

Solve.

22. A sequence of dot figures is shown. The first figure is formed with **3** dots. The second figure is formed with **6** dots. The third figure is formed with **10** dots. How many dots would be needed to form the fifth figure? ________

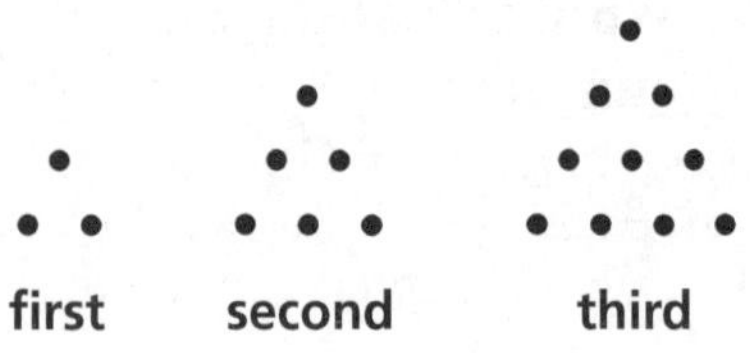

23. A square has two different diagonals. A pentagon has **5**. A hexagon has **9**. How many different diagonals does an octagon, or eight-sided figure, have? (Hint: Draw a picture or find a pattern.) ________

Name ____________________

Cumulative Review
★ Test Prep

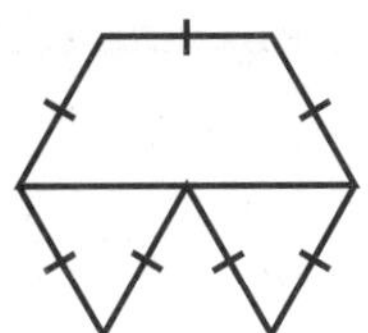

1 **If the perimeter of the triangle on the left is 3 units and the area of the triangle is 1 unit^2 then what is the perimeter and area of the figure on the right?**

A 9 units; 5 units^2

B 7 units; 5 units^2

C 5 units, 7 units^2

D 5 units, 9 units^2

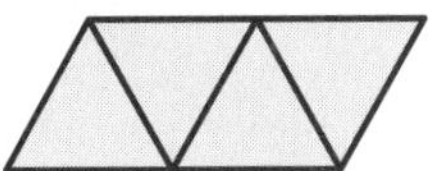

2 **What space figure will the pattern make when cut and folded?**

F equilateral triangle

G cube

H triangular prism

J triangular pyramid

3 **A compact car gets 27.28 miles per gallon. What is that number written as a mixed number?**

F $\frac{27.28}{100}$

G $27\frac{2}{8}$

H $27\frac{28}{10}$

J $27\frac{28}{100}$

4 **Use what you know about the properties of addition. What is the value of the variable n?**
$4 + (99 + 8) = n + (4 + 8)$

F 8 **H** 99

G 12 **J** 107

5 **One piece of ribbon is $3\frac{1}{2}$ feet. Another is about $\frac{5}{6}$ ft shorter. What is a reasonable length for the second piece of ribbon?**

A Less than $2\frac{2}{3}$ ft

B More than 3 ft

C Exactly $2\frac{5}{6}$ ft

D Exactly $4\frac{1}{3}$ ft

6 **Which rectangular prism has the same volume as this cube?**

6 cm, 6 cm, 6 cm

A 4 cm, 12 cm, 3 cm

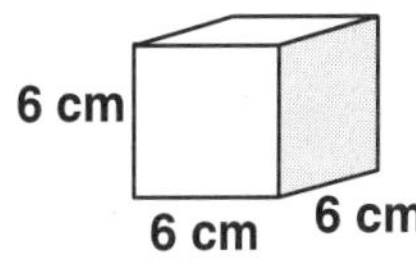

B 10 cm, 4.5 cm, 2 cm

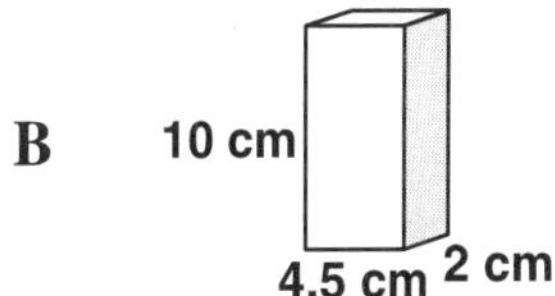

C 4.5 cm, 9 cm, 4 cm

D 9 cm, 8 cm, 3 cm

Line *AB* intersects line *XY* at point *P*. The measure of angle *BPX* is 38°. Use this figure for questions 7–8.

7 Use a protractor. What kind of angle is angle *APB*?

A acute angle

B obtuse angle

C straight angle

D right angle

8 What is the measure of angle *BPY*?

F 38°

G 52°

H 142°

J 322°

9 A bag of oranges weighs 2.5 kilograms, a bag of onions weighs 11.1 kilograms, and a pineapple weighs 0.89 kg. How much do the oranges and pineapple weigh together?

A 13.6 kg

B 11.99 kg

C 11.189 kg

D 2.589 kg

E Not here

10 An inchworm crawled 1.68 m in one day. At this pace, which number sentence shows the number of meters the inchworm will travel in 100 days?

F $10^2 + 1.68 = \square$

G $10^2 \times 1.68 = \square$

H $10^3 \times 1.68 = \square$

J $1.68 \div \square = 10^2$

K $10^2 = 1.68 \times \square$

11 Ilie lives $\frac{3}{5}$ of a mile from school. She walks $\frac{1}{2}$ this distance to get to the bus stop. How far is the bus stop from her house?

A $\frac{1}{10}$ mi

B $\frac{3}{10}$ mi

C $\frac{6}{5}$ mi

D $\frac{11}{10}$ mi

E $1\frac{1}{6}$ mi

12 Every 3 months, a company gives its sales force money for gas based on the average number of miles driven on company business. Mr. Rosen estimates that he has driven 5,839 miles in 65 days. What is the average number of miles per day rounded to the nearest mile?

F 22

G 29

H 89

J 90

K Not here

UNIT 9 • TABLE OF CONTENTS

Ratio and Percent

We will be using this vocabulary:

ratio a comparison between two quantities

percent (%) a special ratio that compares a number to 100

scale drawing a drawing of an object such that the ratio of each length of the object to its corresponding length in the drawing is equal

Dear Family,

During the next few weeks, our math class will be learning about ratios and percents.

You can expect to see homework that provides practice with writing percents as fractions, and fractions as percents. Here is a sample you may want to keep handy to give help if needed.

Writing Percents as Fractions

Example Write **32** percent as a fraction.

1. Write the percent as a fraction with a denominator of **100**. $32\% = \frac{32}{100}$
2. Write the fraction in simplest form. $\frac{32}{100} = \frac{32 \div 4}{100 \div 4} \rightarrow \frac{8}{25}$

Writing Fractions as Percents

Example Write $\frac{3}{4}$ as a percent.

1. Write an equivalent fraction with a denominator of **100**. $\frac{3 \times 25}{4 \times 25} = \frac{75}{100}$
2. Since percent means per hundred, you can think, **75** out of one hundred, then write **75%**. $\frac{75}{100} = 75\%$

During this unit students will need to continue practicing addition, subtraction, multiplication, and division facts.

Sincerely,

Name ____________________

Ratios

STANDARD

Ratios are used to compare two quantities.

Ratios are used to compare two quantities.

The ratio of squares to circles is **5** to **3**.

The numbers in the ratio are called the **terms** of the ratio.

You can write the ratio of squares to circles three ways: **5** to **3**, **5**:**3**, and $\frac{5}{3}$.

Each ratio is read in the same way: **5** to **3**.

Write each ratio three different ways.

1. **3** females to **2** males ____________ **9** cats to **1** dog ____________
2. **6** cakes to **6** pies ____________ **1** table to **4** chairs ____________

Write each ratio three different ways.

3. pentagons to triangles ____________ circles to pentagons ____________
4. circles to triangles ____________ pentagons to circles ____________
5. triangles to pentagons ____________ triangles to circles ____________
6. pentagons to all shapes ____________ all shapes to triangles ____________

STANDARD

You can write a ratio in simplest form the same way you write a fraction in simplest form.

Write the ratio **10** hammers to **5** saws in simplest form.

1. Find the GCF of both terms of the ratio. $\frac{10}{5}$ ← The GCF of **10** and **5** is **5.**
2. Divide each term by the GCF.

$\frac{10 \div 5}{5 \div 5} = \frac{2}{1}$ ← simplest form You can also say the ratio is **2** hammers to **1** saw.

Write each ratio in simplest form three different ways.

7. circles to pentagons

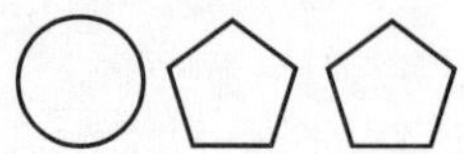

____

squares to circles

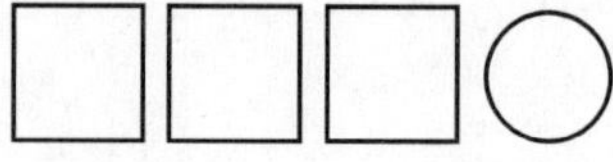

____

hexagons to squares

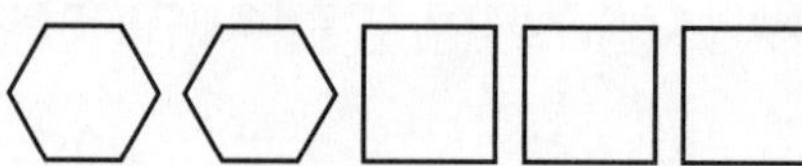

____

Problem Solving
Reasoning

Solve. Write each ratio in simplest form.

8. length of rectangle *A* to length of rectangle *B*

____

9. width of rectangle *A* to width of rectangle *B*

____

10. perimeter of rectangle *A* to perimeter of rectangle *B*

____

11. area of rectangle *A* to area of rectangle *B*

____

2 cm **A** **3 cm**

4 cm **B** **6 cm**

Test Prep ★ Mixed Review

12 **You have four friends. The distances from your house to each of their houses are 3.1 miles, 1.7 miles, 2.6 miles, and 0.2 miles. What is the average distance between your house and your friends' houses?**

A 1.9 mi

B 2 mi

C 2.1 mi

D 2.15 mi

13 **A flower garden is 15 feet long and $2\frac{1}{2}$ feet wide. What is its perimeter?**

F 6 feet

G $17\frac{1}{2}$ feet

H 35 ft

J $37\frac{1}{2}$ feet

Name ______________________

In **2** hours, Mrs. Carr drove **105** miles. If she continued driving at this rate, how far did she drive in **10** hours?

A rate is a special ratio that compares quantities that are in different units, such as miles and hours.

You can use a table to solve a rate problem.

The rate in this problem can be written as:

hours → $\frac{2}{105}$ ← miles

Hours	2	4	6	8	10
Miles	105	210	315	420	525

Mrs. Carr drove **525** miles in **10** hours.

Complete the table. Then use the table to answer the questions.

1. Lucas can read **3** pages in **5** minutes.

Pages	3	6						
Minutes	5	10						

How many pages can Lucas read in **15** minutes? ____________

How long will it take Lucas to read **21** pages? ____________

2. A **5**-pound bag of oranges is on sale for **$2.95**.

Pounds	5					
Cost	$2.95					

What is the cost of **20** pounds of oranges? ____________

A chef has **$15** to spend on oranges. How many pounds of oranges can she buy? ____________

3. A class completes **8** pages of math every **5** days of school.

Pages of Math	8									
Number of Days	5	10	15	20	25	30	35	40	45	50

How many pages will the class complete in **45** days? ____________

How many pages will the class complete in a school year of **180** days? ____________

STANDARD

The **unit price** of an item is the cost of that item *per unit,* such as the cost per pound or the cost per ounce.

Suppose a brand of ketchup you want to buy comes in two sizes:

16 ounces for **$1.59** or **12** ounces for **$1.29.**

To decide which is the **better buy,** you can compare their unit prices. The better buy is the one with the lower unit price.

Find the unit price of each size.

16-ounce bottle:

```
      $.099      Round to $.10
16)$1.590
   -1 44
      150
     -144
        6
```

12-ounce bottle:

```
      $.107      Round to $.11
12)$1.290
    - 1 2
      090
     - 84
        6
```

Since $**.10 per ounce** < $**.11 per ounce,** the **16**-ounce bottle is the better buy.

Circle the better buy in each pair.

4. sports drink

64 ounces for **$2.39** or

20 ounces for **$1.05**

5. frozen cheese pizza

21 ounces for **$4.59** or

10 ounces for **$1.59**

6. peanut butter

18 ounces for **$1.99** or

28 ounces for **$3.59**

Problem Solving Reasoning **Solve.**

7. Suppose you need **12** ounces of chocolate chips for a dessert you are making. A **10**-ounce bag of chips costs **$2.00**, and a **24**-ounce bag costs **$4.19**. What should you buy? Explain.

____

____

Test Prep ★ Mixed Review

8 **What is the prime factorization of 45?**

A 1×45

B 3×15

C 5×9

D $3^2 \times 5$

9 **The diameter of a circle is between 8 cm and 10 cm. What might be the length of the radius?**

F 4 cm

G 4.5 cm

H 8 cm

J 10 cm

Name ______________________________

Equal Ratios

STANDARD

Two ratios are equal if they name the same value.

To write equal ratios, multiply both terms by the same number or divide both terms by the same number.

Multiply to find the equal ratios.

$\frac{6}{9} = \frac{?}{36}$

$\frac{6}{9} = \frac{6 \times 4}{9 \times 4} \rightarrow \frac{24}{36}$

Think: **9 × 4 = 36,** so multiply **6** by **4.**

So, $\frac{6}{9} = \frac{24}{36}$.

Divide to find equal ratios.

$\frac{6}{9} = \frac{2}{?}$

$\frac{6}{9} = \frac{6 \div 3}{9 \div 3} \rightarrow \frac{2}{3}$

Think: **6 ÷ 3 = 2,** so divide **9** by **3.**

So, $\frac{6}{9} = \frac{2}{3}$.

Jana's team scores an average of **3** runs in every **2** innings.
Lisa's team scores an average of **6** runs in every **4** innings.

Are the ratios of runs to innings for both teams equal?

Jana's team $\rightarrow \frac{3}{2} = \frac{3 \times 2}{2 \times 2} \rightarrow \frac{6}{4}$ **Lisa's team**

Since $\frac{3}{2} = \frac{6}{4}$, the ratios are equal.

Determine whether each pair of ratios is equal. Write *yes* or *no*.

1. $\frac{3}{8}, \frac{6}{12}$ ______ $\frac{20}{15}, \frac{4}{3}$ ______ $\frac{1}{4}, \frac{8}{2}$ ______

2. **10:16, 5:4** ______ **9:1, 18:2** ______ **5:9, 15:27** ______

3. **12 to 16, 4 to 3** ______ **7 to 5, 5 to 7** ______ **9 to 3, 3 to 1** ______

Circle the ratio on the right that does *not* equal the ratio on the left.

4. $\frac{3}{4}$ $\frac{9}{12}$ $\frac{6}{8}$ $\frac{15}{16}$ $\frac{12}{16}$

5. **10:8** **20:4** **30:24** **50:40** **40:32**

6. **24 to 30** **12 to 15** **10 to 8** **48 to 60** **4 to 5**

STANDARD

Complete to form equal ratios.

7. $\frac{3}{7} = \frac{\_\_}{21}$ $\frac{10}{12} = \frac{5}{\_\_}$ $\frac{40}{15} = \frac{\_\_}{3}$ $\frac{18}{8} = \frac{\_\_}{4}$

8. $\frac{11}{9} = \frac{22}{\_\_}$ $\frac{1}{5} = \frac{\_\_}{30}$ $\frac{21}{18} = \frac{\_\_}{6}$ $\frac{9}{15} = \frac{3}{\_\_}$

9. $\frac{50}{70} = \frac{5}{\_\_}$ $\frac{7}{3} = \frac{\_\_}{12}$ $\frac{12}{6} = \frac{\_\_}{1}$ $\frac{8}{7} = \frac{\_\_}{21}$

10. $\frac{80}{90} = \frac{8}{\_\_}$ $\frac{28}{32} = \frac{\_\_}{8}$ $\frac{3}{2} = \frac{\_\_}{16}$ $\frac{7}{1} = \frac{\_\_}{6}$

Use the graph to solve each problem.

11. Write the ratio of bales of hay to horses.

4 horses ______ 8 horses ______ 16 horses ______

12. What is the ratio of bales of hay to horses for **4, 8,** and **16** horses in simplest form? ______

13. If the graph continued, how many bales of hay would be needed for **48** horses? ______

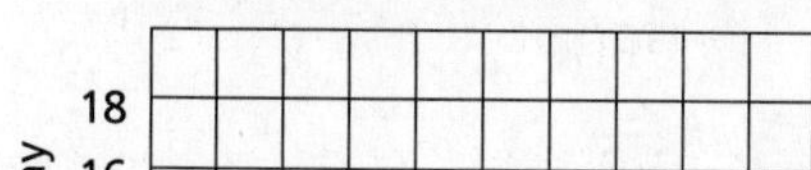
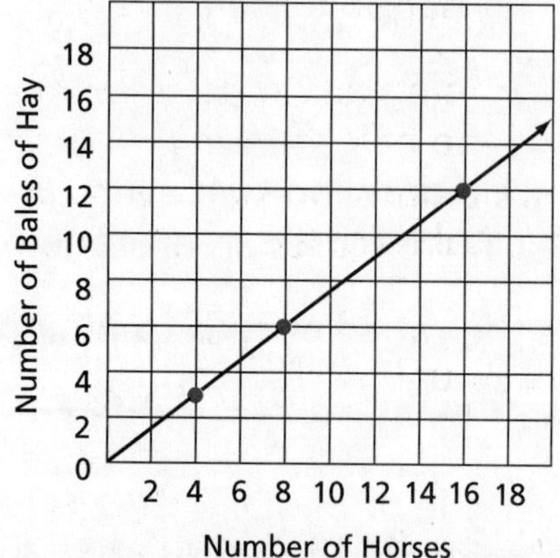

Quick Check

Write the ratio in simplest form in three different ways.

Work Space

14. **14** dogs to **20** cats ______

15. **24** cars to **16** vans ______

16. **95** miles to **40** miles ______

Write the unit price. Give the answer to the nearest cent.

17. **$1.69** for **8** ounces ______

18. **$5.99** for **3** notebooks ______

19. **$6.38** for **24** ounces ______

Complete the pair of equal ratios.

20. $\frac{3}{8} = \frac{\_\_}{40}$ **21.** $\frac{55}{66} = \frac{\_\_}{6}$ **22.** $\frac{7}{4} = \frac{\_\_}{48}$

Name ____________________

Scale Drawing

STANDARD

The picture of the flagpole is smaller than the actual flagpole. The ratio of the height in the picture to the height of the actual flagpole is called the **scale.** The picture is called a **scale drawing**.

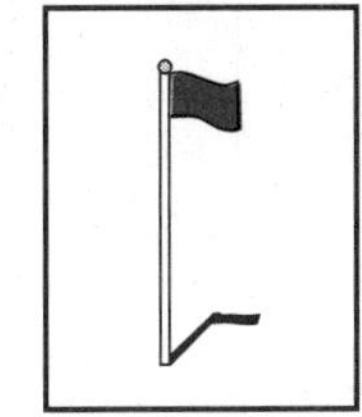

Scale: 1 cm = 3 m

The scale is **1** cm = **3** m.

So, **1** cm in the scale drawing represents **3** m of the actual height.

To find the actual height of the flagpole:

1. Measure the flagpole's height in the drawing. The flagpole is **2** cm tall.
2. Write equal ratios of the height in the scale drawing to the actual height.

height in scale drawing → / actual height → $\frac{1\text{ cm}}{3\text{ m}} = \frac{2\text{ cm}}{?}$ ← height in scale drawing / ← actual height

$\frac{1\text{ cm}}{3\text{ m}} = \frac{2\text{ cm}}{6\text{ m}}$

Think: 1 cm × **2** = **2** cm, so multiply **3** m by **2.**

The actual height of the flagpole is **6** m.

The scale of a map is 1 in. = 50 mi.
Complete each statement.

1. **3** in. represents ______ mi $\qquad$ $\frac{1}{2}$ in. represents ______ mi

2. ______ in. represents **200** mi $\qquad$ ______ in. represents **350** mi

---

The scale of a blueprint is $\frac{1}{8}$ in. = 1 ft.

Complete each statement. Write your answer in simplest form.

3. ______ in. represents **5** ft $\qquad$ ______ in. represents **12** ft

4. $\frac{3}{8}$ in. represents ______ ft $\qquad$ $\frac{5}{16}$ in. represents ______

Complete the table.

5.

Scale length	$\frac{1}{4}$ in.	1 in.	$\frac{1}{2}$ in.	2 in.		$1\frac{1}{2}$ in.		$3\frac{1}{4}$ in.	
Actual length	1 ft	4 ft			$\frac{1}{2}$ ft		11 ft		12 ft

STANDARD

Problem Solving Reasoning

Use the plans for building a bench to answer the questions. The grid lines are $\frac{1}{4}$ in. apart.

6. How long is the actual bench? ________

7. How tall is the actual bench? ________

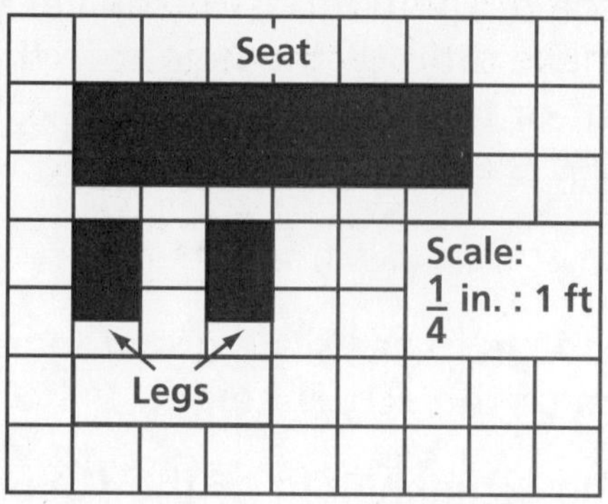

8. What is the area of the surface of the actual bench seat? ________

9. Make a scale drawing to show how the bench pieces could be cut from a **3**-feet by **6**-feet sheet of wood. Be sure to label what scale you use.

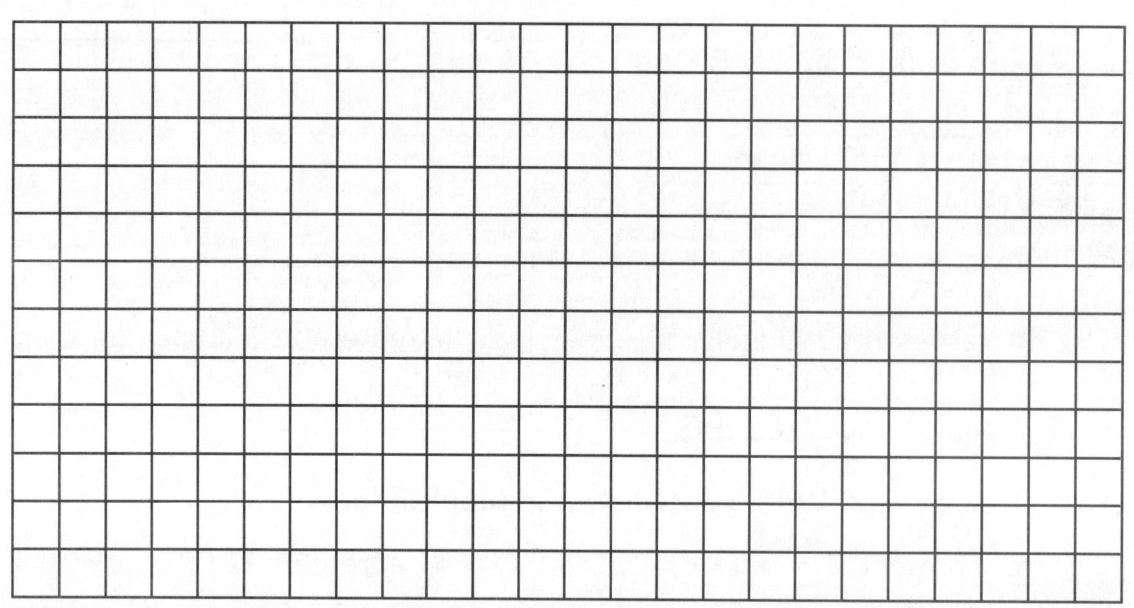

Test Prep ★ Mixed Review

10 Rosa baked two batches of cookies. One batch made $2\frac{2}{3}$ dozen cookies. The other made $3\frac{3}{4}$ dozen cookies. How many dozen cookies did she bake altogether?

A $5\frac{5}{7}$

B $5\frac{7}{12}$

C $6\frac{1}{13}$

D $6\frac{5}{12}$

11 Which number sentence shows the commutative property of addition using decimals?

F $1.2 + 3.7 = 2.1 + 7.3$

G $9.54 + 0 = 9.54$

H $6.45 + 2.35 = 2.35 + 6.45$

J $8.8 + (1.2 + 3.66) = (8.8 + 1.2) + 3.66$

Name ______________________

Problem Solving Strategy: Make a Table

STANDARD

To solve some problems, you may need to make a table to see a pattern.

Problem

In the first week of the season, a soccer team won 2 out of 3 games. By the end of the second week their record of wins to played games was 4 out of 6 games. At the end of the third week it was 6 out of 9 games. At this rate, how many games should the team expect to win after 15 games?

1 Understand **As you reread the problem, ask yourself questions.**

- What do you know about the record of wins to games played?

Each week the record changed.
1st week: 2 out of 3 won
2nd week: 4 out of 6 won
3rd week: 6 out of 9 won

What do you need to find?

____

2 Decide **Choose a method for solving.**

- Try the Make a Table strategy.

What will you label the rows in the table?

____

You should extend the table so you can find the pattern.

3 Solve **Make a table to solve.**

- Complete the table.

Games Played	3	6			
Games Won	2	4			

4 Look back **Check your answer.**

Write your answer below.

Answer: ______________________

STANDARD

Use the Make a Table Strategy or any other strategy you have learned.

1. On a trip of **150** miles, Mr. Gray's car used **5** gallons of gas. At this rate, how many gallons of gas will Mr. Gray need to go **270** miles?

Think: How many miles can be traveled on one gallon?

____

Answer ______________________

2. An architect wants to make a scale drawing of a room that is **12** ft by **20** ft. If the room is **3** in. wide in the scale drawing, find its length in the scale drawing.

Think: How many feet are represented by one inch?

____

Answer ______________________

3. The Camera Corner is having a sale on reprints. You can get **3** reprints for **72¢**. How much will you pay for **9** reprints?

____

4. Jerry paid **$2** sales tax on a coat that he bought for **$50**. How much will the sales tax be on the suit he is buying for **$200**?

____

5. For every half-hour TV show, there are **8** minutes of commercials. How many minutes of commercials are there in **2.5** hours of TV shows?

____

6. Shirley needed **9** rolls of wallpaper for her bedroom. Each roll covered **36** sq ft and cost **$12**. How much did the wallpaper for Shirley's bedroom cost?

____

7. Dana wants to enlarge a **3**-inch by **5**-inch photograph. If the new width will be **12** inches, what will be the new length?

____

8. Caryl used **2** pages in a photo album for **24** photos. She still has to put **60** more photos in the album. How many more pages does she need?

____

9. A punch recipe that serves **20** people calls for **5** cups of pineapple juice to be mixed with **4** cups of orange juice and **8** cups of ginger ale. How many cups of punch would serve **60** people?

____

10. In a survey of **400** people, it was found that **5** out of **8** people like Toasty Bread. How many people surveyed like Toasty Bread?

____

Name ______________________________

Meaning of Percent

STANDARD

Percent is a special ratio that compares a number to **100**.

In the grid, **67** out of **100** squares are shaded. The ratio of shaded squares to all the squares is $\frac{67}{100}$, or **67%**. The symbol % stands for **percent**.

Percent means per hundred.

Write what percent of each grid is shaded.

1. 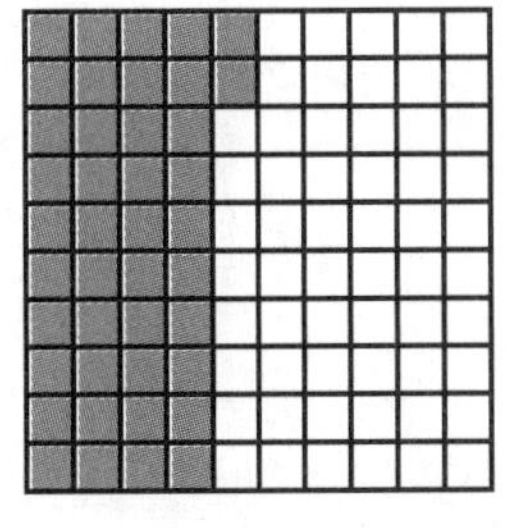 ________ ________  ________

2. 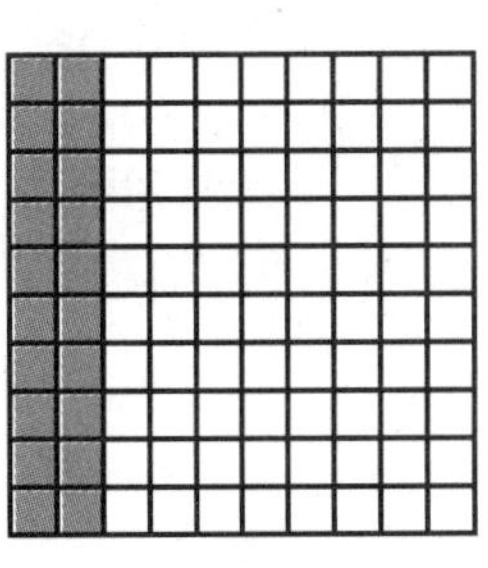 ________ ________ 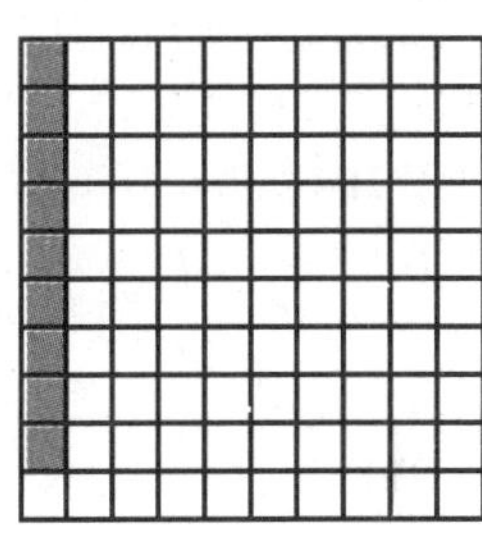 ________

Write each ratio as a percent.

3. $\frac{26}{100}$ ______ $\frac{80}{100}$ ______ $\frac{7}{100}$ ______ $\frac{55}{100}$ ______

4. $\frac{13}{100}$ ______ $\frac{71}{100}$ ______ $\frac{100}{100}$ ______ $\frac{3}{100}$ ______

Write each percent as a ratio.

5. 37% ______ 85% ______ 5% ______ 29% ______

6. 15% ______ 91% ______ 10% ______ 50% ______

STANDARD

Shade each grid to show the percent.

7.

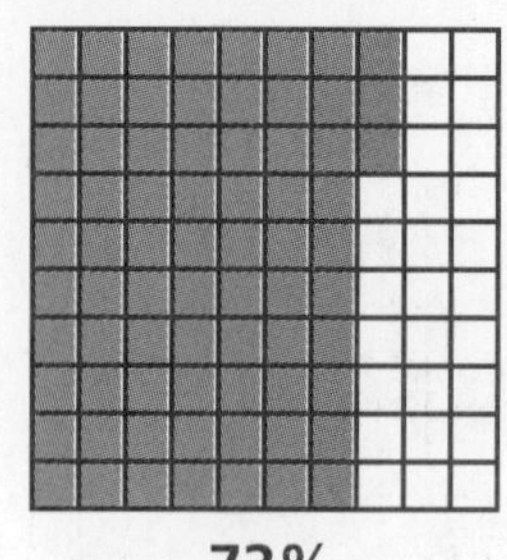

73%

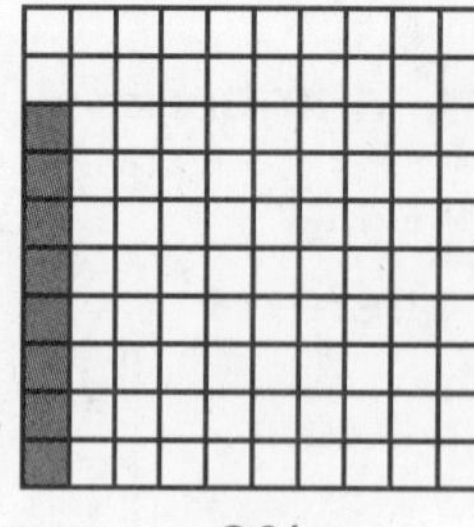

8%

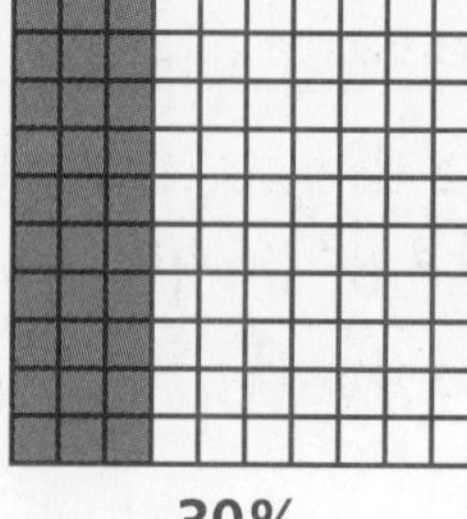

30%

8.

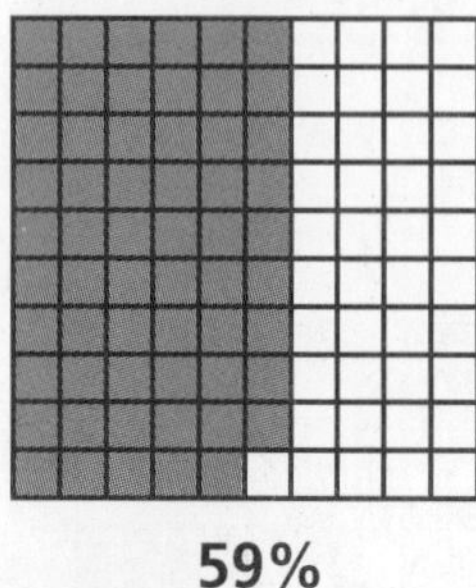

59%

100%

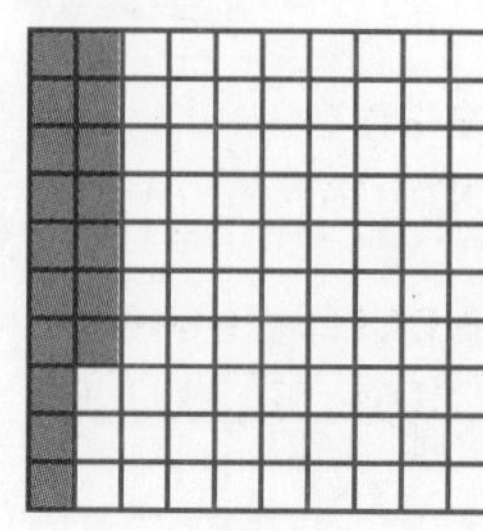

17%

Problem Solving Reasoning **Use the table to solve.**

Kind	Number of Students
Cheese	14
Pepperoni	38
Sausage	27
Vegetable	6
Deluxe	15

Favorite Pizza of 100 Students

9. What percent of the students chose pepperoni pizza? ______

10. What percent of the students chose cheese or sausage pizza? ______

11. What percent of the students did **not** choose vegetable pizza? ______

12. Would it have been possible for the table to show **110%** of the students surveyed? Explain. ______________________

Test Prep ★ Mixed Review

13 Halley is making scarves for a craft fair. Each scarf uses $1\frac{3}{8}$ yards of fabric. How much fabric does she need to make 12 scarves?

A 16 yards

B $16\frac{1}{2}$ yards

C 17 yards

D $17\frac{1}{2}$ yards

14 A 25-pound bag of potatoes costs $9.75. What is the cost of 1 pound of potatoes?

F $.39

G $.49

H $.59

J $.69

Name ______________________________

Fractions and Percent

STANDARD

You can write a **percent** as a **fraction.**

1. Write the percent as a fraction with a denominator of **100.**
2. Write the fraction in simplest form.

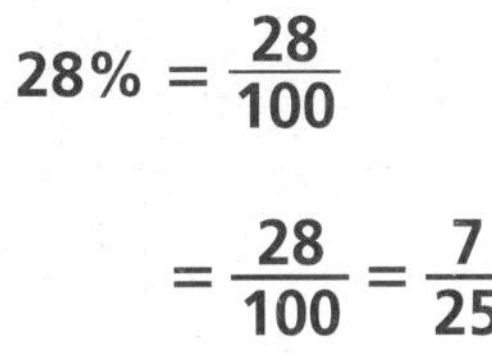

$28\% = \frac{28}{100}$

$= \frac{28}{100} = \frac{7}{25}$

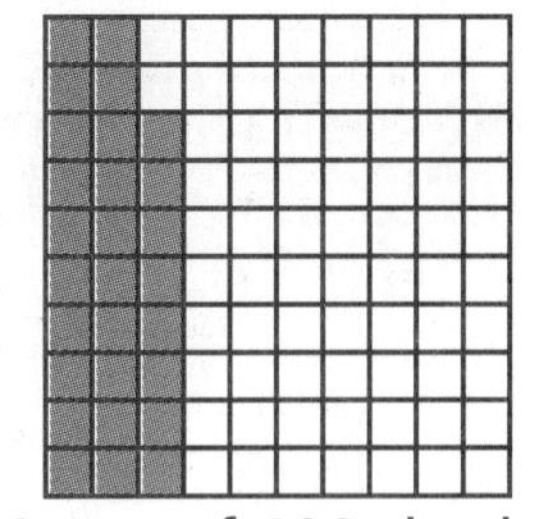

28 out of **100** shaded

You can also write a **fraction** as a **percent.**

1. Write an equivalent fraction with a denominator of **100.**
2. Since percent means per hundred, you can think, **45** out of **100** and write **45%.**

$\frac{9 \times 5}{20 \times 5} = \frac{45}{100}$

$\frac{45}{100} = 45\%$

What part of each grid is shaded? Write a percent and a fraction in simplest form.

1.

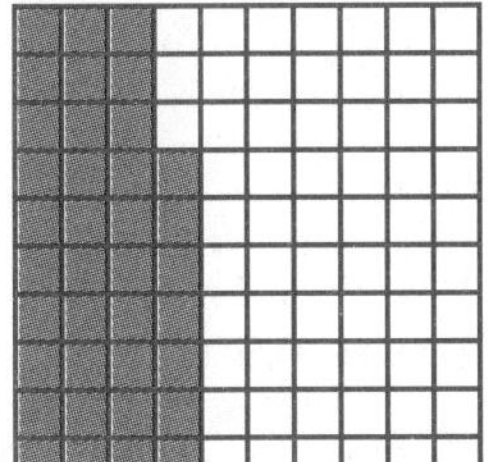

____

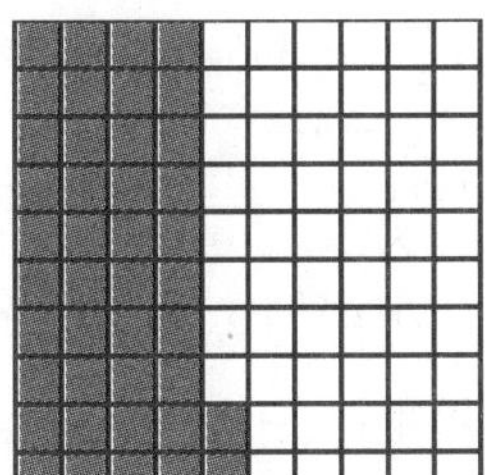

____

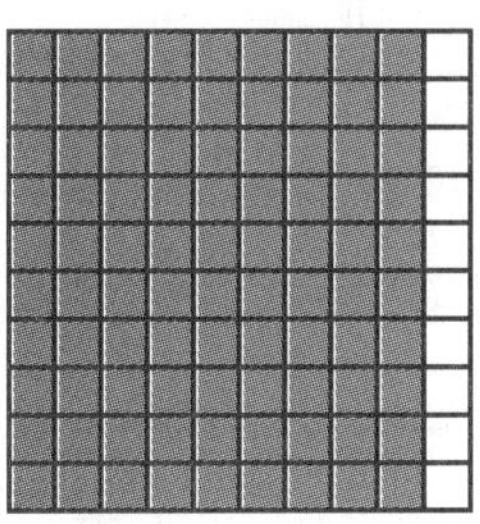

____

What part of each shape is shaded? Write a fraction in simplest form and a percent.

2.

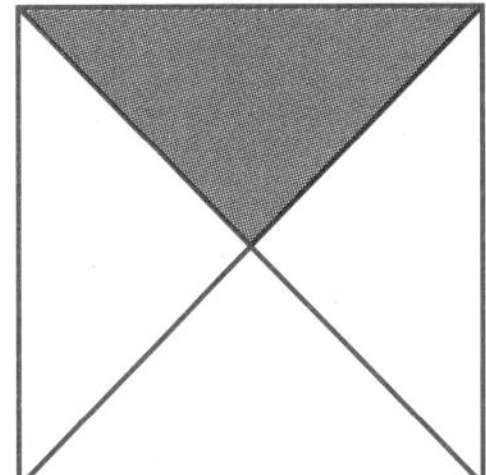

____

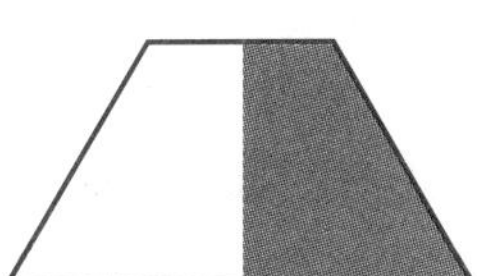

____

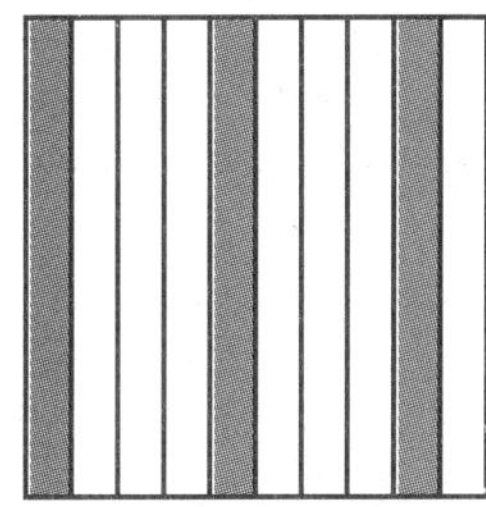

____

3.

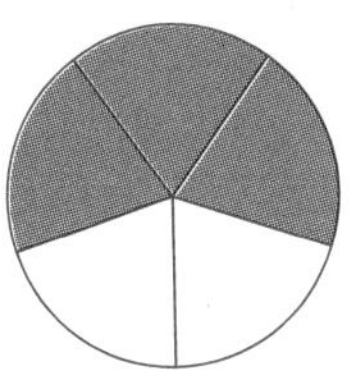

____

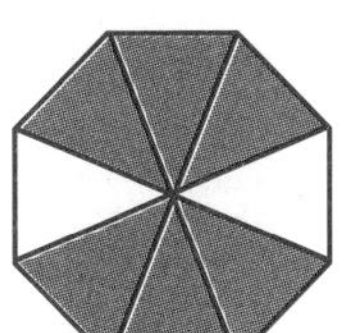

____

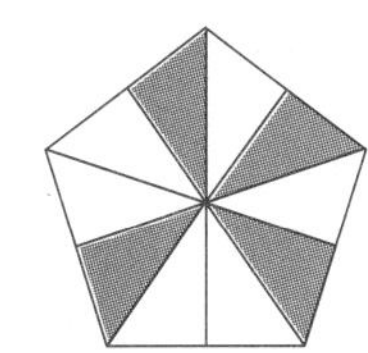

____

STANDARD

Write each percent as a fraction in simplest form.

4. 65% ______ 68% ______ 17% ______ 100% ______ 6% ______

Write each fraction as a percent.

5. $\frac{9}{100}$ ______ $\frac{23}{25}$ ______ $\frac{1}{10}$ ______ $\frac{1}{50}$ ______ $\frac{7}{10}$ ______

Complete the table.

6.

Fraction	$\frac{1}{2}$		$\frac{9}{10}$		$\frac{3}{4}$		$\frac{4}{5}$		$\frac{2}{5}$
Percent		60%		30%		20%		25%	

Problem Solving Reasoning Solve.

7. On a 20-question test, Molly answered 18 questions correctly. What percent of the questions did Molly answer correctly? ______

8. On a 25-question test, Paul answered 19 questions correctly. What percent of the questions did Paul answer **incorrectly?** ______

Quick Check

The scale on a map is 1 in. = 30 mi. Complete the statement.

9. 6 in. represents ______ mi.

10. ______ in. represents 75 mi.

Write the ratio as a percent.

11. $\frac{32}{100}$ ______ **12.** $\frac{9}{100}$ ______ **13.** $\frac{2}{100}$ ______

Write the percent as a fraction in simplest form.

14. 60% ______ **15.** 8% ______ **16.** 59% ______

Write the fraction as a percent.

17. $\frac{3}{4}$ ______ **18.** $\frac{7}{10}$ ______ **19.** $\frac{19}{25}$ ______

Work Space

Name ______________________________

Decimals as Percents and Percents as Decimals

You can write a percent as a decimal.

1. Write the percent as a fraction with a denominator of **100**.
2. Write the fraction as a decimal.

$$49\% = \frac{49}{100} = 0.49$$

49 out of **100** shaded

You can also write a decimal as a percent.

1. Write the decimal as a fraction with a denominator of **100**.
2. Write the fraction as a percent.

$$0.64 = \frac{64}{100}$$

$$\frac{64}{100} = 64\%$$

What part of each grid is shaded? Write a percent and a decimal.

1. 

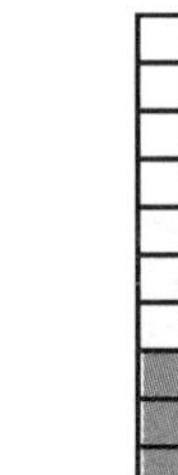

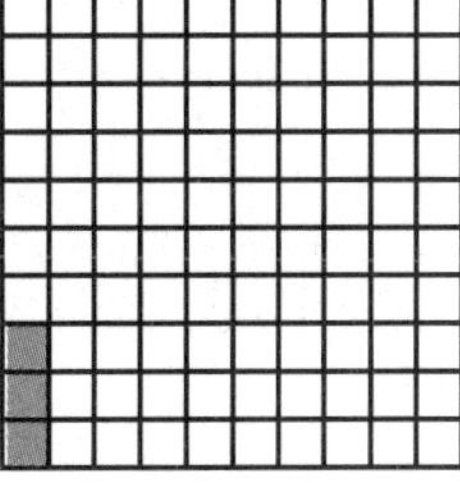

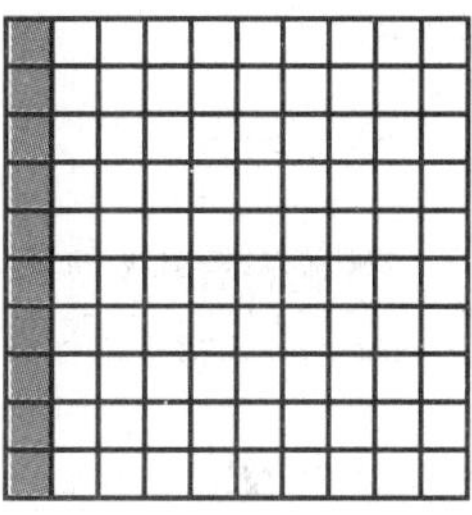

______ ______ ______ ______

______ ______ ______ ______

Write each percent as a decimal.

2. 62% ______ 5% ______ 30% ______ 99% ______

3. 1% ______ 40% ______ 33% ______ 58% ______

4. 6% ______ 21% ______ 100% ______ 60% ______

5. 33% ______ 68% ______ 8% ______ 87% ______

6. 17% ______ 9% ______ 10% ______ 5% ______

STANDARD

Write each decimal as a percent.

7. 0.76 ______ 0.9 ______ 0.02 ______ 0.11 ______

8. 0.6 ______ 0.39 ______ 0.65 ______ 0.01 ______

9. 0.27 ______ 0.08 ______ 0.84 ______ 0.4 ______

10. 0.8 ______ 0.4 ______ 1.00 ______ 0.95 ______

Complete the table.

11.

Decimal			0.3		0.25	0.6		0.2	
Percent	75%	40%		50%			10%		80%

Problem Solving Reasoning

Solve.

12. A race was held last weekend. Nine tenths of the cars finished the race. What percent of the cars did **not** finish the race?

______

13. A car still had **87** hundredths of the race to finish when it developed engine trouble. What percent of the race had it completed?

______

14. Marcus got **45** out of **50** questions correct on a math test. What percent did he get correct?

______

15. A 1-liter juice drink contains **0.10** liter of juice. What percent of the drink is juice?

______

Test Prep ★ Mixed Review

16 The ABC Bottling Company measured the diameter of several bottle caps. Which four of these measurements are listed from least to greatest?

A 2.72 cm, 2.702 cm, 2.707 cm, 2.722 cm

B 2.7 cm, 2.722 cm, 2.702 cm, 2.707 cm

C 2.702 cm, 2.707 cm, 2.72 cm, 2.722 cm

D 2.702 cm, 2.707 cm, 2.722 cm, 2.72 cm

17 A company makes bars of soap. The soap is mixed in large vats, then poured into molds to make 560 bars of soap. The mixture weighs 1,792 ounces. How much does each bar of soap weigh?

F 3 oz

G 3.2 oz

H 30 oz

J 32 oz

Name ______________________________

Fractions, Decimals, and Percents

STANDARD

Fractions, decimals and percents are all related. You know that a number that can be written as a fraction can also be written as a decimal or percent.

Complete the table. Write each fraction in simplest form.

	Fraction	Decimal	Percent
1.		0.37	
2.			48%
3.	$\frac{2}{5}$		
4.			8%
5.	$\frac{1}{10}$		
6.		0.85	
7.			100%
8.	$\frac{11}{20}$		

Write the fraction, decimal, and percent for the point on the number line.

9. 

____

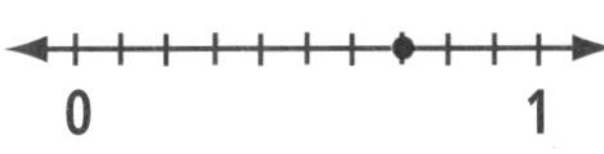

____

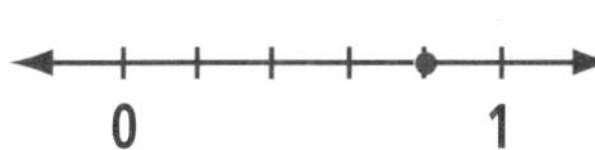

____

10. 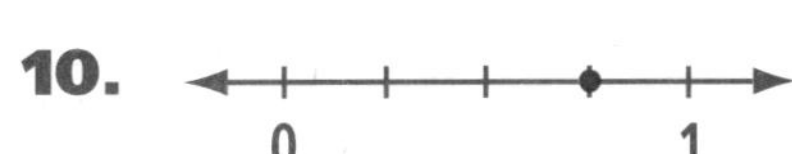

____

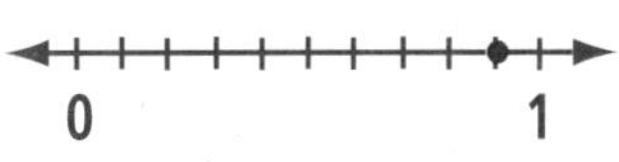

____

0 1
____

11. 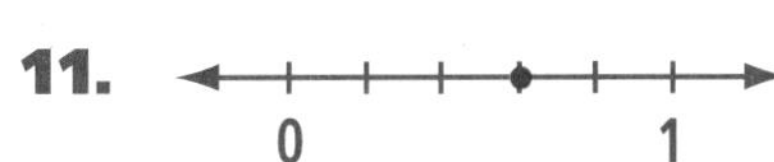

____

____

____

STANDARD

You can compare and order fractions, decimals, and percents. First rewrite them in the same form.

Compare **0.3** ◯ **25%**. Write >, <, or =.

Think: 0.3 = 0.30 = 30%	or	Think: 25% = 0.25
30% (>) 25%		0.3 (>) 0.25
0.3 (>) 25%		0.3 (>) 25%

Compare. Write >, <, or =.

12. $\frac{1}{10}$ ◯ 0.11 $\qquad$ $\frac{3}{5}$ ◯ 53% $\qquad$ 90% ◯ 0.9 $\qquad$ $\frac{18}{25}$ ◯ 72%

13. 0.8 ◯ 88% $\qquad$ 50% ◯ 0.06 $\qquad$ 0.2 ◯ $\frac{1}{5}$ $\qquad$ 70% ◯ $\frac{3}{4}$

Order each set of numbers from least to greatest.

14. 56%, $\frac{1}{2}$, 0.6 $\qquad$ 0.7, $\frac{17}{25}$, 8% $\qquad$ $\frac{3}{4}$, 72%, 0.5

______ $\qquad$ ______ $\qquad$ ______

Problem Solving Reasoning **Solve.**

15. In one class, **0.8** of the students like to play baseball and $\frac{5}{8}$ like to play basketball. Do more students like to play baseball or basketball?

Explain. ______

______

16. In another class, **60%** of the students have a dog and $\frac{2}{3}$ have a cat. Do more students have a dog or a cat?

Explain. ______

______

Test Prep ★ Mixed Review

17 **Which mixed number is equivalent to 2.125?**

A $2\frac{1}{8}$

B $2\frac{3}{25}$

C $2\frac{1}{80}$

D $2\frac{125}{100}$

18 **At birth, Rita's baby sister weighed $7\frac{1}{4}$ pounds. How many ounces is this?**

F 58 ounces

G 87 ounces

H $72\frac{1}{2}$ ounces

J 116 ounces

Name ______________________

Percent of a Number

STANDARD

A pair of inline skates regularly costs **$120.**
They are now on sale for **25%** off.
How much would you save if you bought the skates on sale?

Think: Find **25%** of **$120.**

You can find a percent of a number in different ways.

1. Write the percent as a fraction.

$$25\% = \frac{25}{100}$$
$$= \frac{1}{4}$$

2. Multiply **120** by the fraction.

$$120 \times \frac{1}{4} = \frac{120}{4}$$
$$= 30$$

1. Write the percent as a decimal.

$$25\% = \frac{25}{100}$$
$$= 0.25$$

2. Multiply **$120** by the decimal.

$$\begin{array}{r} \$120 \\ \times\ 0.25 \\ \hline 600 \\ +\ 2400 \\ \hline \$30.00 \end{array}$$

You would save **$30.**

Find each percent.

1. 20% of 75 ________

2. 50% of 64 ________

3. 30% of 270 ________

4. 75% of 60 ________

5. 80% of 45 ________

6. 70% of 700 ________

7. 25% of 3,600 ________

8. 90% of 2,000 ________

9. 40% of 1,500 ________

STANDARD

When an exact amount is not needed, you can estimate the percent of a number.

Think of compatible numbers when you estimate.

52% of 609	13% of 78	21% of 115	74% of 62
Think: 50% of 600 $\frac{1}{2} \times 600 = 300.$	Think: 10% of 80 $\frac{1}{10} \times 80 = 8.$	Think: 20% of 100 $\frac{1}{5} \times 100 = 20.$	Think: 70% of 60 $\frac{7}{10} \times 60 = 42.$

Estimate the percent.

10. 9% of 28 ________ 77% of 16 ________ 48% of 98 ________

11. 59% of 206 ________ 51% of 3,956 ________ 42% of 1,017 ________

Problem Solving Reasoning Solve.

12. A store just received **20** jackets. Of these, **15%** were damaged. How many jackets are **not** damaged?

____

13. A jacket regularly sells for **$78.95**. It is now on sale for **20%** off. Carlos has saved **$55.** Does he have enough money to buy the jacket? Explain.

____

Quick Check

Write the percent as a decimal.

14. 86% ______ **15.** 4% ______ **16.** 30% ______

Write the decimal as a percent.

17. 0.83 ______ **18.** 0.1 ______ **19.** 0.09 ______

Write the numbers in order from least to greatest.

20. 45%, $\frac{2}{5}$, 0.48 ______ **21.** $\frac{2}{3}$, 0.65, 6% ______

Write the percent of the number.

22. 80% of 35 ______ **23.** 30% of 90 ______ **24.** 75% of 56 ______

Work Space

Name ______________________

Problem Solving Application: Use a Circle Graph

STANDARD

This circle graph shows the results of a survey of how often people correspond with family and friends by e-mail. There were 800 people in the survey.

In this lesson, you will use the graph to compare or draw conclusions about data in the graph.

Survey: How often do you use e-mail to correspond with friends and family?

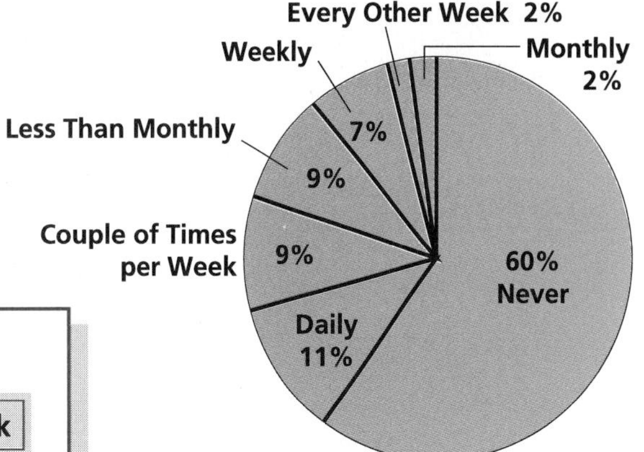

Tips to Remember

1. Understand 2. Decide 3. Solve 4. Look back

- Read the problem carefully. Ask yourself questions about any part that does not make sense. Reread to find answers.
- Compare the labels on the graph with the words and numbers in the problem. Find the facts you need from the graph.
- Ask yourself whether you have solved a problem like this before.

Solve.

1. Is it true that more than half the people have never used e-mail?

Think: What percent is the same as half?

____

Answer ______________________

2. How many people use e-mail at least once a week?

Think: What operations do you need to do to solve this problem?

____

Answer ______________________

3. How many people never use e-mail?

____

4. How many more people use e-mail weekly than monthly?

____

STANDARD

This circle graph shows how the students of the Hancock School raised money to buy a new computer. The total amount raised was **$1,200**.

How Money Was Raised by Students of Hancock School

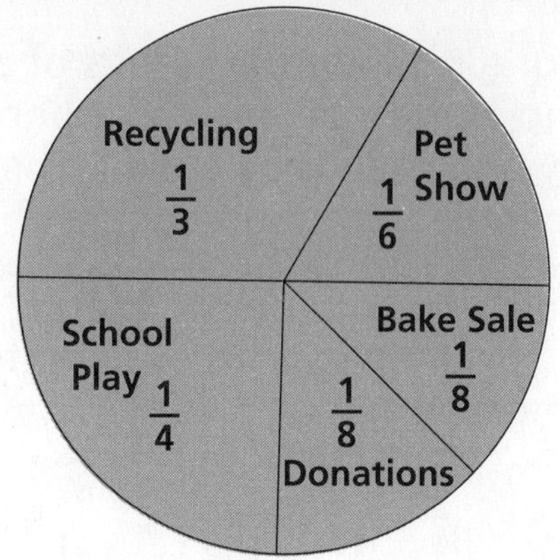

Solve.

5. How was the greatest amount of money raised? How much was raised this way?

____

____

6. Which three ways of raising money for the new computer are together equivalent to **75%** of the money raised?

____

____

7. How much more money was raised from the school play than from the bake sale?

____

8. How much money was raised from the pet show and donations?

____

9. Collect data on the number and types of books you can find in your classroom. Organize your data using the types listed at the right, or choose other types. Make a bar graph of your data.

Some Types of Books
textbook, workbook, reference book, story book

Extend Your Thinking

10. A circle has **360°**. How many degrees are in the Pet Show part of the circle graph?

____

11. Look back at problem 6. Explain the method you used to solve the problem.

____

____

Name ____________________

Unit 9 Review

Write each unit cost. Round your answer to the nearest cent when necessary.

1. 42 oz for **$12.18** ________

2. 6 cans for **$1.49** ________

Use the scale drawing.

3. What is the actual distance between the library and the school? Use a ruler to help decide. ______

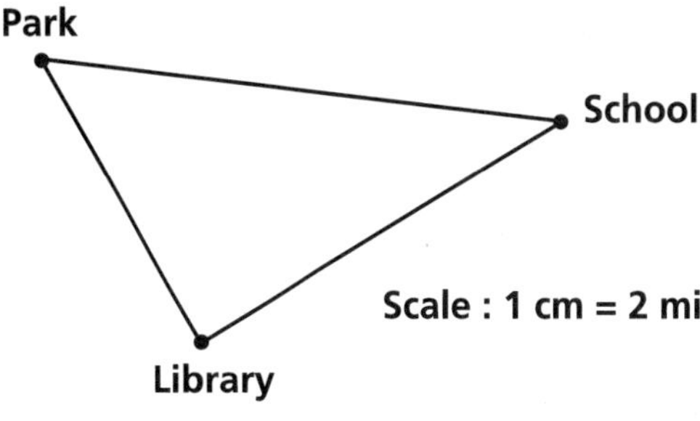

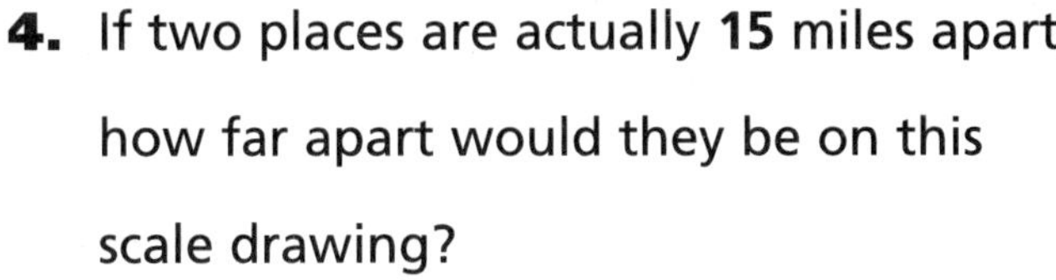

4. If two places are actually **15** miles apart, how far apart would they be on this scale drawing? ________

5. What percent of this grid is shaded? ______

6. What percent is **not** shaded? ______

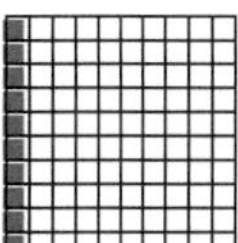

Write each percent as a decimal and fraction in simplest form.
Write each fraction as a decimal and percent.

7. 16% ________

8. 40% ________

9. $\frac{3}{8}$ ________

10. What is **75%** of **120**? ______

11. What is **60%** of **25**? ______

Solve. Use the circle graph.

12. How many students said they would **not** vote for Candidate C?

____

Class Election
20 students surveyed

Candidate A 50%
Candidate B 20%
Candidate C 30%

Solve. Make a table or use another strategy.

13. During a **256** mile trip, an automobile used **8** gallons of gasoline. At that rate, how far can the automobile travel using **12** gallons of gasoline? ________

Name ______________________

Cumulative Review
★ Test Prep

Ms. Li's class recorded the temperature at 11 A.M. every day for two weeks. Use the graph of their data for exercises 1 and 2.

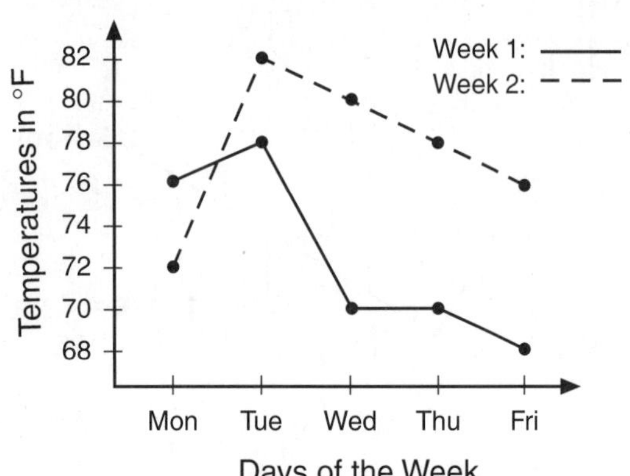

1 **What was the difference in temperature between the two Thursdays?**

A 5°F　　C 7°F

B 6°F　　D 8°F

2 **Between which two days did the temperature have the greatest decrease?**

F Monday and Tuesday, Week 1

G Monday and Tuesday, Week 2

H Tuesday and Wednesday, Week 1

J Tuesday and Wednesday, Week 2

3 **What is the surface area of the prism?**

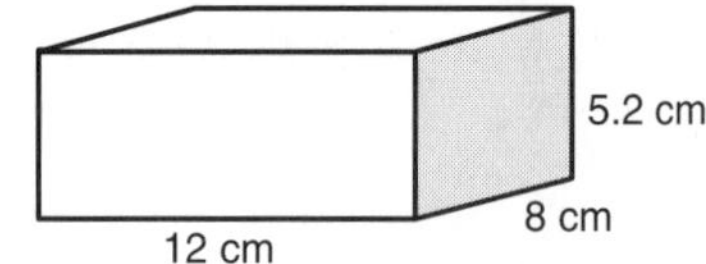

A 200 cm^2　　C 499.2 cm^2

B 400 cm^2　　D 500 cm^2

4 **The sixth grade students at River City are planning a field trip. Of the 150 sixth graders, 68% have decided to go. How many students is this?**

F 48　　H 100

G 68　　J 102　　K Not here

Use the figure below for exercises 5–7.

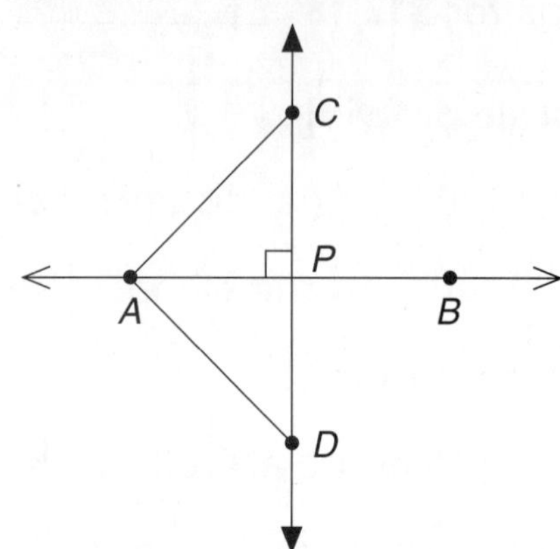

5 **Use your centimeter ruler. How long is $\overline{AB}$?**

A 3 cm　　C 3.4 cm

B 3.2 cm　　D 3.6 cm

6 **Which two lines are perpendicular?**

F $\overline{AD}$ and $\overline{CD}$

G $\overline{AB}$ and $\overline{CD}$

H $\overline{AC}$ and $\overline{CD}$

J $\overline{AB}$ and $\overline{AD}$

7 **Which angle is a right angle?**

A $\angle CAB$　　C $\angle CPB$

B $\angle CAP$　　D $\angle CPD$

8 **What percent of the square is shaded?**

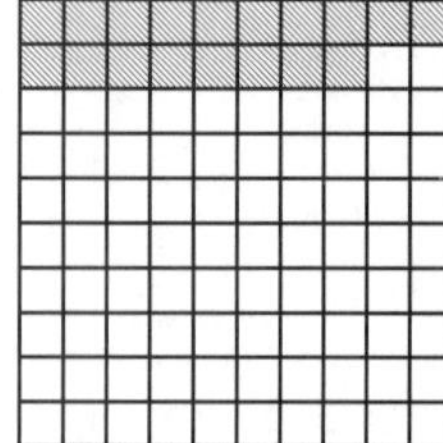

F 9%　　H 82%

G 18%　　J 91%

UNIT 10 • TABLE OF CONTENTS

Data, Statistics, and Probability

We will be using this vocabulary:

average the sum of the numbers in a set of data divided by the number of addends in the set; an average is also called a **mean**

median the middle number in a set of data after the data set has been arranged in order from least to greatest or from greatest to least

mode the number(s) that appear(s) most often in a set of data

range the difference between the greatest and the least number in a set of data

probability the chance that an event will occur

Dear Family,

During the next few weeks, our math class will be learning about data, statistics, and probability.

You can expect to see homework that provides practice with finding the mean and the median. Here is a sample you may want to keep handy to give help if needed.

Mean and Median

Example Find the mean of this set of data: **41, 37, 27, 21, 34.**

1. To find the mean of a set of numbers, first add the numbers. — **41 + 37 + 27 + 21 + 34 = 160**

2. Then divide the sum by the number of addends (or numbers that were added). The quotient or answer is the mean. — **160 ÷ 5 = 32** (32 = mean; 5 = number of addends)

Example Find the median of this set of data: **41, 37, 27, 21, 34.**

1. To find the median of a set of numbers, first order the numbers from least to greatest. — **21 27 34 37 41**

2. Then find the middle number. In this set, 34 is the middle number or median. — **21 27 34 37 41**

If a set of data has two middle numbers, the median is the mean or average of those two numbers.

During this unit, students will need to continue practicing addition and division facts.

Sincerely,

Name ________________________________

Stem-and-Leaf Plots and Histograms

STANDARD

The speed limit near Kim's school is **20** miles per hour. A police officer recorded the speeds at the right for **14** cars.

Speeds of cars (miles per hour)				
18	20	25	25	45
18	32	15	21	10
12	19	30	9	

You can organize this data in a **stem-and-leaf plot.** To understand stem-and-leaf plots, think how the leaves of a plant are connected to the stem. In a stem-and-leaf plot for 2-digit numbers:

- the tens digits form the stem,
- the ones digits form the leaves.

Use these steps to make a stem-and-leaf plot of the data.

1. Write the tens' digits in the stem.

Stem	
0	
1	
2	
3	
4	

2. Write each ones digit to form the leaves.

Stem	Leaves
0	9
1	8 8 5 0 2 9
2	0 5 5 1
3	2 0
4	5

3. Order the leaves from least to greatest.

Stem	Leaves
0	9
1	0 2 5 8 8 9
2	0 1 5 5
3	0 2
4	5

Key: 0|9 means 9 miles per hour

A stem of **0** and a leaf of **9** means that the slowest speed was **9** mph.

A stem of **4** and a leaf of **5** means that the fastest speed was **45** mph.

Use the stem-and-leaf plot to answer each question.

History Test Scores

Stems	Leaves
6	3 5
7	1 6 6 7
8	0 0 2 9
9	2 3 3 5 8

1. What was the greatest score on the history test? _____

2. What was the least test score? _____

3. How many test scores are shown in the plot? _____

4. How many scores were less than **80** ? _____

Refer to the height data in the table.

Height in Inches of West Middle School Teachers
66, 72, 73, 65, 60, 62, 70, 75, 66, 64

5. Complete the stem-and-leaf plot of the data.

Teachers' Height in Inches

Stems	Leaves
_____	_____ _____ _____ _____ _____ _____
_____	_____ _____ _____ _____

6. Look at a ruler to see how long **100** mm is. Then, without looking at the ruler, try to draw a **100** mm line segment. Repeat **10** times. Measure your line segments to the nearest millimeter. Make a stem-and-leaf plot of your measurement data.

STANDARD

A **histogram** is a special bar graph. Look at the histogram for Speed of Cars. The **horizontal scale** shows numbers that represent miles per hour. The **vertical scale** shows the number of cars. There are no spaces between the bars in a histogram.

You can use a stem-and-leaf plot to make a histogram.

1. Draw rectangles around each row of leaves to make bars.
2. Turn the plot so that the bars you drew are vertical.
3. Use the stem as a guide for dividing the data into sets of numbers on the horizontal scale. Each set is called an interval.

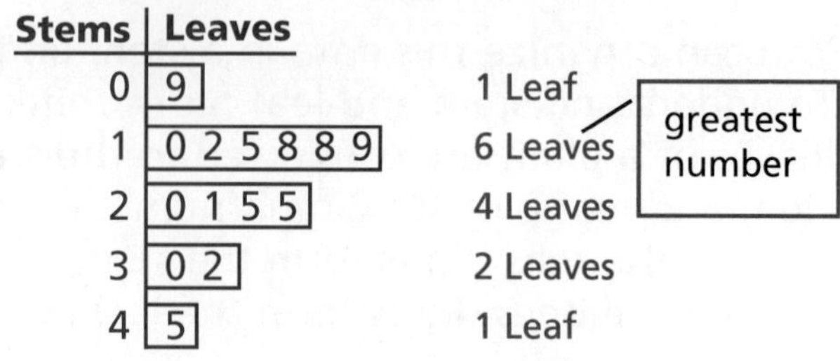

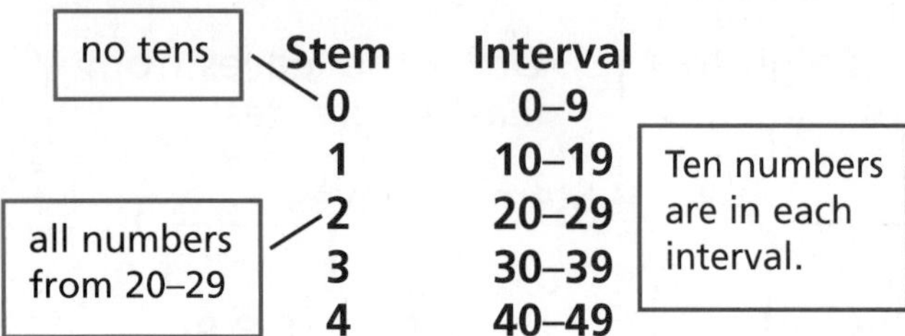

Label the horizontal scale.

4. Since the greatest number of leaves on the plot is 6, make six equal sections on the vertical scale. Label the sections **0–6**. Label the vertical scale.
5. Choose a title. Then shade the bars.

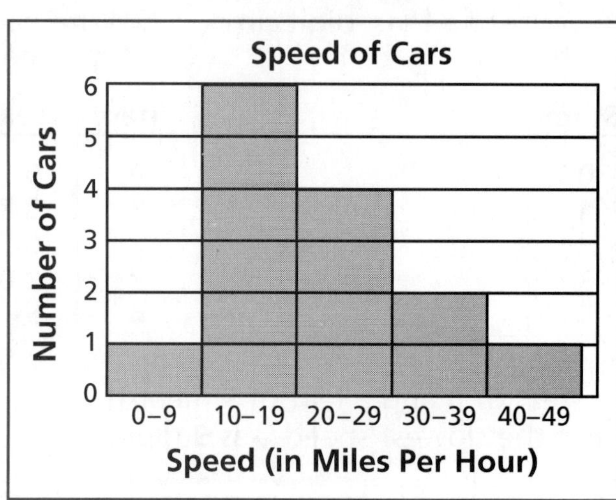

Use the histogram above to answer each question.

7. How many cars had speeds from **20** mph to **29** mph? ______

8. How many cars had speeds from **40** mph to **49** mph? ______

9. Which interval has the least number of speeds? ______

10. How many speeds were greater than or equal to the speed limit of **20** mph? ______

Test Prep ★ Mixed Review

11 **Lena shaded 25 out of 100 squares. What percent of the squares did she shade?**

A 25

B $\frac{1}{4}$

C 0.25%

D 25%

12 **A gift box is in the shape of a cube 8 in. on each side. How much wrapping paper would you need to wrap the box?**

F less than 300 in.^{2}

G less than 384 in.^{2}

H more than 384 in.^{2}

J more than 512 in.^{3}

Name ______________________

Comparing with Graphs

STANDARD

These data show the number of students in each after-school activity.

Students' After-School Activities

Activity	Students
Tennis	40
Softball	45
Basketball	55
Swimming	60
Language Club	33
Baseball	55
Glee Club	28
Chess Club	22

You can make a graph to see the relationships among the data. First, you need to choose the appropriate graph to make.

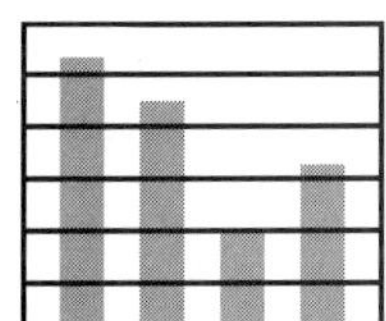

A bar graph is a good choice when the data can be counted.

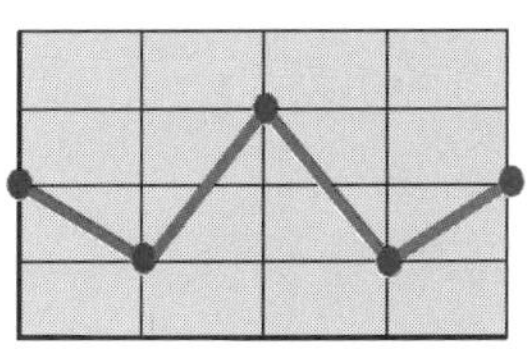

A line graph is appropriate when you want to show changes over time.

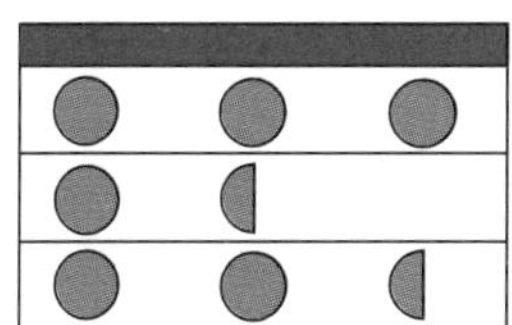

A pictograph is a good choice when the data are in multiples.

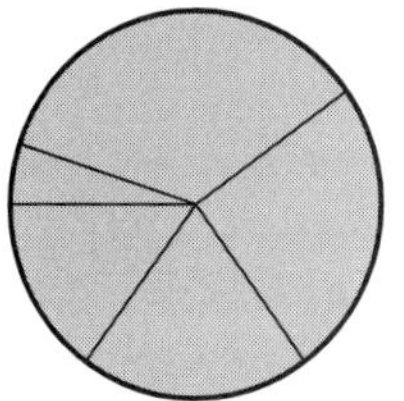

A circle graph is a good choice when the data are part of a whole.

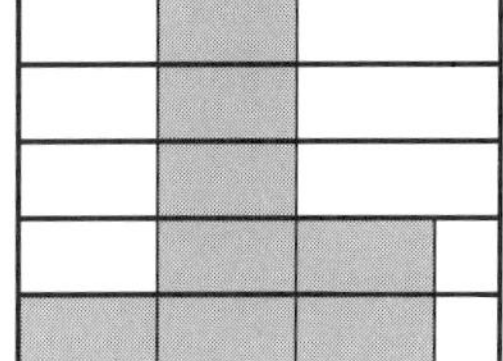

A histogram is a good choice to show how often something happens within a given set of numbers.

Use the data to answer the questions.

1. Which kinds of graphs could represent the data in the table?

____

2. Which kind of graph would **best** represent the after-school data? Explain.

____

3. Which type of graph would you use to show how the number of students in the Chess Club changes throughout the year? Explain.

____

4. Which type of graph would you use to show how many of the Glee Club members are sopranos, altos, tenors, or basses? Explain.

____

STANDARD

Graphs also can be used to show patterns in data.
These two graphs show the weather conditions for a month.

Weather Conditions	
Sunny	○ ○ ○ ○ ○
Cloudy	○ ○
Partly Cloudy	○ ○
Rainy	○
Key	Each ○ = 3 days

Weather Conditions

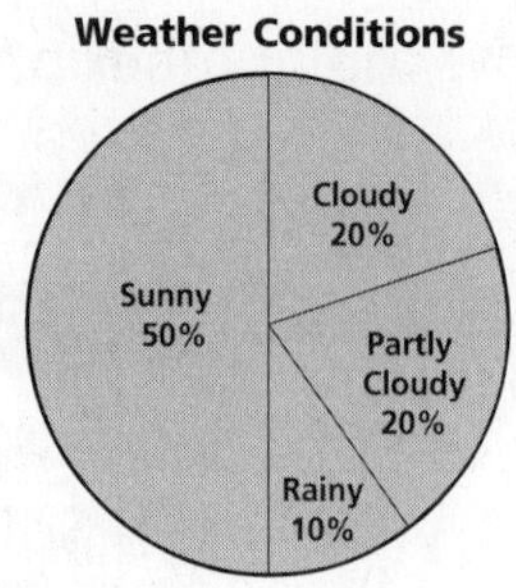

Complete. Tell which graph you used to answer the question.

5. Which months could this data represent? Explain.

____

____

6. True, false, or can't tell? Most days of the month had some sunshine.

____

____

7. By looking at the graphs can you tell that half the days were not sunny? Explain.

____

____

8. Which graph clearly shows the large difference between rainy and sunny days?

____

____

Problem Solving Reasoning Solve. Use the bar graph to answer the question.

9. What might make you think that Kyle sold more buttons than the others?

____

10. How could you change the graph to correctly display the data?

____

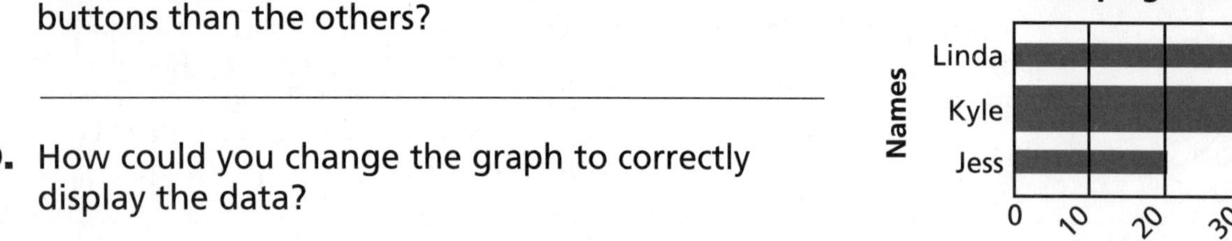

Test Prep ★ Mixed Review

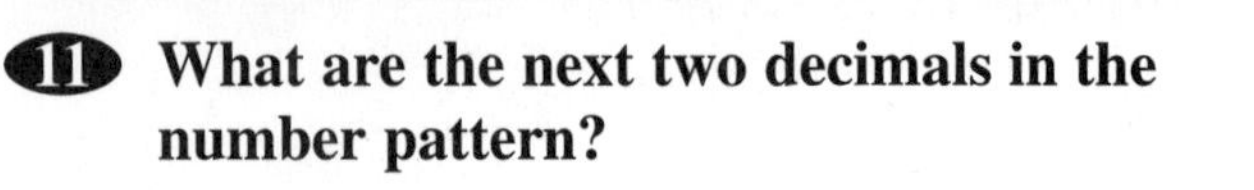

11 **What are the next two decimals in the number pattern?**

5.028, 5.018, ______?, ______?

A 5.0008, 5.008

B 5.008, 4.998

C 5.038, 5.048

D 5.08, 4.98

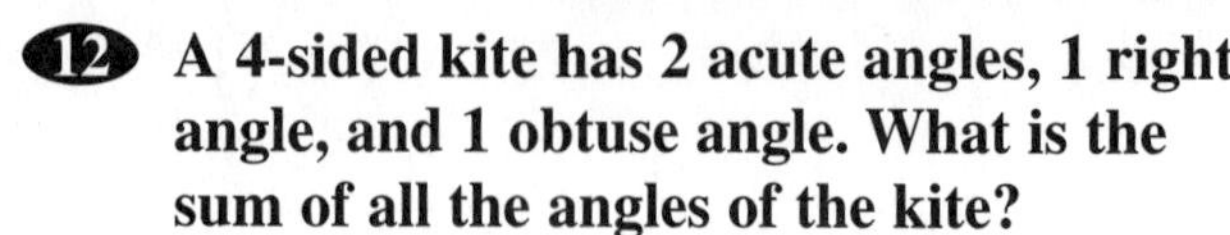

12 **A 4-sided kite has 2 acute angles, 1 right angle, and 1 obtuse angle. What is the sum of all the angles of the kite?**

F 360°

G 270°

H 180°

J 90°

Name ___________________________________

Mean, Median, Mode, and Range

STANDARD

"How many uses for string can you name?" This survey question was asked of **15** students. Their answers are listed below.

The **range, mean, mode,** and **median** are different ways of describing this data.

The **range** is the difference between the greatest and least numbers. **10 − 1 = 9,** so the range is **9.**

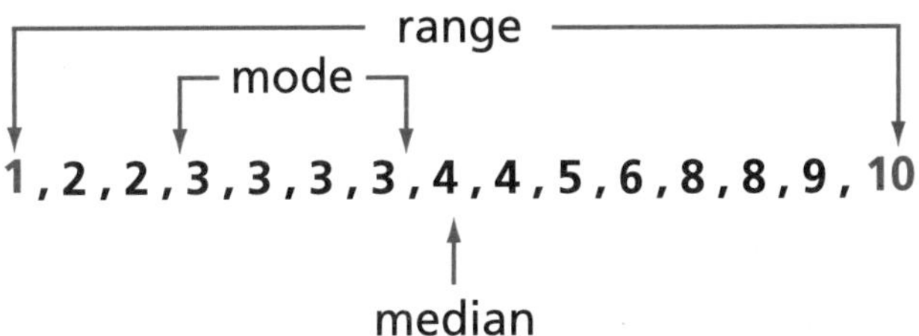

The **mean,** or average, is the sum of the items divided by the number of items. The mean rounded to the nearest tenth is **4.7.**

1 + 2 + 2 + 3 + 3 + 3 + 3 + 4 + 4 + 5 + 6 + 8 + 8 + 9 + 10 = 71

71 ÷ 15 = 4.73

number of students

The **mode** is the number that occurs most often. The mode is **3.** Data may have more than one mode or no mode at all.

The **median** is the middle number when the items are arranged in order. The median for the data above is **4.** In the data below, the median is the mean of the two middle numbers.

3, 7, 8, 9, 11, 14 → 8 + 9 = 17 → 17 ÷ 2 = 8.5

The median is **8.5**

Find the mean, median, range, and mode for each set of data. Round the mean to the nearest tenth. Remember to order the numbers.

1. **10, 12, 15, 15, 10, 9**

mean: ______
median: ______
range: ______
mode: ______

72, 62, 75, 76, 72, 66, 72

mean: ______
median: ______
range: ______
mode: ______

22, 22, 11, 21, 20, 21, 23

mean: ______
median: ______
range: ______
mode: ______

2. **4, 1, 1, 5, 8, 9, 8, 4, 8, 2**

mean: ______
median: ______
range: ______
mode: ______

11, 12, 11, 5, 13, 8, 8, 11

mean: ______
median: ______
range: ______
mode: ______

100, 120, 117, 116, 100

mean: ______
median: ______
range: ______
mode: ______

STANDARD

Problem Solving — Reasoning

Solve. Use the table to answer the questions.

Skateboards	
Style	**Price**
Red	$20
Metallic Blue	$22
Metallic Green	$22
Glow-in-the-Dark	$48
Special Wheels	$52
Extra Features	$75
Deluxe	$98

3. What is the median price? ______

4. What is the range of prices? ______

5. Will adding a **$25** skateboard to the list increase, decrease, or leave the median unchanged? Explain.

______

______

6. Melissa wants to know how much she should save to buy a skateboard. Wilma said, "The price most often seen for a skateboard is **$22**." Tommy said, "The average cost of a skateboard is about **$48**." To whom should Melissa listen? Explain. ______

______

Quick Check

The stem-and-leaf plot shows the fat grams of a cup of nuts. Use the stem-and-leaf plot to answer the questions.

Fat Grams per Cup of Nuts

Stems	Leaves
6	4 7 9
7	2 5 7 7
8	7
9	6

Work Space

7. Peanuts have **72** grams of fat per cup. How many nuts have less than **72** grams of fat? ______

8. In a histogram of the data, which interval would have the highest bar? ______

9. Suppose you want to find the differences between fat grams. Could a line graph of the data help you do this? Explain. ______

10. Suppose that a cup of peanuts has **38** grams of protein and **27** grams of carbohydrate. What kind of graph would you use to compare fat, carbohydrate, and protein grams as part of the total number of grams?

Explain. ______

11. Find the mean, median, mode, and range for the fat data in the completed stem-and-leaf plot.

______

Name ___________________________

According to the Constitution, the President of the United States must be at least 35 years old. This list shows the inaugural ages of all U.S. presidents since **1901.**

Ages: **42, 51, 56, 55, 51, 60, 62, 43, 55, 56, 61, 52, 64, 46, 69, 54, 51**

A **line plot** can be used to order lists of data. To make a line plot, first make a number line. Then put an X above each number as many times as the number appears in the list.

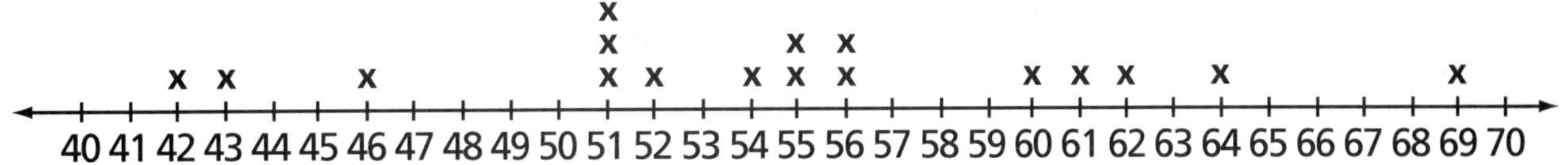

Use the line plot to answer these questions about the data.

1. Explain how to find the range of the data. What is the range?

____

2. Vice President Theodore Roosevelt became president upon the death of William McKinley in 1901. He was the youngest president inaugurated. How old was he then? ________

3. The next-youngest president was John F. Kennedy. How old was he at his inauguration in 1961? ________

4. Ronald Reagan was the oldest president at his inauguration in 1981. How old was he then? ________

5. The greatest number of presidents were inaugurated at what age? ____

6. What is the median of these presidents' ages at inauguration? ____

7. What is the mean of these presidents' ages at inauguration? Round your answer to the nearest tenth. ____

8. What is the mode of the ages? ____

9. If **42**, **43**, and **69** are removed from this list of data, how does the mean change? Explain. ___________________________

STANDARD

A line plot also allows you to see the *shape* of the data.If you draw a line above the *X*s, you can see that the data curve up and down.

A **cluster** is a group of data on a line plot that are close together.

A **gap** is a space between data on a line plot.

An **outlier** is a data point on either end of a line plot that is very far away from the other values.

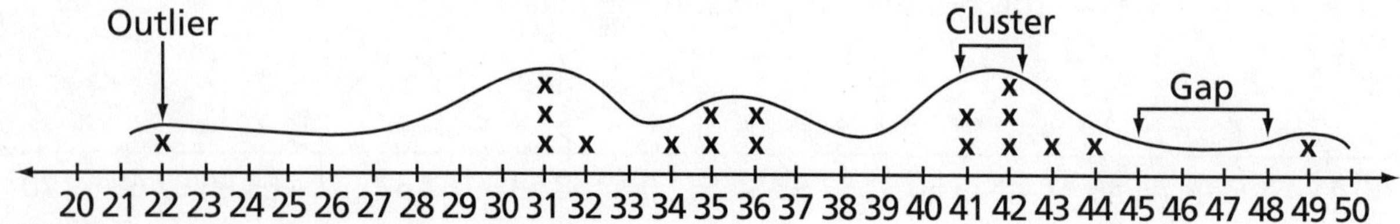

Use the line plot to answer each question.

10. There are **3** clusters in this line plot. Between which numbers are the clusters? ______ and ______

11. Name **2** outliers in this line plot.______ and ______

12. Name the **4** gaps in this line plot. ______ to ______; at ______; ______ to ______; ______ to ______

13. What is the mode of the data? ______ and ______

14. What is the range of the data? ______

Problem Solving
Reasoning

Solve.

15. Could eliminating outliers from a set of data affect the range, median, mode, or mean? Explain.

____

____

Test Prep ★ Mixed Review

16 At what time do the hands of a clock form a right angle?

A 8:00

B 8:30

C 9:00

D 9:30

17 On a number line, which point would be to the right of 0.7?

F $\frac{70}{1,000}$

G $\frac{699}{1,000}$

H $\frac{700}{1,000}$

J $\frac{770}{1,000}$

Name ______________________________

Problem Solving Application: Too Much Information

STANDARD

Some problems give more facts than you need. In a problem with too many facts, you have to select only the information you need.

Tips to Remember

1. Understand	2. Decide	3. Solve	4. Look back

- Write down the facts in the problem. Decide whether there are extra facts.
- Read each problem more than once. Circle the important words and numbers. Cross out the words and numbers that you don't need.
- Think about each fact in the problem. Ask yourself: Is this an extra fact? Or do I need it to find a solution?

Cross out the extra information. Then solve the problem.

1. The girls basketball team scored the following points in their games: **65, 52, 59, 48,** and **66.** The boys basketball team scored these points in their games: **47, 71, 69, 55,** and **53**. What was the average number of points scored by the boys basketball team?

Think: What information do you need to solve the problem? What information is extra?

____

____

____

____

____

____

Answer ______________________________

2. On a math quiz, **11** students scored **100, 7** students scored **90, 6** students scored **80,** and **4** students scored **70.** Two students were absent from math class and didn't take the quiz. What was the range of the scores on the quiz?

Think: What information do you need to find the range? What information is not necessary?

____

____

____

____

____

____

Answer ______________________________

STANDARD

Cross out the extra information. Then solve the problem.

3. On her science tests, Ana scored **80, 93, 87** and **96.** On her math tests, Ana scored **100, 84, 89,** and **79.** Ana's English average was **95.** What was Ana's science average?

____

4. There are **6** people in the Jones family. There are **2** sons and **2** daughters, who are twins. Their ages are **32, 34, 3, 7, 10,** and **3.** What is the median age in this family?

____

5. Brian bought some CDs for **$14.00** each. He counted the number of tracks on each and found them to be **12, 13, 18, 15, 11, 16,** and **13.** What was the mode of the number of tracks on the CDs?

____

6. A class made a line plot of the number of books read by each student. The teacher read 10 books. Five students read **8** books each. Three students read **5** books each. Ten students read **9** books each. What was the mode?

____

7. Sandy made a stem-and-leaf plot of the prime numbers between **1** and **32.** The numbers in the stem-and-leaf plot were **2, 3, 5, 7, 11, 13, 17, 19, 23, 29,** and **31.** What was the median of the numbers?

____

8. Mr. Green keeps a log of how many miles he can go on a tank of gas. He averages **23** miles per gallon. The entries in his log are **325, 336, 320, 308,** and **297.** What is the range of the mileage?

____

Extend Your Thinking

9. Look back at problem 3. What was the difference between Ana's science average and her math average?

____

10. Look back at problem 5. What was the average price per track on the CDs that Brian bought?

____

11. Explain how you decided what was extra information in problem 7.

____

____

12. Explain how you formed the answer to problem 4.

____

____

Name ______________________

Probability

STANDARD

The measure of the possibility that something may or may not happen is called **probability**.

A probability of 0 means that it is *impossible* for an event to happen.

A probability of 1 means that an event is *certain* to happen.

A probability between **0** and **1** means an event may or may not happen.

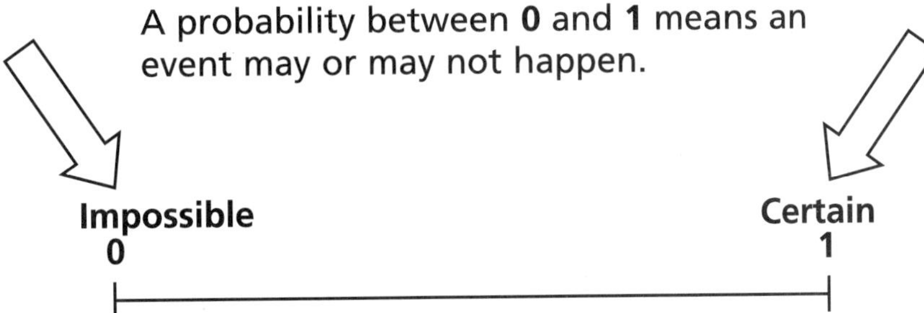

Choose *0, 1,* or *between 0 and 1* to describe each probability.

1. A person's name contains the letter *a*. ______

2. You will sleep sometime during your lifetime. ______

3. Tomorrow's date is October 14, 1925. ______

4. On your next birthday you will be **34** years old. ______

5. You will toss a **6** if you toss a cube numbered **1, 2, 3, 4, 5, 6**. ______

6. You will toss a **1, 2, 3, 4, 5,** or **6** if you toss a cube numbered **1, 2, 3, 4, 5, 6**. ______

Circle the letter of the event that has the greater chance of happening.

7. **a.** You will attend school next year. **b.** You will graduate from high school next year.

8. **a.** Tossing a **4** on a cube numbered **1, 2, 3, 4, 5, 6**. **b.** Tossing a **4** on a cube numbered **2, 2, 4, 4, 6, 6**.

9. **a.** Tossing a coin and getting tails. **b.** Tossing a coin and getting heads or tails.

Change each sentence so that the probability of each event happening is 1.

10. You can find a herd of sheep in your classroom. ______

______

11. You can toss a **2** on a cube numbered **3, 4, 5, 6, 7, 8**. ______

______

12. It will be exactly three o'clock four different times today. ______

______

STANDARD

Suppose these squares were placed inside the bag.

13. Name a letter of the alphabet that has a probability of **0** of being drawn from the bag. ________

14. Name a letter that has a greater chance of being drawn than **Y**. ________

15. Of the letters **X, Y,** and **Z,** which letter has the least chance of being drawn? ________

Problem Solving
Reasoning

Solve.

16. Conduct an experiment. Follow these steps.

1. Make **10** two-inch-squares of paper. Label **5** squares **X, 3** squares **Y,** and **2** squares **Z.** Place them in a paper bag.
2. Without looking, draw a square from the bag and record the result on the tally chart. Put the square back into the bag.
3. Repeat Step 2 forty-nine times more.

Paper Squares		
Letter	**Tally**	**Total**
X		
Y		
Z		

17. Which result(s) occurred most often? ________

Quick Check

Use the line plot about class quiz scores to complete.

Work Space

18. What are the mean and median scores? Round the mean to the nearest tenth.

____

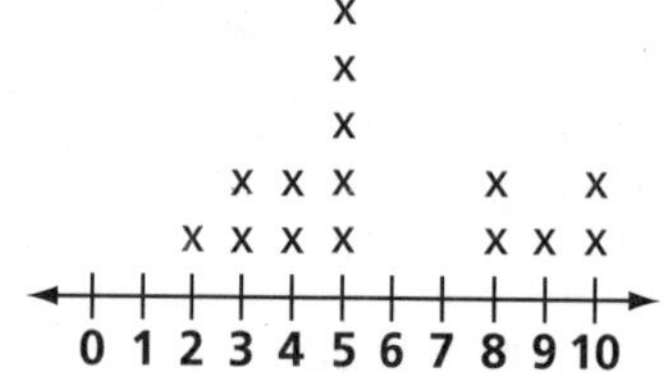

19. Suppose a student got a score of **15**. Would this score be considered a cluster, a gap, or an outlier? Explain.

____

Suppose you have cards numbered 0–9.
Choose *0, 1,* or *between 0 and 1* to describe the probability.

20. Picking a **5**. ________

21. Picking a **10**. ________

Name ______________________________

Problem Solving Strategy: Make a List

STANDARD

An organized list can sometimes help you find the answer to a problem.

Problem

Alex, Barika, and Clara sit in the front row. Make a list to find how many different ways they can be seated.

---

1 Understand **As you reread the problem, ask yourself questions.**

- What do you know about Alex, Barika, and Clara?

  They all sit in the front row.

  What do you need to find out?

  ____

---

2 Decide **Choose a method for solving the problem. Try the strategy Make a List.**

- If Alex is in the first seat, who can be in the seat next to him? ______________________________

---

3 Solve **Make a list to show the possible ways they can sit.**

Alex in first seat: ABC or ____________.

Barika in first seat: BAC or ____________.

Clara in first seat: CAB or ____________.

---

4 Look back **Check your answer.**
Write your answer below.

- Are there any other possible seating arrangements?

  ____

  List all the possibilities.

  Answer: ______________________________

  ____

STANDARD

Solve. Use the Make a List strategy or any other strategy you have learned.

1. A deli offers lunch specials. For **$3.79,** you can choose a cheese, tuna, or bologna sandwich and a macaroni or potato salad. What lunch specials are available?

Think: Could you order macaroni salad with each sandwich?

____

Answer ______________________

2. I have a number cube with the numbers **1, 2, 3, 4, 5,** and **6** on it. If I toss a nickel and toss the number cube, what are all the possible outcomes?

Think: How many outcomes are possible with a nickel?

____

Answer ______________________

____

3. A hamburger can be ordered with or without cheese, with or without ketchup, and with or without pickles. How many different ways can you order the hamburger?

____

4. A bag contains **56** marbles. Ten are red, **18** are blue, **15** are yellow, and the rest are green. How many green marbles are in the bag?

____

5. A rectangle has a perimeter of **30** in. Its length is twice its width. What are the dimensions of the rectangle?

____

6. A rectangular garden measured in whole feet has an area of **24** ft^2. What is the greatest length of fencing needed to put a fence around the garden?

____

7. A family room in the shape of a square measures **15** ft on each side. How much will it cost to carpet the family room if carpeting sells for **$19** per square yard?

____

8. The results of a skating survey showed that **15** students like to use in-line skates, **12** students like to ice skate, and **4** like to do both. How many students were surveyed?

____

9. How many different ways can Kate, Leo, Mike, and Nan be standing in line for the movies?

____

10. Emma scored **88** and **85** on two quizzes. How many points does she need to score on the next quiz to have an average quiz score of **90**?

____

Name ______________________________

A result of a probability experiment is an **outcome.**

To find the *probability* of an event, or how likely it is to occur, use this ratio:

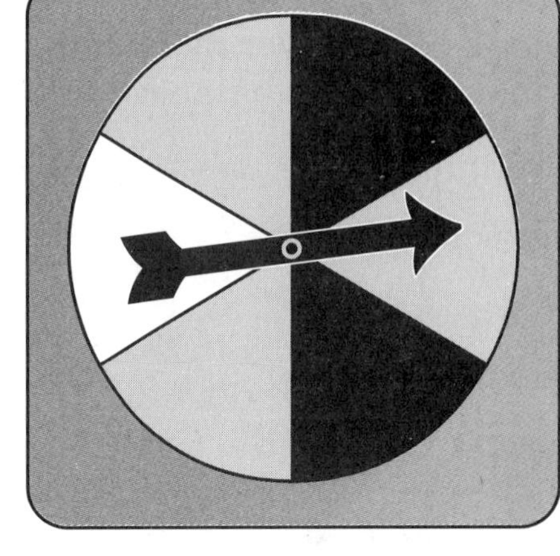

Probability (P) = $\frac{\text{number of favorable outcomes}}{\text{total number of possible outcomes}}$

- The probability that this spinner will point to white is $\frac{1}{6}$. There is one white section on the spinner, or **1** favorable outcome. There are six sections on the spinner altogether, or **6** possible outcomes.

- The probability that the spinner will point to gray is $\frac{3}{6}$. Out of **6** possible outcomes, **3** sections are gray, or favorable.

It is **more likely** that the spinner will point to gray than to white because $\frac{3}{6} > \frac{1}{6}$

Use the spinner below to answer questions 1–6.

1. What is the total number of possible outcomes on the spinner? ______

2. How many sections are labeled **A**? ______

T?______ **S**? ______

Suppose the spinner is spun once.
Write each ratio in simplest form.

3. What is the probability of the spinner pointing to **A**? ______ out of ______ or ______

4. What is the probability of the spinner pointing to **S**? ______ out of ______ or ______

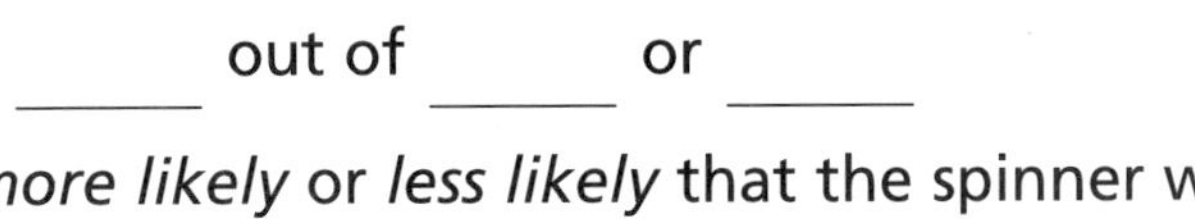

5. Is it *more likely* or *less likely* that the spinner will point to **A** than to **S**? Explain. ______________________________

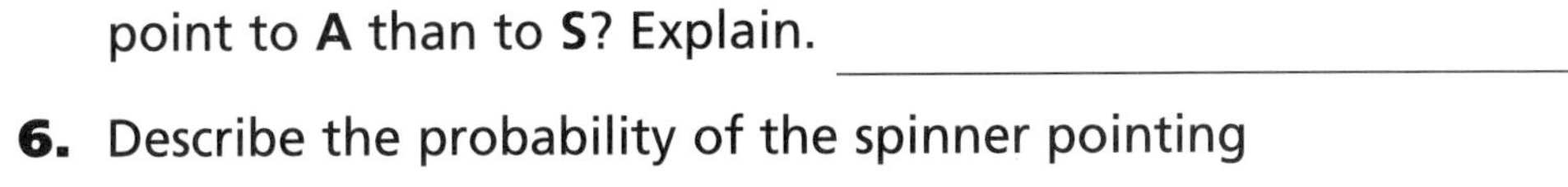

6. Describe the probability of the spinner pointing to **A**, **T**, or **S**. ____________

STANDARD

Suppose a number cube is tossed once. The cube is numbered 1, 2, 3, 4, 5, 6. Write each ratio in simplest form.

7. What is the probability of tossing a **6**? _____ out of _____ or _____

8. What is the probability of tossing a **3** or a **6**? _____ out of _____ or _____

9. What is the probability of tossing an even number? _____ out of _____ or _____

When each player in a game has an equal probability of winning, the game is said to be *fair.* Write *fair* or *unfair.*

10. The player with the greatest number of **2**'s wins the game.
Isabella tossed a 6-sided cube numbered **1, 2, 3, 4, 5, 6.**
Roman tossed a 6-sided cube numbered **1, 2, 3, 4, 5, 6.** __________

11. The player with the greatest number of **3**'s wins the game.
Hanna tossed a 6-sided cube numbered **1, 2, 3, 4, 5, 6.**
Noah tossed a 6-sided cube numbered **3, 4, 5, 3, 7, 3.** __________

Problem Solving
Reasoning

Solve.

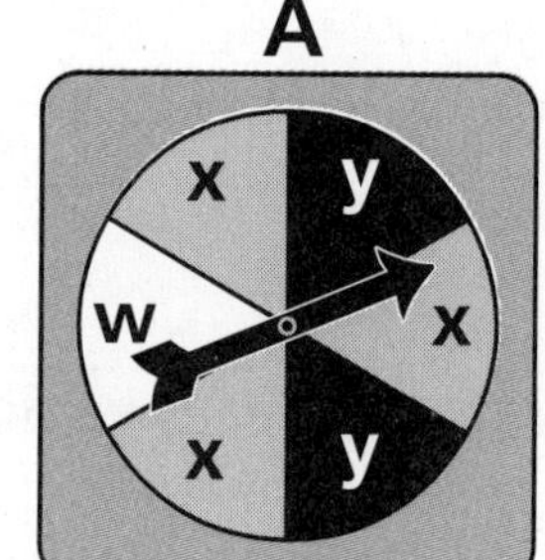

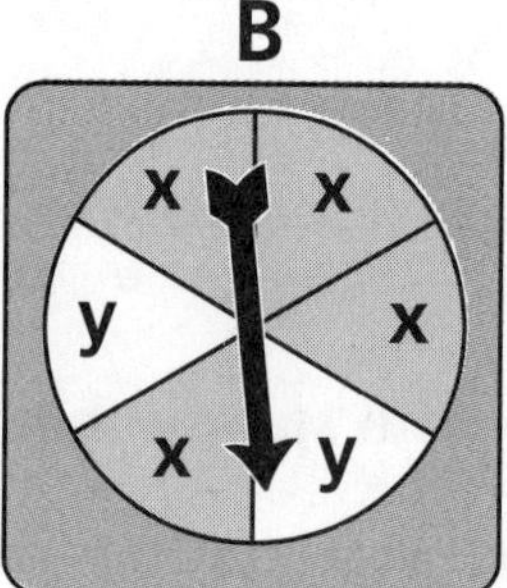

12. On which spinner is **w** an impossible outcome? Explain. __________

____

13. Which spinner has a $\frac{1}{3}$ probability of pointing to **y**? __________

14. Which spinner is least likely to point to **x**? Explain. __________

15. On a separate piece of paper, draw a spinner with 2 possible outcomes: **P** and **R**. Arrange the sections, **P** and **R**, so that the spinner is more likely to point to **P** than to **R**.

Test Prep ★ Mixed Review

16 **What kind of graph is appropriate to use to compare the price differences for lettuce over a 6 month period?**

A line graph
B bar graph
C circle graph
D line plot

17 **A class made a circle graph to show how they spent a $55.00 budget for a party. The section for decorations was 8% of the circle. About how much money does that section stand for?**

F Less than $4.00
G Between $4.00 and $6.00
H Between $6.00 and $8.00
J More than $8.00

Name ______________________________

Using Probability

STANDARD

You can use a small part of a large group of data to represent the whole group. The small part is called a **sample**. Then you can use the sample to make predictions about the large group.

Suppose there are **100** cookies in a box. There are chocolate chip, sugar, and raisin cookies. You can predict how many of each type are in the box by studying a sample.

Without looking, you take a sample of **10** cookies out of the box and use the table at the right to record the number of each type of cookie.

You can use the data in the table to make a prediction about all of the cookies in the box.

Cookies		
Cookie	**Tally**	**Total**
Chocolate chip	|||	3
Sugar	||	2
Raisin	𝍸	5

Number of chocolate chip cookies in the sample → $\frac{3}{10} = \frac{?}{100}$ ← Number of chocolate chip cookies in the box
Number of cookies sampled → ← Number of cookies in the box

Multiply by **10** to find an equal ratio.

$$\frac{3 \times 10}{10 \times 10} = \frac{30}{100}$$

You can predict that there are **30** chocolate chip cookies out of **100** cookies in the box.

Based on the sample, the probability of getting a chocolate chip cookie is $\frac{3}{10}$.

Use the sample data above to answer each question.

1. What is the number of sugar cookies in the sample? ______
2. What ratio can you write to compare the number of sugar cookies in the sample with the total number of cookies in the sample? ______
3. How many sugar cookies do you predict are in the box? Explain.

____

4. How many raisin cookies would you predict are in the box? Explain.

____

5. Suppose the box contained **200** cookies. In an experiment the same sample as above was the outcome. Predict how many chocolate chip cookies would be in the box. ______

STANDARD

Perform each probability experiment. Then answer each question.

6. Toss a coin fifty times. Record each outcome. Based on your sample, what is the probability of the coin landing heads up? Tails up?

____

7. Use a cube numbered **1, 2, 3, 4, 5,** and **6.** Toss it fifty times. Record each outcome. Based on your sample, what is the probability of tossing an odd number?

____

Problem Solving
Reasoning

Solve.

8. A class is divided into **8** study groups, numbered **1–8**. Every student is randomly assigned to one of the **8** groups. You want to be assigned to a group whose number is less than **6**.

Name the favorable outcomes: _______________

What is the total number of possible outcomes? _______________

What is the probability of being assigned to a group whose number is less than **6**? _____

Quick Check

A number cube is numbered 1, 2, 3, 4, 5, 6. Write each probability in simplest form.

Work Space

9. The probability of tossing a **2**. _____

10. The probability of tossing a number greater than **2**. _____

11. The probability of tossing an odd number that is greater than **2**. _____

A spinner has 3 colors (red, blue, and yellow) and 6 sections. You spin the spinner 9 times and make this tally:

Red	Blue	Yellow
||||	|||	||

12. What ratio can you write to describe the number of times you spun blue in the sample? _____

13. Based on the sample, how many sections of the spinner would you predict are blue? _____

14. Based on the sample, how many sections of the spinner would you predict are red? Yellow? _____

Name ______________________________

Use the data about ages of teachers at West Middle School to answer the questions.

Ages of West School Teachers
36, 32, 41, 25, 25, 48, 40, 42, 22, 27,
30, 32, 40, 46, 44, 28, 28, 25, 39, 42,

Stem	Leaves
2	
3	
4	

1. Use the data to complete the stem-and-leaf plot.
2. Use the stem-and-leaf plot to help you draw a histogram.
3. What is the mean age of the teachers? ______
4. What is the mode of the age of teachers? ______
5. What is the range of ages for the teachers? ______
6. What is the median age of all the teachers? ______

Use the spinner to answer the question.

7. If you spun this spinner **100** times, how many times would you predict it would point to **M**? Explain.

____

____

8. A penny, a nickel, and a dime are tossed at the same time. On another sheet of paper, show all of the possible outcomes that can occur. What is the probability of the outcome (Heads, Heads, Heads)?

____

A book mark is in the shape of a parallelogram. Use your centimeter ruler to help you answer questions 1 and 2.

1 **Measure the parallelogram to the nearest millimeter. What is the perimeter of the book mark to the nearest mm?**

A 12.6 **C** 162

B 18 **D** 180

2 **What is the area of the book mark rounded to the nearest cm^2?**

F 1,944 **H** 15

G 145.8 **J** 14.6

3 **The science club found the average monthly temperature from October through May and made a line graph. The temperatures, in order from October through May, are 18°C, 13°C, 10°C, 3°C, 5°C, 13°C, 19°C, and 26°C. What two months on the graph would show the same temperature?**

A October, February

B November, March

C December, April

D January, May

4 **Sandro has 12 blue pencils and 8 red pencils. He wants to divide the pencils into boxes so that each box has the same number of red and the same number of blue pencils. What is the greatest number of boxes he can make?**

F 2 **H** 6

G 4 **J** 8 **K** NH

5 **Amber caught a $3\frac{1}{2}$ lb. fish. The record for the day was a $10\frac{1}{4}$ lb. fish. How much more did the record fish weigh?**

A $13\frac{3}{4}$ lb **C** $7\frac{1}{4}$ lb **E** $6\frac{1}{8}$ lb

B $6\frac{3}{4}$ lb **D** $6\frac{5}{8}$ lb

6 **A baby was 3.5 kilograms at birth. While the baby was in the hospital, he lost 0.2 kilogram. Before going home, he gained 0.3 kilogram. How many kilograms was the baby when he went home?**

F 2.5 **H** 6.3 **K** Not here

G 4 **J** 8.5

7 **Tajma's mother is a travel agent and she brings extra posters home. Of the 72 posters Tajma has, 25% of the posters are sites in Asia while $\frac{1}{3}$ of the posters are of sites in the United States. How many more posters of the United States does she have than posters of Asia?**

A $\frac{7}{12}$ **C** 6 **E** 42

B $\frac{1}{12}$ **D** 36

8 **Ravi worked $2\frac{1}{2}$ h on his scout project on Friday, $4\frac{1}{2}$ h on Saturday, and $3\frac{3}{4}$ h on Sunday. What are the mean and median times he worked?**

F $2\frac{1}{2}$ h, $3\frac{1}{2}$ h

G 3 h, $3\frac{1}{2}$ h

H $3\frac{1}{6}$ h, $3\frac{5}{6}$ h

J $3\frac{1}{2}$ h, $3\frac{3}{4}$ h

K NH

UNIT 11 • TABLE OF CONTENTS

Algebra: Integers, and the Coordinate Plane

We will be using this vocabulary:

integers the set of numbers that includes positive and negative whole numbers and 0

coordinate plane a grid with horizontal and vertical number lines that intersect at the origin

origin the point where the x- and y-axes of the coordinate plane intersect

quadrant one of four sections in the coordinate plane

Dear Family,

During the next few weeks, our math class will be learning about integers and the coordinate plane.

You can expect to see homework that provides practice in ordering integers. Here is a sample you may want to keep handy to give help if needed.

Ordering Integers

Integers are the set of numbers that include positive whole numbers, negative whole numbers, and zero, for example: **⁻2, ⁻1, 0, 1, 2.**

Example Here are steps for ordering the set of integers **⁻1, 5,** and **⁻4** from greatest to least.

1. One way to order integers is to use a number line.

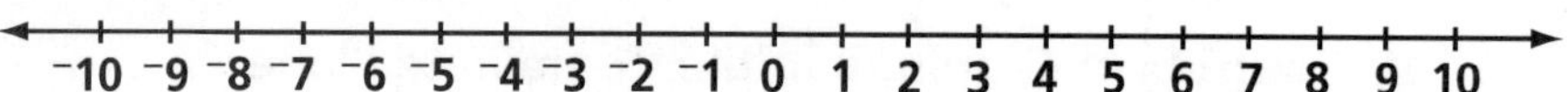

2. Locate the integers on the number line.

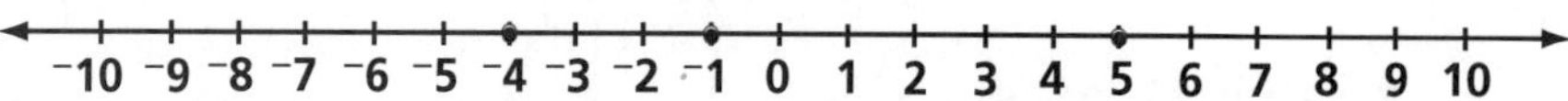

3. Compare and order the integers. On a number line, the integer farthest to the right is greatest and the integer farthest to the left is least. So the integers from greatest to least are: **5, ⁻1, ⁻4.**

During this unit, students will need to practice comparing and ordering integers as well as add, subtract, multiply, and divide with integers.

Sincerely,

Name ____________________

Positive and Negative Numbers

STANDARD

Words have opposites. Some examples are: *enter* a room and *leave* a room, *stand up* and *sit down*, and *in* and *out.* In mathematics, numbers have opposites too.

Whole numbers greater than **0** are **positive numbers.** Their opposites are whole numbers less than **0,** called **negative numbers.**

Positive numbers, negative numbers, and **0** make up a set of numbers called integers.

$$\ldots {}^{-}7, {}^{-}6, {}^{-}5, {}^{-}4, {}^{-}3, {}^{-}2, {}^{-}1, 0, 1, 2, 3, 4, 5, 6, 7 \ldots$$

negative integers (⁻7 through ⁻1) — **positive integers** (1 through 7)

0 is neither positive nor negative.

A positive number may or may not have a positive sign (+) in front of it. A negative sign (–) must always be placed in front of a negative number.

The number ⁺**5** is read "positive **5.**" Its opposite, ⁻**5,** is read "negative **5.**"

Write the opposite.

1. **50** feet up ____________ lose **5** lb ____________

2. **6** m below sea level ____________ add **9** cups ____________

3. move back **2** units ____________ **20** years ago ____________

4. **60** km south ____________ **5** miles east ____________

5. to the right **6** in. ____________ multiply by **8** ____________

Write *yes* if the number is an integer. Write *no* if it is not.

6. **50** ______ **⁻1,000** ______ $\frac{1}{2}$ ______ **0** ______

7. **2** ______ **3.2** ______ **⁻6.58** ______ **⁻402** ______

Write the opposite of each integer.

8. **7** ______ **⁻9** ______ **250** ______ **⁻1** ______

9. **15** ______ **⁻101** ______ **64** ______ **0** ______

10. **⁻91** ______ **4,678** ______ **2** ______ **13** ______

STANDARD

Represent each situation with an integer.

11. 14 degrees below zero ______

Rita owes $15. ______

12. Sam grew 3 inches. ______

Myron lost 2 books. ______

13. water level 4 m below normal ______

10 pennies saved ______

14. gain of 15 feet ______

loss of 5 gallons ______

Problem Solving
Reasoning

Solve.

15. The fifth grade class held a bake sale. Their expenses were $24. They earned $48. Write each money amount as an integer.

______

16. A football player ran with the football two times. The first time he gained 8 yards. The second time he lost 3 yards. Write the gain and loss as integers.

______

17. One night the temperature fell 14 degrees from midnight to 5 A.M. Then it rose 21 degrees from 5 A.M. to noon. Write the rise and fall of the temperature as integers.

______

18. On Monday the stock of Zip Company rose 12 points, then it fell 8 points on Tuesday. Write the rise and fall of the stock prices as integers.

______

19. Look at your answers to rows 6 and 7 on page 281. Which numbers are not integers? Explain.

______

______

20. Use the number line on page 281. Find 6 and $^{-}6$. How many units from zero is each integer? Write a rule that describes the location of opposites on the number line.

______

______

Test Prep ★ Mixed Review

21 Which number sentence is true?

A 957 mL > 9.2 L

B 1.94 m < 20.2 cm

C 0.15 kL < 110 L

D 9.14 g > 892 mg

22 A test had 50 items and Hakim got 48 correct. What percent did he get correct?

F 98%

G 96%

H 90%

J 48%

Name ______________________________

Integers on a Number Line

STANDARD

You can use a thermometer to help you understand integers.

1. The temperatures that are above zero are written with positive numbers.

2. The temperatures that are below zero are written with negative numbers.

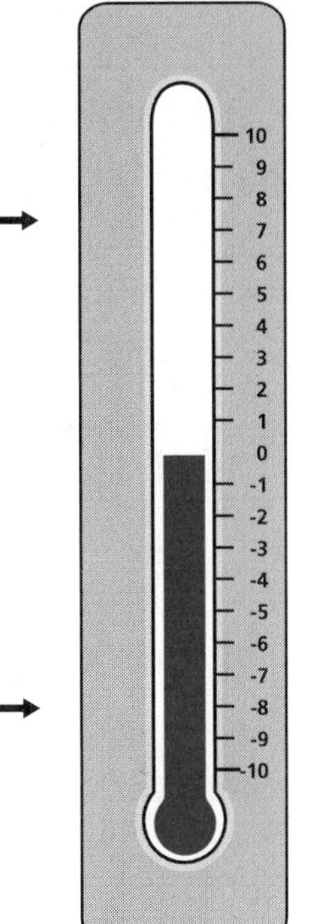

5° above zero is written: 5°. You can read it as "positive five degrees."

5° below zero is written: ⁻5°. You can read it as "negative five degrees."

A number line can also help you understand integers.

Negative integers are less than 0.

Zero is neither positive nor negative.

Positive integers are greater than 0.

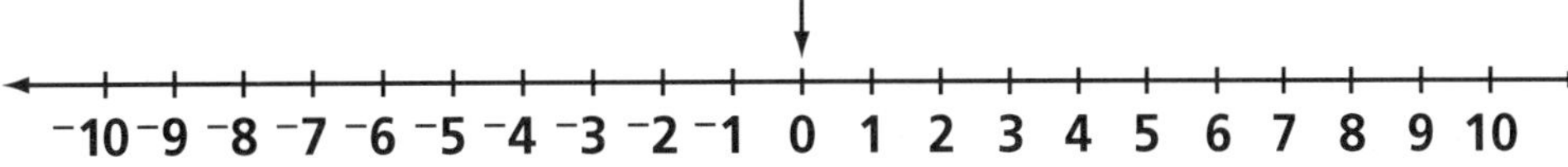

Write the integer that represents each temperature.

1. 8 degrees below zero ______ 3 degrees above zero ______

2. 2 degrees above zero ______ 9 degrees below zero ______

Compare the temperatures. Write the colder temperature.

3. ⁻8° or 3° ______ ⁻10° or 0° ______ 8° or 3° ______

4. ⁻8° or ⁻3° ______ ⁻1° or ⁻5° ______ ⁻10° or 2° ______

How many integers are *between* these integers?

5. ⁻3 and 3 ______ ⁻1 and ⁻9 ______ ⁻6 and 5 ______

STANDARD

The **coordinate** of a point on a number line is the number that identifies the location of the point.

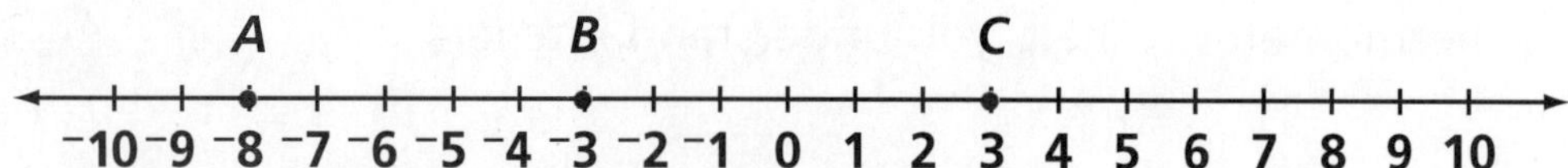

The coordinate or location of point *A* is ⁻**8**, of point *B* is ⁻**3**, and of point *C* is **3**.

Name the coordinate of each point on the number line.

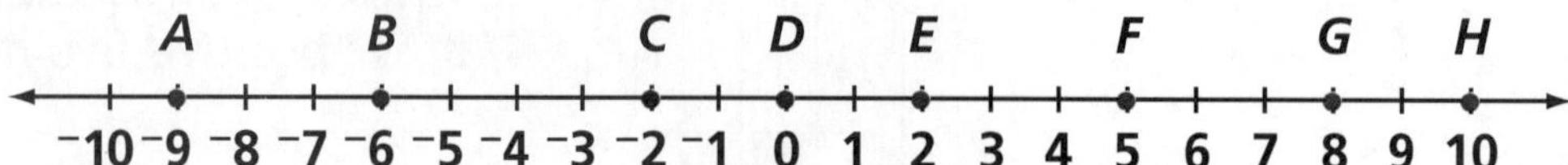

6. *A* ______ *B* ______ *C* ______ *D* ______

7. *E* ______ *F* ______ *G* ______ *H* ______

Locate and label each point on the number line.

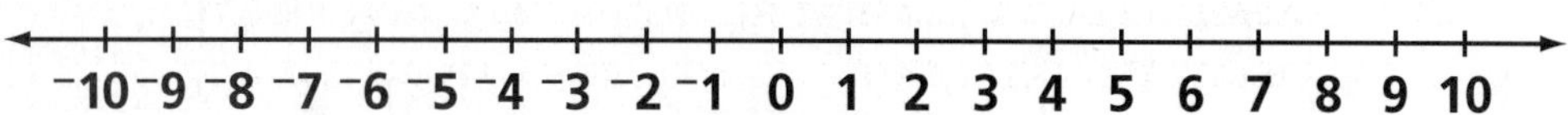

8. *A* at ⁻**8** *B* at **7** *C* at **4** *D* at ⁻**5**

9. *E* at **1** *G* at ⁻**3** *H* at **0** *I* at ⁻**10**

Problem Solving Reasoning **Solve.**

10. How many negative integers are greater than ⁻**6**?

______

11. How many integers are both greater than ⁻**3** and less than **3**?

______

12. On the number line for rows **8** and **9** above, what are the next **4** negative integers?

______

Test Prep ★ Mixed Review

13 What is the value of this expression?

$$\left(\frac{8}{15} \times \frac{2}{9}\right) \div \frac{8}{9}$$

A $\frac{64}{81}$

B $\frac{8}{9}$

C $\frac{2}{15}$

D $\frac{2}{9}$

14 6.8 in.^{3} could represent the dimension of what?

F the perimeter of a box top

G the size of the picture on the front of the box

H the sum of the areas of all the faces of the box

J how much cereal the box will hold

Name ______________________________

Comparing and Ordering Integers

STANDARD

The numbers on a number line *increase* as you move *to the right.* The numbers $^{-}8$ and **4** are labeled on the number line below. You can see **4** is to the right of $^{-}$**8.**

Words: four is greater than negative eight

Symbols: **4** > $^{-}$**8**

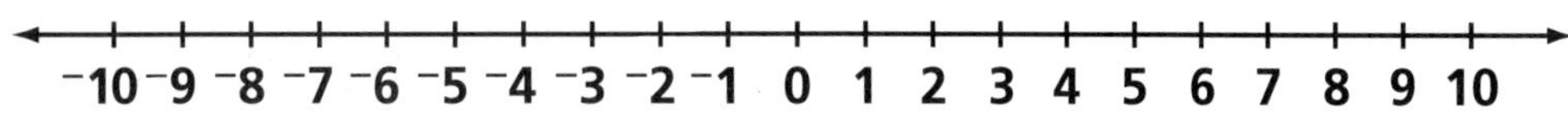

The numbers on a number line *decrease* as you move *to the left.* You can see $^{-}$**8** is to the left of **4.**

Words: negative eight is less than four

Symbols: $^{-}$**8** < **4**

Use > or < to compare the integers.

1. 8 ◯ 7 $\qquad$ $^{-}1$ ◯ $^{-}2$ $\qquad$ $^{-}3$ ◯ 5 $\qquad$ 9 ◯ $^{-}10$

2. $^{-}6$ ◯ 0 $\qquad$ 5 ◯ $^{-}5$ $\qquad$ $^{-}2$ ◯ $^{-}8$ $\qquad$ 5 ◯ 9

Graph the numbers on the number line.
Then order the numbers from *greatest* to *least.*

3. 6, 0, $^{-}3$, 1

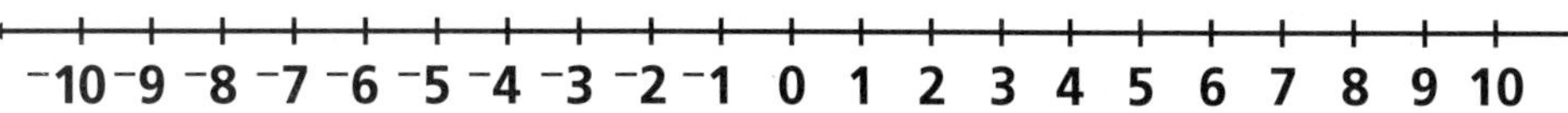

____

4. 4, $^{-}1$, $^{-}6$, $^{-}5$

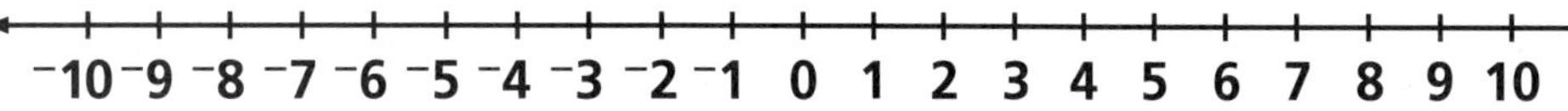

____

5. $^{-}10$, 5, 3, $^{-}9$, $^{-}3$

$^{-}10$ $^{-}9$ $^{-}8$ $^{-}7$ $^{-}6$ $^{-}5$ $^{-}4$ $^{-}3$ $^{-}2$ $^{-}1$ 0 1 2 3 4 5 6 7 8 9 10

____

6. 0, $^{-}2$, $^{-}1$, 1

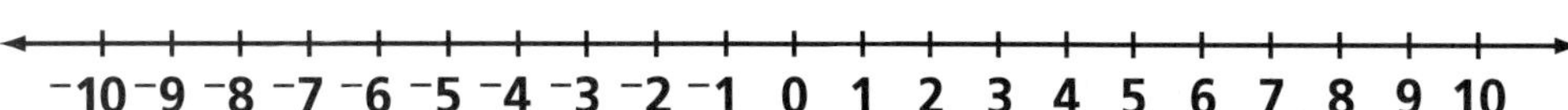

____

7. 8, $^{-}7$, 6, $^{-}5$

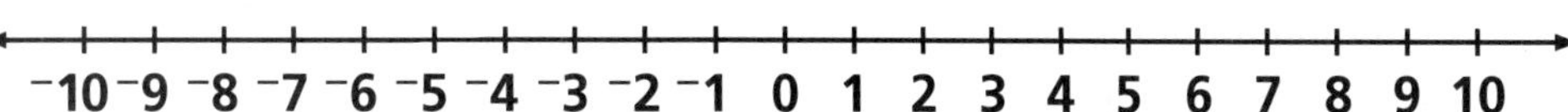

____

STANDARD

Any number that can be shown as the quotient of two integers is called a **rational number**. Rational numbers include fractions, mixed numbers, and *some* decimals.

Remember: A fraction is another way to show division.

Examples: **2 Think:** $\frac{2}{1}$ **or 2 ÷ 1 = 2** **0.25 Think:** $\frac{25}{100}$ **or 25 ÷ 100 = 0.25**

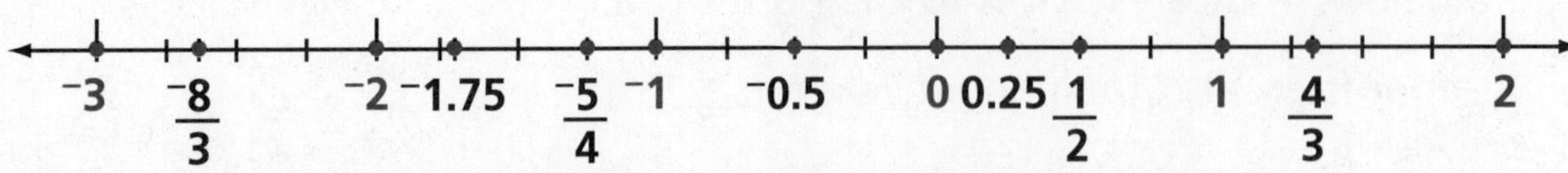

You can use a number line to compare and order rational numbers.

$\frac{-8}{3}$ is to the left of **⁻1.75.**	**⁻1** is to the right of **⁻1.75.**	So, the numbers ordered from least to greatest are:
$\frac{-8}{3}$ < **⁻1.75**	**⁻1 > ⁻1.75**	$\frac{-8}{3}$, **⁻1.75, ⁻1.**

Graph the numbers. Then order them from *greatest* to *least*.

8. ⁻1 2 $\frac{3}{4}$ $\frac{-3}{4}$ 0

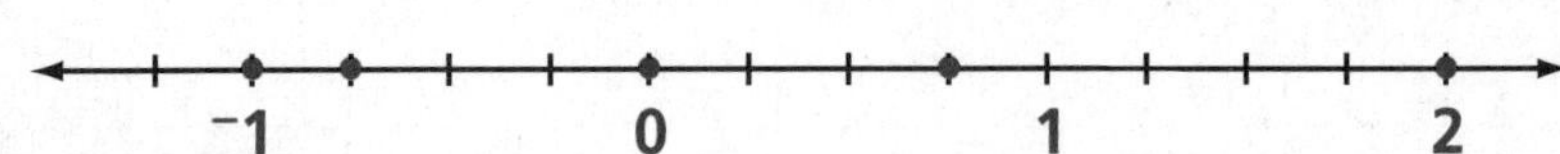

____

9. 2 ⁻1 ⁻0.5 0.75 ⁻1.75

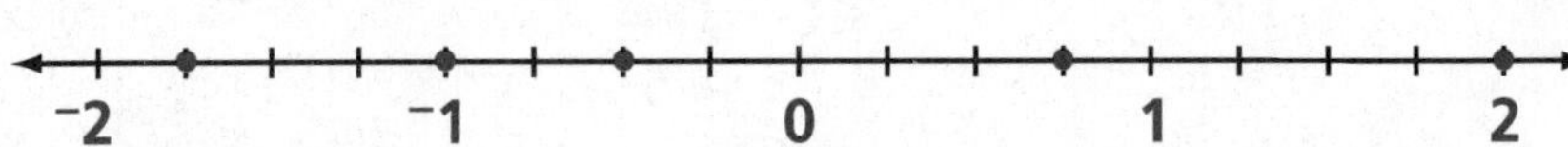

____

Quick Check

Write each number as an integer. Then write the opposite.

Work Space

10. down 3 floors ______ ______

11. loss of 7 gallons ______ ______

12. the opposite of ⁻4 ______ ______

Locate and label each point on the number line.

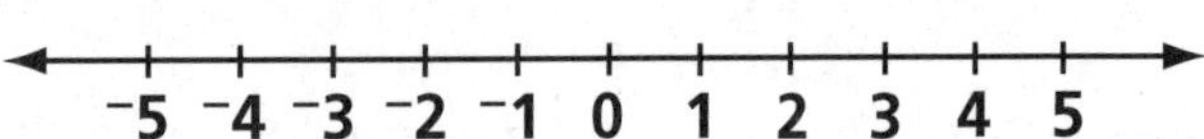

13. C at ⁻4 **14.** *A* at ⁻1 **15.** *B* at 2

Use > or < to compare. Draw a number line if you need to.

16. ⁻4 ◯ 4 **17.** ⁻9 ◯ ⁻10 **18.** $\frac{-3}{4}$ ◯ $\frac{2}{5}$

19. Write the numbers $\frac{8}{10}$, ⁻1$\frac{3}{4}$, ⁻3, 9, ⁻10, 6, 0.7 in order from least to greatest. ______________

Name ____________________

The Coordinate Plane

Two number lines form the **coordinate plane.**

The horizontal number line is called the ***x-axis***. The vertical number line is called the ***y-axis***.

The axes cross at the **origin** and divide the plane into 4 **quadrants**, numbered I, II, III, and IV.

An ***ordered pair*** represents a **coordinate** or location on a coordinate plane.

To locate a point on the grid, follow these steps.

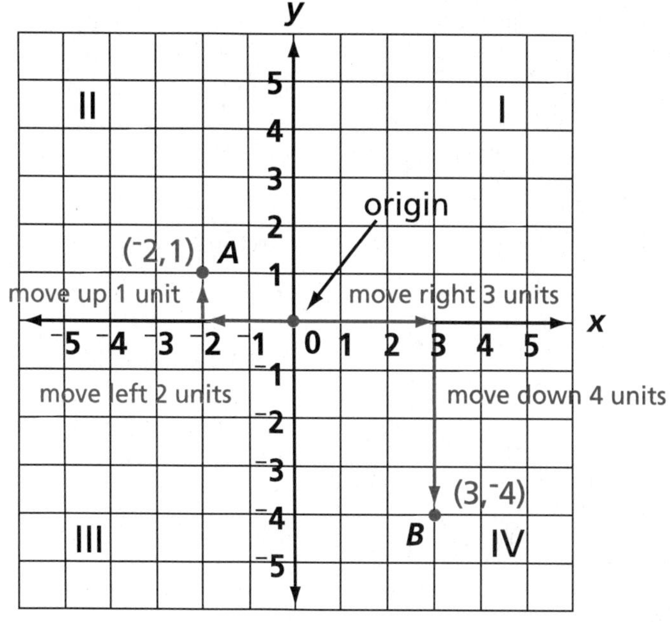

1. Start at the origin.
2. Look at the first number of the ordered pair, **x**. If it is *positive* move *right* that number of units. If it is *negative* move *left*.
3. Look at the second number of the ordered pair, ***y***. If it is *positive* move *up* that number of units. If it is *negative* move *down*.

move left **2** ↘ *x*, *y* ↙ move up **1**
(⁻**2**, **1**)

The point located at (⁻**2**, **1**) is ***A***.

move right **3** ↘ *x*, *y* ↙ move down **4**
(**3**, ⁻**4**)

The point located at (**3**, ⁻**4**) is ***B***.

Circle the set of directions that best describes the location of the ordered pair.

1. (⁻2, 5)	right **2**, down **5**	left **2**, up **5**	right **5**, down **2**
2. (⁻3, ⁻2)	right **3**, left **2**	right **3**, right **2**	left **3**, down **2**
3. (4, ⁻1)	right **4**, down **1**	left **1**, up **4**	left **4**, down **1**
4. (3, 2)	right **3**, left **2**	right **3**, up **2**	left **3**, down **2**

STANDARD

Write the letter of the point at each location.

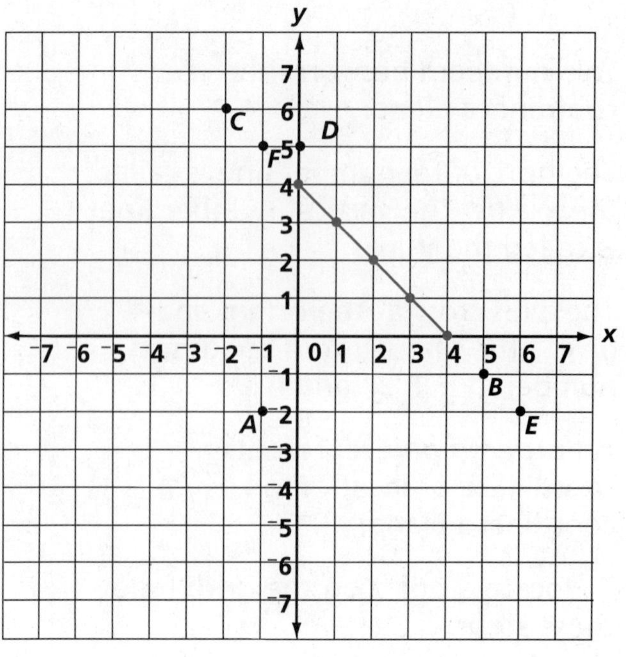

5. (−2, 6) ______ (−1, −2) ______

6. (0, 5) ______ (5, −1) ______

7. (−1, 5) ______ (6, −2) ______

Look at the table for the equation $x + y = 4$.
Think: What 2 numbers equal 4?
Then complete the table and write the ordered pairs (x, y).

8. $x + y = 4$

x	y
0	4
1	
2	

Ordered Pairs

(x, y)
(0, 4)
(1,)
(,)
(,)
(,)

9. Graph the ordered pairs from exercise 8 on the coordinate plane.
a. Connect the points to form a line segment.

b. Extend the line segment in both directions.
What other ordered pairs are on this line segment?

____

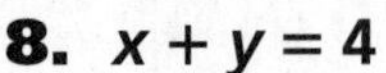

Solve.

10. Give an ordered pair for another point that is on a line segment that connects (0, 3), (1, 2), and (2, 1) but extends in both directions.

____

Test Prep ★ Mixed Review

11 Some students measured a segment as 6.71 cm, 6 cm, and 5.9 cm. What is the mean length to the nearest mm?

A 62 mm

B 62 cm

C 6 cm

D 6 mm

12 Which number in this list has the greatest value? $\frac{5}{4}$ 75% 1.54 $\frac{72}{100}$

F $\frac{5}{4}$

G 75%

H 1.54

J $\frac{72}{100}$

Name ______________________

Adding Integers

STANDARD

You can use a number line to add integers.

Follow these steps when adding integers on a number line.

1. Start at the location of the first addend.
2. To add a positive number, move that number of units to the *right*. To add a negative number, move that number of units to the *left*.
3. The answer is where you stop on the number line.

Begin at **⁻2.**
Move **3** units right. So, **⁻2 + 3 = 1.**

⁻2 + 3 = ?

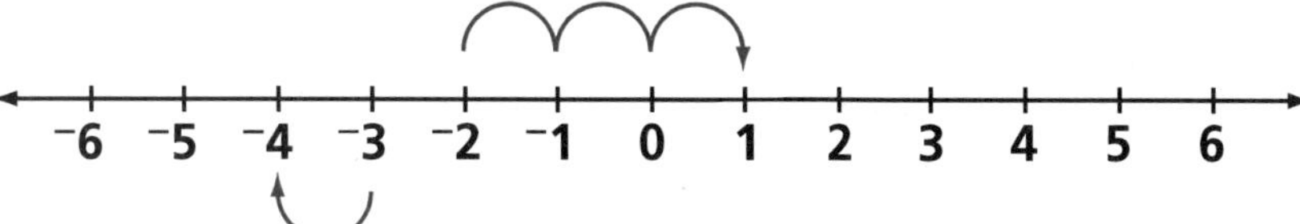

⁻3 + ⁻1 = ?

Begin at **⁻3.**
Move **1** unit left. So, **⁻3 + ⁻1 = ⁻4.**

Use the number line to find the sum of the integers.

1. ⁻1 + 4 Begin at _____, move 4 units __________. The sum is _____.

2. 3 + ⁻5 Begin at _____, move _____ units left. The sum is _____.

3. ⁻1 + ⁻4 Begin at _____, move _____ units __________. The sum is _____.

4. 2 + 3 Begin at _____, move _____ units __________. The sum is _____.

5. ⁻2 + ⁻4 Begin at _____, move _____ units __________. The sum is _____.

6. ⁻6 + 6 Begin at _____, move _____ units __________. The sum is _____.

Find the sum. Use the number line when necessary.

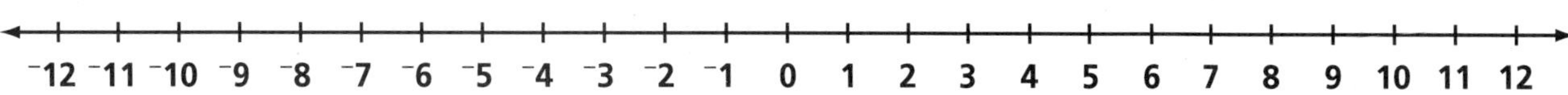

7. 3 + 7 = _____ 3 + ⁻7 = _____ ⁻3 + 7 = _____ ⁻3 + ⁻7 = _____

8. 8 + ⁻8 = _____ 2 + ⁻5 = _____ 1 + ⁻1 = _____ 8 + ⁻3 = _____

9. 10 + ⁻7 = _____ ⁻10 + 7 = _____ 6 + ⁻8 = _____ ⁻4 + ⁻4 = _____

STANDARD

Find the sum.

10. $^-3 + {}^-3 =$ ____ $6 + 2 =$ ____ $4 + {}^-4 =$ ____ $0 + {}^-5 =$ ____

11. $^-3 + 21 =$ ____ $^-9 + {}^-5 =$ ____ $17 + {}^-9 =$ ____ $^-17 + {}^-5 =$ ____

12. $^-15 + {}^-3 =$ ____ $^-5 + 2 =$ ____ $^-4 + {}^-4 =$ ____ $7 + {}^-5 =$ ____

13. $28 + {}^-2 =$ ____ $45 + {}^-2 =$ ____ $^-39 + {}^-4 =$ ____ $10 + {}^-35 =$ ____

14. $^-43 + {}^-21 =$ ____ $^-16 + 2 =$ ____ $4 + {}^-24 =$ ____ $^-25 + 25 =$ ____

15. $^-23 + {}^-3 =$ ____ $16 + 22 =$ ____ $14 + {}^-4 =$ ____ $50 + {}^-45 =$ ____

16. $^-1 + 2 + 3 =$ ____ $3 + {}^-7 + {}^-2 =$ ____ $^-1 + {}^-3 + {}^-4 =$ ____

17. $3 + 5 + 1 =$ ____ $^-1 + {}^-7 + 9 =$ ____ $6 + {}^-6 + 5 =$ ____

Problem Solving
Reasoning

Solve.

18. Is the sum of two negative numbers positive or negative? ____

19. When adding a positive number and a negative number, is the sum greater than or less than the positive number? ____

20. What is the sum of two opposites? ____

21. When $x = 2$ and $y = 0$, then $x + y$ equals 2. Name 3 other pairs of numbers for x and y that will also equal 2 when added.

____

Test Prep ★ Mixed Review

22 Which figure is a parallelogram that has all its sides congruent but not all its angles congruent?

A equilateral triangle *ABC*

B square *WXYZ*

C rhombus *JKLM*

D pentagon *QRSTU*

23 There are 192 seats set up for a 2:30 p.m. meeting. As of 2:00 p.m., only 75% of the seats were filled. How many empty seats are there?

F $38\frac{2}{5}$

G 48

H 144

J 768

Name ____________________

Subtracting Integers

STANDARD

Follow these steps when subtracting integers on a number line.

1. Rewrite the subtraction equation as an addition equation:
   a. Do *not* change the first number.
   b. Change the subtraction sign to an addition sign.
   c. Change the second number to its opposite.
2. Start at the location of the first addend.
3. To add a *positive* number, move that number of units to the *right.* To add a *negative* number, move that number of units to the *left.*
4. The answer is where you stop on the number line.

You can rewrite a subtraction equation as an addition equation by using *opposites.*
- The opposite of $^-$ is $^+$.
- The opposite of **4** is **$^-4$**.
- The opposite of **$^-8$** is **8**.

$^-2 - {}^-3 = ?$ Think: $^-2 + 3 = ?$

Start at **$^-2$**.
Move **3** units right. So, **$^-2 - {}^-3 = 1$.**

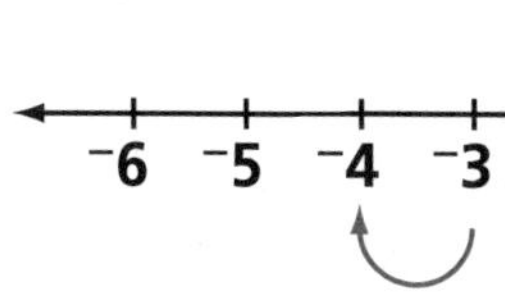

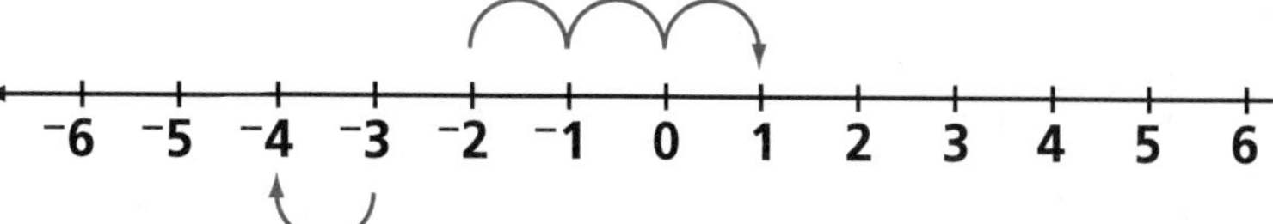

$^-3 - 1 = ?$ Think: $^-3 + {}^-1 = ?$

Start at **$^-3$**.
Move **1** unit left. So, **$^-3 - 1 = {}^-4$.**

Find each difference. Use the number line above to help you.

1. 5 − 6 → 5 + $^-6$ Start at ______, move **6** units ________. Then **5 − 6** is ______.
2. $^-3$ − 4 → ______ + $^-4$ Start at ______, move **4** units ________. Then **$^-3$ − 4** is ______.
3. 4 − $^-2$ → 4 + ______ Start at ______, move **2** units ________. Then **4 − $^-2$** is ______.

Find each difference.

4. 3 − 7 = ______ + ______ → ______ 3 − $^-7$ = ______ + ______ → ______
5. 8 − $^-8$ = ______ + ______ → ______ 2 − $^-5$ = ______ + ______ → ______
6. $^-10$ − $^-7$ = ______ + ______ → ______ $^-10$ − 7 = ______ + ______ → ______
7. $^-3$ − $^-3$ = ______ + ______ → ______ 6 − 2 = ______ + ______ → ______

STANDARD

You know that subtraction and addition are related. You can use addition properties to help you subtract more than two integers.

- Rewrite the subtraction expression as a related addition expression. Use properties to add.

$^-3 - {^-1} - 5 \rightarrow {^-3} + 1 + {^-5} \rightarrow ({^-3} + {^-5}) + 1$

$^-8 + 1$

$^-7$

Commutative Property

The sum is the same if you change the order of the addends.

$^-5 - {^-5} + 2 \rightarrow {^-5} + 5 + 2 \rightarrow 0 + 2$

2

The sum of opposites is 0.

Zero Property

When you add **0** to a number the result is that number.

Use properties to find the value of the expressions.

8. $^-1 - 2 - 3 =$ ______ $3 + {^-7} - {^-2} =$ ______ $^-1 - {^-3} + {^-4} =$ ______

9. $3 - 5 + 1 =$ ______ $^-1 - {^-7} + 9 =$ ______ $6 + {^-6} - 5 =$ ______

10. $^-2 - {^-3} + 2 =$ ______ $^-1 - {^-7} - 9 =$ ______ $^-6 + 13 - 7 =$ ______

11. How can changing the order of the addends in $^-62 - 18 + 62$ help you find its value more quickly?

____

Quick Check

What ordered pair is being described?

12. Start at (0, 0). Go right **2**, then go down **4**. ______

13. Start at (0, 0). Go left **4**, then go up **2**. ______

14. Start at (0, 0). Go down **5**. ______

Add.

15. $7 + {^-3}$ ______ **16.** $^-3 + {^-9}$ ______

17. $32 + {^-32} + {^-4}$ ______

Use properties to find the value of the expression.

18. $^-5 - {^-3}$ ______ **19.** $3 - {^-6}$ ______

20. $7 - 8$ ______

Work Space

Name ______________________________

Problem Solving Strategy: Work Backward

STANDARD

You may need to use the strategy Work Backward to solve some problems.

Problem

Lori is thinking of a mystery number. If she multiplies the number by 3 and then adds 4, the result is 25. What is Lori's mystery number?

1 Understand

Try to rewrite what you know in your own words.

- What do you know about Lori's mystery number?

  If I multiply the mystery number by 3 and add 4 to it, the answer is 25.

  What do you need to find?

  ____

2 Decide

Choose a method for solving.

- Try the strategy Work Backward.

  What is the result of the operations on Lori's mystery number?

  ____

  What operations did Lori use to get the result?

  ____

3 Solve

Organize the information, then solve.

Inverse of addition is ________	Subtract **4**. **25 − 4 =** ______
Inverse of multiplication is ________	Divide by **3**. **21 ÷ 3 =** ______
Mystery Number	______

4 Look back

Check your answer.

Start with 7. Multiply it by 3. Then add 4. What is your result?

____

STANDARD

Use the Work Backward strategy or any other strategy you have learned.

1. Bruce is thinking of a mystery number. If he divides it by **9** and then subtracts **7** from it, the result is **1**. What number is Bruce thinking of?

Think: What is the inverse of subtraction? Division?

____

Answer ______________________

2. Allison bought some cassettes by mail order. Each cassette cost **$7**. There was an additional charge of **$4** per order for shipping costs. The total bill came to **$53**. How many cassettes did Allison buy?

Think: Is the additional charge one amount or many amounts?

____

Answer ______________________

3. Bethany left her office and went up **2** floors to work in the library. At lunch time, she left the library and went down **3** floors to the cafeteria. After lunch, she went up **4** floors to the mailroom on the **9**th floor. On what floor is Bethany's office?

____

4. Jack bought **3** jars of gravy. He used a coupon good for **$0.75** off **3** jars of gravy. He gave the cashier a **$5**-dollar bill. She gave him **$0.68** in change. How much did each jar of gravy cost before the coupon?

____

5. Amy checked the temperature every hour between **10:00** and **2:00**. At **11:00**, the temperature had risen **1** degree. At noon, it had risen **2** more degrees. At **1:00**, the temperature dropped **1** degree. At **2:00**, it dropped **2** more degrees and the thermometer read **68°** F. What was the temperature at **10:00**?

____

6. During the month of May, Bob made the following deposits to and withdrawals from his savings account. On May 3, he put in **$65**. On May 8, he took out **$85**. On May 15, he put in **$35**. On May 27, he put in **$49**. At the end of the month, he had **$659** in his account. How much did he have in the account at the beginning of May?

____

7. On Wednesday, $\frac{1}{2}$ the tickets for a raffle were sold. On Thursday an additional **54** tickets were sold. There were **21** unsold tickets. How many raffle tickets were there in all?

____

8. In his third game Greg bowled **194**. His score in the second game was **8** more than in the first game, and his score in the third game was **19** more than in the first game. What did Greg bowl in the second game?

____

Name ______________________

Multiplying Integers

STANDARD

You can think of multiplication as repeated addition.

- Think of repeated addition to find the product of a *negative* integer and a *positive* integer.

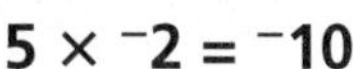

$5 \times {}^-2 = {}^-10$

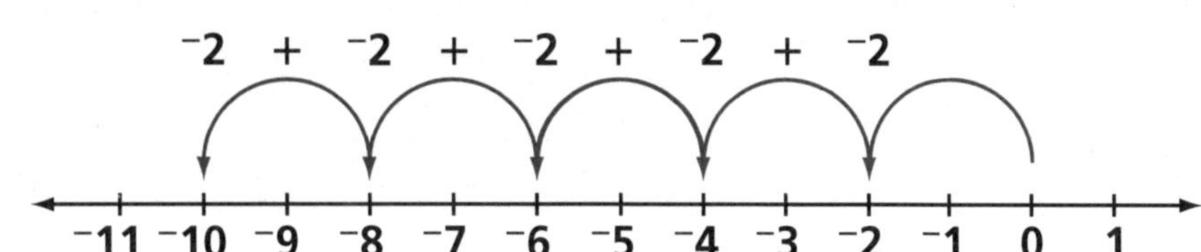

- The product of a *negative* integer and a *negative* integer is a positive integer. $^-5 \times {}^-2 = 10$

Follow these rules when multiplying integers.

The product of two numbers with the **same sign** is **positive.**

positive × positive = positive	$3 \times 2 = 6$	$a \cdot b = ab$
negative × negative = positive	$^-3 \times {}^-2 = 6$	$^-a \cdot {}^-b = ab$

The product of two numbers with **different signs** is **negative.**

positive × negative = negative	$3 \times {}^-2 = {}^-6$	$a \cdot {}^-b = {}^-ab$
negative × positive = negative	$^-3 \times 2 = {}^-6$	$^-a \cdot b = {}^-ab$

Circle the sign of each product.

1. 8×5	+	–	**2.** $^-8 \times 5$	+	–	**3.** $^-3 \times {}^-8$	+	–
$^-4 \times {}^-5$	+	–	$6 \times {}^-1$	+	–	$^-3 \times 8$	+	–
1×50	+	–	$^-3 \times {}^-9$	+	–	$3 \times {}^-8$	+	–

Find each product.

4. $8 \times 5 =$ ______ $^-8 \times 5 =$ ______ $^-3 \times {}^-8 =$ ______ $^-3 \times 0 =$ ______

5. $n \cdot {}^-5 =$ ______ $6 \times {}^-1 =$ ______ $^-3 \times 8 =$ ______ $0 \times 8 =$ ______

6. $1 \times 50 =$ ______ $^-3 \times {}^-9 =$ ______ $3 \times {}^-8 =$ ______ $1 \times {}^-5 =$ ______

7. $7 \times 6 =$ ______ $^-5 \times 7 =$ ______ $y \cdot {}^-8 =$ ______ $4 \times {}^-9 =$ ______

8. $^-11 \times {}^-2 =$ ______ $25 \cdot m =$ ______ $^-16 \times {}^-3 =$ ______ $^-35 \times 4 =$ ______

9. $^-11 \times {}^-4 =$ ______ $^-17 \times 3 =$ ______ $15 \times {}^-4 =$ ______ $^-19 \times {}^-2 =$ ______

STANDARD

Multiplication properties can help you find the product of more than two integers.

Commutative Property

$^-5 \times 24 \times {}^-2$
$(^-5 \times {}^-2) \times 24$
10×24
240

$^-2 \cdot x \cdot {}^-3$
$(^-2 \cdot {}^-3) \cdot x$
$6x$

The order in which numbers are multiplied does not change the product.

Distributive Property

$^-3 \times (1 + {}^-8)$
$(^-3 \times 1) + (^-3 \times {}^-8)$
$^-3 + 24$
21

$a \cdot (2 + {}^-4) = (a \cdot 2) + (a \cdot {}^-4)$
$a \cdot {}^-2 = 2a + {}^-4a$
$^-2a = 2a - 4a$
$^-2a = {}^-2a$

The product of a factor and a sum is the same as multiplying each addend by the factor and adding those products.

Property of Zero

$^-23 \times {}^-16 \times 0 = 0$ $\quad$ $^-n \times 0 = 0$

When a number is multiplied by zero, the product is always zero.

Property of One

$1 \times {}^-12 = {}^-12$ $\quad$ $1 \cdot {}^-5 \cdot y = {}^-5y$

When a number is multiplied by one, the product is that number.

Find the product. Use the properties of multiplication.

10. $^-4 \times 10 \times 2 =$ ______ $\quad$ $^-4y \times {}^-64 \times 0 =$ ______ $\quad$ $2 \times (^-8 \times {}^-2) =$ ______

11. $^-5 \times {}^-48 \times {}^-2 =$ ______ $\quad$ $2 \times (^-8 + n) =$ ______ $\quad$ $^-14 \times 4 \times 1 =$ ______

12. $(t \cdot {}^-7) + (t \cdot 8) =$ ______ $\quad$ $^-10 \times {}^-10 \times 33 =$ ______ $\quad$ $^-23 \times b \times 0 =$ ______

13. $4 \times 6 \times 50 =$ ______ $\quad$ $(^-3 \times {}^-11) + (^-3 \times 11) =$ ______ $\quad$ $^-4 \times 1 \times 38 =$ ______

Problem Solving
Reasoning

Solve.

14. The temperature in Bob's home was **68**°F when the furnace stopped working. The temperature dropped **5**° every hour. If it continues to drop at this rate, what can you say about the temperature in Bob's home after **6** hours?

____

Test Prep ★ Mixed Review

15 In a game, Barbara's score was 2. Then she gained 3 points, lost 5 points, and then lost 1 point. What was her final score?

A $^-3$

B $^-1$

C 1

D 3

16 Isabel's aunt Nina is three times as old as Isabel is. Nina is 30. Which equation could you use to find out Isabel's age?

F $30 = 3 \times a$

G $30 \times 3 = a$

H $30 \times a = 3$

J $3 + a = 30$

Name ______________________

Dividing Integers

STANDARD

You can use these rules when dividing integers.

The quotient of two numbers with the **same sign** is **positive.**

positive ÷ positive = positive $6 \div 2 = 3$

negative ÷ negative = positive $^-6 \div {}^-2 = 3$

The quotient of two numbers with **different signs** is **negative.**

positive ÷ negative = negative $6 \div {}^-2 = {}^-3$

negative ÷ positive = negative $^-6 \div 2 = {}^-3$

Circle the sign of the quotient.

1. $18 \div {}^-2$ + −

$^-24 \div {}^-6$ + −

$^-63 \div 9$ + −

2. $^-18 \div 2$ + −

$66 \div {}^-11$ + −

$^-9 \div {}^-3$ + −

3. $^-18 \div {}^-2$ + −

$^-54 \div 9$ + −

$^-20 \div {}^-4$ + −

Find each quotient.

4. $18 \div {}^-2 =$ ____ $^-18 \div 2 =$ ____ $^-18 \div {}^-2 =$ ____ $^-3 \div 1 =$ ____

5. $^-24 \div {}^-6 =$ ____ $66 \div {}^-11 =$ ____ $^-54 \div 9 =$ ____ $8 \div {}^-1 =$ ____

6. $^-63 \div 9 =$ ____ $^-9 \div {}^-3 =$ ____ $^-20 \div {}^-4 =$ ____ $^-5 \div 1 =$ ____

7. $^-21 \div {}^-7 =$ ____ $25 \div {}^-5 =$ ____ $^-16 \div {}^-4 =$ ____ $^-35 \div 7 =$ ____

Circle the value of the variable that makes the equation true.

8. $^-24 \div x = 6$ $x = 4$ $x = {}^-4$

$m \div 12 = {}^-12$ $m = 144$ $m = {}^-144$

$45 \div 1 = r$ $r = 45$ $r = {}^-45$

$^-1 \div y = {}^-1$ $y = 1$ $y = {}^-1$

9. $64 \div {}^-8 = y$ $y = 8$ $y = {}^-8$

$^-55 \div {}^-5 = b$ $b = 11$ $b = {}^-11$

$^-72 \div t = {}^-9$ $t = 8$ $t = {}^-8$

$g \div {}^-3 = 33$ $g = 99$ $g = {}^-99$

Write the value of *m* that balances each equation.

10. $^-44 \div m = 4$ $m =$ ____

$^-72 \div m = {}^-8$ $m =$ ____

11. $m \div {}^-6 = 6$ $m =$ ____

$^-80 \div {}^-4 = m$ $m =$ ____

STANDARD

To find the value of an expression with integers and more than one operation, you must follow the **order of operations.**

Order of Operations
First, complete all the operations inside the parentheses. Second, multiply and divide from left to right. Third, add and subtract from left to right.

Example

$\frac{(^-5 + 3) \times (^-9 + ^-1)}{^-2}$ Complete the operations inside the parentheses. $^-5 + 3 = ^-2$ and $^-9 + ^-1 = ^-10$

$\frac{^-2 \times ^-10}{^-2}$ Multiply. $^-2 \times ^-10 = 20$

$\frac{20}{^-2} = ^-10$ Simplify. $20 \div ^-2 = ^-10$

Find the value of each expression.

12. $\frac{(^-8 + ^-12)}{2}$ ______ $3 \times (6 \div ^-2)$ ______ $(^-4 - 6) \times (9 \div ^-3)$ ______

13. $\frac{(^-8 \div ^-2)}{4}$ ______ $\frac{^-10 \div (6 + ^-1)}{2}$ ______ $\frac{^-4 \times 6 + ^-3}{(9 \div ^-3)}$ ______

Problem Solving
Reasoning

Solve.

14. The low temperatures this week were as follows: **31°**, **18°**, **⁻5°**, **⁻2°**, **13°**, **17°**, and **⁻2°**. What was the mean or average low temperature?

______

15. Kendra received **$5** each day for **5** days for walking her neighbor's puppy. She deposited **$7** in her bank account. Then she divided the remainder of what she earned evenly into **3** envelopes, one marked movies, another marked vacation, and the third marked presents. How much money did she put into the envelope marked vacation?

______

Test Prep ★ Mixed Review

16 Suppose you are on a number line and you start at ⁻2, then jump 5 spaces in the negative direction. Where do you land?

A 7

B 3

C ⁻5

D ⁻7

17 You are staying at a friend's house for 5 days. You pack 3 pairs of pants of different colors and 4 T-shirts of different colors. How many different outfits can you make that combine pants and a T-shirt?

F 12 G 15

H 18 J 20

Name ___________________________

Graphing in the Coordinate Plane

STANDARD

You can write a **function** or **rule** that tells how to find ordered pairs. The rule shows how to use one or more operations with a number (*x*) to get a second number (*y*).

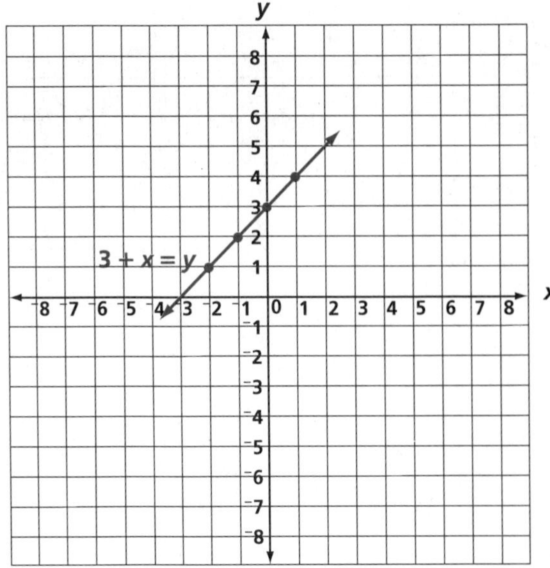

- An example of a rule is: **3 + *x* = *y***

  It tells you to "add **3** to ***x*** to get ***y***."

  So when ***x* = 2**, replace ***x*** with **2** in the rule to find ***y***.

$$\overset{x}{3 + 2} = \overset{y}{5}$$

- Notice that you can write an ordered pair using the values that you found with the rule:

  ***x* = 2** and ***y* = 5**   ordered pair → **(2,5)**

You can use a rule and a table to find other ordered pairs. The table below is called a **function table**. It shows that you start with a value for ***x***, then replace ***x*** in the rule with that value to find ***y***.

Rule: 3 + *x* = *y*			Ordered Pair
x	3+*x*	*y*	(*x*, *y*)
⁻2	3+⁻2	1	(⁻2, 1)
⁻1	3+⁻1	2	(⁻1, 2)
0	3+0	3	(0, 3)
1	3+1	4	(1, 4)

Can you see patterns in the table?

If you graph the ordered pairs and connect the points, a line is formed. So you can say that the graph of **3 + *x* = *y*** is a straight line.

Complete each function table.

1.

Rule: 2 + *x* = *y*			Ordered Pair
x	2 + *x*	*y*	(*x*, *y*)
1	2 + 1		(1,)
2	2 +		(,)
3	2 +		(,)
4	2 +		(,)

2.

Rule: 3 − *x* = *y*			Ordered Pair
x	3 − *x*	*y*	(*x*, *y*)
⁻2	3 − ⁻2		(,)
0	3 −		(,)
2	3 −		(,)
4	3 −		(,)

3. Graph the ordered pairs from Exercises 1 and 2 on the grid above. Connect the points. Draw arrowheads on both ends of each figure to show that they are lines. Label each line with the correct rule.

STANDARD

Complete each function table. Then graph the ordered pairs. Connect the points to draw lines. Label each line with the correct rule.

4. Rule: $2 - x = y$

x	$2 - x$	y	Ordered Pair (x, y)
1	2 −		(,)
2	2 −		(,)
3	2 −		(,)
4	2 −		(,)

5. Rule: $x + 5 = y$

x	$x + 5$	y	Ordered Pair (x, y)
$^{-}8$	+ 5		(,)
$^{-}5$	+ 5		(,)
$^{-}3$	+ 5		(,)
0	+ 5		(,)

Use this grid for exercises 4–5.

6. Rule: $1 - x = y$

x	$1 - x$	y	Ordered Pair (x, y)
$^{-}1$	1 −		(,)
0	1 −		(,)
1	1 −		(,)
2	1 −		(,)

7. Rule: $^{-}2 \times x = y$

x	$^{-}2 \times x$	y	Ordered Pair (x, y)
$^{-}3$	$^{-}2$ ×		(,)
0	$^{-}2$ ×		(,)
3	$^{-}2$ ×		(,)
4	$^{-}2$ ×		(,)

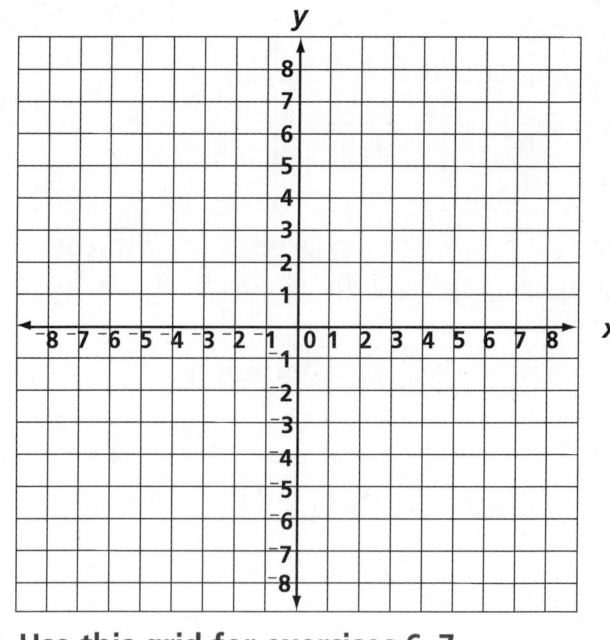

Use this grid for exercises 6–7.

Name ____________________

STANDARD

You can find the rule for the line that is on this coordinate grid. Follow these steps.

1. Find at least **3** points on the line. Make a table. Write ordered pairs for the points.

(x, y)
$(^-2, ^-1)$
$(0, 1)$
$(2, 3)$
$(4, 5)$

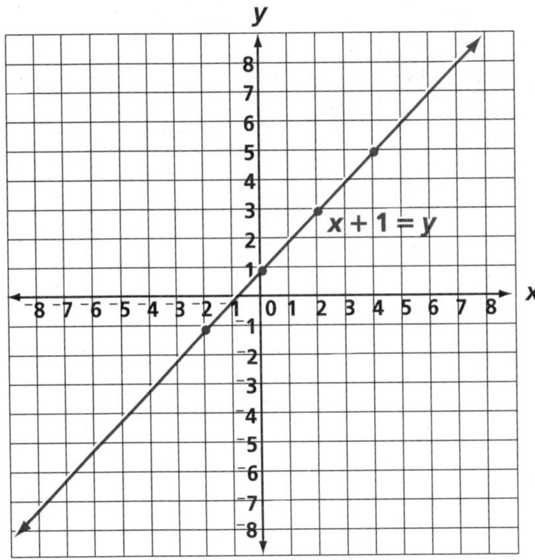

2. Study the pattern in the table. Use words to describe the pattern.
   Add **1** to **x**. Then, **x + 1** is **y**.

3. Write an equation using symbols. $x + 1 = y$.

4. Check the equation. Replace **x** and **y** with the values in the table.
   $x + 1 = y \rightarrow {}^-2 + 1 = {}^-1$
   The equation is true, so $x + 1 = y$ is correct.

Complete the tables for lines *A* and *B*. Give the rule in words. Then write the equation for the line.

8. Line *A*

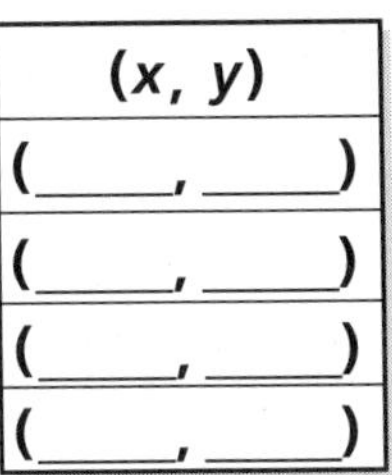

(x, y)
(____, ____)
(____, ____)
(____, ____)
(____, ____)

Rule in words: ____________________

____

The equation: ____________

9. Line *B*

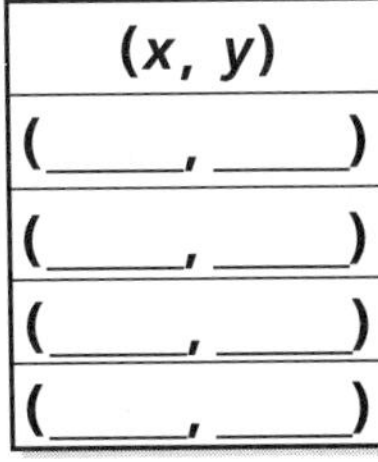

(x, y)
(____, ____)
(____, ____)
(____, ____)
(____, ____)

Rule in words: ____________________

____

The equation: ____________

STANDARD

Complete the table for Line *A*.
Give the rule in words.
Then write the equation for the line.

10. Line *A*

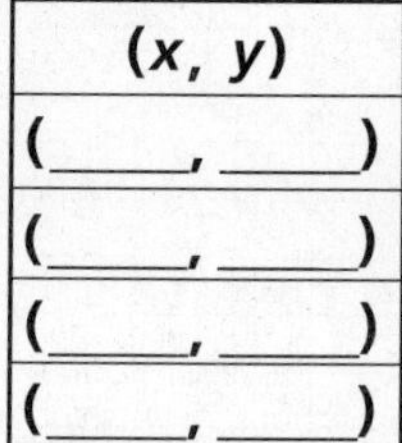

(x, y)
(____, ____)
(____, ____)
(____, ____)
(____, ____)

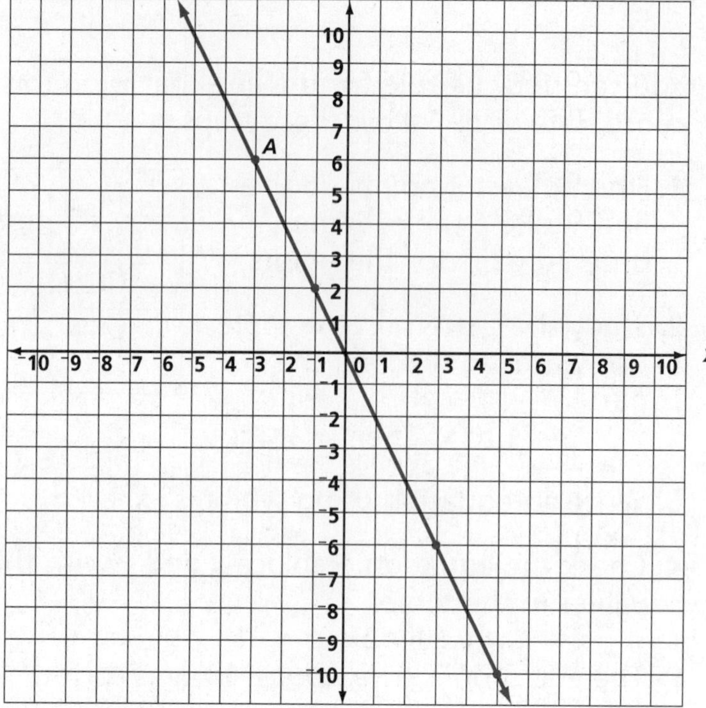

Rule in words: ____________________

____

The equation: ______________

Problem Solving Reasoning **Solve.**

11. Tim planted a tree. After **1** year, the tree was **1** foot tall. After **2** years, it was **2** feet tall. After **5** years, it was **5** feet tall. Name **3** ordered pairs that could be used to graph the growth of the tree.

____

12. How tall would you expect Tim's tree to be in **10** years? ____________

Quick Check

Find each product or quotient.

Work Space

13. $^-8 \times 5$ ______

$2 \times {}^-16$ ______

$^-4 \times {}^-12$ ______

14. $^-28 \div 7$ ______

$36 \div {}^-9$ ______

$^-55 \div {}^-11$ ______

Complete.

15. Write an equation for this rule: The first number (x) times **3** is the second number (y). __________

16. The point (3, ______) lies on the line of the equation in Exercise 10. Use the graph to complete the ordered pair.

Name ______________________________

Problem Solving Application: Choose the Operation

STANDARD

When solving a problem, often you have to decide which mathematical operation to use.

In this lesson, you will need to choose the correct operation when solving problems involving integers.

Tips to Remember

1. Understand 2. Decide 3. Solve 4. Look back

- Predict the answer. Then solve the problem. Compare your answer with your prediction.
- Find the action in the problem. Which operation shows the action best: addition, subtraction, multiplication, or division?
- Try to remember a real-life situation like the one described in the problem. What do you remember that might help you find a solution?

Choose the correct operation. Then solve.

1. On Saturday, the lowest temperature was **$^-4$°F**. On Sunday the lowest temperature was **$^-6$°F**. Which is the correct operation for finding how much higher the temperature was on Saturday?

a. $^-4 - (^-6)$ **b.** $^-6 - (^-4)$

c. $^-4 + (^-6)$ **d.** $^-4 \times {}^-6$

Think: You are comparing two temperatures. Should you add or subtract?

____

____

Answer ______________________________

2. The temperature at noon was **0°F**. It dropped **2°F** per hour from noon to **4:00** P.M. Which is the correct operation to find the temperature at **4:00** P.M.?

a. $^-2 - 4$ **b.** $^-2 + 4$

c. $^-2 \times 4$ **d.** $4 \div {}^-2$

Think: How many degrees does the temperature drop each hour? What operation does this suggest?

____

____

Answer ______________________________

STANDARD

Choose the correct operation. Then solve.

3. Jessica's score was $^{-}6$ points. In the next game she scored **8** points. What is the correct operation to find Jessica's score now?

a. $^{-}6 + 8$ b. $^{-}6 - 8$

c. $^{-}6 \times 8$ d. $8 - (^{-}6)$

____

4. Jaime's score was **0**. He scored $^{-}3$ points in each of the next **4** games. What is the correct operation to find Jaime's score now?

a. $^{-}3 + 4$ b. $^{-}3 - 4$

c. $^{-}4 \times {}^{-}3$ d. $^{-}3 \times 4$

____

5. A football team lost **24** yards over **4** plays. What is the correct operation to find the average number of yards the team lost per play?

a. $^{-}24 \times 4$ b. $^{-}24 \div 4$

c. $^{-}24 + 4$ d. $^{-}24 - 4$

____

6. The temperature was **2**°F at midnight. At **3:00** A.M. it had dropped to $^{-}$**1**°F. What is the correct operation to find the number of degrees the temperature had dropped?

a. $2 - 1$ b. $2 + (^{-}1)$

c. $2 \times (^{-}1)$ d. $2 - (^{-}1)$

____

7. In golf, **par** is the number of strokes it should take to complete a hole. A golfer's score was **4** under par. On the next hole, he scored **2** over par. What is the correct operation to find the golfer's score now?

a. $^{-}4 \div 2$ b. $^{-}4 \times 2$

c. $^{-}4 + 2$ d. $^{-}4 - 2$

____

8. Arnold finished a golf game **5** strokes over par. Lee finished **4** strokes under par. What is the correct operation to find how many more golf strokes Arnold made than Lee?

a. $5 - (^{-}4)$ b. $^{-}4 - 5$

c. $5 \times (^{-}4)$ d. $5 + (^{-}4)$

____

Extend Your Thinking

9. Look back at problem 3. Suppose Jessica scored the following points in the next three games: $^{-}$**4**, **1**, $^{-}$**2**. What would be Jessica's score now?

____

10. Look back at problem 6. Suppose that the temperature rose steadily **1**°F every hour from **3:00** A.M. until **9:00** A.M. What would be the temperature at **9:00** A.M.?

____

Name ______________________

Unit 11 Review

Write the opposite of each integer.

1. 4 ____ **2.** $^{-}2$ ____ **3.** 551 ____ **4.** $^{-}9$ ____

Graph the following integers on the number line.
Then order them from *greatest* to *least*.

5. $^{-}8, 8, 2, ^{-}1$ ____________

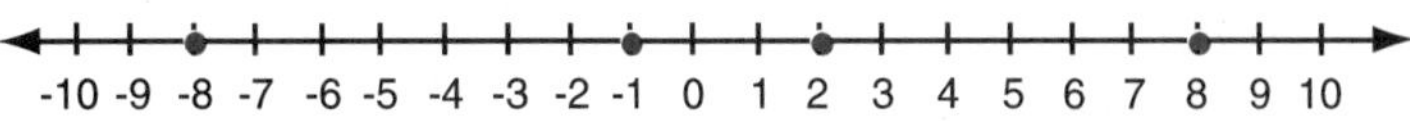

Use the coordinate graph for exercises 6 and 7.

6. Write the ordered pair for each point.

Point *A* ____ Point *B* ____ Point *C* ____

7. Connect the points and extend the line in both directions. Write the equation for the line. ____

____

8. Is (24, 25) a point on the line? Explain. ________

____

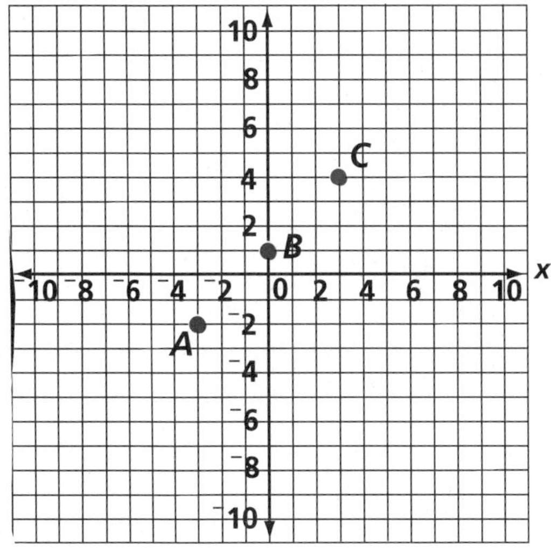

Write each sum, difference, product, or quotient.

9. $5 - 9 =$ ____ **10.** $5 + ^{-}9 =$ ____ **11.** $^{-}5 - 9 =$ ____ **12.** $^{-}5 - ^{-}9 =$ ____

13. $^{-}5 + ^{-}5 =$ ____ **14.** $5 - ^{-}9 =$ ____ **15.** $6 + ^{-}6 =$ ____ **16.** $3 + ^{-}1 =$ ____

17. $7 \times 5 =$ ____ **18.** $^{-}8 \div 4 =$ ____ **19.** $^{-}7 \times ^{-}6 =$ ____ **20.** $^{-}3 \div ^{-}3 =$ ____

21. $14 \div ^{-}7 =$ ____ **22.** $5 \times ^{-}1 =$ ____ **23.** $^{-}16 \div ^{-}8 =$ ____ **24.** $0 \times ^{-}1 =$ ____

Problem Solving Reasoning Solve.

25. The temperature in one city is **$^{-}2$°F** and in another city is **$^{-}9$°F** colder.

What is the temperature in the coldest city? ____

26. What number added to **75** is **65** and divided by **2** is **$^{-}5$**? ____

Name ________________________________

The streets of the town of Brightsville form a grid. Use the grid to answer questions 1 and 2.

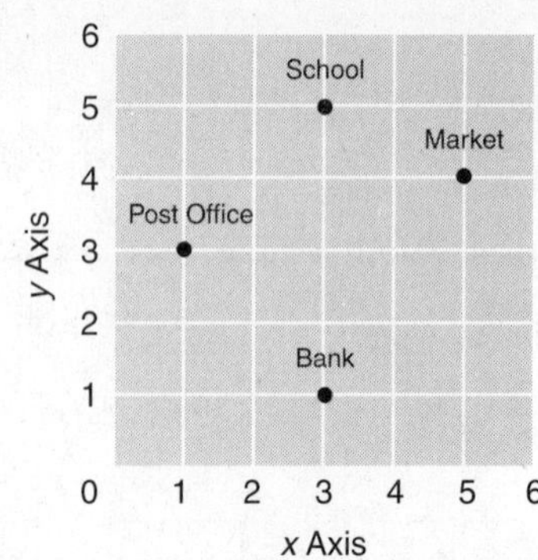

1 **Which best represents the coordinates of the school on the map?**

A (1, 3) **C** (3, 5)

B (3, 1) **D** (5, 4)

2 **Which set of directions could you use to go from the school to your house which is located at ($^-1$, $^-1$)?**

F left 2, down 2

G left 2, down 6

H left 4, down 2

J left 4, down 6

3 **The number line is a scale drawing of a street 1 mile long. Suppose you live at point *B*. The Meliks live $\frac{1}{4}$ mile to the left of you. The Rosens live less than $\frac{1}{4}$ mile to the right of you. Which points represent the Meliks and the Rosens?**

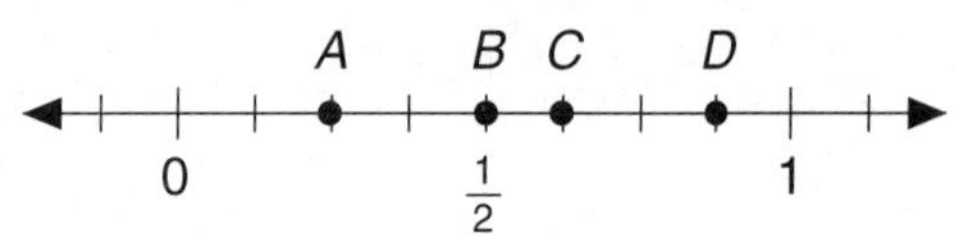

A *A*, *C* **C** *C*, *A*

B *A*, *D* **D** *C*, *D*

4 **Which expression does not have a value of 6 when $n = 3$?**

F $60 \div (n^2 + 1)$

G $(6 \div n) \times 3$

H $600 \div (4 \times n - 2)$

J $(6 - n) + (30 \div 10)$

5 **Which numbers would you use to complete the table of ordered pairs for the rule $^-5 \times x = y$?**

x	y
5	-25
1	-5
0	0
-1	
-3	

A 5, 15 **C** $^-5$, $^-15$

B $^-5$, 15 **D** $^-5$, $^-25$

6 **A package of batteries that cost $8.49 was on sale for $6.89. The computer club bought a dozen packages. How much did they spend?**

F $101.88

G $89.88

H $82.68

J $71.92

K Not here

7 **What is the value of this expression?**
$^-4 \times (8 + {}^-11) \div 2$

A $^-36$ **C** $^-6$ **E** 6

B $^-7$ **D** 4

Tables of Measures

Metric System

Prefixes

kilo (k)	=	1,000		
hecto (h)	=	100		
deka (da)	=	10		
deci (d)	=	0.1	=	$\frac{1}{10}$
centi (c)	=	0.01	=	$\frac{1}{100}$
milli (m)	=	0.001	=	$\frac{1}{1,000}$

Length

1 kilometer (km)	=	1,000 meters (m)
1 hectometer (hm)	=	100 meters
1 dekameter (dam)	=	10 meters
1 decimeter (dm)	=	0.1 meter
1 centimeter (cm)	=	0.01 meter
1 millimeter (mm)	=	0.001 meter

Capacity

1 kiloliter (kL)	=	1,000 liters (L)
1 hectoliter (hL)	=	100 liters
1 dekaliter (daL)	=	10 liters
1 deciliter (dL)	=	0.1 liter
1 centiliter (cL)	=	0.01 liter
1 milliliter (mL)	=	0.001 liter

Mass

1 kilogram (kg)	=	1,000 grams (g)
1 hectogram (hg)	=	100 grams
1 dekagram (dag)	=	10 grams
1 decigram (dg)	=	0.1 gram
1 centigram (cg)	=	0.01 gram
1 milligram (mg)	=	0.001 gram

Customary System

Length

1 foot (ft)	=	12 inches (in.)
1 yard (yd)	=	3 feet
1 yard	=	36 inches
1 mile (mi)	=	5,280 feet

Capacity

1 tablespoon (tbs)	=	3 teaspoons (tsp)
1 fluid ounce (fl oz)	=	2 tablespoons
1 cup (c)	=	8 fluid ounces
1 pint (pt)	=	2 cups
1 pint	=	16 fluid ounces
1 quart (qt)	=	2 pints
1 gallon (gal)	=	4 quarts

Weight

1 pound (lb)	=	16 ounces (oz)
1 ton (T)	=	2,000 pounds

Area

1 square foot (ft^2)	=	144 square inches ($in.^2$)
1 square yard (yd^2)	=	9 square feet
1 acre (A)	=	4,840 square yards
1 square mile (mi^2)	=	640 acres

Other Measures

Time

1 minute (min)	=	60 seconds (s)
1 hour (h)	=	60 minutes
1 day (d)	=	24 hours
1 week (wk)	=	7 days
1 month (mo)	≈	4 weeks
1 year (yr)	=	12 months
1 year	=	52 weeks
1 year	=	365 days
1 leap year	=	366 days
1 decade	=	10 years
1 century	=	100 years

Counting

1 dozen (doz)	=	12 things
1 score	=	20 things
1 gross (gro)	=	12 dozen
1 gross	=	144 things

Geometric Formulas

Rectangle

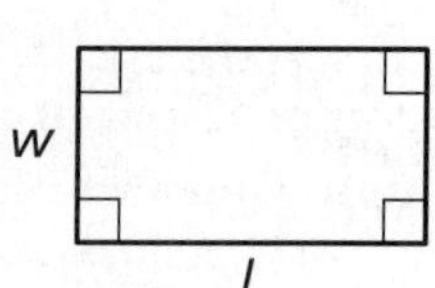

Perimeter:
$P = 2(l + w)$

Area:
$A = lw$

Square

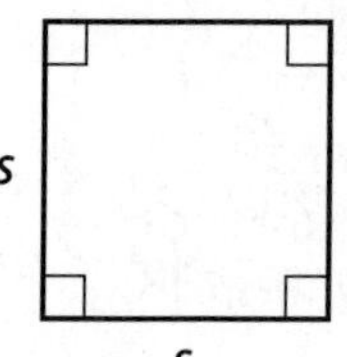

Perimeter:
$P = 4s$

Area:
$A = s^2$

Parallelogram

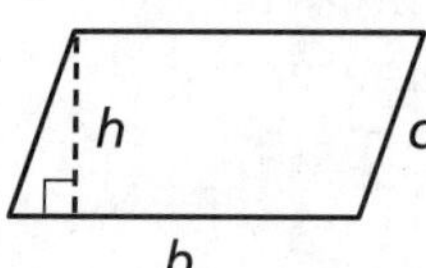

Perimeter:
$P = 2(b + c)$

Area:
$A = bh$

Right Triangle

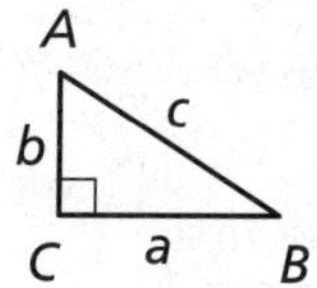

Perimeter:
$P = a + b + c$

Area:
$A = \frac{1}{2}ba$

Triangle

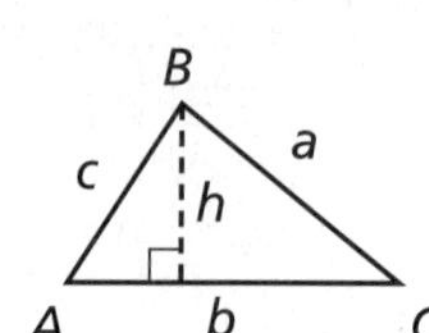

Perimeter:
$P = a + b + c$

Area:
$A = \frac{1}{2}bh$

Rectangular Prism

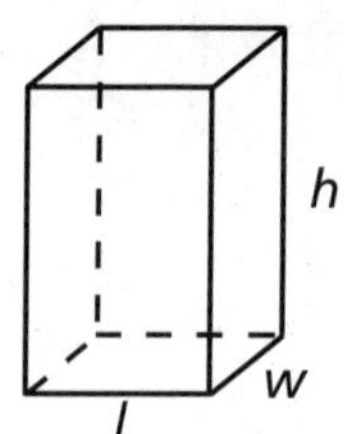

Surface Area:
$SA = 2(lw + wh + lh)$

Volume:
$V = lwh$

Cube

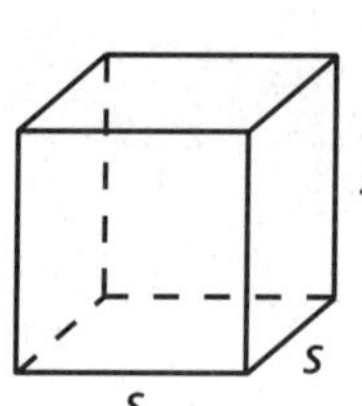

Surface Area:
$SA = 6s^2$

Volume:
$V = s^3$

Glossary

A

acute angle An angle whose measure is less than 90°

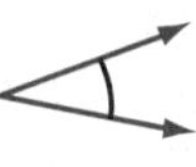

acute triangle A triangle whose largest angle is an acute angle

addend A number to be added in an addition expression

adding 0 property Adding zero to any number does not change the number.
Examples: $7 + 0 = 7$ and $n + 0 = n$

addition The arithmetic operation that combines two numbers
Example:

```
 23 ← addend
+13 ← addend
 36   sum
```

algebraic expression (see expression)

altitude (of a plane figure) A segment of a triangle or parallelogram that is perpendicular to the base. In a triangle one endpoint is the vertex opposite the base.

angle A geometric figure formed by two rays with a common endpoint. The angle below can be named either ∠ABC or ∠B.

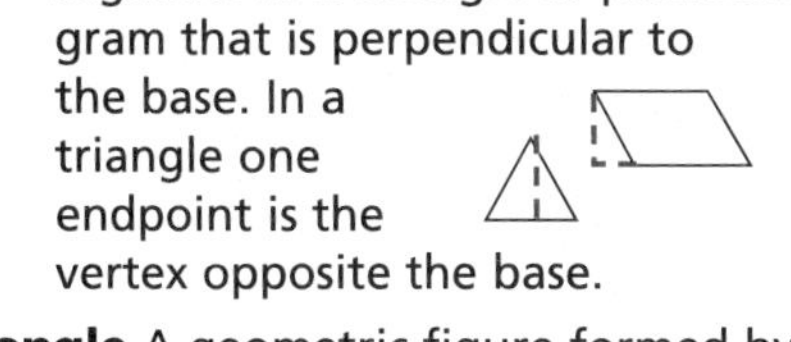

angle *ABC* or ∠ *ABC*

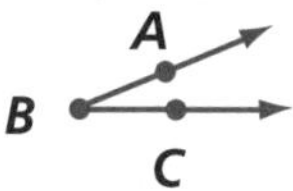

area A measure of the number of square units in a region or a surface

associative property of addition (also called the grouping property of addition) Changing the grouping of the addends does not change the sum.
Example: $(37 + 95) + 5 = 37 + (95 + 5) = 137$

associative property of multiplication (also called the grouping property of multiplication) Changing the grouping of the factors does not change the product.
Example:
$(25 \times 5) \times 2 = 27 \times (5 \times 2) = 270$

average (or mean) A measure of central tendency. It is computed by adding all the items of data and dividing by the number of items.

axis (see *x-axis*, *y-axis*) A reference line on a graph

B

bar graph A pictorial representation of data that uses lengths of bars to show the information

base (of an exponent) The number that is used as a factor when evaluating powers
Example: $3^4 = 3 \times 3 \times 3 \times 3$
The base is 3.

base (of a geometric figure) A side or face in a plane or solid figure

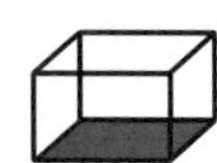

billion The number 1,000 million or 1,000,000,000

C

capacity The maximum amount of liquid that a container can hold

Celsius temperature scale (°C) The temperature scale in the metric system in which the freezing temperature of water is 0°C and the boiling temperature of water is 100°C.

center (see *circle*)

centi- A prefix meaning one hundredth
Example: A centimeter is 0.01 meter.

central angle An angle whose vertex is the center of a circle

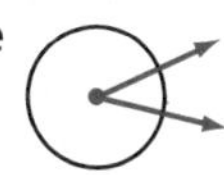

certain event An event that will always occur, such as "The sun will rise tomorrow morning." The probability of a certain event is 1.

chord A segment joining any two points on a circle

circle A plane figure that has all of its points the same distance from a given point called the center

circle graph A pictorial representation of data that uses sections of a circle to show the information

cluster Several items of data grouped into a small interval

common denominator A denominator used when adding two or more fractions with unlike denominators. Any common multiple of the given denominators can be used to write equivalent fractions.
Example: Some common denominators of $\frac{1}{2}$ and $\frac{1}{3}$ are 6, 12, 18, 24,...

common factor A number that is a factor of two or more whole numbers
Example: 1, 2, 3, and 6 are common factors of 12 and 18.

common multiple A number that is a multiple of two or more whole numbers
Example: Common multiples of 3 and 4 are 12, 24, 36,...

commutative property of addition (also called the order property of addition) Changing the order of the addends does not change the sum.
Example: $3 + 4 = 4 + 3 = 7$

commutative property of multiplication (also called the order property of multiplication) Changing the order of the factors does not change the product.
Example: $3 \times 5 = 5 \times 3 = 15$

compass A tool used to construct circles and other figures

compatible numbers Numbers used to make estimates. They are easy to work with mentally and are close to the given numbers.

composite number A number with three or more factors
Example: 9 is composite, because its factors are 1, 3, and 9.

cone A space figure with one flat, circular surface and one curved surface

congruent figures Figures that have exactly the same size and shape. In congruent polygons, corresponding angles are congruent and corresponding sides are congruent.

coordinate Each number of an ordered pair
Example: (4, 6) has a first coordinate of 4 and a second coordinate of 6.

coordinate plane A grid with number lines used to locate points in a plane

counting number Any of the numbers 1, 2, 3, 4, and so on

cube A rectangular prism whose faces are all congruent squares

customary system of measurement The system of measurement currently used in the United States

cylinder A space figure with two congruent circular bases joined by a single curved surface

D

data Numerical information

deci- A prefix that means one tenth
Example: A decimeter is 0.1 meter.

decimal A number that uses place value to indicate parts of a whole. The decimal point separates the whole number digits from the digits representing parts of a whole.
Example: The decimal

represents the number three and 67 hundredths.

decimal point (see *decimal*)

degree A unit of measure of temperature or of an angle

denominator The numeral below the fraction bar in a fraction. It tells how many parts are in the whole.

diagonal A segment joining two vertices of a polygon that is not a side

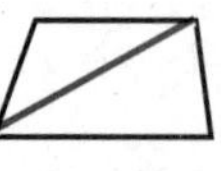

diameter A chord of a circle that contains the center

difference The answer to a subtraction problem

digit Any of the symbols used to write numerals. In the base 10 system, they are 1, 2, 3, 4, 5, 6, 7, 8, 9, and 0.

distance The length of a path between two points

distributive property The same answer is obtained whether you add first and then multiply or multiply first and then add.
Example: $3 \times (20 + 7) = 3 \times 20 + 3 \times 7 = 81$

dividend The number that is divided

divisible A number is divisible by another number if there is no remainder when they are divided.
Example: 4, 16, and 640 are all divisible by 4.

division An operation that divides a set into equal sets.
Example:

quotient → 10 R5 ← remainder
divisor → 6)65 ← divident

divisor The number that is divided by

double-bar graph A bar graph that compares two sets of data by using two bars for each category

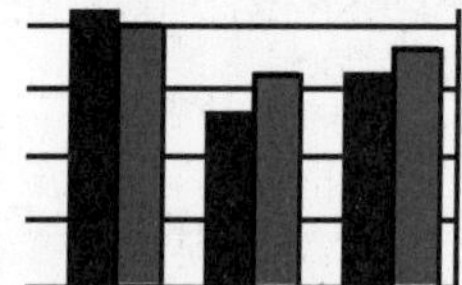

double-line graph A line graph that compares two sets of data by using one line for each set

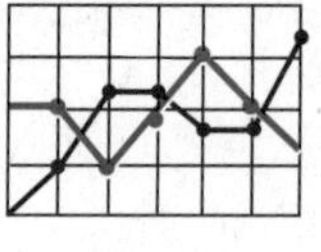

E

edge A line segment that is the intersection of two faces of a space figure

elapsed time A measure of the time that passes between the beginning and end of an event
Example: The elapsed time between 9:30 A.M. and 2:15 P.M. is 4 hours 45 minutes.

endpoint A point at the end of a line segment or ray

equally likely Outcomes of an experiment that have an equal chance of occurring
Example: A spinner is divided into 6 congruent sections. Each section is an equally likely outcome of a spin.

equation A number sentence that says that two expressions have the same value. It may be true, false, or open.
Example: $3 + 7 = 10$ is true; $3 + 7 = 7$ is false, and $3 + n = 10$ is open.

equilateral triangle A triangle with three congruent sides

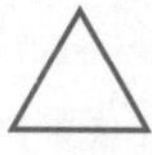

equivalent fractions Two or more fractions that represent the same number.
Example: $\frac{1}{2} = \frac{2}{4} = \frac{3}{6} = \frac{4}{8}$

estimate To find a approximate solution mentally by using numbers that are close to the original numbers and easy to work with mentally
Example: To estimate 47 + 32, add the rounded numbers 50 + 30. The estimated sum is about 80.

evaluate To find the value of an expression

even number A whole number that is divisible by 2

event Any outcome or set of outcomes of an experiment

expanded form A number written so that each digit is expressed as a power of 10 instead of by its position in the numeral
Example:

Expanded forms for 316:

300 + 10 + 6

(3 × 100) + (1 × 10) + (6 × 1)

exponent A number that tells how many times a base is to be used as a factor.
Example: 3^4 represents the product {3 × 3 × 3 × 3}
4 factors

exponent form A number expressed as a power
Example: Exponent forms of 64 are 2^6 and 8^2

expression A number, symbol, or combination of numbers and symbols that represents a mathematical quantity
Examples: $(7 + 3) \div 5$ or $6 \times n$

F

face A flat surface that is a side of a space figure

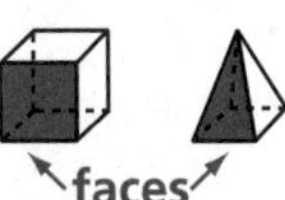

factor A number to be multiplied in a multiplication expression

factor (of a number) A counting number that exactly divides another number
Example: The numbers 1, 2, 3, 4, 6, and 12 are all factors of 12.

factor tree A diagram used to show the prime factors of a composite number

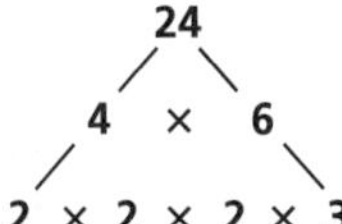

Fahrenheit temperature scale (°F) The temperature scale in the customary system in which the freezing temperature of water is 32°F and the boiling temperature of water is 212°F.

formula An equation that expresses a mathematical relationship
Example: A formula for area A of a rectangle with length l and width w is $A = l \times w$

fraction A number such as $\frac{1}{2}$ or $\frac{3}{4}$ that is used to express a part of a region or set

frequency The number of times an event occurs

function A set of ordered pairs

G

gap A characteristic of data. It is a significant interval that contains no data.

graph A pictorial representation of a data set or equation

greatest common factor (GCF) The greatest number that is a factor of each of two or more numbers.
Example: The greatest common factor of 24 and 30 is 6.

grouping symbol Parentheses or other symbols that indicate the grouping of numbers or terms in an expression

H

heptagon A polygon that has 7 sides

hexagon A polygon that has 6 sides

histogram A type of bar graph that shows frequencies over intervals

I

impossible event In probability, an event that cannot take place, such as "A prime number is also a composite number." The probability of an impossible event is 0.

inequality A number sentence that states that two numbers or expressions are greater than (>), less than (<), or not equal to (≠).
Examples: $3 + 6 < 10$ is read "Three plus six is less than 10."
$5 + 7 \neq 10$ is read "Five plus seven is not equal to 10."

integer The set of numbers containing all the whole numbers and their opposites

intersecting lines Line that cross each other or that have points in common

interval One of the equal sized divisions on a histogram or other graph scale

inverse operations An operation that undoes the results of another operation. For example, addition and subtraction are inverse operations, as are multiplication and division.

isosceles triangle A triangle with at least two congruent sides

J–K–L

key (of a pictograph) An indication of what a single symbol on the graph represents

kilo- A prefix meaning 1000.
Example: A kilogram is 1000 grams.

least common denominator (LCD) The least number that is a common denominator of two or more fractions. It is the least common multiple of the denominators of each of the fractions.
Example: The least common denominator of $\frac{1}{2}$ and $\frac{2}{3}$ is 6.

least common multiple (LCM) The least number that is a common multiple of two or more numbers
Example: 12 is the least common multiple of 3 and 4.

line A set of points that extends endlessly in two opposite directions

line graph A pictorial representation of data that shows changes over time using line segments

line plot A pictorial representation of a small set of data along a number line. Each data item is represented with an "X" placed above a number on the line

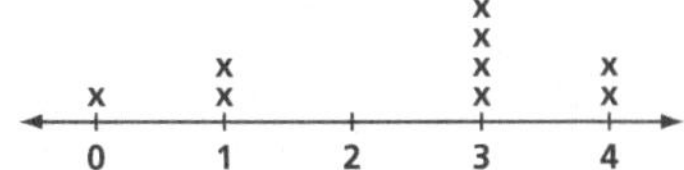

line segment A part of a line that has two endpoints

M

mass The amount of matter in an object. Some units of mass are milligram, gram, and kilogram.

mean The average of a set of data. It is found by adding each item of data and dividing by the number of items.
Example: 4 is the mean of 2, 4, 5, and 5.

median The middle point of the data when they are arranged from least to greatest. If there is an odd number of data items, it is the middle number. If there is an even number of data items, it is the mean of the two middle numbers.
Example: 4.5 is the median of 2, 4, 5, 5.

metric system of measurement An international system of measurement that uses the meter, liter, gram, and degrees Celsius as the basic units of measure

milli- A prefix meaning one thousandth
Example: A milliliter is 0.001 liter

mixed decimal A decimal, such as $0.83\frac{1}{3}$, that ends with a fraction

mixed number A number, such as $2\frac{2}{3}$ that is made up of a fraction less than one and a whole number

mode The number (or numbers) that occurs most often in a set of data. If every number occurs only once, the data has no mode.
Example: 5 is the mode of 2, 4, 5, 5.

multiple of a number The product of the number and any whole number.
Example: The multiples of 4 are 0, 4, 8, 12, 16, . . .

multiplication An operation that expresses repeated addition of the same number
Example: 12 ← factor
× 4 ← factor
48 ← product

multiplying by 1 property Multiplying any number by 1 is equal to that number.
Example: 0.3 × 1 = 0.3

multiplying by 0 property Multiplying any number by 0 is equal to 0.
Example: $\frac{1}{4} \times 0 = 0$

N

negative integer A number such as −1, −2, −3, and so on that is less than 0

number line A line that has its points labeled with numbers (called coordinates) such as whole numbers, integers, fractions, and so on

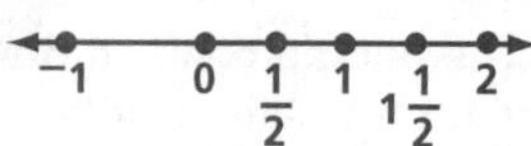

number pattern An ordered set of numbers that seems to have a rule or pattern for finding the next number
Example: 1, 4, 7, 10, . . .is a number pattern whose rule is "add 3" to find the next number

numeral A name or symbol for a number

numerator The number over the bar in a fraction. It tells how many parts of the whole are under discussion.

numerical expression An expression that contains only numbers, symbols of operation, and grouping symbols
Example: (7 + 4) × 6

O

obtuse angle An angle whose measure is greater than 90° and less than 180°

obtuse triangle A triangle whose largest angle is obtuse

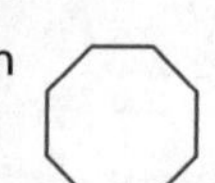

octagon A polygon that has 8 sides

odd number A whole number that is not divisible by 2

open equation An equation that contains a variable

opposites Two numbers whose sum is 0. They are also called additive inverses.
Examples: 2 and −2 are opposites.

order of operations The rules that define the order in which the operations in an expression are to be evaluated. They are:
1 First work within parentheses
2 Next evaluate powers
3 Multiply and divide from left to right
4 Finally, add and subtract from left to right

ordered pair A pair of numbers used to locate a point in a coordinate plane. The first number is the horizontal distance from the origin; the second number is the vertical distance.

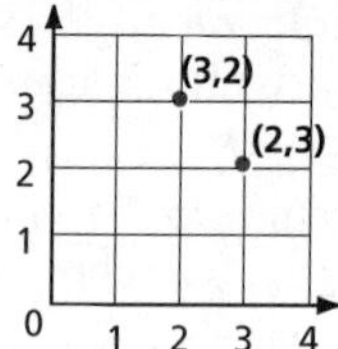

origin The point on a coordinate grid at which the two axes meet. Its coordinates are (0, 0).

outcome A result in a probability experiment

outlier An item of data that is significantly greater or less than all the other items of data

P

parallel lines Two lines in the same plane that do not intersect

parallelogram A quadrilateral that has its opposite sides parallel and congruent

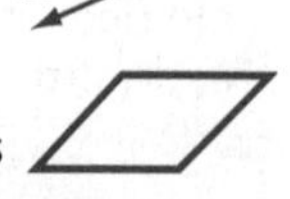

pentagon A polygon with 5 sides

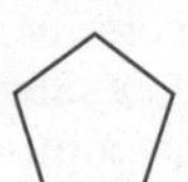

percent A ratio that compares a number to 100
Example: 39% is $\frac{39}{100}$.

percentage The result obtained by multiplying a quantity by a percent

perimeter The distance around a polygon. It is found by adding the lengths of all the sides.

period Each group of three digits seen in a number written in standard form
Example: In the number 306,789, 245, the millions period is 306, the thousands period is 789, and 245 is the ones period.

perpendicular lines Two lines that intersect to form right angles

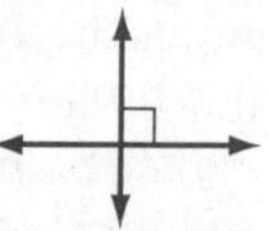

pictograph A pictorial representation of data that uses a single symbol or to represent multiples of a quantity

place-value system A system of numeration in which the value of a digit depends on its position in the numeral

plane A smooth flat surface that extends infinitely in all directions on the surface

plane figure A figure whose points are all in the same plane

point A location in space. It is represented by a dot.
• A point A

polygon A plane figure composed of line segments that meet only at their endpoints. The segments must form a closed figure.

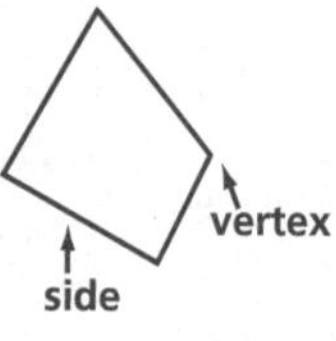

positive integer A counting number such as 1, 2, 3, ... that is greater than 0

power A number that can be expressed using a single base and exponent.
Example: 32 is a power of 2; it is the fifth power of 2.

prime factorization Expressing a number as a product of prime numbers
Example: $36 = 2 \times 2 \times 3 \times 3$ or $2^2 \times 3^2$

prime number A whole number greater than 1 that has exactly two factors, itself and 1
Example: $2 = 2 \times 1$

prism A space figure that has two congruent, parallel bases that are joined by parallelograms. A prism is named by the shape of its bases.

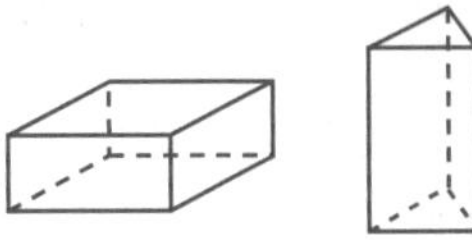

probability A number between 0 and 1 used to describe how likely an event is to happen; a measure of chance

product The answer to a multplication problem

protractor A tool used to measure and draw angles

pyramid A space figure whose base is a polygon and whose other faces are triangles that share a common vertex. A pyramid is named by the shape of its base.

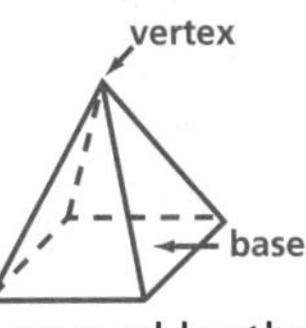

Q

quadrant One of the four sections of a coordinate plane formed by the axes. They are numbered counterclockwise starting from the upper right quadrant.

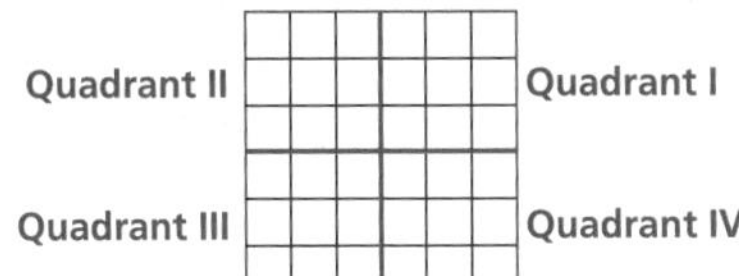

quadrilateral A polygon that has four sides

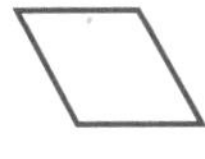

quotient The answer in a division problem

R

radius A segment from any point on a circle to its center; also the length of this segment

range The difference between the least and greatest numbers in a set of data
Example: The range of the data 2, 4, 5, 5 is $5 - 2 = 3$.

rate A ratio in which unlike quantities are being compared, such as words per minute or feet per second

ratio A comparison of two quantities using division
Example: 3 : 4, 3 to 4, or $\frac{3}{4}$

ray A part of a line that has one endpoint. When naming it, the endpoint is used first.

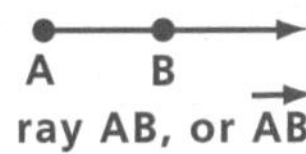

reciprocals Two numbers whose product is 1. They are also called multiplicative inverses.
Examples: 2 and $\frac{1}{2}$ $1\frac{3}{4}$ and $\frac{4}{7}$

rectangle A parallelogram that has four right angles

rectangular prism A space figure all of whose faces are rectangles

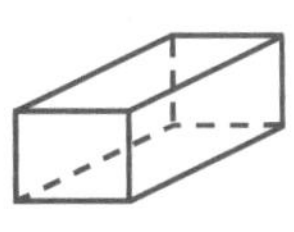

regular polygon A polygon that has all sides congruent and all angles congruent

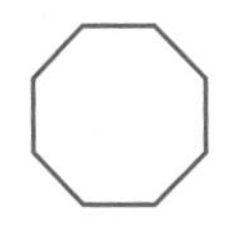

remainder The number that is left over in a division problem

rhombus A parallelogram that has all of its sides congruent

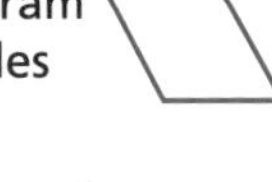

right angle An angle whose measure is 90°

right triangle A triangle whose largest angle is a right angle

rounding a number Replacing an exact number by another number that is easier to use or compute with
Examples: 12,501 rounded to the nearest hundred is 12,500.
4.386 rounded to the nearest hundredth is 4.39.

S

scale drawing A picture or diagram that is exactly the same shape as another but of a different size. Each distance in the drawing is in the same ratio as the corresponding distance in the original.

scale factor The ratio in a scale drawing or other similar figures that compares the scale drawing dimensions to the actual dimensions

segment (see *line segment*)

scalene triangle A triangle that has no congruent sides

semicircle Half of a circle

sequence Numbers arranged according to some pattern or rule

side of an angle One of the rays that make up an angle

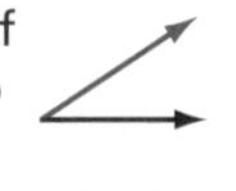

side of a polygon One of the line segments that make up a polygon

similar figures Two figures that have the same shape but not necessarily the same size. In similar polygons, corresponding angles are congruent and corresponding sides are proportional.

simplest form A fraction less than 1 in which the numerator and denominator have no common factors except 1, or a mixed number in which the fractional part is in simplest form
Examples:
$\frac{5}{10} = \frac{1}{2}$ $2\frac{6}{9} = 2\frac{2}{3}$ $\frac{12}{4} = 3$

solve an equation To find the value of the variable (called the solution) that makes an open equation true

space The set of all points

space figure A figure that is not entirely in one plane

sphere A space figure that has all of its points the same distance from a point, called the center.

square A rectangle that has all its sides congruent

standard form A number that is expressed as a base 10 numeral
Example: 3,126 is the standard form of the number three thousand, one hundred twenty-six.

stem-and-leaf plot A way to arrange data by place value. The front digit or digits are called stems, the last digit or digits are called leaves.

Example: This plot shows the following data:

82, 82, 87, 95, 112, 113

stem	leaves
8	2 2 7
9	5
10	
11	2 3

straight angle An angle whose measure is 180°

substitution Replacing one symbol by another.
Example: A number such as 5 can be substituted for n in the expression $15 \div n$

subtraction An arithmetic operation that takes away a given amount
Example:

$$\begin{array}{r} 345 \\ -122 \\ \hline 223 \end{array} \leftarrow \text{difference}$$

sum The answer to an addition problem

surface area The total area of all the faces or surfaces of a space figure

T

term (of a ratio) Either of the two numbers of a ratio

trapezoid A quadrilateral that has exactly one pair of parallel sides

tree diagram A organized way of listing all the possible outcomes of an experiment

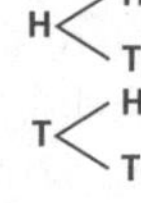

triangle A polygon that has three sides

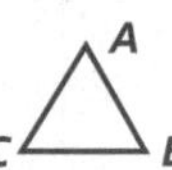

U

unit A fixed quantity used as a standard for length, area, volume, weight, and so on

unit fraction A fraction with a numerator of 1
Examples: $\frac{1}{3}$ and $\frac{1}{7}$

unit price The cost of a single unit of an item
Example: $3 per pound for hamburger meat

unit rate A rate whose second term is a single unit, such as 50 miles per hour

V

variable A letter that is used to represent one or more numbers

variable expression An expression that contains one or more variables

vertex The common point where two sides or edges meet (plural: vertices)

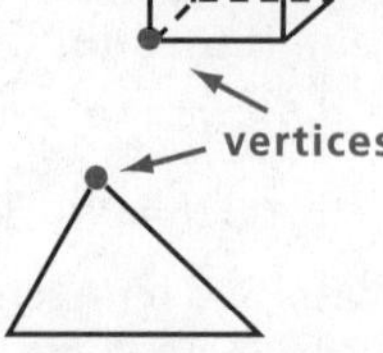

volume A measure of the space within a closed figure in space

W–X–Y–Z

whole number Any of the numbers 0, 1, 2, 3, . . .

***x*-axis** The horizontal number line on a coordinate plane

***y*-axis** The vertical number line on a coordinate plane

zero power of a number The zero power of any number that is not zero is 1.
Example: $10^0 = 1$

Symbols

$<$	is less than
$>$	is greater than
$=$	is equal to
$\neq$	is not equal to
n	variable or placeholder
$+$	plus, addition symbol
$-$	minus, subtraction symbol
$\times$	times, multiplication symbol
$\cdot$	times, multiplication symbol
$\div$	divided by, division symbol
5^4	5 to the fourth power, or $5 \times 5 \times 5 \times 5$
°	degree
(2, 3)	the ordered pair 2, 3
A	point A
$\overleftrightarrow{AB}$	line AB
$\overline{AB}$	segment AB
$\overrightarrow{AB}$	ray AB
$\angle$	angle
$\cong$	is congruent to
$\perp$	is perpendicular to
$\parallel$	is parallel to
Δ	triangle
$a : b$	the ratio of a to b
%	percent
$P(A)$	The probability of event A
$^{+}5$	positive five
$^{-}5$	negative five